THREADS OF HISTORY
THE TAPESTRIES AT BLENHEIM PALACE

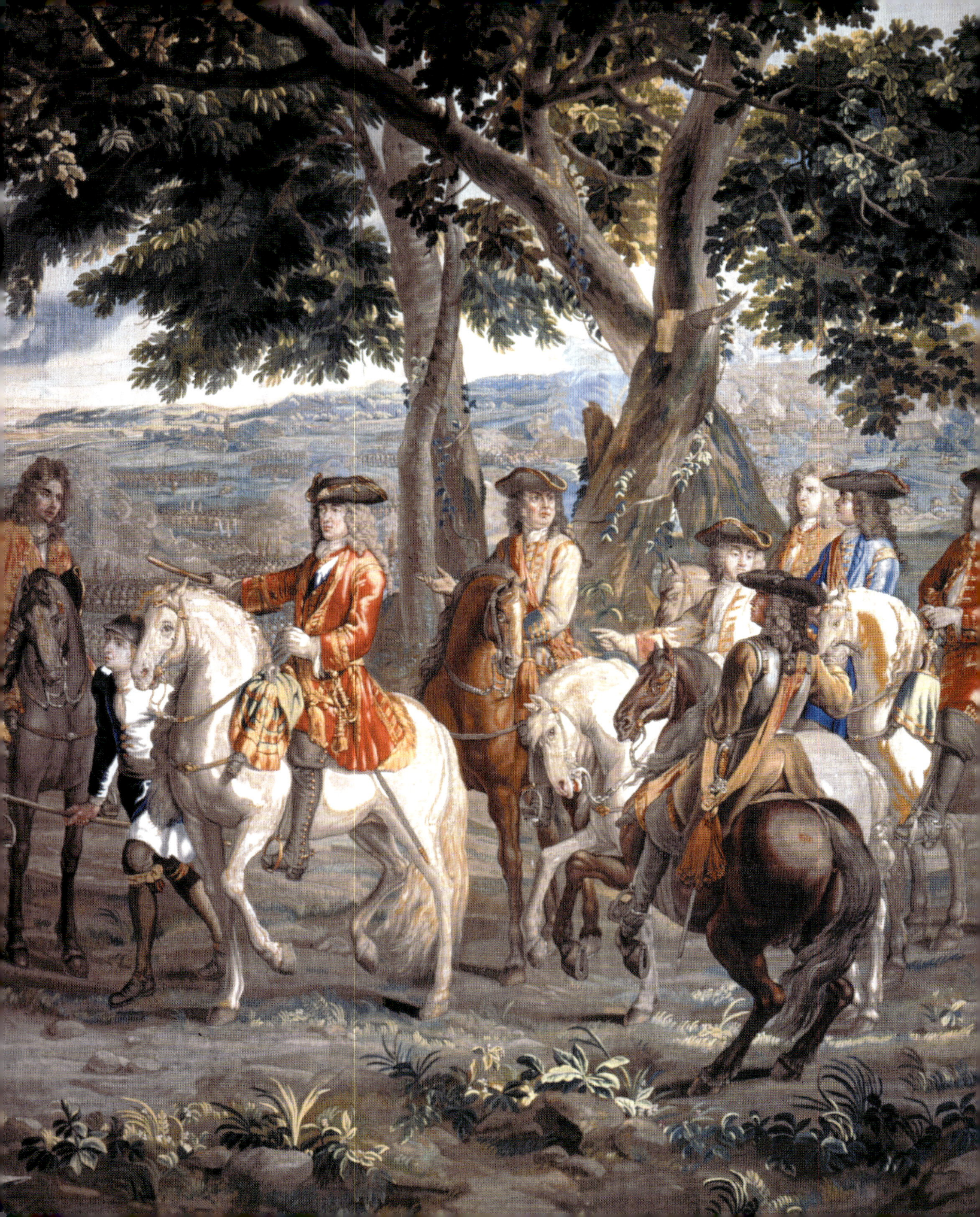

THREADS OF HISTORY
THE TAPESTRIES AT BLENHEIM PALACE

Jeri Bapasola

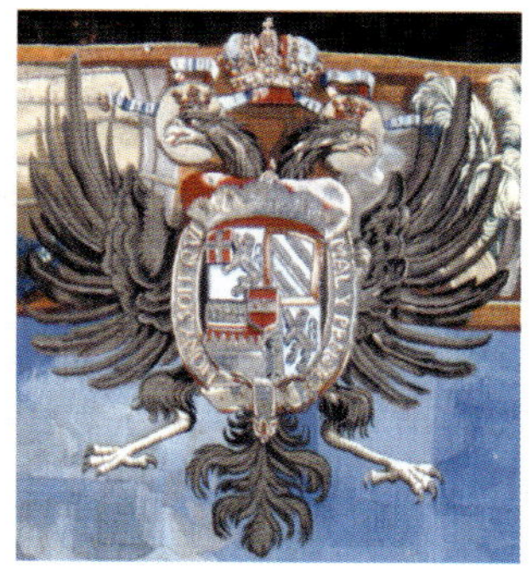

British Library Cataloguing-in-Publication Data.
A catalogue record for this book is available from the British Library

ISBN 0 899889 18 2

Lightmoor Press is an imprint of Black Dwarf Lightmoor
Unit 144b, Lydney Industrial Estate, Harbour Road, Lydney, Gloucestershire, GL15 4EJ
telephone 01993 773927
website: www.lightmoor.co.uk

Printed by The Alden Press, Oxford

Dedicated to the memory of David Chandler and Harold Yexley
with admiration and affection.

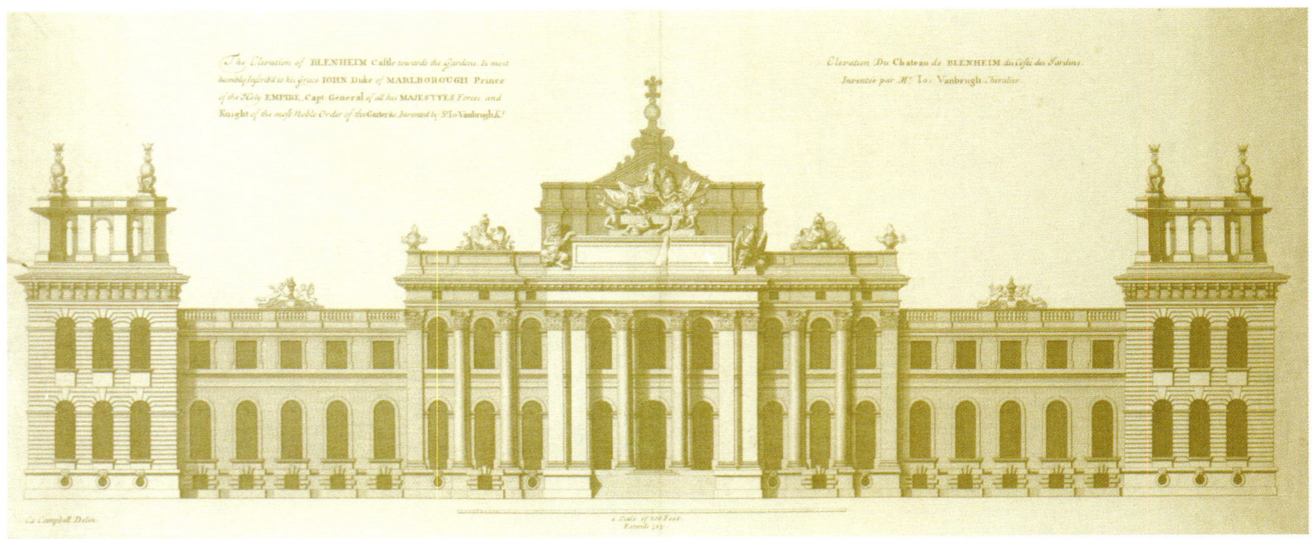

CONTENTS

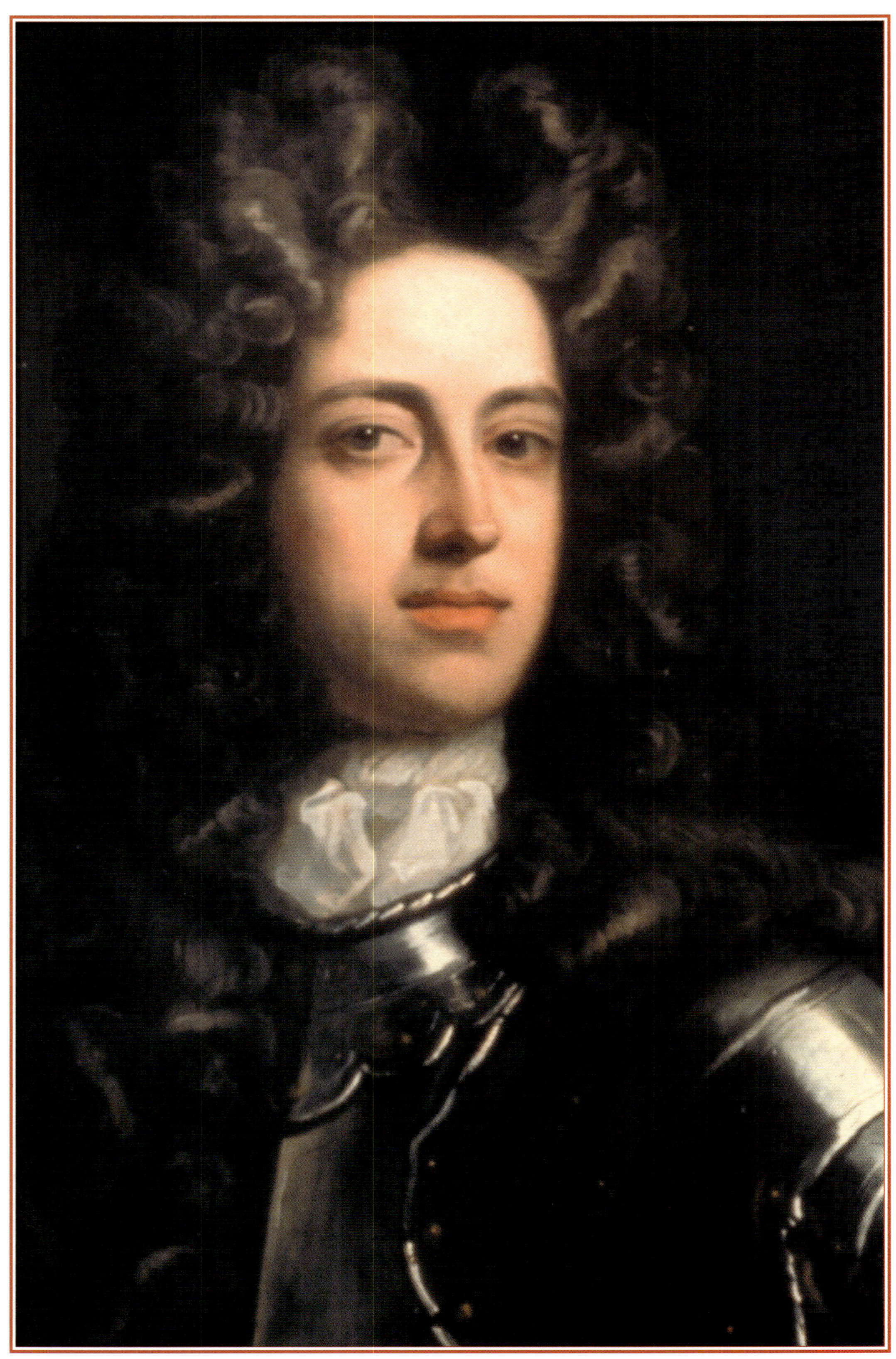

John Churchill,
Duke of Marlborough
by Closterman (detail).

PREFACE

THE tapestries at Blenheim Palace are remarkable in many ways: for their design and variety, for the beauty and quality of their craftsmanship and for their significance in recording aspects of British military history. But what is equally important regarding these tapestries and in particular the set entitled the *Victories of the Duke of Marlborough*, is that they still belong to the family and are even now displayed in the house for which they were commissioned and where they were always intended to be hung. It is far more usual for sets of tapestries not to survive due to imperfect storage conditions or being lost through fire or damp; or else to continue to exist in other locations as a result of distribution amongst heirs. However, while some of the original Blenheim tapestries have indeed been lost or may have been disposed of, four near complete sets of tapestry commissioned by John Churchill almost three hundred years ago still survive in situ, the detailed scenes full of activity, and the yet vibrant colours evidence of the very high quality of these works of art: the Duke of Marlborough's woven legacy.

At Blenheim about four years ago, I was fortunate in being invited by the librarian to work on archival documents at the Palace. This was instrumental in motivating my subsequent research of the history of the tapestry collection. In the preparation of this book I have mainly drawn on primary source material but for specific parts of my research I am indebted to the publications of Alan Wace, Guy Delmarcel, Koen Brosens, Wendy Hefford and David Chandler whose previous scholarship has made my task that little bit easier.

Alan Wace's study *The Marlborough Tapestries at Blenheim Palace and their relation to other military tapestries of the War of the Spanish Succession* was written in the 1930s when he was head of the department of textiles in the Victoria & Albert Museum. He was assisted by H. C. Marillier, the then managing director of the Morris Tapestry Works, who painstakingly compiled a multi volume subject catalogue of tapestries which remains a valuable source of information. For various reasons their work remained unpublished until 1968 when Helen Wace posthumously arranged for her husband's manuscript to be printed. Wace principally discusses two sets of martial tapestries at Blenheim, the *Art of War* and Marlborough's *Victories*. As far as the *Victories* are concerned, it would appear that Wace did not gain access to archival material and he assumed that the *Ramillies* panel was never woven. He also mistakenly believed that Marlborough's *Art of War* set had been gifted to him. However, his work in comparing all the existing sets of *Art of War* tapestries in various locations still remains a fundamental source of reference.

Wendy Hefford, also in the department of textiles at the Victoria & Albert Museum, made the breakthrough on the *Ramillies* tapestry and supplemented the information available on the Blenheim tapestries when she undertook research in the Blenheim archives to help date some *Art of War* tapestries bequeathed to the Museum in 1972. She published her findings in an article entitled *Some Problems concerning the Art of War Tapestries* in the Bulletin de Liaison (No. 41/ 42, 1975 – I et II) of the Centre International d'Etude des Textiles Anciens,

Lyon in which she makes useful comparisons between the 'first' and 'second' version *Art of War* tapestries and Marlborough's *Victories* set.

Subsequently, no specific archival work was undertaken on the tapestries at Blenheim, although ironically, the documents became more easily accessible in 1978 when the bulk of the Blenheim archives, including the papers of John and Sarah Churchill, first Duke and Duchess of Marlborough, were acquired by the British Library (in lieu of tax on the estate of the 10th Duke of Marlborough who died in March 1972). The Blenheim Papers at the British Library are the single most important primary source of information pertaining to the reign of Queen Anne. They are now carefully preserved and arranged into hundreds of bound volumes. Only a very few manuscripts from this early period have remained in the Long Library and the muniments room at Blenheim Palace itself and it is these documents which are referred to in the notes as being from the Blenheim archives.

The established reference works on Flemish tapestry production were Alphonse Wauter's *Essai historique sur les tapisseries et les tapissiers de haute et de basse lisse de Bruxelles* (1876-1878) and Jean Denuce's 1936 publication *Antwerp Art Tapestry and Trade*. More recently, historical scholarship has been greatly advanced by several Belgian researchers. The eminent scholar of Flemish tapestry Professor Dr Guy Delmarcel has published a great number of articles and books, the most important of which, in covering the period under review, was his masterly survey, *Flemish Tapestries* (1999). Further archival research undertaken by Dr. Koen Brosens resulted in an article on the Flemish weaver Judocus de Vos (*Studies in the Decorative Arts* Vol. IX, No. 2, 2002) and valuable information is also provided in his 2004 publication, *A Contextual Study of Brussels Tapestry 1670-1770 – The Dye Works and Tapestry Workshop of Urbanus Leyniers (1674-1747)*.

With regard to the research of the military aspects of this work and to discover why John Churchill is often regarded as the greatest soldier of his time, a quantity of both primary and secondary sources were consulted. I list only those books which were repeatedly employed. First, the monumental biography published in 4 volumes between 1933 and 1938 by his equally illustrious descendant, Winston S. Churchill, entitled *Marlborough : His Life and Times*. Then, the extensive subsequent work of Dr. David G. Chandler, military historian at Sandhurst: *Marlborough as Military Commander* (1973), *The Art of Warfare in the Age of Marlborough* (1976), and *Military Memoirs of Marlborough's Campaigns 1702-1712* (1968), all of which were regularly turned to and drawn upon.

Some sections of this book, including the history and production of tapestry, are directed towards the more general reader. The primary function of this work however, is to present for the first time a contextual study of the Duke of Marlborough's tapestry commissions, taking into account the substantial amount of newly discovered archival information. At Blenheim, we are fortunate in having a remarkable and unique tapestry collection: it has been a joy to unravel some of these threads of history.

NOTES : PRIMARY SOURCE MATERIAL

SPELLING

Spelling during this period was not standardised and was often little more than a phonetic rendering of a particular word. The Duke of Marlborough was a notoriously bad and erratic speller, while the Duchess, although less well educated, was at least consistent in her spelling. On the other hand, the Duke had an extremely legible hand whilst the Duchess's handwriting is much harder to distinguish; her words seem to fly on the page. In quoting from old documents and letters, the original manuscript text has been preserved without any modernisation of the spelling or grammar. Incomplete words have been filled in within brackets. Quotations from texts written in foreign languages have been translated into English.

DATING

The calendar reform set out by Pope Gregory XIII in 1582 was not adopted in England until 1752 by which time there was an 11-day difference between the 'new' Gregorian calendar and the 'old' Julian one. English dating till the mid 18th century was known as 'old style' (O.S.) whereas in the rest of Europe, 'new style' (N.S.) prevailed. So, for example: 2nd August 1704 (O.S.) was 13th August 1704 (N.S.). The dates quoted in this book are as written on the original documents, bearing in mind that those written in England were in O.S. and those written on the continent, sometimes by the same person, were in N.S. It is also worth mentioning that the O.S. year started on Lady Day, 25th March, rather than 1st January, which was the beginning of the N.S. year. So, for example: 24th March 1703 (O.S.) would be followed by 25th March 1704 (O.S.).

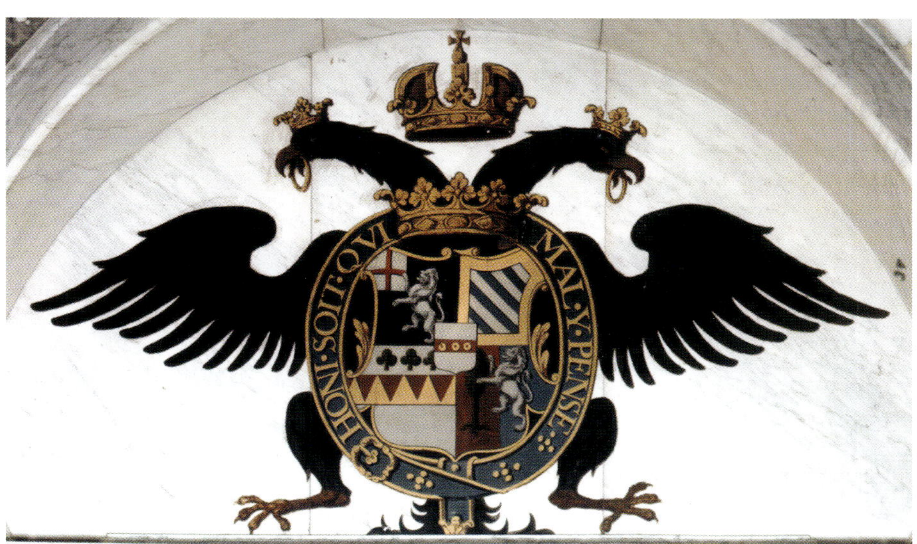

Armorial bearing of John Churchill, 1st Duke of Marlborough.

Map of Europe circa 1700

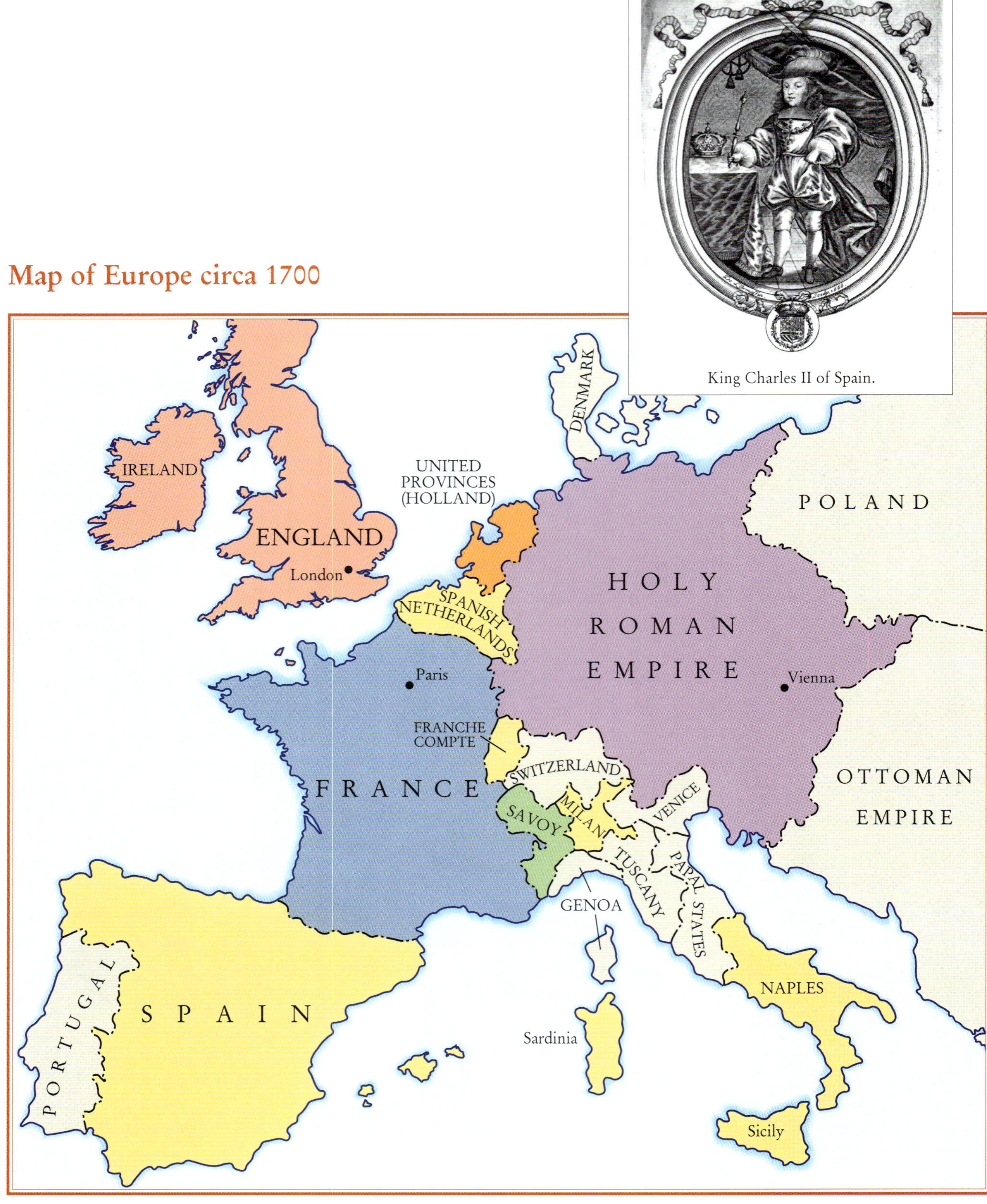

King Charles II of Spain.

Chapter One

SETTING THE SCENE

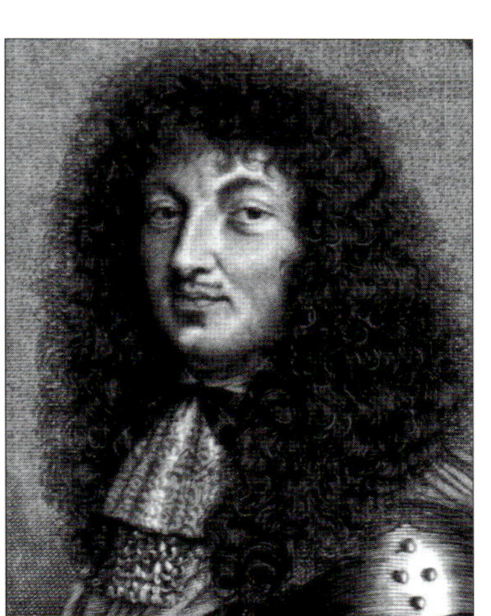

King Louis XIV.

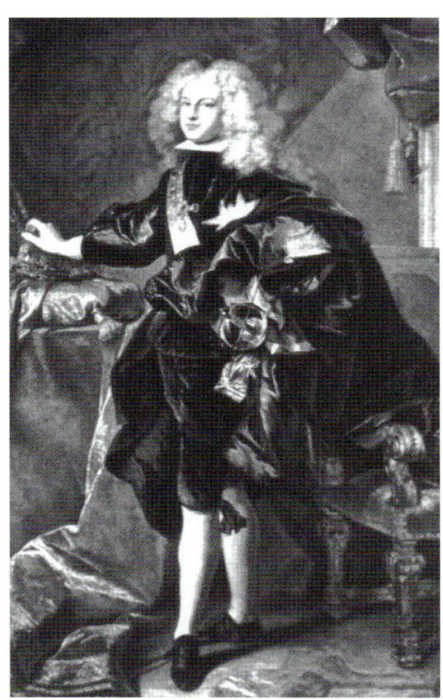

Philip of Anjou, King Philip V of Spain.

IN the spring of 1708 John Churchill, Duke of Marlborough, Captain General of the English and Allied armies was on campaign in Flanders when on 14th May he wrote to his wife from Brussels *"I have been to see the hangings for your apartment and mine, as much as are done of them I think are very fine. I shall not send them over til the Winter unless you desire them. I shou'd be glad at your leasure you wou'd be providing everything that may be necessary for furnishing those two apartments that you wou'd direct Van Brook [Vanbrugh] to finish the breaks between the Windows in the great Cabinett with looking glasses, for I am resolv'd to furnish that roome with the finest picturs I can gett..."* [1]

This was not the first time the Duke had been preoccupied with the finishing and furnishing of Blenheim, the grand baroque palace that was being built for him at public expense under the supervision of the architect John Vanbrugh. The ancient royal hunting estate outside the small Oxfordshire village of Woodstock and the funds for constructing a house there had been granted by Queen Anne after the Duke's great victory in 1704 at the Battle of Blenheim. This decisive battle ended the notion that Louis XIV's French army was invincible and marked the turning point in the War of the Spanish Succession, which was being fought on several fronts in Europe.

The reasons for the war were complex but hinged around the attempt to settle the Spanish succession at the death of the childless King of Spain, Charles II. There were three claimants to his throne and the division of the vast Spanish empire was determined by treaties negotiated between the major powers in Europe in the years leading up to the Spanish King's death in 1700. Despite the efforts to reconcile many conflicting interests, the dying King, in an attempt to keep his empire intact, named in his will Louis XIV's grandson Philip Duke of Anjou as his heir, abrogating the previously negotiated settlements.

War was now almost inevitable as Louis XIV decided to accept the terms of the will over the implementation of the Partition Treaties.[2] Proclaiming his grandson King Philip V of Spain, Louis attacked and occupied several fortresses and towns in the Spanish Netherlands, situated to the north of France (in present day Belgium). This action threatened not only Dutch security but also the balance of power in Europe. So, to limit French ambitions and to prevent Louis XIV from subjugating Europe, a Grand Alliance was formed between England, the United Provinces (Holland), some German dominions, and the Holy Roman Empire (a confederation of states headed by the Austrian Habsburgs).

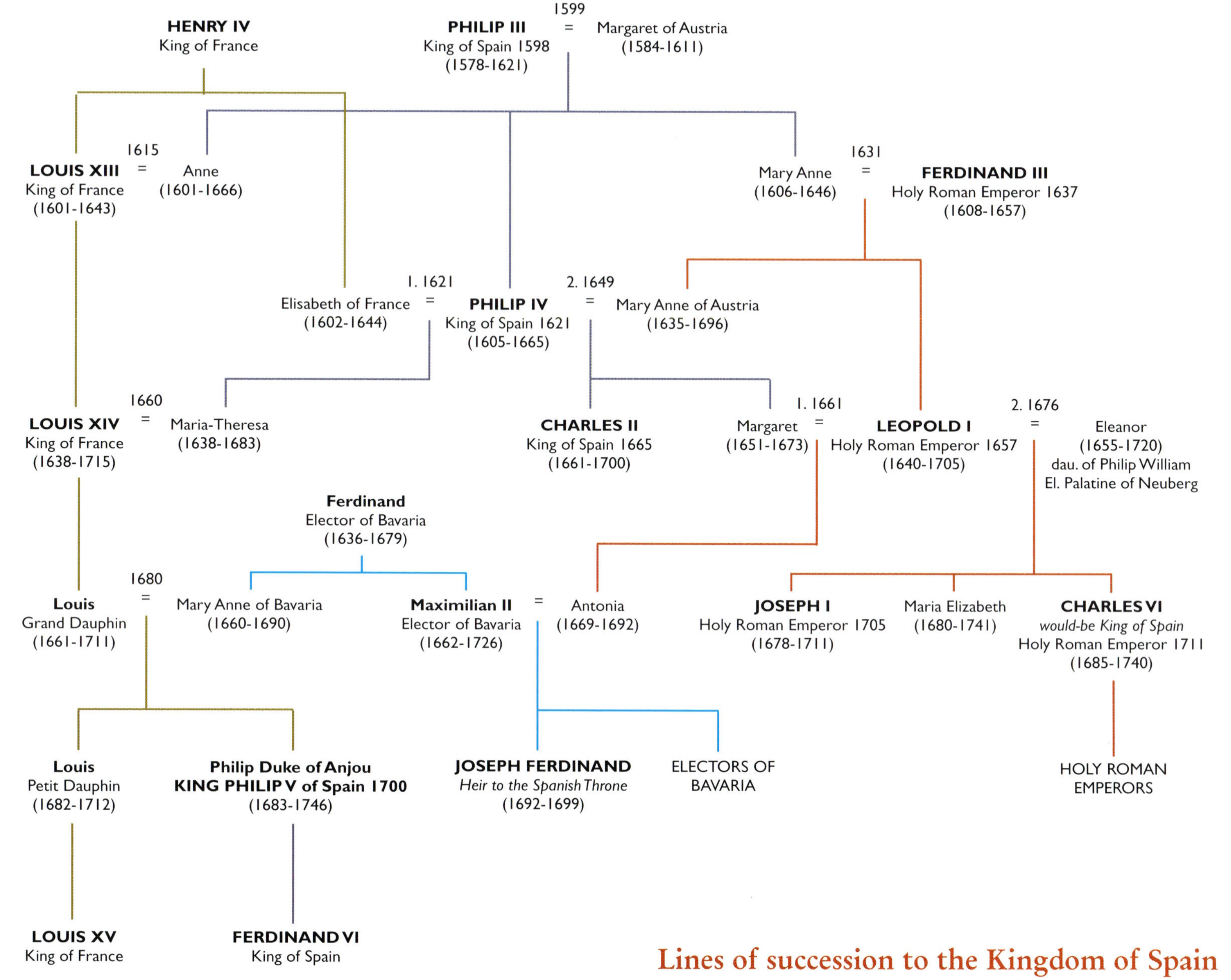

HENRY IV
King of France

PHILIP III
King of Spain 1598
(1578-1621)
1599 = Margaret of Austria
(1584-1611)

LOUIS XIII
King of France
(1601-1643)
1615 = Anne
(1601-1666)

Mary Anne
(1606-1646)
1631 =
FERDINAND III
Holy Roman Emperor 1637
(1608-1657)

Elisabeth of France
(1602-1644)
1. 1621 =
PHILIP IV
King of Spain 1621
(1605-1665)
2. 1649 = Mary Anne of Austria
(1635-1696)

LOUIS XIV
King of France
(1638-1715)
1660 = Maria-Theresa
(1638-1683)

CHARLES II
King of Spain 1665
(1661-1700)

Margaret
(1651-1673)
1. 1661 =
LEOPOLD I
Holy Roman Emperor 1657
(1640-1705)
2. 1676 = Eleanor
(1655-1720)
dau. of Philip William
El. Palatine of Neuberg

Ferdinand
Elector of Bavaria
(1636-1679)

Louis
Grand Dauphin
(1661-1711)
1680 =
Mary Anne of Bavaria
(1660-1690)

Maximilian II
Elector of Bavaria
(1662-1726)
= Antonia
(1669-1692)

JOSEPH I
Holy Roman Emperor 1705
(1678-1711)

Maria Elizabeth
(1680-1741)

CHARLES VI
would-be King of Spain
Holy Roman Emperor 1711
(1685-1740)

Louis
Petit Dauphin
(1682-1712)

Philip Duke of Anjou
KING PHILIP V of Spain 1700
(1683-1746)

JOSEPH FERDINAND
Heir to the Spanish Throne
(1692-1699)

ELECTORS OF
BAVARIA

HOLY ROMAN
EMPERORS

LOUIS XV
King of France

FERDINAND VI
King of Spain

Lines of succession to the Kingdom of Spain

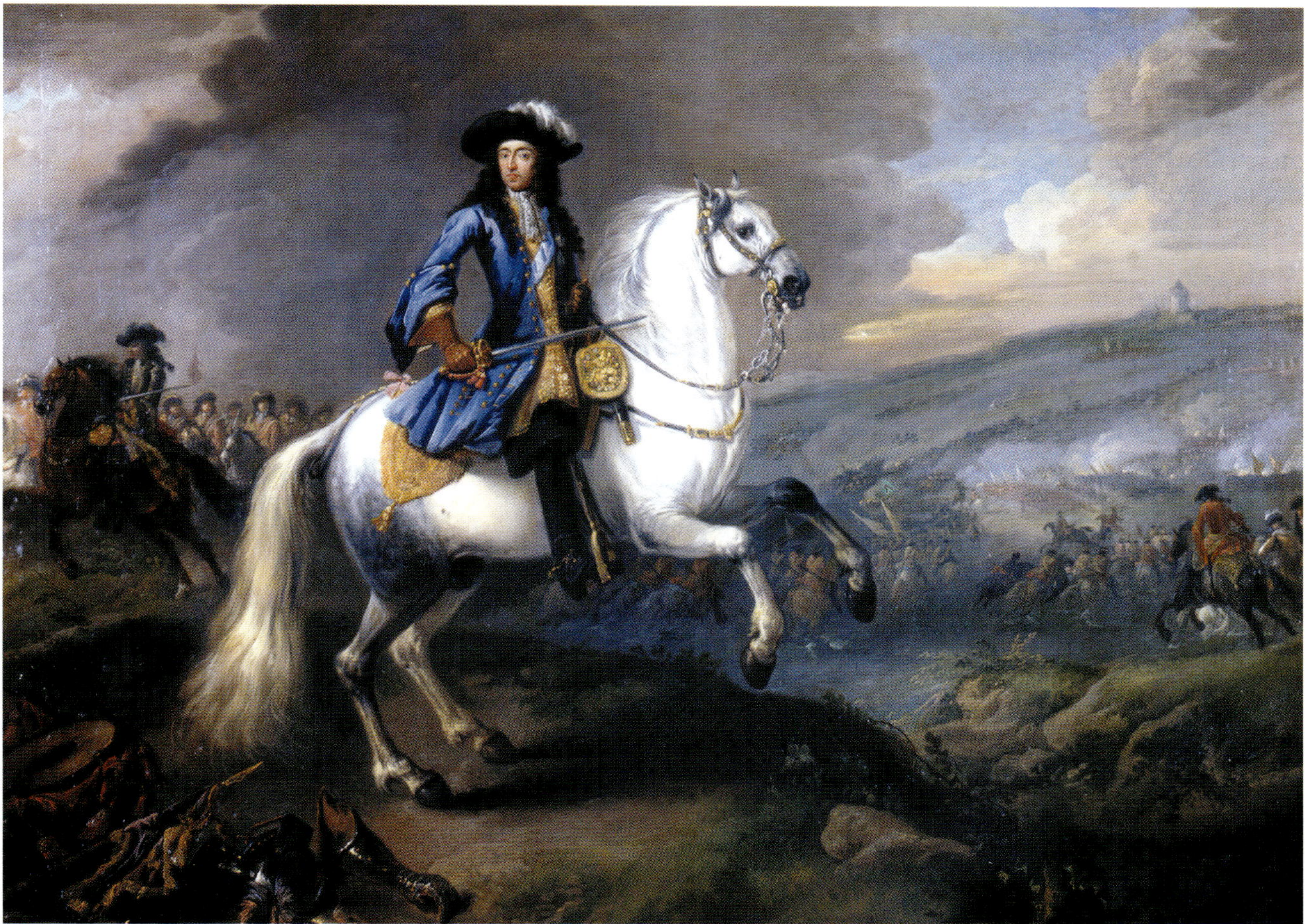

King William III by Jan Wyck.

King William III (who had joined in the negotiations of both Partition Treaties), might not have been able to convince parliament in England of the need to go to war had Louis XIV not provoked deep religious outrage in England by publicly acknowledging, in September 1701, that the rightful claimant to the English throne was the exiled King James II's catholic son, James Edward Stuart (the Old Pretender).

When King William died in March 1702 and Queen Anne ascended the English throne, John Churchill, then Earl of Marlborough,[3] was sent to the continent to negotiate with the Dutch and other states forming the Alliance and war was declared against France and Spain in May 1702. In July, Churchill, aged 52, was appointed Captain-General of the Allied forces and soon afterwards Master General of the Ordinance.

The war lasted a decade and was punctuated at regular intervals with major battles and victories for the Allies led by Marlborough in Flanders: the most successful was at Blenheim in 1704, the most profitable at Ramillies in 1706, the most daring at Oudenarde in 1708 and the most costly at Malplaquet in 1709. Apart from these four major battles, almost thirty fortresses were besieged and taken, not to mention several other successful minor actions and combats. However, on the Spanish front things did not go as well for the Allies and after ten years of fighting, England was war weary, the country was dominated by party politics and Marlborough's position was undermined by his enemies at home. The new administration desired peace at any cost and a negotiated settlement ended the hostilities in 1713 when the Peace of Utrecht was signed.

The Battle of Blenheim had not only been a turning point in the War of the Spanish Succession, raising a question mark over the previously held notion of French superiority and invincibility, but it was also, more importantly, the dawn of a long period of expansion and consolidation which saw Britain's rise to spectacular achievement on the world stage. The political and economic scene had been set by this remarkable victory, followed by further successes gained by Marlborough with almost mechanical accomplishment which would lead to Britain being pushed, for the first time, from the edge of Europe into the centre of the global stage. The resultant subsequent growth of trade routes and an ambitious programme of empire building through colonisation meant that by the end of the eighteenth century, the map of the world had been redrawn and British supremacy within it was unquestioned.

In the early 1700s the Marlboroughs were the most powerful political family in England. John Churchill, an ambitious and able man, born outside the traditional aristocratic governing class, had been able to rise to a position of prominence. By the end of his career he had become the greatest military commander of his time. His pre-eminence as Captain General of the English army, along with his wife Sarah's envied position as Queen Anne's favourite at Court, was a passport to their social and material success. Their importance

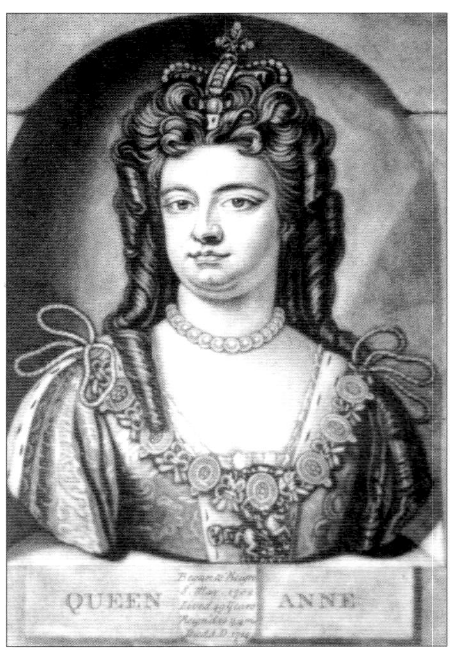

Queen Anne.

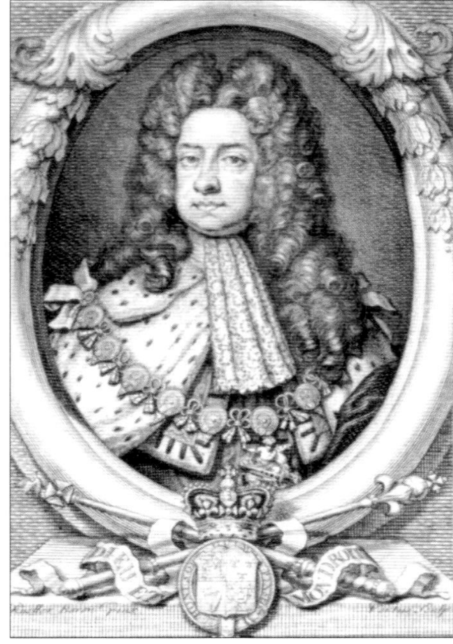

King George I.

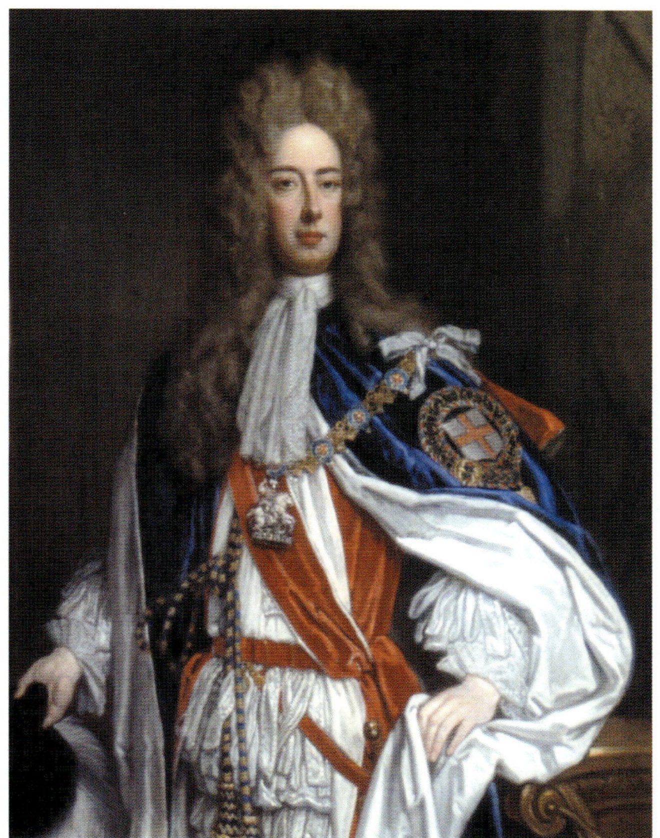

John Churchill, Duke of Marlborough
by Sir Godfrey Kneller.

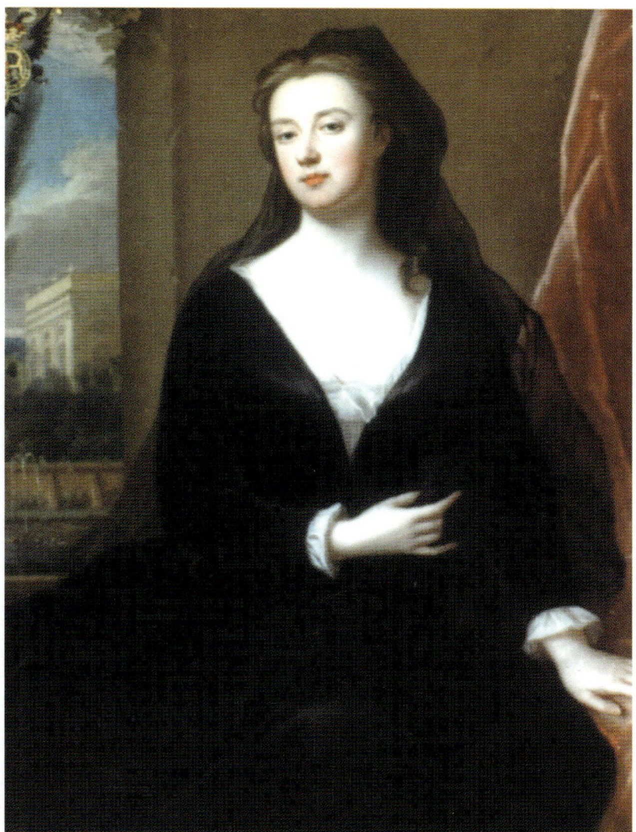

Sarah Churchill, Duchess of Marlborough
attributed to Charles Jervas.

and influence at the heart of government was to continue for many years until political and personal differences triggered Sarah's eventual fall from royal esteem. This resulted in the Marlboroughs being dismissed from all their significant offices in the last years of the Queen's reign, only returning to favour once more, for a short time, when George I came to the throne in 1714.

John Churchill's victories count amongst the greatest moments in British military history even today, 300 years after the Battle of Blenheim. The house he had built and so splendidly furnished stands as a monument to his achievement. Alexander the Great once said "*It is a lovely thing to live with courage and die leaving an everlasting fame*" : John Churchill's legacy still endures through his tapestries, some of which are Blenheim Palace's most important surviving historical records of his military accomplishments.

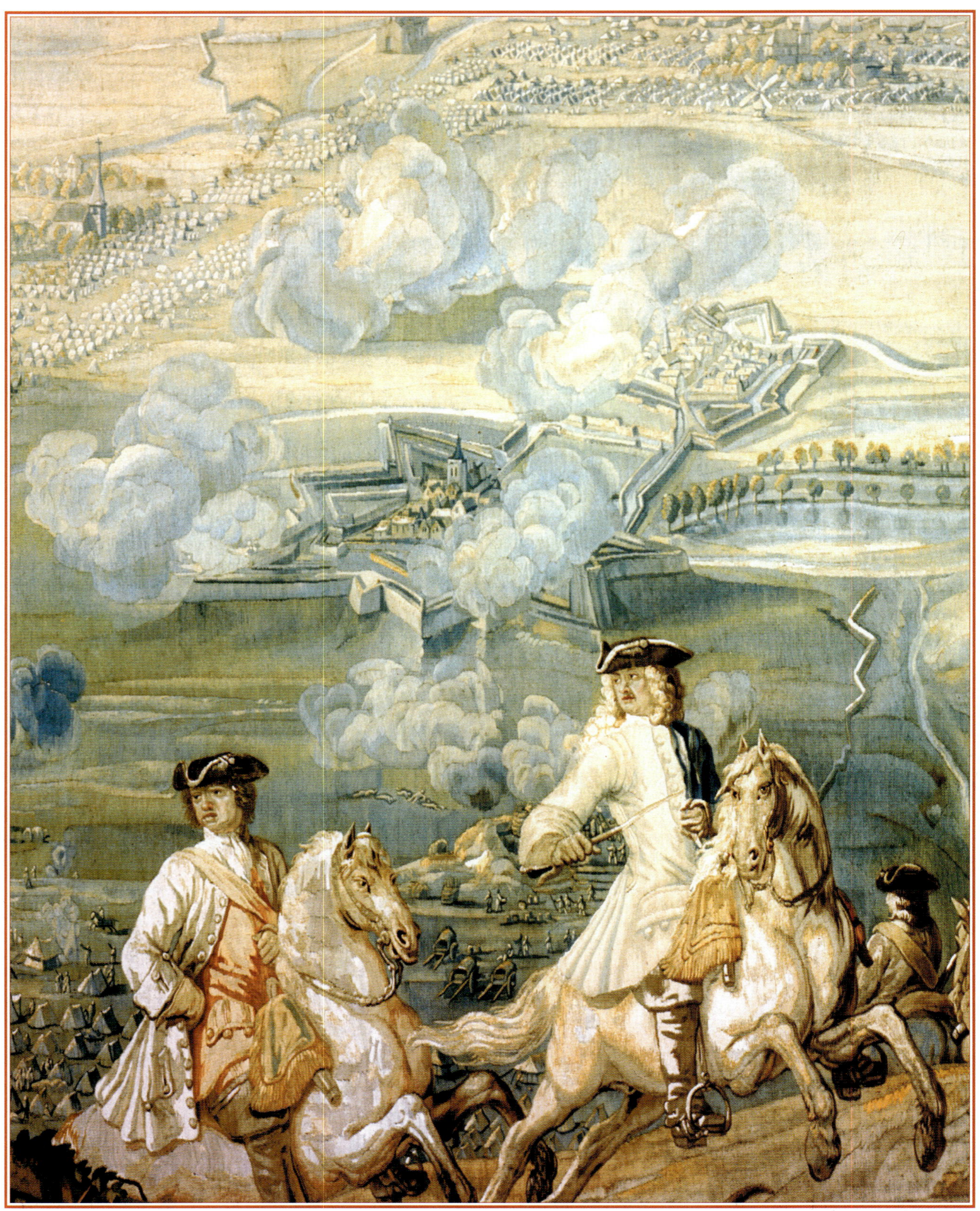

Chapter Two

TAPESTRY DESIGN & PRODUCTION TECHNIQUE

ORIGINALLY, tapestries were an essential part of the furnishing of royal households, great expenditure being lavished on them to promote both the image and the authority of the monarch and his entourage. These possessions were acquired to confirm not only the high status and power but also the wealth of those who commissioned them.

Military subjects had always been popular for representation in tapestry. Martial tapestries sometimes formed part of the court propaganda, as they were more suited to a demonstration of stately power than other decorative editions. In the late fourteenth century, the great patron of tapestry, Philip the Bold, Duke of Burgundy,[4] commissioned exclusive tapestry creations celebrating his achievements. But such specific contemporary events enacting moments of great drama in the life of the patron were not the frequently chosen option as this required designs specially made to order which were expensive to produce and were usually of limited interest to other potential customers beyond the original patron. Apart from exceptionally wealthy nobles who were able to afford to commission their own sets of newly designed tapestries, the trade in martial tapestries (as in other more decorative sets) was led by entrepreneurial merchants who commissioned new designs. For commercial reasons the scenes depicted were chosen predominantly from classical, mythical or historical warfare (such as the History of Troy, of Clovis, of Caesar or of the legendary Alexander), which would have a broader appeal and from which they could make several other editions for a variety of clients who would be able to chose either the heroes or the concepts with which they wished to be associated.

Louis XIV, King of France (1643-1715), revived the tradition of ordering exclusive tapestries of contemporary military subjects. In a specially commissioned set of fourteen panels which related the great events of his reign (the *Histoire du Roi* series), half represented his battles and sieges. These were designed by Charles Le Brun and were woven at the Royal Manufactory of the Gobelins, established in 1662 by Jean-Baptiste Colbert, Louis's Minister of Finance. The production of tapestries, furniture, paintings and other works of art in silver, gold and bronze at the Gobelins was entirely reserved for royal commissions, either to be displayed and used in the palaces and other residences of the King and the royal family or for gifts offered by them. The factory closed down due to financial difficulty in 1694 and recommenced production on a commercial basis in 1699, the second phase of its operation, but only to produce tapestries.[5] The manufactory at Beauvais was founded by Colbert in 1664 and supplied the open market with tapestries. Production in both these centres flourished and presented significant competition for the long established Flemish weavers.

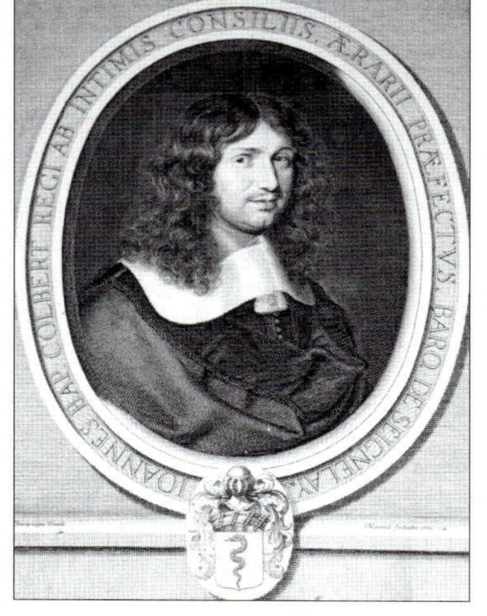

Jean-Baptiste Colbert.

Facing page :
Detail from the *Bouchain III* tapestry.

The decoration of the interiors of palaces built by royalty and the aristocracy often constituted an important part of their legacy and consequently the vogue for contemporary battle tapestries found equal favour with King Christian V of Denmark, King Charles XI of Sweden and the Elector Max Emmanuel of Bavaria to name but a few. While French tapestry workshops had been busy producing panels glorifying Louis XIV, all of his rivals, including King William III,[6] the Duke of Marlborough and Prince Eugene of Savoy, patronised the workshops of Flemish weavers.

For a variety of reasons (beyond the scope of this book), royal patronage of tapestry commissioning slowed down in the early eighteenth century and the aristocracy became the principal customers of tapestry workshops. Flemish tapestry production now particularly focused on meeting the tastes and requirements of this increasingly powerful and wealthy class of nobles. On her accession, Queen Anne acquired a substantial collection of tapestries (mainly consisting of the great antique tapestries purchased by Henry VIII and later additions made under Charles II and William III) but she is not known to have commissioned a single new tapestry during her twelve-year reign. On the other hand, the Duke of Marlborough was an important client of the Flemish workshops and obtained from them several sets of tapestries from 1705 to 1717. Of the six sets of tapestries the Duke is known to have commissioned, no less than three were ordered with military subjects, all brilliantly designed and executed, serving to immortalise the greatness of his martial achievement.

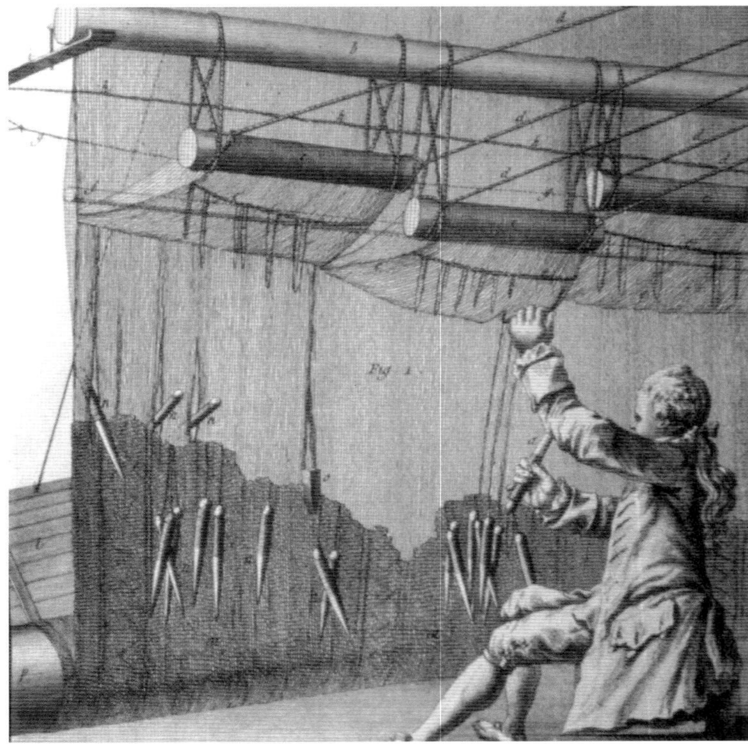

View of a high-warp tapestry weaver at work.

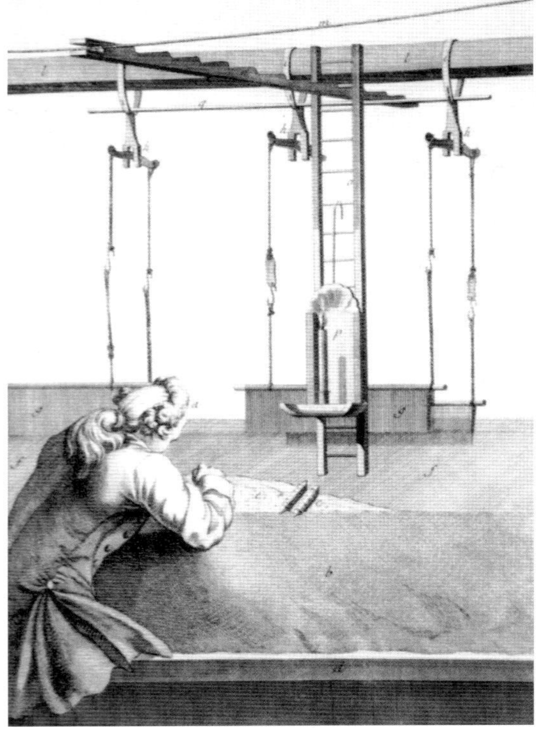

View of a low-warp tapestry weaver at work.

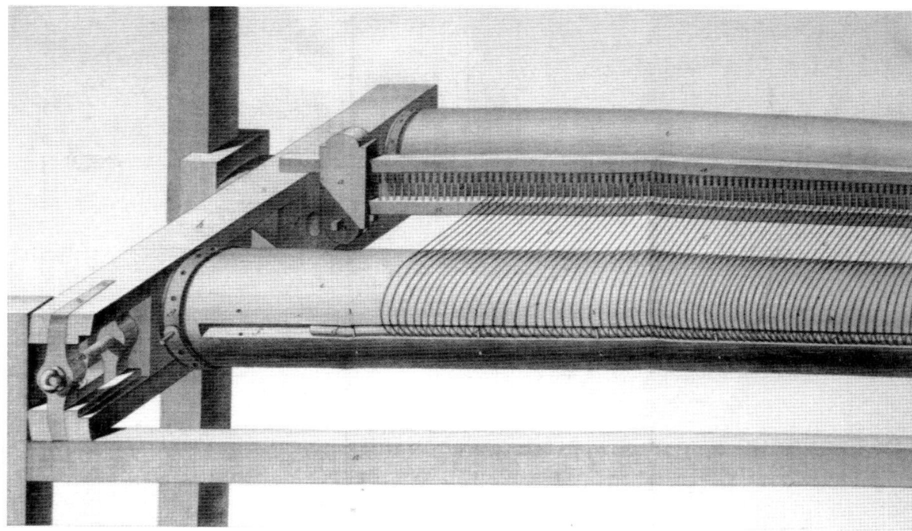

Tapestry is a form of textile woven by hand on a loom where the weaver builds up the pattern or design using coloured threads on a base of plain threads. Flemish weavers followed a tradition of low-warp (*basse-lisse*) tapestry manufacture, using a horizontal loom with foot operated treadles. French weavers employed this technique as well as the high-warp (*haute-lisse*) technique on a vertical loom. It is virtually impossible to distinguish on which type of loom a finished tapestry has been woven.

Whichever loom was used, a tapestry was formed on it by the weaving of lengthwise plain threads (warps) with crosswise coloured threads (wefts) in a specific manner to form a panel. The tapestry was woven horizontally from left to right with the weaver working on the reverse of the panel.

The loom consisted of two wooden rollers between which plain warp threads, usually of undyed wool, were fixed. The weaving process was undertaken to form the picture by passing bobbins or shuttles of different coloured weft threads through specific sections of the warps according to

Below : A bobbin of coloured (weft) thread being passed under a section of the warp.

Below right : The coloured weft threads are pressed firmly together by means of a comb-like tool.

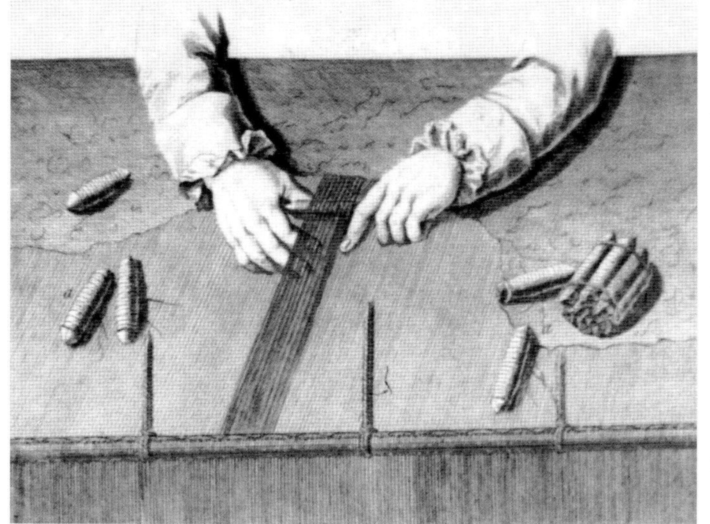

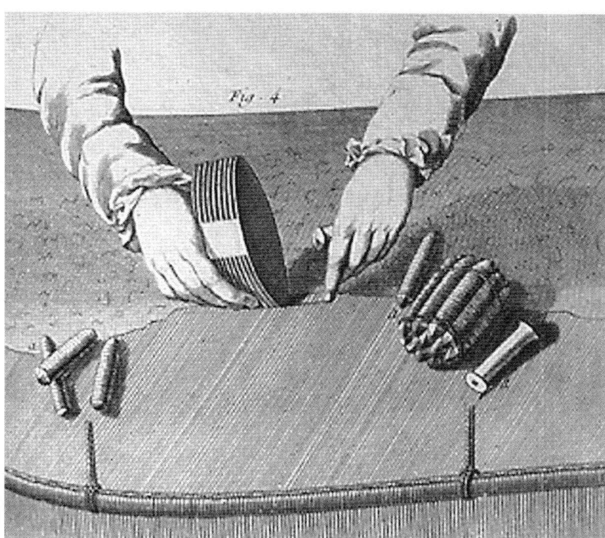

the design of the tapestry. The weft threads were finer threads, usually of wool but sometimes of silk for highlighted areas and in richer tapestries, of silver and gold. The wefts were passed both over and under the warps, in an alternating sequence, and were then beaten tightly down with a comb-like tool so as to completely cover the warps.

Weaving was a slow and laborious process but the low warp method of production had the advantage of being quicker to operate as the weaver also used his feet to control treadles that were linked to drawstrings to open up spaces between the warp threads. The bobbins of coloured weft threads could then be passed quickly and easily through these spaces (called sheds) as he had both hands free. In contrast, the high warp weaver had to use his hands for every move of the weaving operation. A tapestry on a low warp loom would normally take only about two thirds of the time required for the same panel to be woven on a high warp loom, so proving more economical to produce.

The dimensions of a tapestry panel depended on both artistic and technical considerations. The artist would produce or adapt a design in accordance with the patron's requirements but the ultimate size of a tapestry panel was also technically limited by the span of the loom. Warp threads the width of

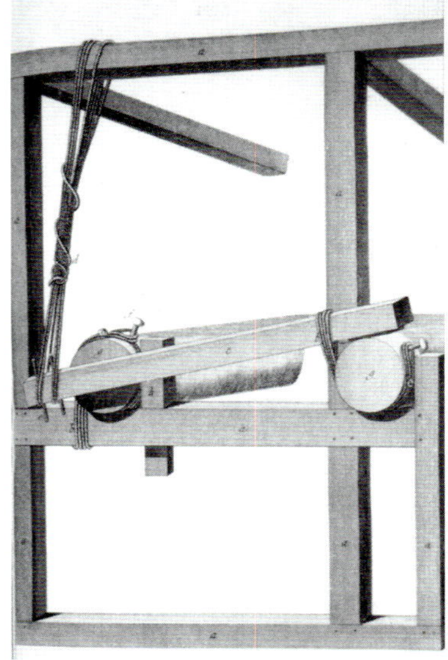

A side view of a low warp loom. The warp threads were tensioned between the two cylinders.

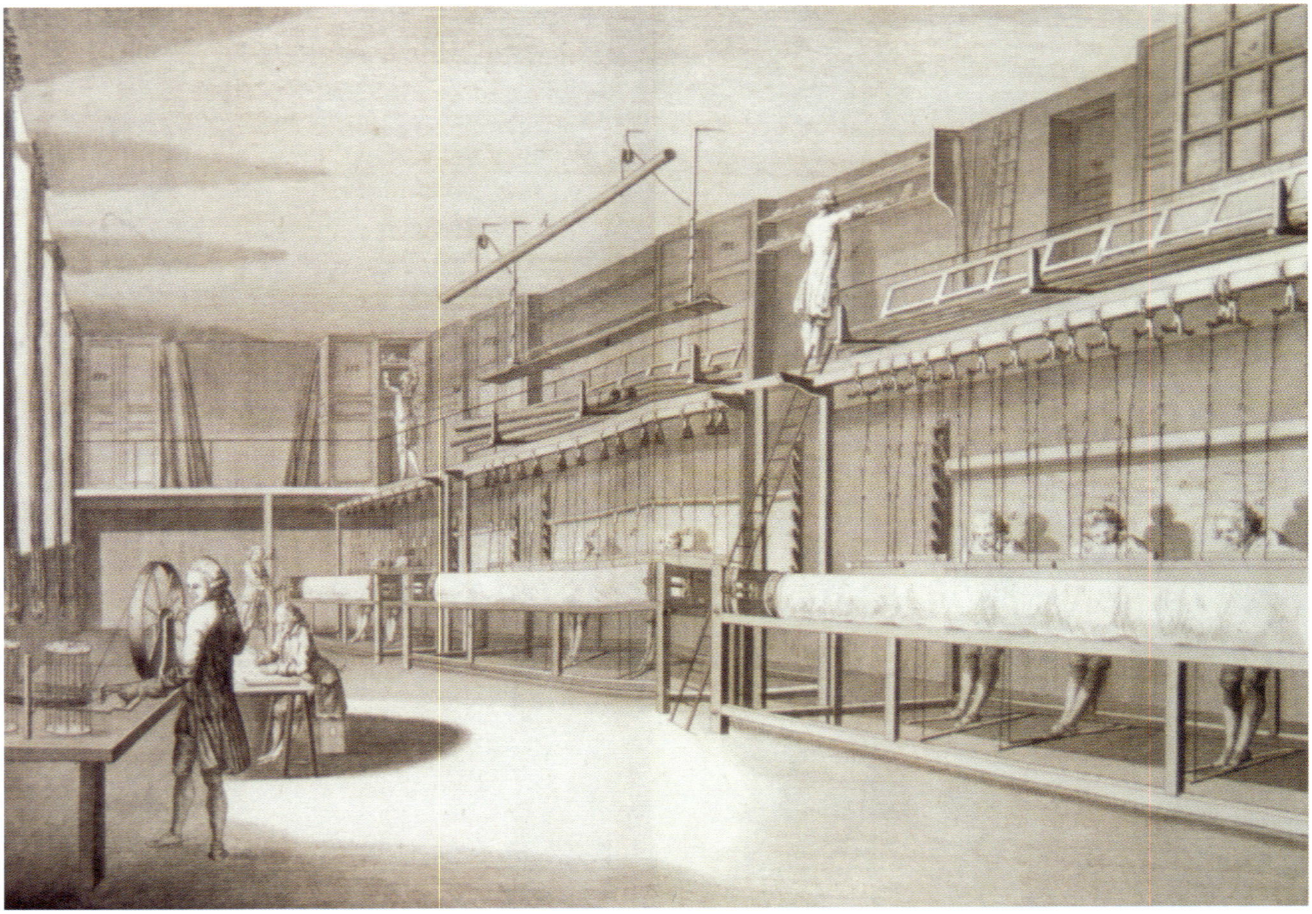

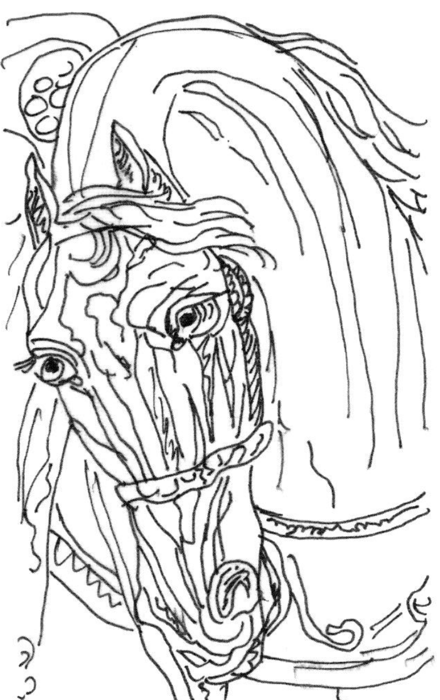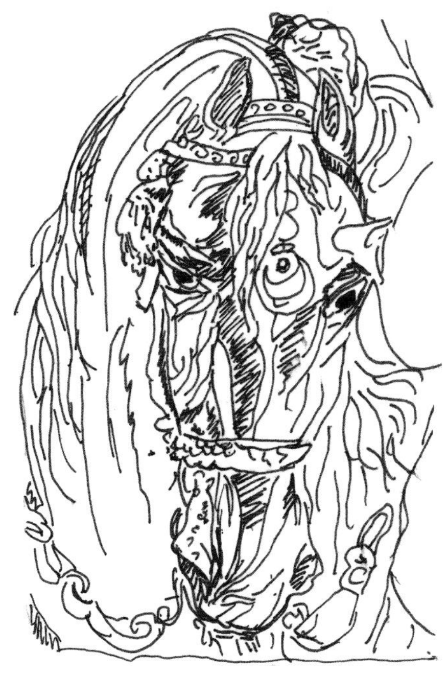

the tapestry panel were rolled onto the loom. This was an operation that necessitated a certain skill as the entire panel had to be woven with these threads at the same tension throughout. The height of the tapestry was established by the number of warp threads fixed along the span of the rollers. In the seventeenth and early eighteenth centuries, the very finest tapestries had roughly 20-25 warps per inch (8-10 warps per cm). The maximum height that could be accommodated was roughly 15 feet (450cms). Once the height of the tapestry was fixed, it could be repeated for each of the panels in the series, ensuring the floor to ceiling dimensions remained the same for the entire set, whatever the width of each panel.

The method of weaving also affected the way the cartoon was made and used. Derived from the Italian word '*cartone*' (meaning a strong piece of paper), the cartoon was a full-scale picture where the composition and colouring was worked out in detail and from which the weaver copied the artist's design. As the weaver's model, it was a purely functional work of art, an intermediate but crucial step in the production of a tapestry from its initial design to the finished woven panel.

The cartoon was produced by gluing together several sheets of paper to create the actual dimensions of the tapestry panel. The design of the tapestry was then drawn or painted onto the paper using watercolours. For the low warp method, the cartoon was cut up vertically into narrow sections, generally about $2^{1}/_{2}$ feet (75-80cms) wide. This was done carefully to avoid cutting through a face or any other significant areas where specialist weavers might be employed. The cartoon strips were placed under the warp threads of the loom where the weaver worked on the rear of the tapestry, thereby producing a panel that was the mirror image of the cartoon.

Innovatory new methods in cartoon drawing and working technique were initiated by Rubens in the early 17th century. Rubens painted his cartoons in oil on actual-size canvases.[7] These paintings were not cut up into strips, but a coloured copy was made on paper and divided into sections which the weavers used under the loom. Both techniques of cartoon preparation were in use at the time the Blenheim Palace tapestries were produced, although according to Dr. Brosens, in the first half of the eighteenth century, cartoons painted in oil on canvas rather than watercolour on paper were predominant in the production of Flemish tapestry.

An obvious disadvantage of the low warp technique caused by the cartoon being placed under the warp was that the workman, being only able to see a small section of the cartoon at any one time through the warps, though able to reproduce every detail in the work, was only able to judge the whole composition by referring to a sketch or small painting of it. He did not see the final result until the tapestry was completed and taken off the loom, by which time it was too time consuming and too expensive and therefore too late to remedy any mistakes.*

This method of employment of the cartoon allowed tapestry production to have many variations. Used many times if the composition was a popular one, cartoons were also copied, leased or sold. They could be altered when re-used for a different client or another destination, every edition allowing for a variety of alternatives in not only the final design but also in colour and in the detail of the decorative borders. Sections could be added or omitted depending on the requirement and size of each individual commission. For example, in a document from the Blenheim archives, the suppliers indicate to the Duke of Marlborough that one of the cartoons in the *History of Alexander* set "*... can be made into two or three sections, being 36 feet 5 inches, representing the Battle and Capture of Porus*".[8]

As already mentioned, the low warp weaver's technique produced a tapestry panel that was the mirror image of the cartoon. The cartoon artists had to be aware of the direction and sense of the final picture in producing the cartoon where the entire design was reversed. For example, in the set now called the *Victories of the Duke of Marlborough*, if the tapestry required the Duke's right hand to be raised, holding out his commander's baton, then the cartoon artist had to ensure that the left hand was drawn raised. This compensation was done

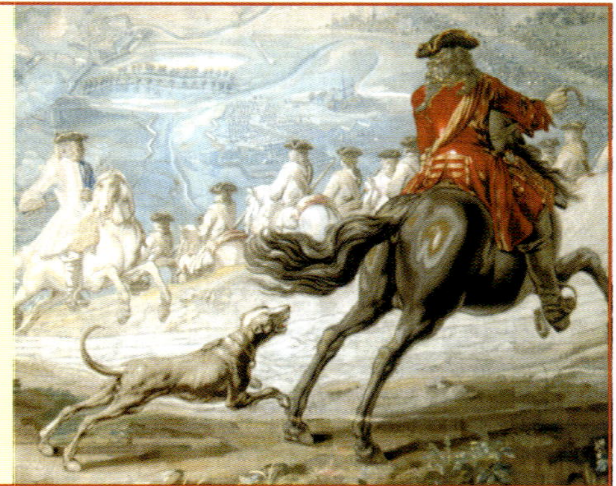

* This appears to be the most likely explanation for the curious dog (which seems to be galloping and has horses hooves) in the *Bouchain III* panel of the *Victories* set: all the other animals in the set are horses.

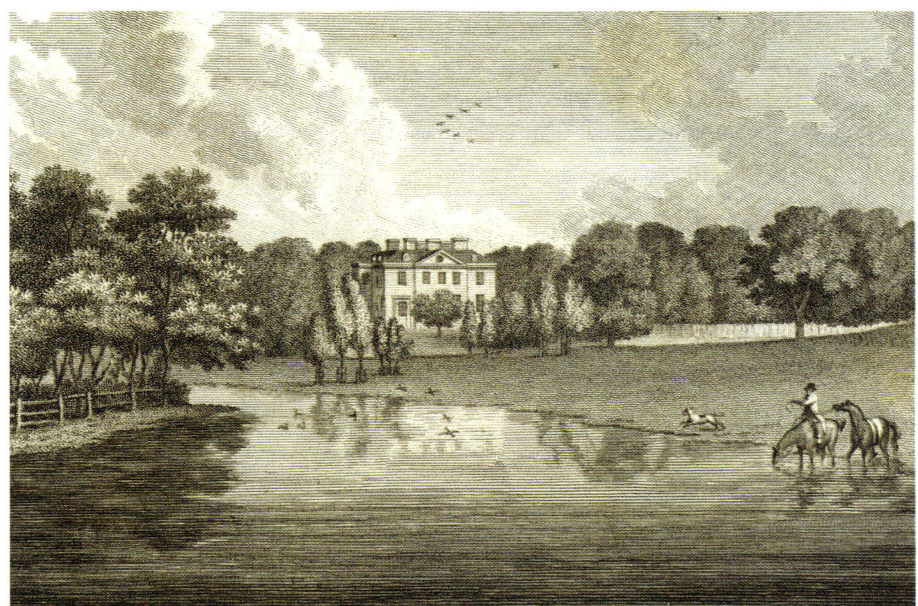

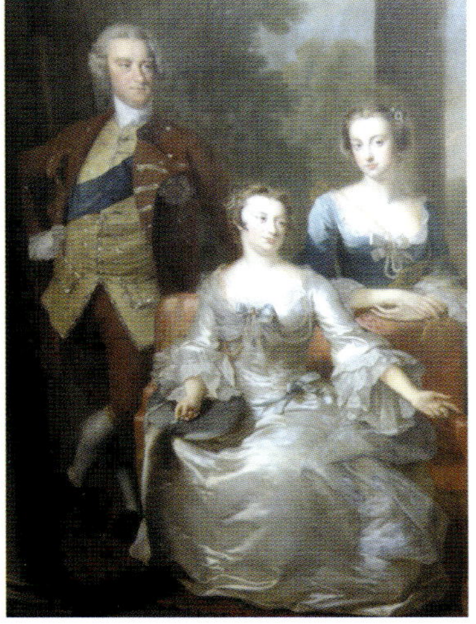

Charles, 3rd Duke of Marlborough
by Hudson (detail).

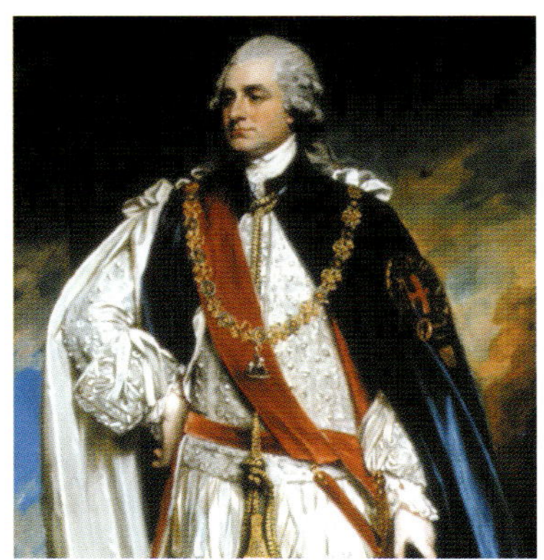

George, 4th Duke of Marlborough
by Romney (detail).

not only for gesture but also for facial representation, costume or dress, as well as for any inscriptions. It was not unusual practice because craftsmen of other media, such as engraving, were also faced with a similar problem of the eventual reversal of their composition.

This method of production was employed in the design of any newly commissioned set of tapestries including the spectacular tapestry series at Blenheim called the *Victories of the Duke of Marlborough*. Because of the way cartoons were used and often re-used so many times until they were completely worn, most of them have perished. Nonetheless, a search for any surviving designs for Marlborough's tapestries led to the very exciting discovery of a painting by de Hondt that belongs in the British Government art collection today. Entitled *Marlborough at the Battle of Bouchain*,[9] it is the design for the small *Bouchain* tapestry in the *Victories* set of the Blenheim collection. More importantly, the picture must have been enlarged and transferred in reverse to a full scale cartoon for the tapestry, because the painting is in the same direction as the tapestry.

Although the existence of this painting has previously gone unnoticed, it was part of the family's art collection and was known to be hung at Langley Park. Langley was an old 17th century mansion built by Sir Robert Kederminster on an estate near Slough which ironically was once the home of Abigail Masham, Sarah Churchill's rival at court, before it was purchased in 1738 by the 3rd Duke of Marlborough. In 1788, the 4th Duke sold the estate to Sir Robert Bateson Harvey, a magistrate and MP for Buckinghamshire. This painting, amongst other things, remained the property of the Harvey family until the last Lady Harvey's death in 1935. Mr. Morgan Grenville, her grandson and heir then disposed of the estate. The picture was acquired by the Property Services Agency of the former Department of the Environment in 1977 and now forms part of the Government art collection.

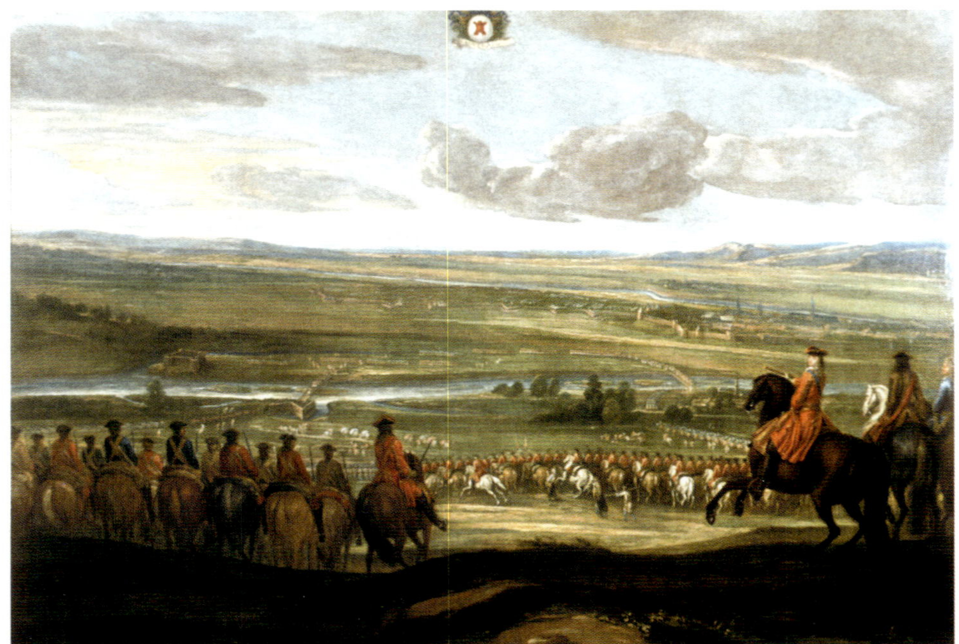

The painting measures 4ft 6in. high (137cms) by 6ft 3in. wide (191cms), while the corresponding tapestry is 14ft 6in. high (442cms) by 12ft 5in. wide (378cms). The increase in the scale of the composition and the necessary additional stretching of the image along its vertical axis has allowed the cartoon artists to produce a very detailed and broadened rendering of the topography which is not as evident in the painted work. It is also interesting that in the painting John Churchill is not at all recognisable, while in the tapestry his portrait is quite convincingly rendered. The accurate depiction of faces was done at the cartoon stage of the production process with auxiliary cartoons being used by highly skilled weavers for the individual heads made from portraits supplied by the patrons themselves.

In Louis XIV's *Histoire du Roi* series, fourteen different portraits were specially painted for the depiction of important characters included in the tapestry panels[10] but this was not a common practice and would only have been undertaken in exceptionally prestigious commissions. Judocus de Vos, the master weaver who undertook the Duke's *Victories* commission is known to have reassured him of the quality of portraiture he might expect in his tapestries, writing to him from Brussels, "*I will examine yet again that there is nothing missing from the drawing of Your Highness's portrait*".[11]

The Duke of Marlborough did not purchase the cartoons for his tapestries although these had been offered to him for a payment of 5,000 florins.[12] On 26th August 1717, Sarah, Duchess of Marlborough (who occupied herself in conducting the Duke's business in his last years after he suffered a stroke), wrote in a letter to Lord Cadogan "... *I hope there was some bargain made with the Tapistry man that he might not impose as most of these people are apt to do. But when he is not left to him self I know hee has sold the same Designs at very reasonable prices...*".[13]

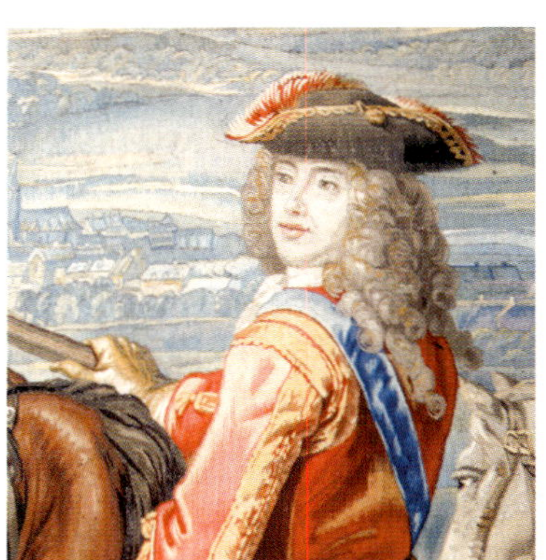

John Churchill's portrait in the *Bouchain II* tapestry.

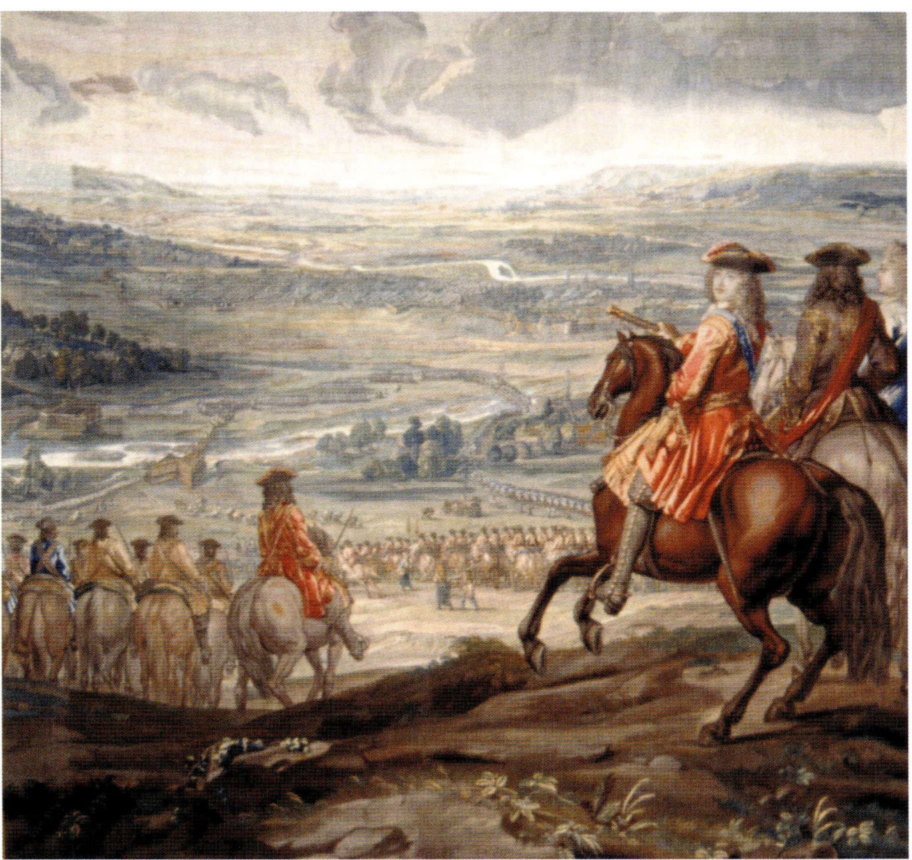

The *Bouchain II* tapestry.

The designs she refers to were the cartoons for the *Victories* set which were adapted and reused by the weavers. They formed a part of the series of martial tapestries depicting general scenes of warfare called the 'second version' *Art of War* tapestries.[14] This series comprised a total of fourteen panels, eight based on the 'first version' i.e. *Campement, Faschinade, Embuscade, Pillage, La Marche, Fouragement, Rencontre, Attacque* and six smaller ones which were based on the Duke of Marlborough's *Victories*.[15] Panels from both the first and second versions of the *Art of War* set were commissioned by several of the Duke's generals[16] for their own homes, including Lord Cobham (Stowe), Lord Cadogan (Caversham), the Duke of Argyll (Inverary), Major-General Richard Lumley the Earl of Scarborough (Stanstead), Lord Orkney (Cliveden), and General Webb (Biddesden).[17]

Ironically, the second *Art of War* series was quite shrewdly marketed by the Flemish weavers not only to Marlborough's friends but also to his enemies in the War of the Spanish Succession, such as the Elector of Bavaria, Max Emmanuel, who commissioned several panels in the early 1720s for his newly completed palace at Schleissheim. A further set was later commissioned by Augustus the Strong, King of Saxony, in 1724 for his palace at Dresden.[18] Each of these subsequent sets was woven with some variations in both design detail and colour and in the trophy borders which were usually composed of flags, drums, armour, weapons and other military accoutrements.

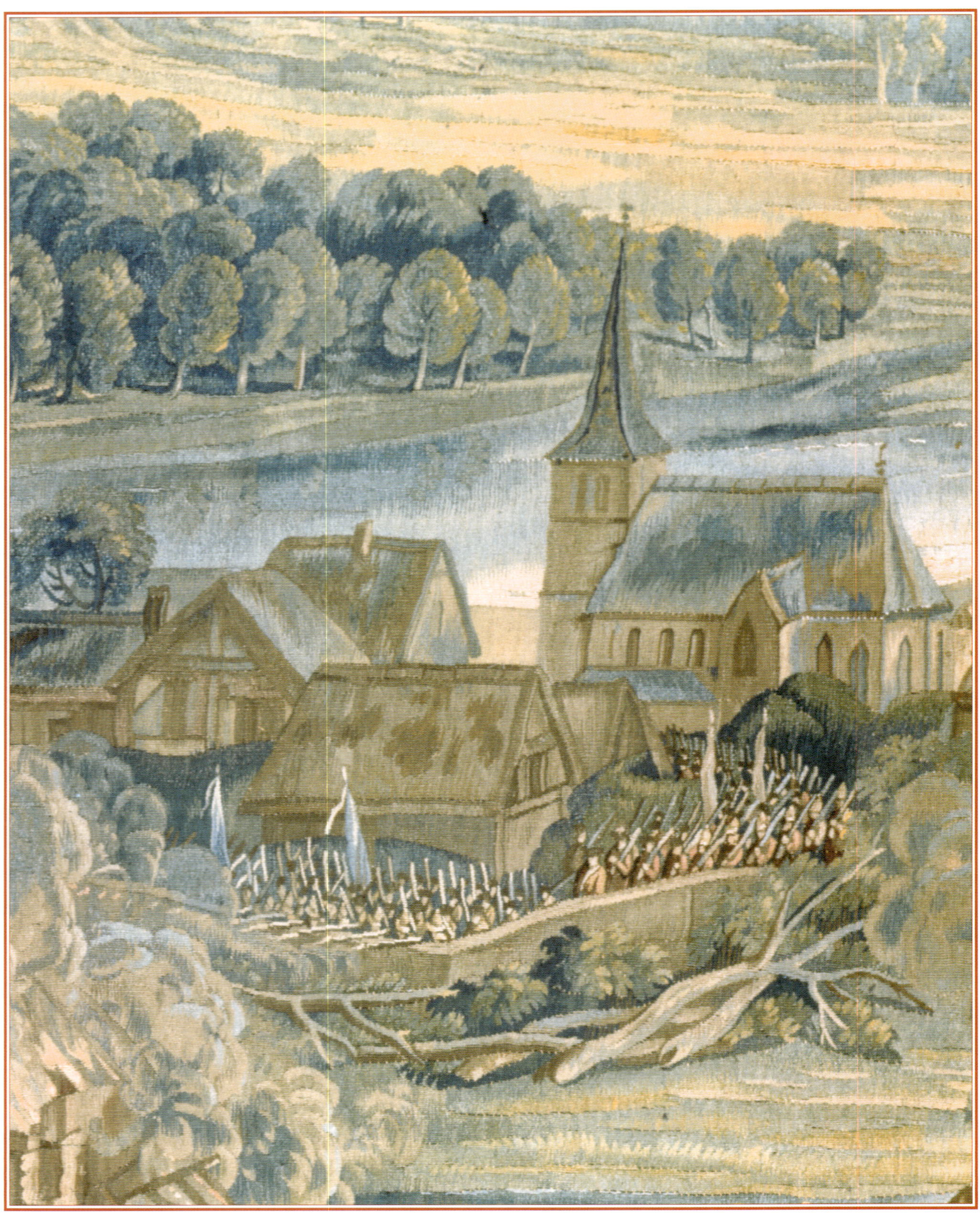

Chapter Three

FLEMISH TAPESTRY WORKSHOPS AND JUDOCUS DE VOS

TAPESTRY weaving was highly labour intensive. The width of looms varied but on a loom which was roughly 11½ feet (350cms) wide, three weavers (*leggewerkers*) could sit side by side, producing just over two running feet (70cms) of tapestry per man per month.[19]

The pay of Flemish weavers varied greatly according to skill. 'Common work' (backgrounds) was paid for at the lowest rate, next came landscape, but the highest rate was paid to those weavers who were able to carry out 'facework' (anatomies and faces), which obviously required the most skill. There is no existing documentation on the rates of pay earned by the different classes of weavers but the general assumption is that a highly skilled weaver was paid about one florin a day.[20]

The signature that appeared on the tapestry belonged to the head of the workshop or the master weaver. While the names of some master weavers are known to us through surviving documents and some skilled workers are listed in Brussels guild registers, the vast majority of this talented workforce remains anonymous.

The master weaver usually owned the workshop and was in charge of its operation for both production and payments. He was in part also a financier, able to make the monetary investment required up front in tapestry production where the cost of raw materials was high and the process of weaving from a complicated pattern was laborious and slow. He made contracts with clients and supplied sets as stock to dealers or factors for re-sale on the open market or in the *Tapissierspand* (tapestry maker's hall). The

The rate of exchange in 1705 was, on average, 10½ to 11 Flemish florins to the English pound.

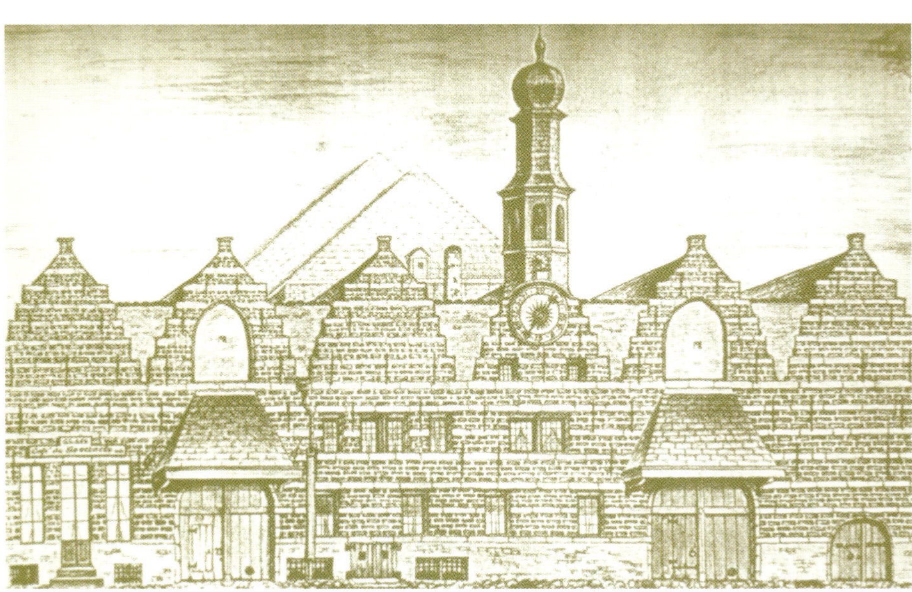

The *Tapissierspand* (tapestry maker's hall) in Antwerp taken from a contemporary print.

Facing page :
Detail from the *Blenheim* tapestry.

Antwerp *pand* [21] was a sales room established in 1553 which was open for business daily (except Sundays and holidays) and was the largest market not only for finished tapestries, but also for everything associated with tapestry production.

The master weaver worked with designers, artists and cartoon painters; he purchased the dyes, the wools, the silks, the gold and silver threads, and he also decided which tapestries would be set up on the various looms within the workshop and which weavers to employ. It is generally presumed that the workmen were paid by the hour on a daily wage basis[22] and sometimes different weavers were called in as required to execute different parts of any single tapestry.

The workshop usually operated a staggered production dependent on the numbers of looms it had at its disposal. A number of tapestries could be woven concurrently on different looms. Larger sets of tapestries with more than six pieces were not normally undertaken together but were woven in groups of two to four. In large workshops, if a set was being produced to be sold 'off the peg' as stock and a new bespoke order was received, the weavers interrupted their work to start production of the new order, leaving the other looms idle for a period of time. This meant that all the looms of the workshop were not tied up on any particular set at once or for any specific customer at the same time. This procedure had its basis in the economics of running the workshop, for it was normal that although the master weaver was paid a deposit of roughly one third of the value of the commission when it was placed in order to cover his costs, he would sometimes be kept waiting for the balance of his money on completion of the work.

The materials used in the weaving were of great importance for their quality counted as much as the fineness of the cartoon along with the skill of the weavers in ensuring the merit of a tapestry panel and its resultant cost. The best workshops used well-dyed fine quality silk and wool wefts, on a foundation of strong woollen or linen warps. Wools and silks for the wefts were dyed before they were woven, the colours being provided by dyers.

Two views of dyer's workshops in the eighteenth century.

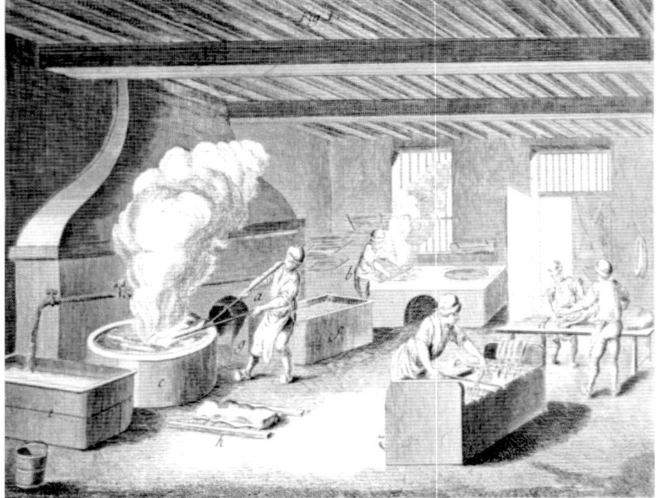

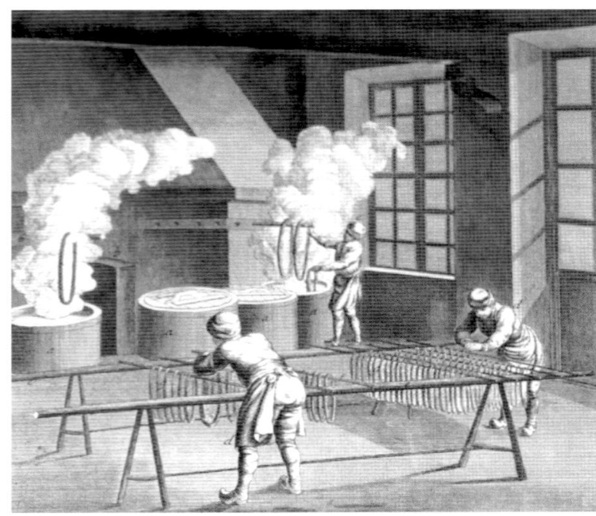

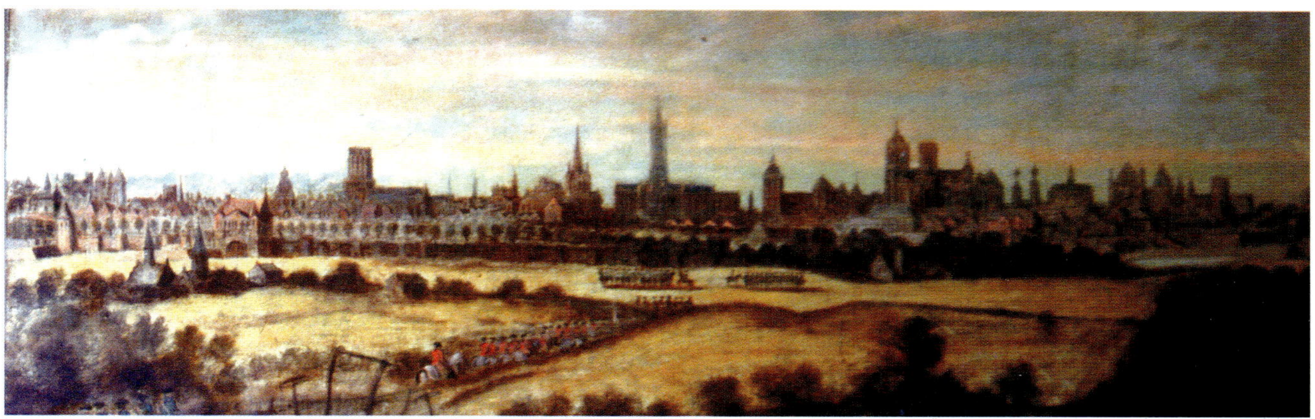

View of Brussels in the early eighteenth century.

The range of colours had vastly expanded as dyers adapted their palettes to match those of painters and a variety of new dyes were produced to create a much wider mixture of tonal effects.

As far as Flemish tapestry production was concerned, in Brussels, from 16th May 1528 all tapestries larger than 6 square ells (2.81 sq. m) were subject to inspection to stop the practice of adding colour with chalk, ink or paint after the weaving of a panel was completed. It had become compulsory for weavers to weave in the town mark, a red shield with a capital B on either side (Brabant and Brussels), as well as the monogram or signature of the master weaver. By 1544 this ruling had been extended to all tapestry production centres in the Low Countries. Further development of the industry meant that from 1656 it was possible for the tapestry merchants to display their goods in the Brussels *pand* set up for this purpose. Previously they had been able to sell their goods either through their workshops, or by sending them to Antwerp (either to the biennial fair or to the marketplace at the *pand)* or at the annual fair at Bergen op Zoom.[23]

At the beginning of the seventeenth century there were probably about 100 master weavers and 1,500 workmen registered in Brussels.[24] However, excessive production, unsatisfactory colouring due to bad dyeing techniques, competition from the Gobelins, Beauvais and Mortlake factories, and the emigration of many skilled Flemish weavers to other European tapestry centres, resulted in a decline in Flemish tapestry production after 1670. In 1695, King Louis XIV ordered Marshal Villeroy to bombard the city of Brussels and this mortar attack led to the city centre being almost completely

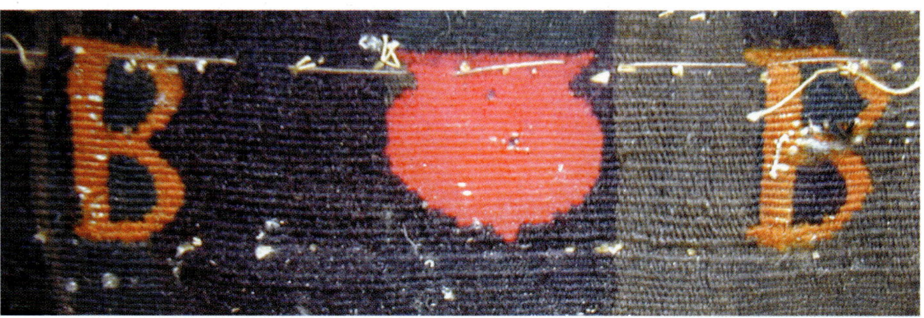

The Brabant-Brussels mark.

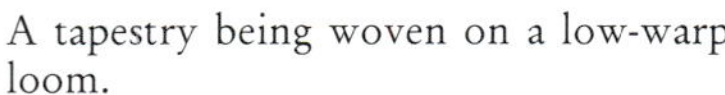
A tapestry being woven on a low-warp loom.

destroyed by fire. As a result, at the turn of the eighteenth century there were only a very few weaver's workshops of any significance left in operation, their number had dropped to nine master weavers who owned a total of 53 looms and employed around 150 workmen.[25] Judocus de Vos was one of these master weavers.

Judocus de Vos was born in 1661. He was the son of Marcus de Vos,[26] a Brussels tapestry weaver who operated a workshop from the mid 17th century and was the dean of the tapestry makers craft guild in 1663, and for several years after.[27] As a young man, it is thought Judocus served his apprenticeship at the Gobelins and returned to Brussels around 1684 where he continued to work in his father's workshop. He received his 'privileges' on 29th August 1705.[28] (The Flemish paid taxes on four areas of consumption: flour, meat, wine, and beer. Exemption from this taxation was granted to those 'privileged' businessmen whose activity made an important contribution to the local economy and because they paid the wages of a certain number of workmen, usually four or more.)

Employing twelve looms, Judocus de Vos was the owner of Brussels' largest

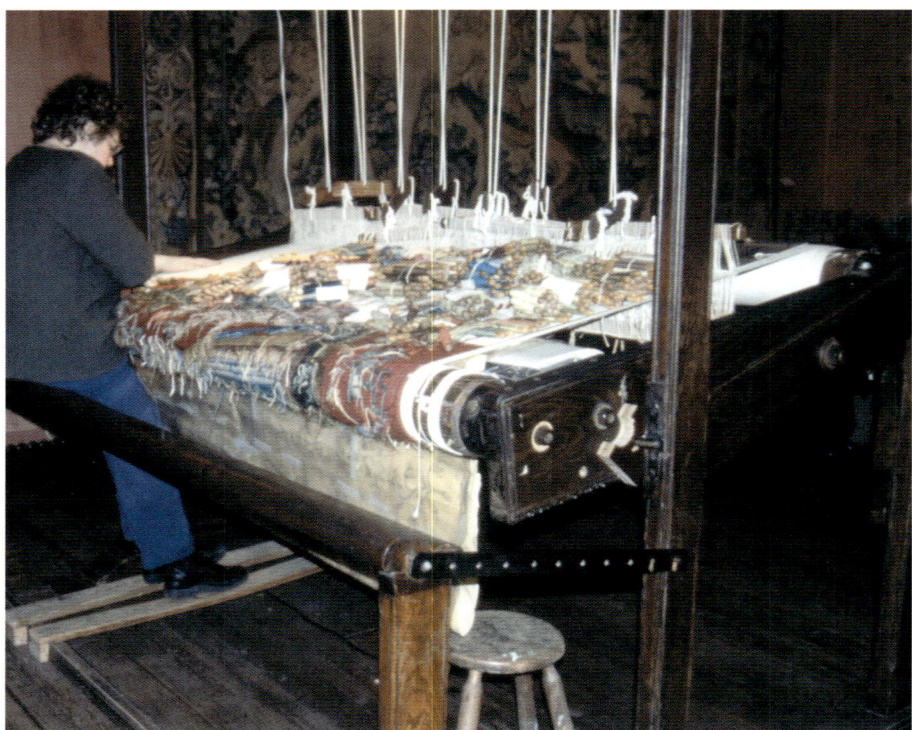

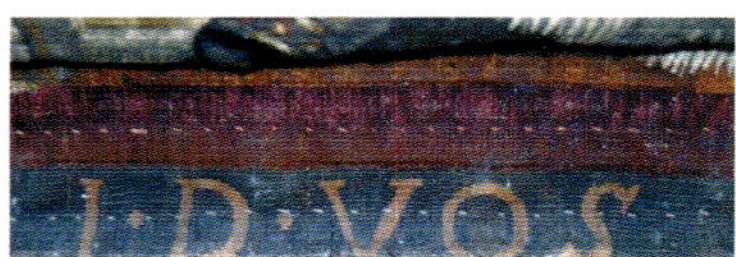

The maker's mark of Judocus de Vos from the selvedge of the *Wynendael* tapestry.

The maker's mark of Judocus de Vos from the selvedge of the *Donauworth* tapestry.

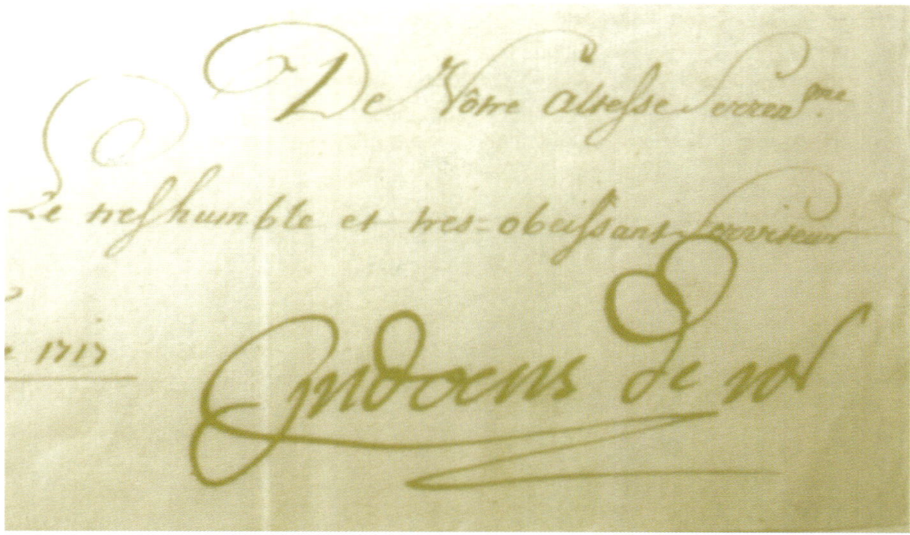

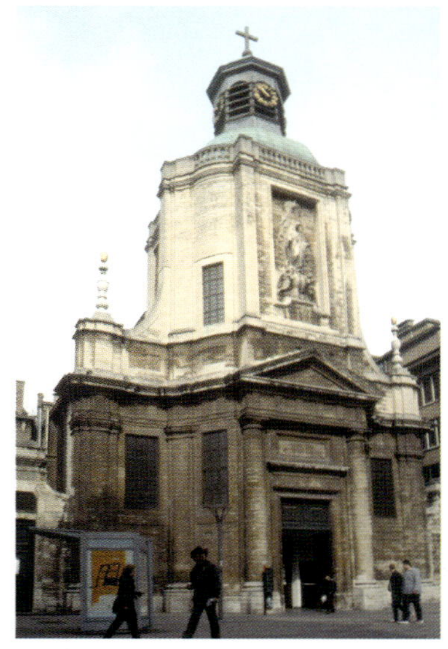

The church of Notre Dame du Finistere in Rue Neuve in Brussels.

workshop from 1703-1707. He produced many different tapestry designs of which six were special commissions and included the *Virtues* and the *Victories* sets for the Duke of Marlborough. De Vos was known to have not only sub-contracted tapestry work but also acted as a dealer and distributor of work from various Oudenarde workshops via the Antwerp based firm of Nicolaas Naulaerts.[29] He also traded in tapestries made by other weavers based in Brussels and Antwerp.

De Vos married Johanna Maria Verheylewegen in Brussels on 9th September 1685 at the church of Notre Dame du Finistere in Rue Neuve. They had four daughters and two sons. The family lived in Rue Neuve from 1715 onwards. Judocus died at the age of 73, in February 1734, after suffering a long illness and was buried in the same church where he had been married. After his death, his brother Jan-Frans de Vos continued the workshop and was recorded as still having eight looms in 1736.

The Duke of Marlborough was one of Judocus de Vos's most important patrons, ordering over two dozen tapestry panels from him between 1707 and 1717, but for his initial commissions the Duke made contracts through dealers and financiers who were associated jointly in the production of his tapestries.

The maker's mark of Judocus de Vos from the selvedge of the *Lines of Brabant* tapestry.

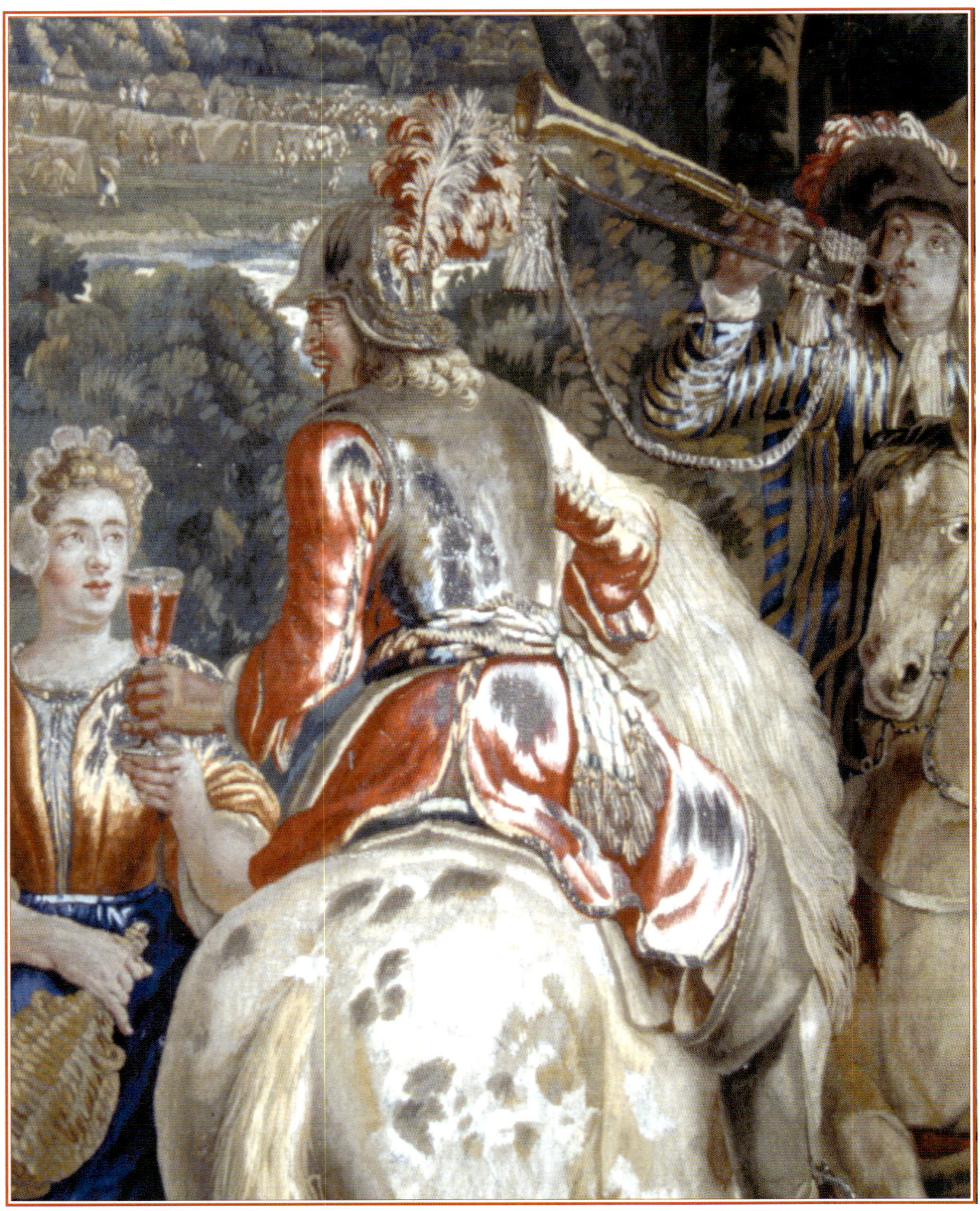

Chapter Four

MARLBOROUGH'S EARLY TAPESTRY COMMISSIONS

THE first set of tapestries to be ordered by the Duke of Marlborough was the *Art of War*, a series containing images of warfare not identified with any particular campaign or illustrating any specific event but representing various general scenes from army life both in camp and in active service in the field.

This 'first version' *Art of War* series had been designed in 1696 by the Flemish artist Lambert de Hondt[30] for Maximilian Emmanuel (1662-1726) the Elector of Bavaria, who was also Governor General of the Southern Netherlands from 1692-1701 and remained as Louis XIV's representative in the Duchy of Brabant until May 1706 when the whole area was ceded to the Allies after the Battle of Ramillies.

The series was called *Art of War* from the description in a document which detailed an order placed in 1700 for King William III of England ("*Exercitie van den Oorloghe*").[31] The set comprised eight panels entitled *Campement, Faschinade, Embuscade, Pillage, La Marche, Fouragement, Rencontre* and *Attacque*. Seven editions of this set are known to have been woven from 1696 onwards, including one for the Duke of Marlborough.[32]

No surviving documents have been found within the Blenheim archives in connection with this order which has led to erroneous assumptions being made that the set was gifted to the Duke.[33] However, a study of the records of the Antwerp based firm of tapestry dealer Nicholaas Naulaerts has revealed that this was not the case.[34]

Nicholaas Naulaerts was a prominent merchant who had built up a thriving business in tapestry production and export in the late seventeenth and early eighteenth centuries. As well as having a substantial establishment in Antwerp, he set up depots and had agents working on his behalf in several other towns. A leading figure in Flemish trade of the time, he is also known to have dealt in various luxuries such as wines, tobaccos, gilt-leather and silks but the principal area of business always remained the supply of sets of tapestry. The firm dealt regularly with all of the well-known Antwerp, Brussels and Oudenarde based tapestry workers, sometimes paying them in raw materials like silks and wools rather than in coin because of the illiquidity of monetary exchange and the structure of credit networks at the time. It was a generally accepted custom for several workshops to collaborate on the execution of large orders; common ties of patronage were an established business reality. By the turn of the century Nicholaas Naulaerts had engaged his son-in-law Frans Blommaerts in his business, a few years before his death in September 1703.

The *Art of War* set for the Duke of Marlborough was contracted by Nicholaas' son, Jan-Frans Naulaerts, along with Frans Blommaerts.

According to the firm's register, an entry dated 2nd November 1705[35] records an order being placed by "*General Marlborough*" for nine tapestry panels of "*Fructus Belli [Art of War]*" measuring 268½ ells. (The Flemish ell was 27 inches or 69.56cms). It goes on to state that the commission was assigned to the weavers "*Jeronimus de Clerck and Vander Beurcht*". It was not habitual for the weavers of tapestries to be named in the contractual detail unless they ran well-established and significant workshops.

A second entry dated 9th November 1706[36] lists the details of the panels in the "*set of tapestries representing the Fruits of War very richly worked with gold and silver*" ordered by the Duke of Marlborough, with the individual measurements of each panel as well as a calculation of amounts charged, also mentioning the payment of an advance of 2,000 florins which had been received by the firm through Mr. Sweet. Benjamin Sweet was the deputy-paymaster for the English army in Flanders and regularly handled money on the Duke of Marlborough's account.

The tapestries ordered were *La Marche, La Bataille [Embuscade], La Siege d'une ville [Attacque], Ou on coupe les facines [Faschinade], Rencontre, Les Campements, Fouragement,* and two panels called *Pillage*.[37] The latter were selected portions from the *Pillage* cartoon, making a total of nine rather than the usual number of eight tapestry panels that comprised this series. As has already been explained, it was fairly common for weavers to adapt and use the cartoons in their possession to fit their client's requirements.

The dimensions of the tapestries mentioned in the records state that the three largest panels, all at 14 feet wide, were *La Marche, Embuscade,* and *Rencontre.* Next, at 12 feet wide each, were *Faschinade* and *Attacque.* Another pair, both at 9 feet wide, was *Campement* and *Fouragement,* and finally the truncated pair from *Pillage* each measured 4 feet in width. The height of the tapestries was set at 14½ feet (442cms) throughout.

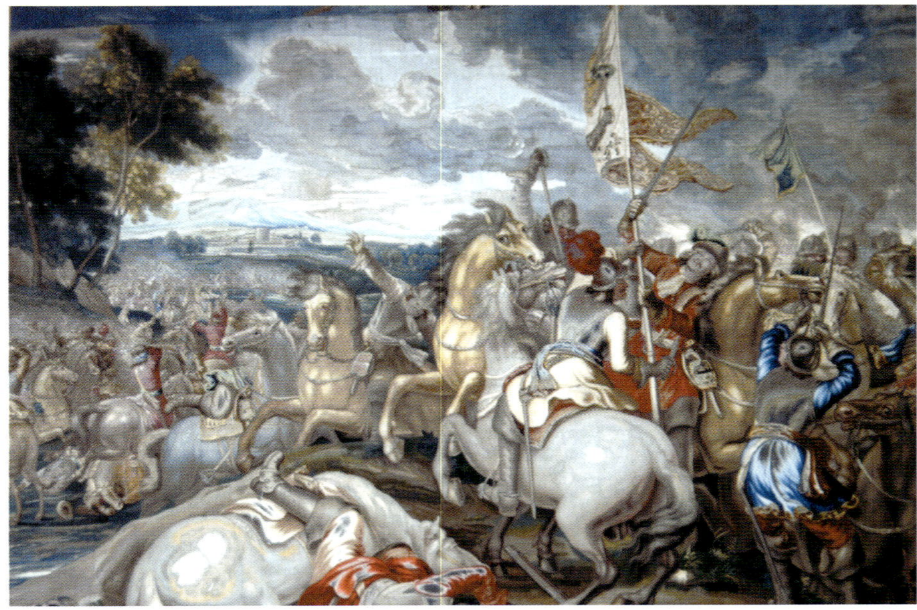

The *Rencontre* tapestry.

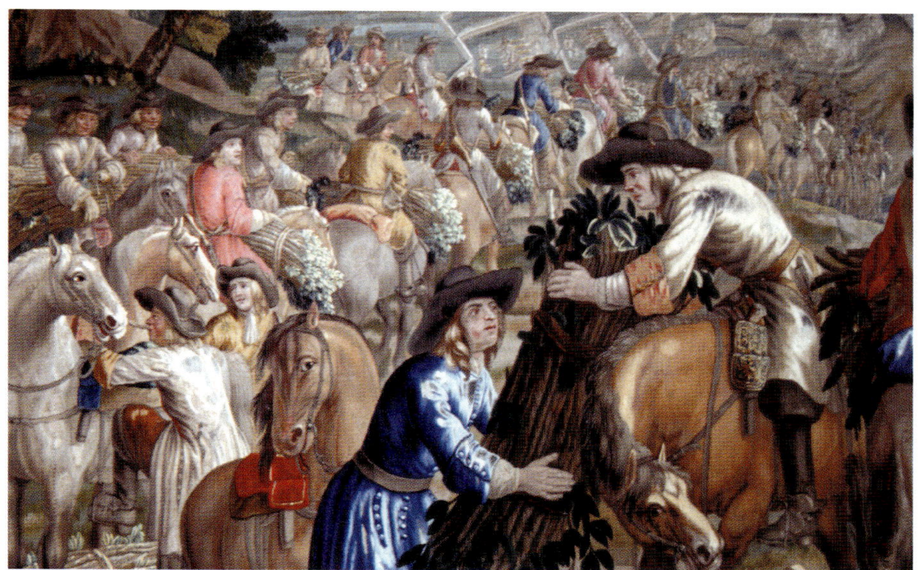

The entry dated 2nd November 1705 also states that Naulaerts and Blommaerts would pay the weavers a rate of 19 florins per ell, but the firm charged the Duke 24 florins per ell, their surcharge or commission thus amounting to 5 florins per ell. The nine tapestry panels cost a total of 6,502 florins 10 styvers (the rate of conversion in 1705 was on average $10\frac{1}{2}$ to 11 Flemish florins to the English pound). Added to this was the price of commissioning a specially painted border* (382 florins 10 styvers), and a fee (18 florins) for a portrait of the Duke. This portrait would have been used in the panel entitled *La Marche* which is the only panel in the first *Art of War* series that glorifies the commanding general. A document in the Blenheim Papers dated 10th February 1709[38] confirms that the specially designed bold trophy borders were executed by "*Van Orla*", who presumably was the artist Jan Van Orley.

Van Orley was born in Brussels on 4th January 1665 and died there on 22nd February 1735. Taught his trade by his father Pierre and his uncle Jerome, he became an established Brussels history painter, a prolific designer of tapestries and painter of tapestry cartoons, supplying most of the requirements of the Van der Borcht workshops.

---

* There is some doubt as to whether John Churchill paid for the designs of the specially made borders which were used for his first commission – the *Art of War* set – and then adapted and reused later for his last commission – the *Victories* set. The Naulaerts daybook (ff. 159 & 162) shows the borders charged to the Duke's account on 9th November 1706 and they were presumably paid for with the *Art of War* tapestry commission. When the Duke asked the dealers to pass on the border designs to Judocus de Vos they seem to have charged him again, as in a document dated 10th February 1709 they added a remark stating that the Duke did not want to pay (BL Add. Mss. 61,348 f. 83). This has led to an ambiguity as to whether the Duke paid once or not at all for the borders. Payment or an agreement of some kind must have been made, as the Duke is not known to have employed the Naulaerts firm again after February 1709 and the borders were given to Judocus de Vos who adapted and reused them for the *Victories* tapestries.

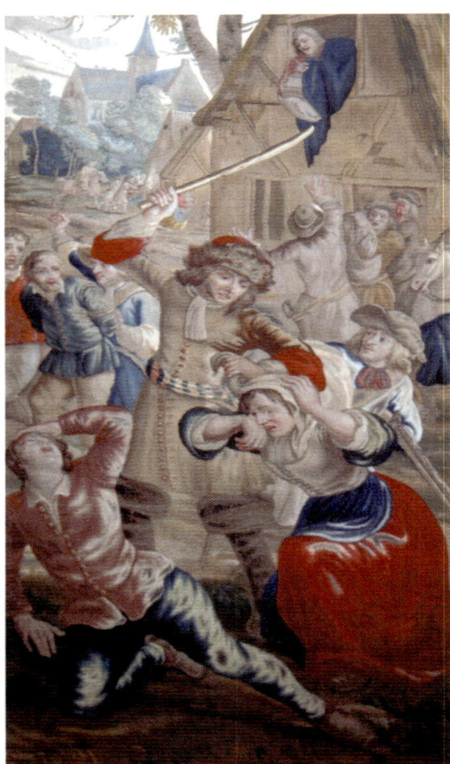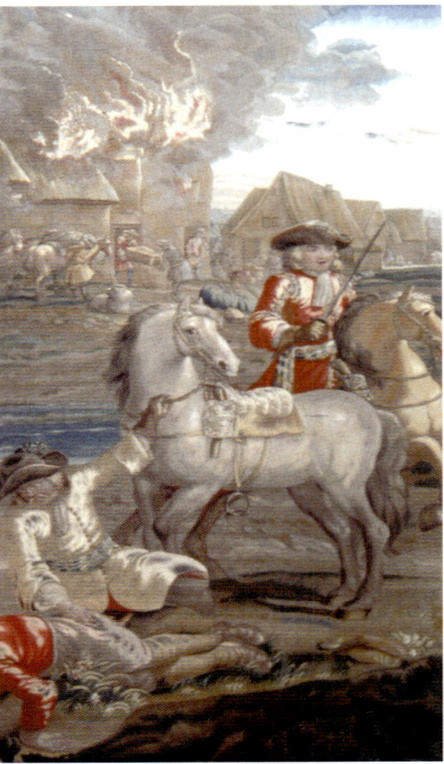

As these tapestries had been ordered not only as decorative wall coverings but also to underline his military prestige, John Churchill almost certainly wanted to ensure the highest quality of weaving for his first commission. In a letter dated 25th April 1706, he requested his wife to have sent over to his army headquarters, as a sample, one panel from the set of ten tapestries she had received in December 1704 as a gift from the Electress of Hanover[39] "... *when the yackt returns for Lord Hallifax I must desire you wou'd send on[e] of the peeces of Pr[incess] Sophia hangings which has little figures in itt, for the man at Bruxels is obliged to make my hangings of the same fines [fineness]*".[40] A further letter written from Cambron on October 18th reveals that this sample had still not arrived after five months, "... *I am sorry to tell you that the Peece of Hanging you sent by Lady Portland is not as yet to be found, there housekeeper saying it was sent to Ld Albemarle but at my arrival at the Hague I hope to find it, but for fear of the worst you will send another little peace by Capt. Sanders, for the bargain that is made for the new hangings is that they are to be of the same fines [fineness], with those of the Electories [Electress], so that if there be one peece finer than the others I desire that may be sent, and if you can let me know which peece it was that was sent by Lady Portland, so that if it shou'd be lost, that I may have another made*".[41]

It was probably too late in any case for this piece of tapestry to be used as a sample since the weaving was completed by November 1706. The set of nine panels had been finished in a short space of time – about 12 months – which may be due to the fact that two of Brussels' pre-eminent workshops were involved in the production.

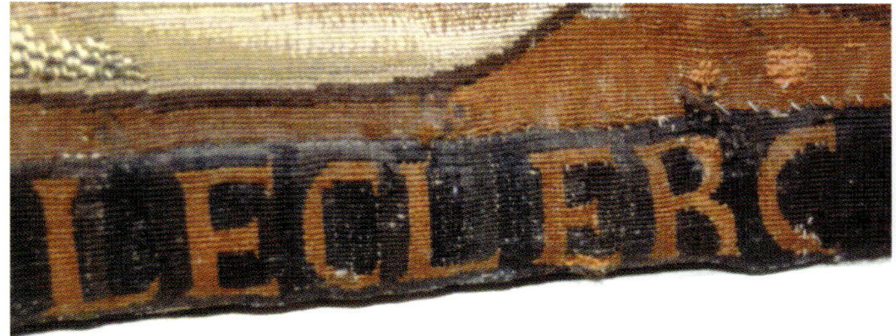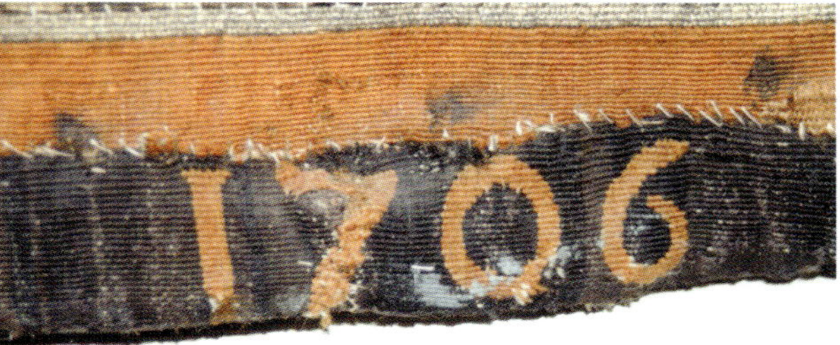

Details from the selvedge of the *Rencontre* tapestry.

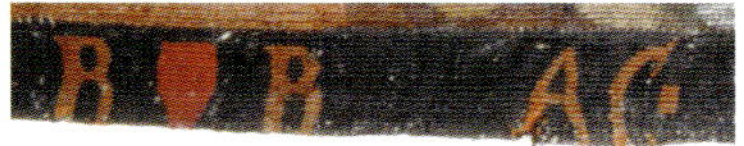

The A.C. and B-B marks from the selvedge of the *Campement* tapestry.

The master weavers of this set were the well established and highly regarded Brussels tapestry makers, Jasper Van der Borcht and Jerome Le Clerc. The lower selvedge of *Campement* bears the Brabant-Brussels mark and the maker's mark – A.C. This was the signature known to have been used by Jasper (Gaspar) Van der Borcht and sometimes thought to have also been employed by his father, Jacob Van der Borcht. They styled themselves A.C. or A. Castro, a play on words, as Castro was the Latin word for castle and Van der Borcht, the Dutch equivalent. This distinguished their work from another less well-established family of weavers with the same name.[42]

The Van der Borchts had an extremely successful workshop in Brussels which was run in partnership with another accomplished tapestry weaver, Jerome (Hieronymus) Le Clerc who was in business for a considerable length of time, from 1677 to 1718. The lower selvedge of the *Rencontre* panel bears the signature of Le Clerc, the Brabant-Brussels mark and the date 1706, the date when the panel was woven.

All the panels of this set bear John Churchill's coat of arms in the centre of the top border. The wide decorative borders, designed by Jan Van Orley, are filled with guns, saddles, arms and armour, trumpets, drums and other military motifs, appropriately framing the subjects in the centre of each panel. The two *Pillage* panels have borders only at the top and bottom, which, in addition to their size, is an indication that they were intended to be *entrefenetres* (panels filling the wall spaces between windows).

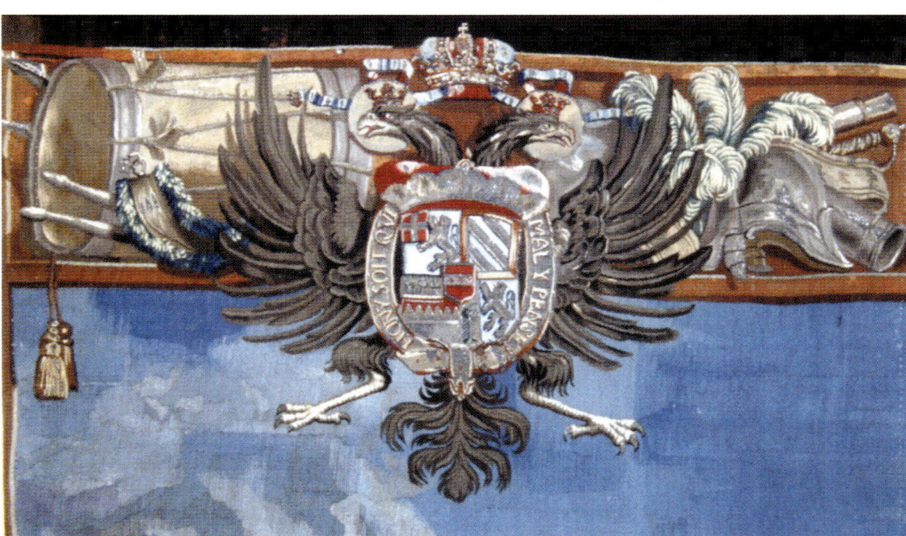

Top border of a *Pillage* entrefenetre showing the Duke's coat of arms.

The Duke's *Art of War* tapestries, as is known from documentary evidence as well as from the surviving panels at Blenheim Palace, were woven in wool and silk and highlighted with silver and gold threads. These were silk threads with a thin filament of silver or silver gilt or gold wrapped spirally around. The use of these threads when weaving tapestries produced a brilliant lustre when they were new, adding not only to the richness of appearance of the panel but also to the cost of the work. To make these threads dazzle more, especially when illuminated by candlelight, the weavers sometimes produced a ripple or basketweave effect on the surface of the tapestry by alternating four metallic wefts over three or four warps. However, the exposed silver eventually tarnished and the woven area ended up as a blackish patch.

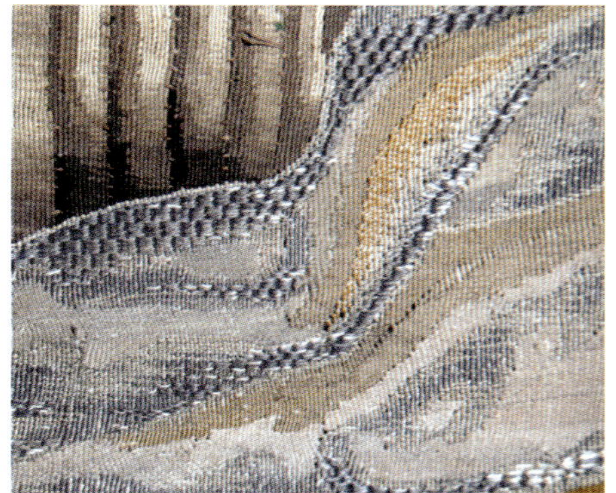
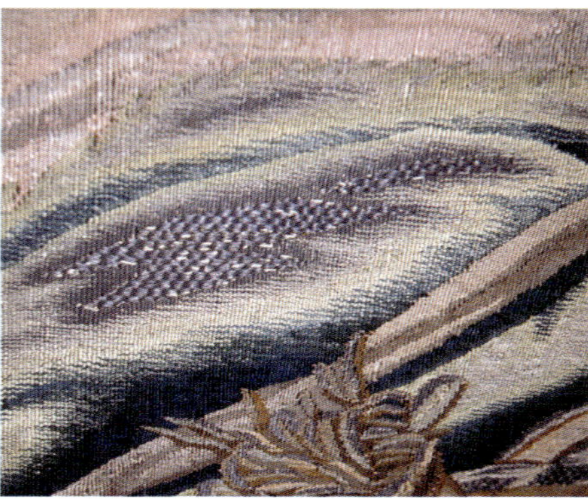
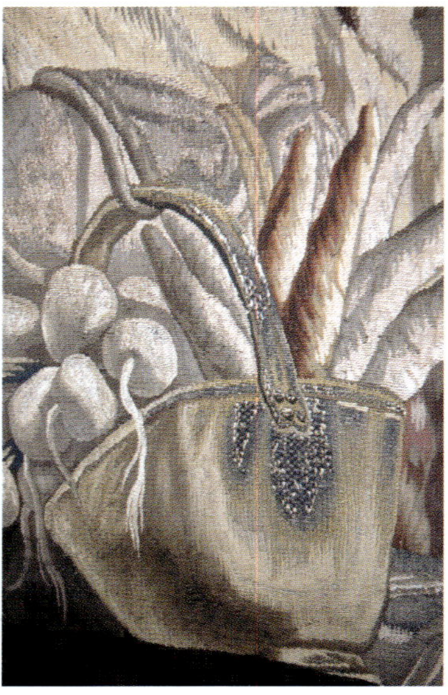

Details from the *Art of War* tapestries showing the use of metallic threads and the basketweave technique.

John Churchill did not care for this gold and silver effect. He wrote as much in a letter to his wife on 1st November 1706, "*the hangings I had made att Bruxelles are finish'd and the greatest fault I find with them is their having to[o] much silver and gold in them, however I hope you will like them. If I had received the measures of the apartement you and I are to live in I shou'd have bespoke some more, but now you may see these, and be the better able to tell me what alterations you will have made in the next and I believe you will be of my opinion to have no silver or gold*".[43]

We know that the *Art of War* tapestries were ordered by the Duke and were intended to be displayed in the private apartments at Blenheim Palace. From the Duke's letter we also know that he lacked the exact dimensions for their rooms in the east wing where the private apartments were located, indicating that the order was placed at a very early stage in the plans for the building.

Queen Anne had made the Marlboroughs aware of her intention to gift them the Manor of Woodstock on 17th January 1705 and a Bill was hastily passed through both Houses of Parliament within three weeks. At some point soon afterwards the Queen suggested that payment would be made for a suitable house to be constructed, since the only buildings on the estate were a small number of keeper's lodges and the remains of the old manor house. At first, the funding of the building was kept a closely guarded secret so as not to arouse jealousy at Court of this further generosity to the Marlboroughs. On June 9th 1705 the architect John Vanbrugh was officially authorised by the Lord Treasurer, Sidney Godolphin, to make contracts with workmen.[44] In July, Sir Christopher Wren (then Master of the Queen's Works) estimated the building would cost £100,000 - more than twice the amount originally planned. The Duchess was shocked and thought it was too large a sum to be paid, but relented on seeing that the Duke had quite set his heart on the project. However, when building work started later in 1705, Vanbrugh continued to make changes to his increasingly extravagant designs, resulting in many difficulties for the Marlboroughs in the years to come (and a massive cost overrun).

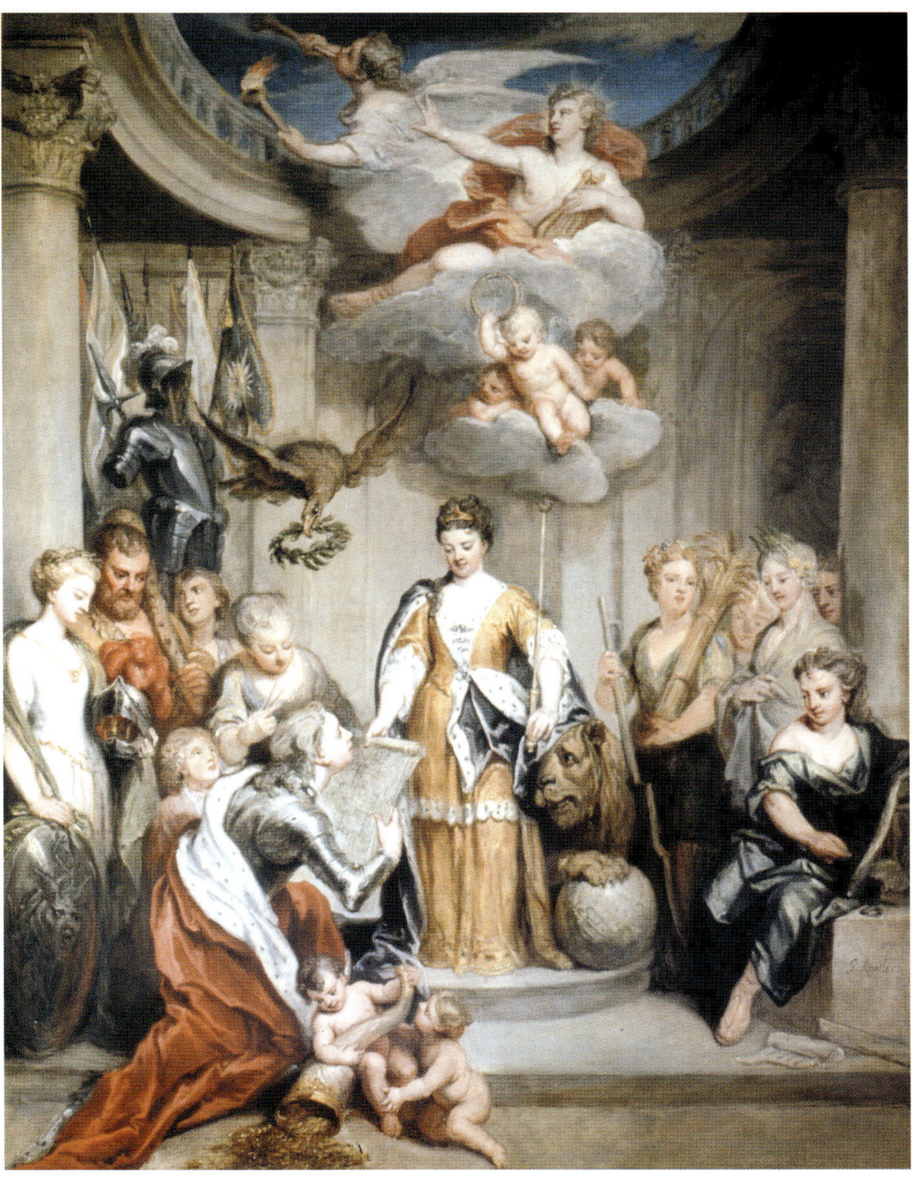

Military Merit by Sir Godfrey Kneller. This allegorical painting shows Queen Anne presenting Blenheim Palace to the victorious Duke of Marlborough.

The fact that the Duke did not have accurate dimensions of their apartments in the east wing when the order was placed for the tapestries has subsequently led to three of the surviving panels – *Rencontre, Attacque,* and *Campement* – being folded up by just over a foot each (roughly 31-36cms) to allow them to fit vertically into the wall spaces where they hang. This is the only set of tapestries currently at Blenheim Palace which encounters this problem, all the other sets ordered by the Duke, as we shall see, were made to exact dimensions provided by the architect.

The shipment of the set of nine tapestries was dispatched to England in mid November 1706 along with several other works of art the Duke had either bought or been gifted and which included a large equestrian portrait of King Charles I on horseback by Van Dyck.[45] On 19th November 1706, the Customs Commissioners were informed that several cases of pictures and hangings had arrived in London and were to be opened at the Duke of Marlborough's lodgings at St. James's.[46] At this time there were tariffs and duties payable on Flemish luxury goods like lace, linen and draperies which were brought into England. The Duke had already informed the Duchess in a letter from Rotterdam dated 8th November that "*I am so fond of some pictures I shall bring with mee, that I could wish you had a place for them til the gallerie at Woodstock be finished*". It took more than twelve years before some of these pictures and tapestries were finally hung in the east wing at Blenheim. Today only five tapestries of this set have survived – they are *Rencontre, Attacque,* and *Campement* and the cut down pair of *Pillage*. The fate of the other tapestries is not known.

The Duke went on to use the Naulaerts firm once more, in 1707, ordering two further sets of tapestries from them. At this time, with a large number of his military victories yet to take place, John Churchill had not thought of commissioning a set based on his own triumphs, that would come later. For the moment, he perhaps viewed his accomplishments more through association with the legendary Greek hero Alexander. So, for his own suite of rooms in the east wing of Blenheim Palace he intended to hang the series entitled the *History of Alexander the Great* and for his wife's apartments, a series of *Teniers peasants*.

On the 11th of April 1707, at the start of another campaign in Flanders, Marlborough wrote to Sarah "*pray lett me have the measures of the Hangings which I am to bespeak for yours and my apartement*".[47] John Vanbrugh, the architect of Blenheim Palace was called upon to provide exact dimensions so that the tapestries would fit perfectly into their intended wall spaces. A very detailed list was made up and sent to the Duke.[48] This contained not only the dimensions each panel was required to be on each wall within each room, (there were three rooms specified, two for the Duke and one for the Duchess), but it also meticulously mentioned the direction from which the daylight would fall on each of the panels. The Duke was satisfied with what he had received and wrote again from Brussels on May 4th "*...the measures of the roomes are so well explain'd that I believe itt will be an advantage to the hangings*".[49]

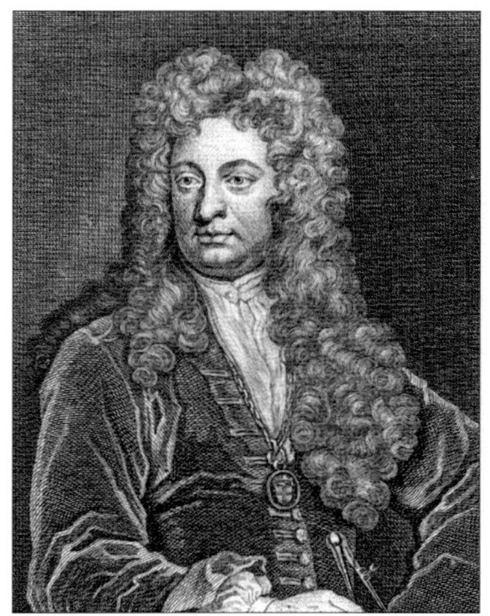

John Vanbrugh.

Vanbrugh's notes of the work required to be carried out on the interiors of the private apartments provide the following details:

"Grand Cabinet: the ceiling to be flatt with plain pannells and no fretwork...the piers between the windows to be with looking glass as high as the springing [of the arches of the windows]. The rest of the room to be wainscoted for Hangings...

Lord Duke's Drawing Room: Wainscoated with deal if for hangings...

Lady Dutchesses Long Closet: wainscoted for hangings...

Lady Dutchesses Bedroom: wainscoted with deal for Hangings and Marble Chimney".[50]

Floor plan of the 1st Duke and Duchess's apartments at Blenheim, circa 1719.

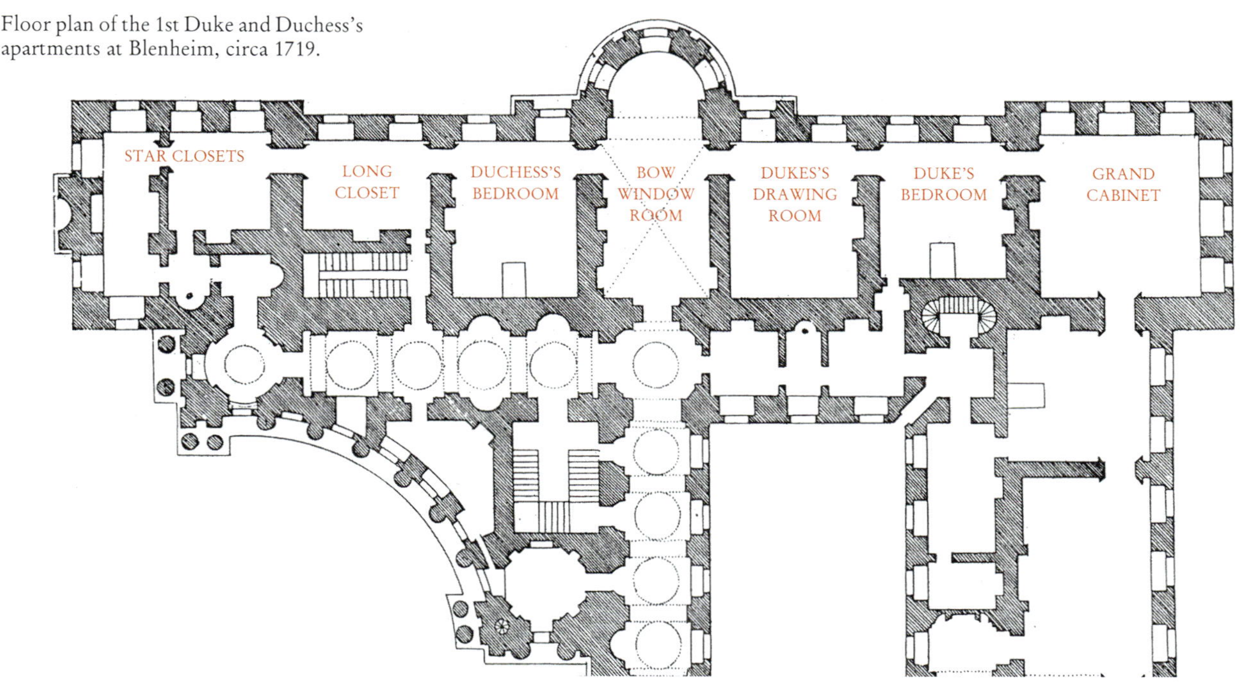

And so while work on the building progressed in England, the Duke was busy in Flanders, not only at the head of his army carefully carrying out military manoeuvres but also aggressively acquiring a substantial number of fine works of art for the decoration of his new house.

The tapestry series called the *History of Alexander the Great* comprised hangings illustrating a variety of scenes from the life of the legendary Greek hero. By commissioning this set the Duke of Marlborough followed the convention of making an allusion to military glory and his own virtues. This tradition had been revived by Louis XIV, whose example may have inspired Marlborough. By 1707 the Duke had gained two celebrated victories against the Sun King, first at Blenheim in 1704 and then at Ramillies in 1706. He perhaps considered himself equally if not more worthy of comparison to Alexander than his nemesis, for whom this tapestry series had originally been designed.

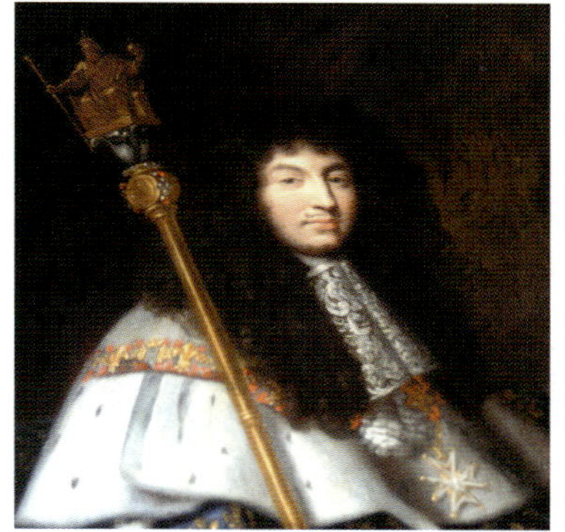
King Louis XIV.

No victor in world history had left a legacy comparable with that of Alexander, a military genius whose story readily supplied painters with subjects for monumental works of art depicting his outstanding and well chronicled performances on the battlefield. These included his defeat of the Persian King Darius, his protection of the royal ladies, his triumphal entry into Babylon, his great march eastwards into Asia and the capture of King Porus.

It is not surprising that John Churchill identified himself with this ancient warrior: Alexander was characteristically able to adjust to the unexpected. Keeping his plans flexible and producing a swift response to changes in the enemy's tactics, Alexander had a comprehensive grasp of detail. He made several long marches (often at night) and was a master of strategy and surprise. He had an extraordinary relationship with his army and was genuinely interested in the predicament of the common soldier fighting under his leadership. All these qualities were also true of John Churchill.

The designer of the *Alexander* series was the French painter Charles Le Brun (1619-1690). Well established by the 1650s as a great decorative painter, he was responsible for several sets of large history paintings which were later translated into tapestries. Le Brun's paintings were circulated throughout Europe in the form of engravings: he was one of the few artists who received a rare royal privilege allowing him to control the copying of his images and

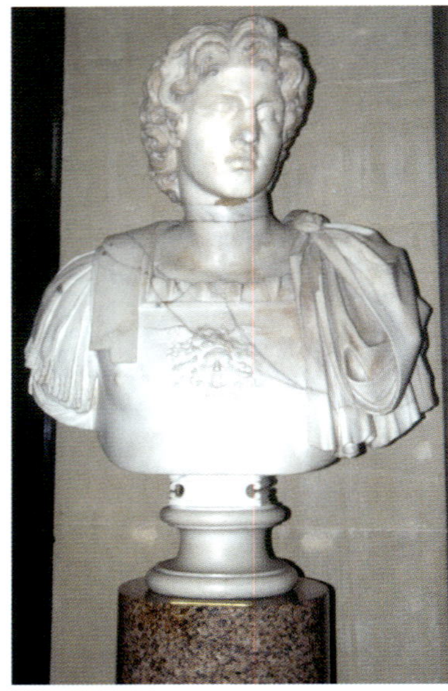

Marble bust of Alexander the Great.

The *Babylon* tapestry.

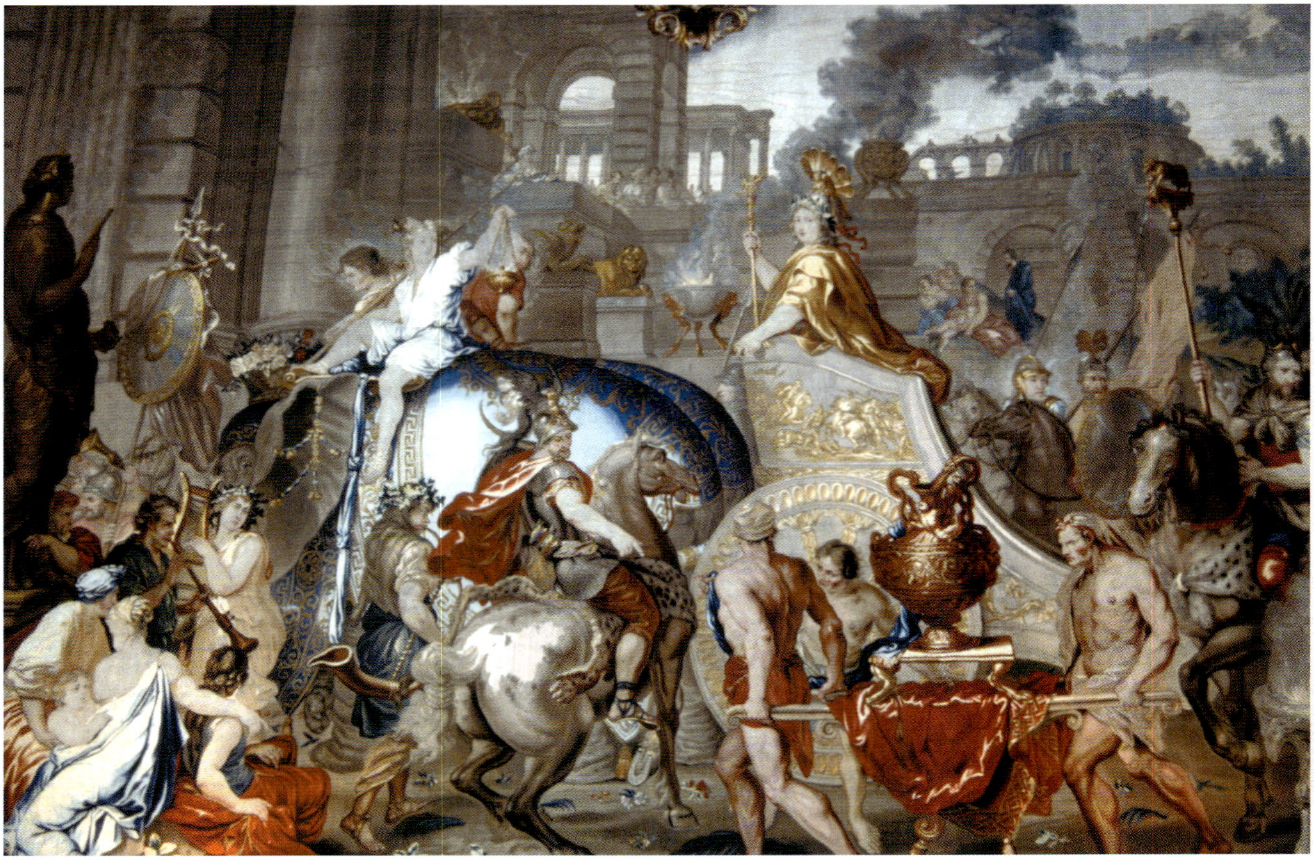

The *Granicus* tapestry.

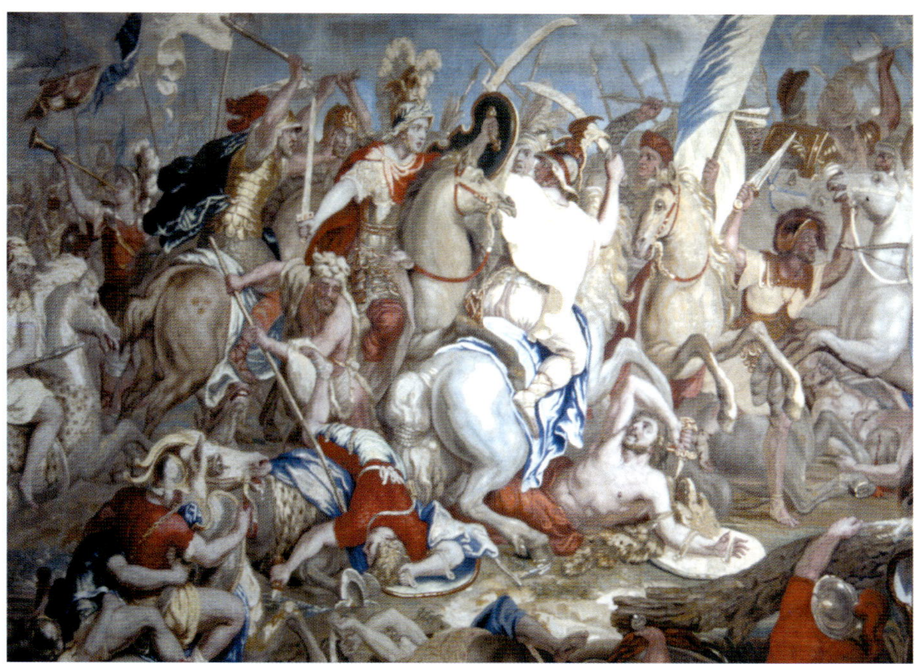

prevent their unauthorised reproduction. By 1664 he was in charge of Louis XIV's collections of works of art, confirmed as *Premier Peintre du Roi* (court painter) and at about the same time took over as the director of the Gobelins manufactory. The *History of Alexander the Great* was one of Le Brun's best known works for tapestry art, the depiction of Alexander's military exploits originally conceived as a historical tribute to Louis XIV's victories. Le Brun painted four enormous pictures, each approximately 40 feet wide, representing *The Passage of the Granicus*, *The Battle of Arbella*, *The Defeat of Porus*, and *Alexander's triumphal entrance into Babylon*. An earlier work entitled *The Queens of Persia* (or *The Tent of Darius*) also formed a part of the *Alexander* tapestry series.[51] The paintings were created between 1661 and 1668, then cartoons were produced for the tapestries and the first set was woven at the Gobelins in 1680.

Scenes from the life of *Alexander* were repeatedly commissioned by clients of both French and Flemish tapestry workshops. Previously, for other sets of decorative tapestries designed by Le Brun, the original French cartoons were sent to Flemish workshops for the production of further sets.[52] However, for the *Alexander* tapestries, the French workshops produced their sets from Le Brun's designs, while the sets woven by Flemish weavers in the early eighteenth century were from designs based on prints of the series which had been produced by Gerard Edelincks and Gerard Audrans between 1672-78.[53] In their sets, the Flemish weavers also began to introduce new subjects from Alexander's life which had not been painted by Le Brun.

The Duke of Marlborough commissioned a total of twelve tapestries from the *Alexander* series, although to begin with, in 1707, an order was placed for just eight panels. "*My Glasses* (mirrors the Duke had ordered from France) *are come to Bruxelles*", he noted to Sarah on June 30th from his camp at

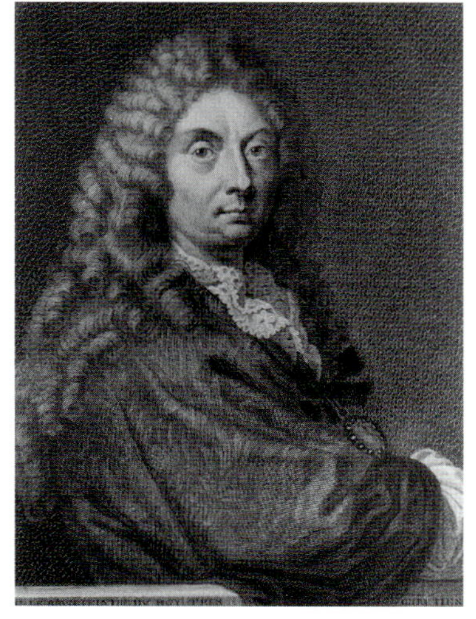

Charles Le Brun.

Meldert, "*and I have bespoke the Hangings, for one of my greatest pleasures is in doing all that in me lyes that we may as soon as is possible enjoye that happy time of being quietly together, which I think of with pleasure as often as I have my thoughts free to myself*".[54]

In July the same year discussions with all concerned for the new sets of tapestries must have been in their final stages, for on the 21st of that month the Duke wrote home with some urgency "*... my head is full of things that are displeasing that I am at this time a very improper judge of what wou'd be best for the work at Woodstock, for really I begine to dispaire of having any quietness there, or anywhere else... I shall write about the hangings, and I hope there is time enough to make them of the higt [height] you desire...*"[55] Four days later he had made a decision regarding the measurements, "*... I had write about the hangings, but have had no answer, but shall keep them to the first dimentions since you think that will be best...*"[56]

The tapestry contract,[57] written in French, still exists in the archives, specifying the exact dimensions of each of the eight panels ordered, the height being fixed at $13^1/_2$ feet (411cms), and also that the ducal coat of arms be incorporated within the border. It further states that the set had to be completed as quickly as possible and preferably within ten months. Additionally, there is reference to the quality of the weaving, stipulating "*the same fineness as those panels delivered earlier [Art of War] but without any gold or silver*". The price of the weaving was fixed at 22 florins per ell, a lower price than the Duke's *Art of War* tapestries which had contained gold and silver threads.

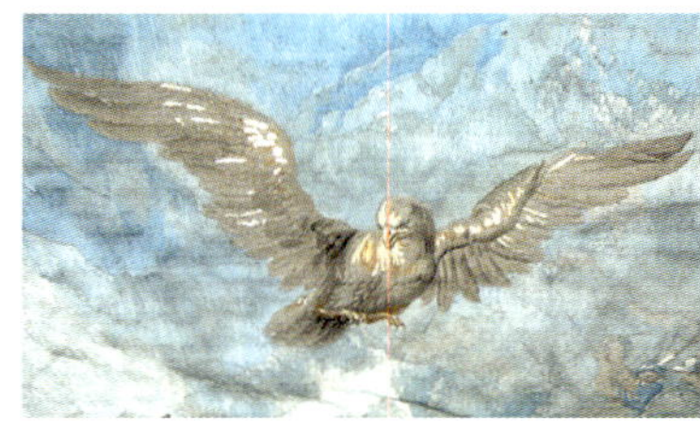

Detail from the *Arbella* tapestry.

The *Arbella* tapestry.

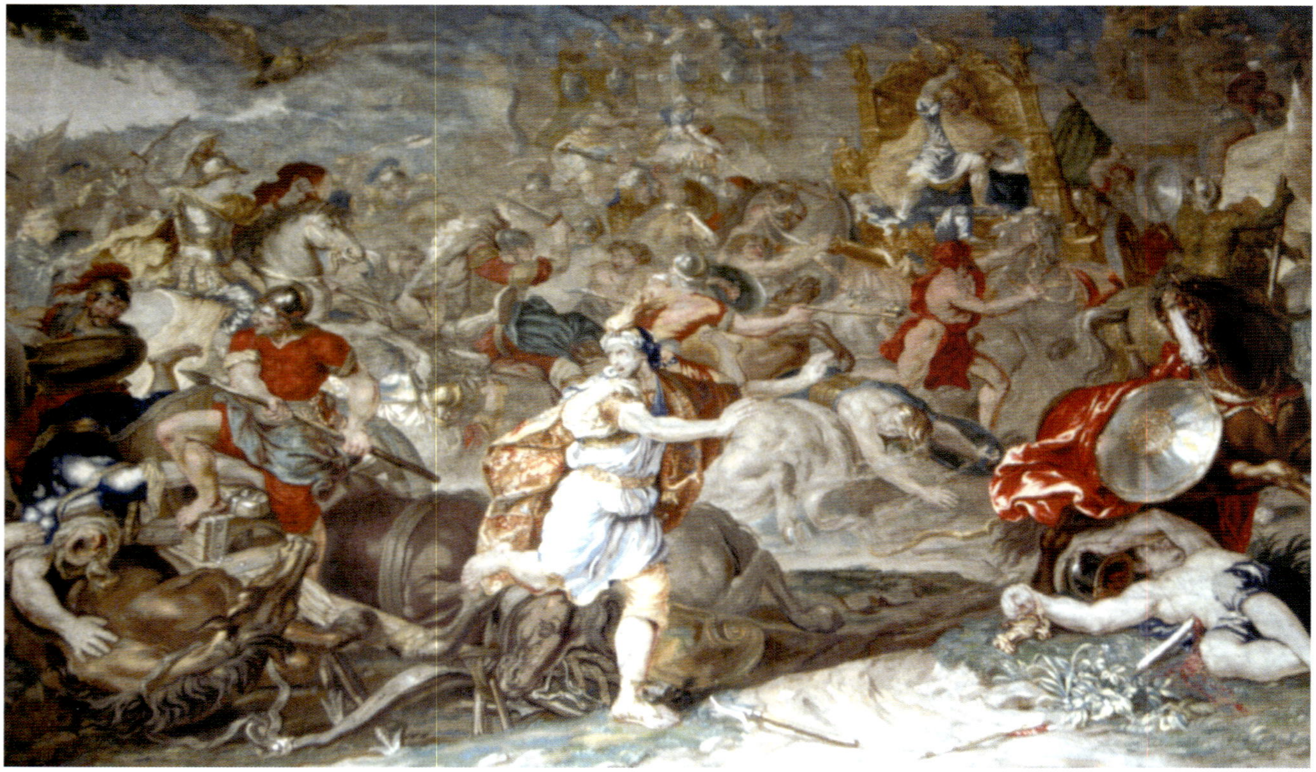

The contract also included an order for another set of tapestries which is no longer extant in the Blenheim collection. This was a set of four tapestries called *Teniers Peasants* which illustrated scenes of country people who were portrayed going about their daily activities or recreations within a rural setting. The series was inspired by the paintings of the well-known Flemish artist David Teniers the Younger (1610-1690). The dimensions for this set were specified as two large panels about 20 feet wide, two smaller panels about 10 feet wide, all being the same height – 10 feet 11 inches (332cms). The cost of weaving the *Peasants* was fixed at the slightly cheaper rate of 18 florins per ell. The location and fate of these tapestries is not known today, but originally they were destined for the Duchess's apartments.

Payment terms for both sets were also laid out in the contract. The Duke would pay one third of the estimated amount in advance and the balance on delivery. On 12th September 1707, from the army's camp at Helchin, Adam Cardonnel (the Duke's field secretary) sent word to Benjamin Sweet "*I pray you will pay to Monsieur Naulaerts or order the sum of 2,800 guilders currant money of Holland which being an advance for Two Setts of Hangings he is to make for my Lord Duke. You are to take the like security as formerly that in case the Hangings when made are not approv'd and accepted by his Grace that then the said sume paid in advance shall be return'd*".[58] The payment was made within ten days.

A statement of account[59] itemizing the completion of and delivery to the Duke of several sets of tapestries lists the different panels which were produced but with no mention of where they were made or who the weavers were. A small detail, but one perhaps not altogether undeserving of attention, is revealed in the Naulaerts daybook. In the entry pertaining to the Duke's commission in June 1707 is a note that "*Clerck will undertake the Peasants for 15 florins, the Alexander for 18 florins, without gold*".[60]

It is not entirely clear what happened next, but another entry in the firm's records dated 19th September 1707[61] states quite emphatically that a sub-contract was made between Judocus de Vos on one part and J.J. Naulaerts and F. Blommaerts on the other part for two tapestry sets, one of *Peasants* and the other of *Alexander*, both for the Duke of Marlborough. The rate fixed in this sub-contract for both sets was 15 florins per ell.

It is unlikely that de Vos undercut Le Clerck to obtain the commission. A more probable explanation is that once the Duke had chosen the designs he wished to have made up into tapestries, Naulaerts and Blommaerts found that they did not own all of the corresponding cartoons. The Naulaerts firm very likely used cartoons designed by Peter Ykens, assisted by Peter Spierinckx (who painted the landscapes) and Jasper Verbruggen (who was responsible for the flora).[62] De Vos must have had his own set of *Alexander* cartoons (perhaps executed by the two other known designers of the *Alexander* series, Lodewijk Van Schoor and Jacobus Van der Heyden)[63] which included the ones the dealers were missing and may have insisted either that he be paid for their use, or that he be given a share of the work. The entry in the firm's daybook substantiates this to some extent where it reveals that both parties agreed to supply each other the cartoons without any charge

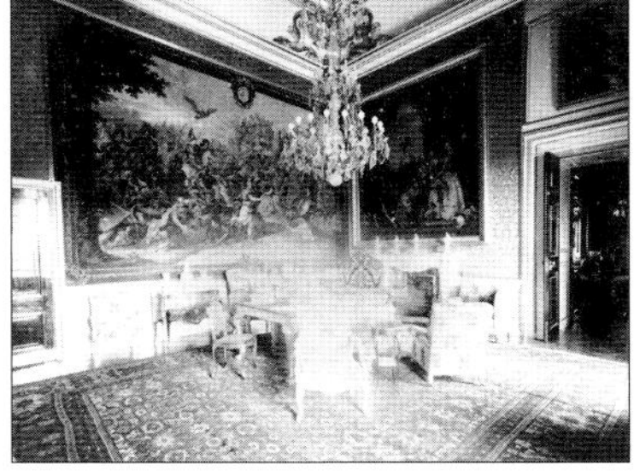

Old photograph circa 1890 showing the *Arbella* tapestry hanging in the present Green Drawing Room.

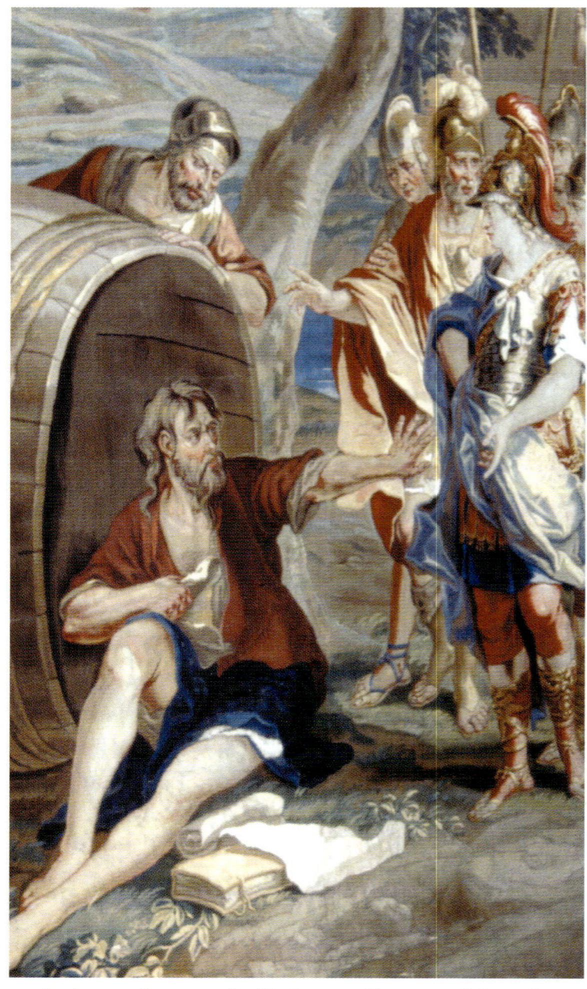
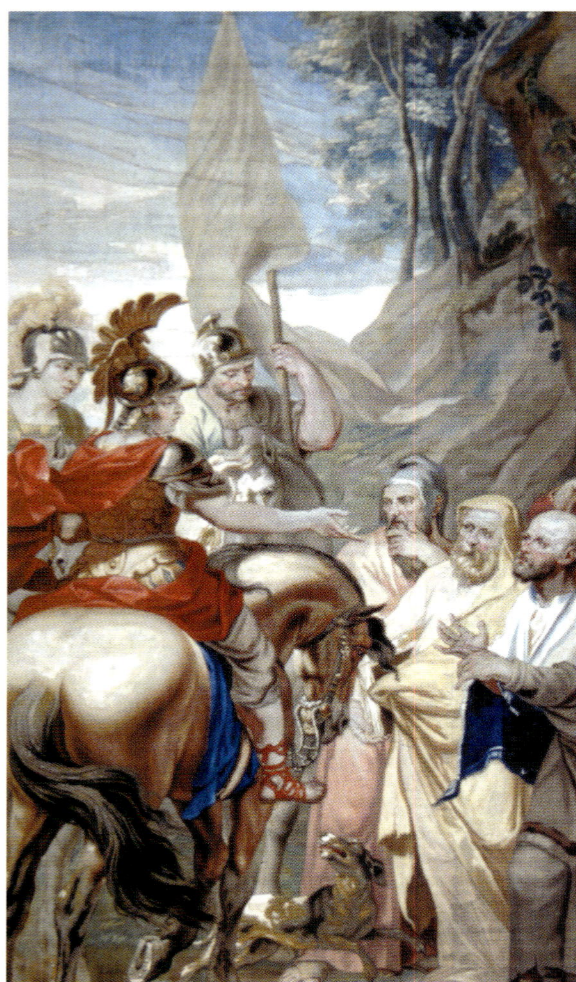

Above left : The *Diogenes* tapestry.
Above right : The *Philosophes* tapestry.

and share the work.[64] According to this sub-contract, only four *Alexander* tapestries were to be made by de Vos, the other four were presumably committed to another workshop.

The documents list the details of the set as follows : the largest panel, 21 feet wide, was *La Bataille de Darius.* Next, at 20 feet wide each, were *Le passage de la Riviere Granicus,* and *la nouvelle piece etant la bataille de Porus.* A further large panel at 17¹/₂ feet was *l'entrée triumphale en Babilone.* Two panels called *l'assemblee du reste* and *le Pillage* were each 5 feet wide, and finally another pair, *ou on prend les Prisonniers* and *Porus mene Prisonnier* measured 6 feet in width.[65]

The archives reveal that some of the panels had been completed by the winter of 1708,[66] and that all the tapestries were delivered on the 10th of February 1709[67] (not in ten months as per the contract but in just under eighteen months). The final payment was made on 9th April 1709.[68] The Duke seemed pleased with the hangings he had received, writing to Sarah from the Abbey of Loos on 24th June "*... the two suites of hangings which were made at Bruxelles by Vanbroukes [Vanbrugh's] measures cost me above eight hundred pounds, so that if possible they shou'd serve for the roomes they were intend'd for, being sure in England there can be none had so good and fine*".[69]

However, despite the Duke's apparent satisfaction, something seems to have occurred in the course of production of this order which prompted Marlborough not to use the firm of Naulaerts and Blommaerts again. Perhaps the confusion over the selection of the cartoons and the sub-contracting of weavers leading to the subsequent delay in delivery played a part, or, more likely, the Duke simply decided to cut out the middlemen and place his future orders through the weaver's workshop. Whatever the reason, he ordered four more *Alexander* tapestries directly from de Vos in the summer of 1709.[70] The tapestries are described as *La famille de Darius aux pieds d'Alexandre, Les Philosophes par devant Alexandre, Diogenes etant assis dans son tonneau* and *Alexandre descendant de son cheval et embrasse son pere.*[71] The records reveal that these four panels were delivered on 28th November 1710.[72]

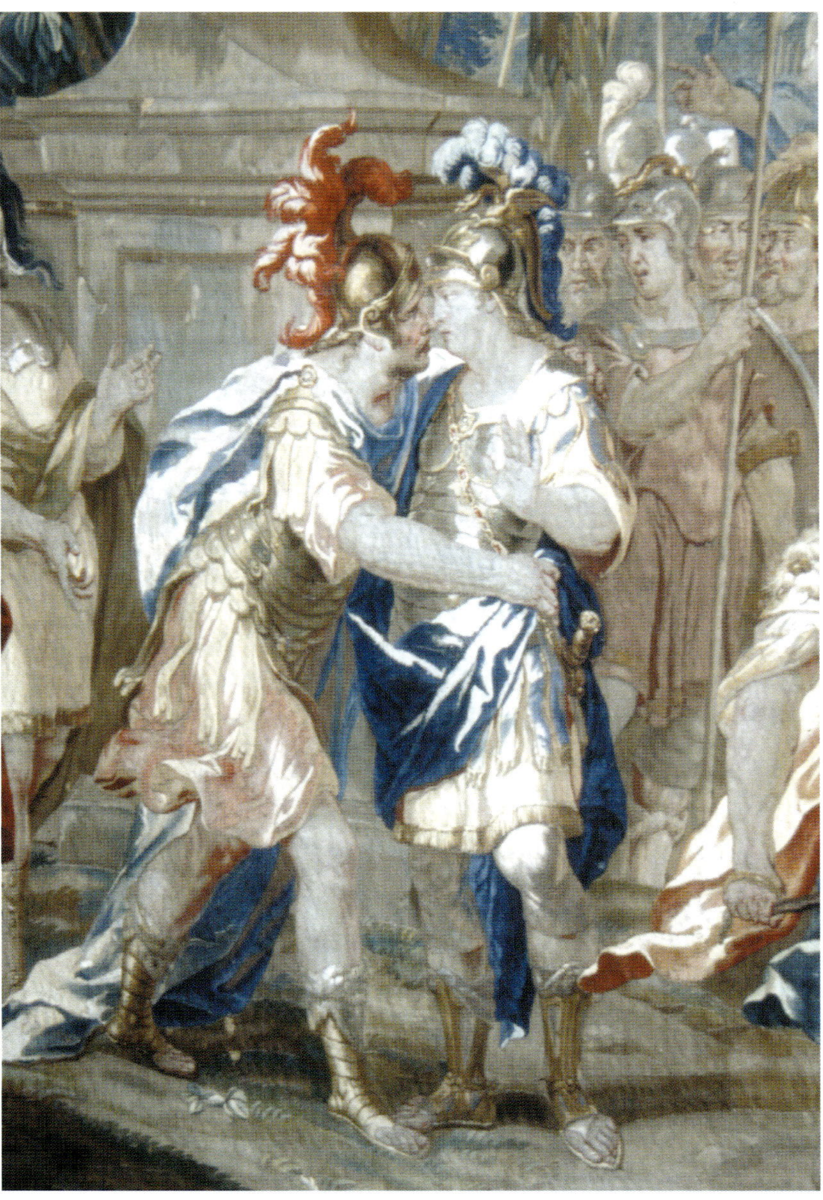

Tapestry detail showing Alexander greeting his father.

Quite apart from the puzzle of attribution of the weavers responsible for some of the *Alexander* tapestries, a visual examination of the panels led to the discovery that in four of the surviving works at Blenheim, the ducal coat of arms has been skilfully added into the top border rather than woven as an integral part of the tapestry. The four panels in question – *Les Philosophes par devant Alexandre, Diogenes etant assis dans son tonneau, La Bataille de Darius [Arbella]* and *Le passage de la Riviere Granicus* – are not connected with any particular part of the two separate commissions, which adds to the ambiguity surrounding the making of this set. The border of each panel is a woven imitation of a carved and gilded frame, following the fashion of the time.[73] Several of the surviving panels have been cut down on one or both sides or folded up to fit into the wall spaces where they now hang. But even after almost 300 years, there is nothing lacklustre in the appearance of this set which is entirely homogeneous, and virtually identical in quality.

The entire commission of twelve tapestries was originally hung in three rooms at Blenheim Palace: the Bow Window Room, the Duke's drawing room and the Duke's bedchamber. Today, eight *Alexander* tapestries survive in the Palace's collection and the other four are only known through documentation.

A laborious search to trace any of the tapestries known to have been commissioned by John Churchill but which are missing from the Blenheim collection today satisfyingly revealed the existence of a panel at Berkeley Castle. This tapestry was found to correspond in size to the hanging called *la nouvelle piece etant la bataille de Porus* had it been complete with its borders. John Churchill's coat of arms is woven as an integral part of the tapestry and has therefore survived even after the borders were removed at some point during its life.

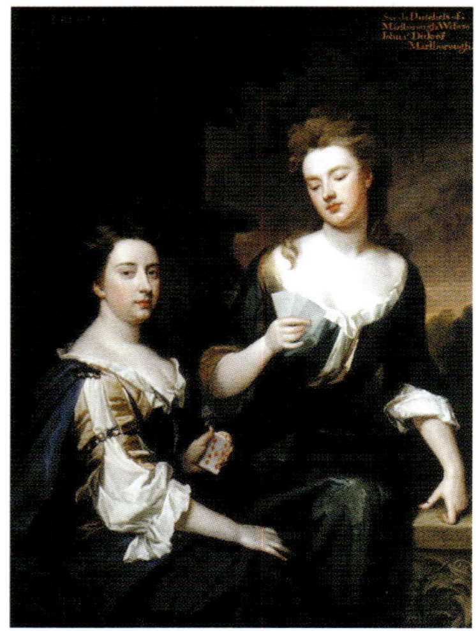

Sarah, Duchess of Marlborough and Lady Fitzharding by Sir Godfrey Kneller.

Details showing the added-in coat of arms on the *Arbella* tapestry.

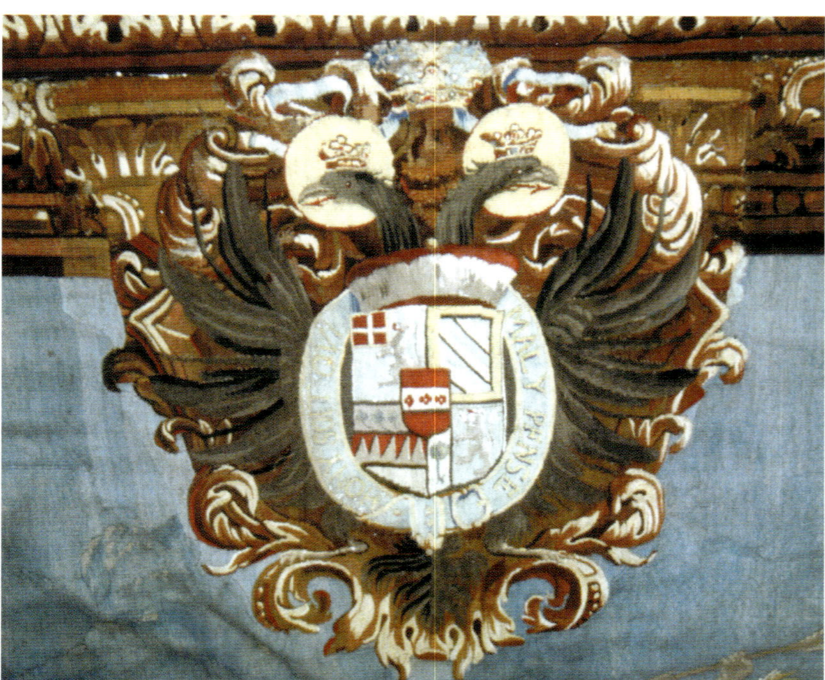

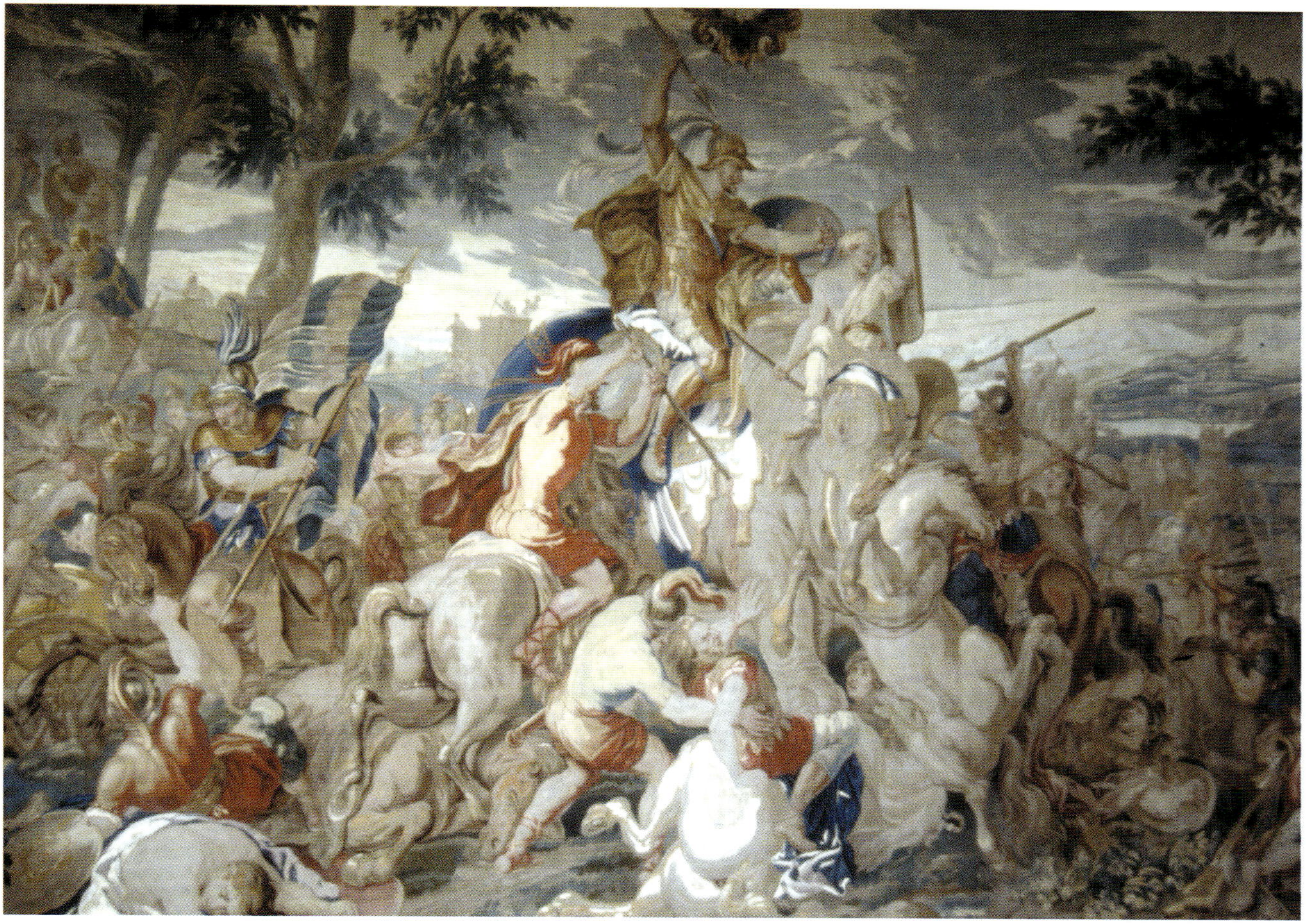

The *Porus* tapestry [*Battle of Hydaspes*].

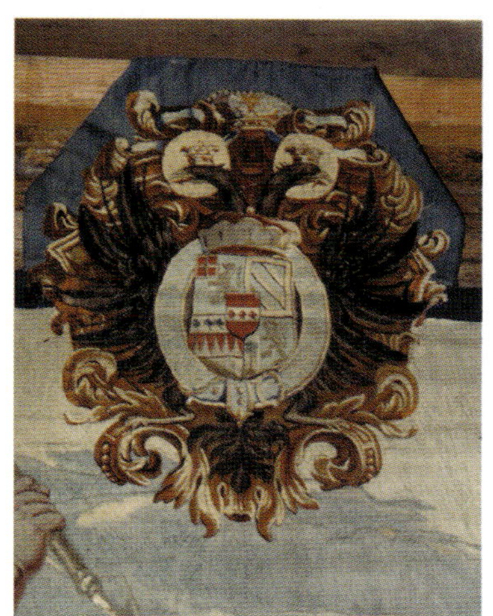

Detail showing John Churchill's coat of arms on the *Porus* tapestry panel at Berkeley Castle.

It is also not known when or in what circumstances the panel left Blenheim to become part of the Berkeley collection. The only link between the two families known to exist dates back 300 years to the friendship between Sarah Churchill and Lady Fitzharding. Lady Fitzharding was Barbara Berkeley, Sarah's closest childhood friend, who married Captain John Berkeley, 4th Viscount Fitzharding of Berehaven and Baron Berkeley of Rathdowne.

While the friendship between the two women endured, it is improbable that the tapestry would have found its way to its new home during the lifetime of Lady Fitzharding as she died in 1708, at which date the panel had not been received by the Churchills and Blenheim Palace was still under construction.

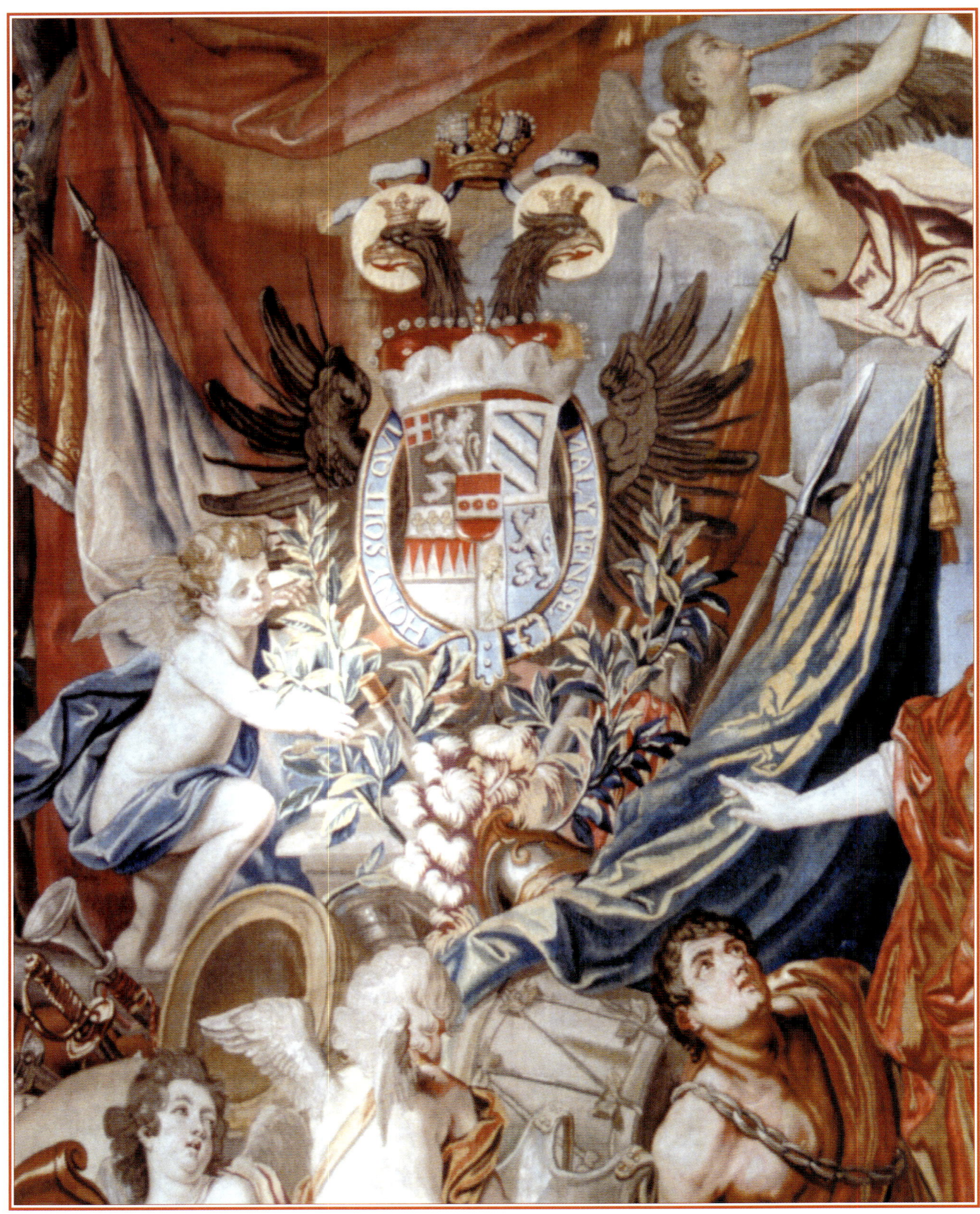

Chapter Five

MARLBOROUGH'S LATER TAPESTRY COMMISSIONS

JOHN Churchill and his wife Sarah had a great passion for collecting. Their activities focused both on making purchases of existing works of art as well as commissioning new ones. The design and purpose of Blenheim Palace was always intended to be more than the provision of a comfortable domestic residence, it was in effect to stand as a monument to the glory of Queen Anne through the military genius of the Duke of Marlborough. In this respect the choice of his later tapestry commissions would prove to be significant.

In 1709, the Duchess herself undertook to have a new London residence constructed. She appointed Sir Christopher Wren as architect, with the specific brief to make her home *"strong, plain and convenient"* and so Marlborough House in Pall Mall bore no resemblance whatever to Blenheim. However, with two new homes now being built simultaneously, the Duke enthusiastically stepped up his spending on works of art to fill them.

On July 11th 1709, preoccupied with both houses, he wrote to his wife from his army camp *"I approve of all you have done, but for fear of mistakes I desire you will give order that the stables which are already covered shou'd be finish'd so that the horses and sarvants might be in that building, I believe you can't be to[o] carefull of hindering Vanbruck [Vanbrugh] from begining new foundations for nothing is so good as the finishing of what is order'd. I am desirous that you would send me the exact measures of the roomes in your House in London which you desier shou'd be furnish'd with Tapestry. I also desire of you that you*

Blenheim Palace, north front

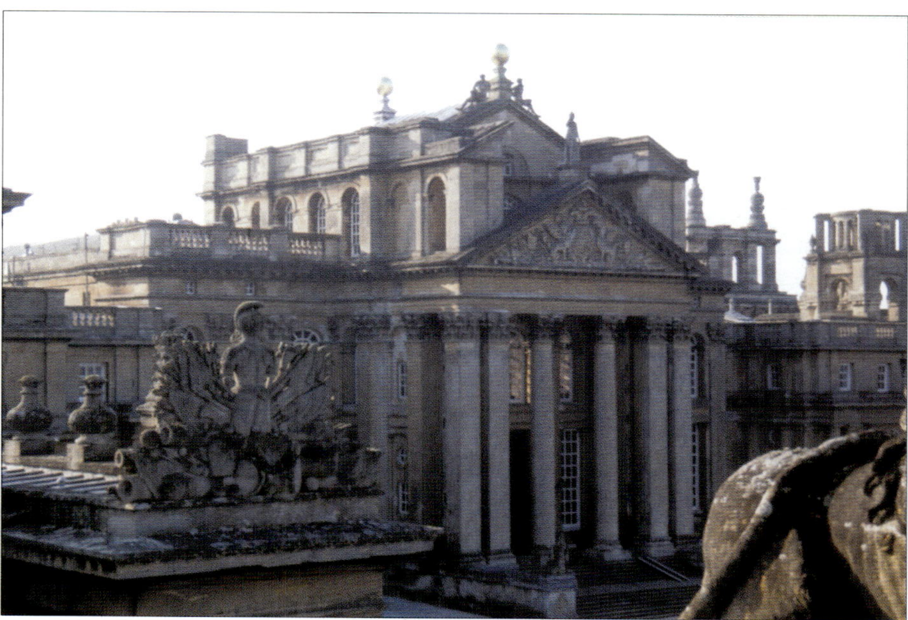

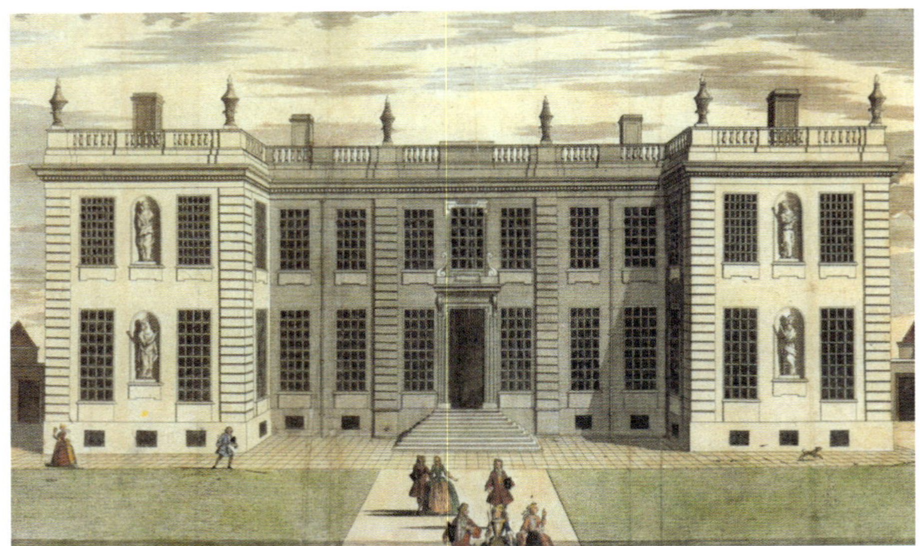

will gett me the exact measures for the great roome as well as all the others that are between the Sallon and the grande Cabinet and that I may have all these measures as soon as possible".[74]

To furnish and decorate some of the vast rooms at both houses in London and Woodstock, the Duke is known to have ordered three further sets of tapestries from the Flemish master weaver, Judocus de Vos. First, a set called the *Pleasures of the Gods*, followed by another important commission called the *Virtues* and the last but most significant set of martial tapestries, the series now called *The Victories of the Duke of Marlborough*. Although he dealt directly with de Vos for these last three sets, John Churchill, nevertheless, was influenced by and relied on the offices of an intermediary, His Excellency the Count Sinzendorf.[75]

Philippe Louis Wenzel Count Sinzendorf, a diplomat and statesman, was the Austrian Emperor's envoy to Versailles from 1699-1701 and Court Chancellor in Vienna from 1702-1713. He was the Imperial Plenipotentiary at the Hague in 1709 and at Utrecht in 1713. From 1705, he also held the post of Protector of the Viennese Imperial Academy of Arts.

As Ambassador to the French court at Versailles, he would certainly have appreciated and been inspired by Louis XIV's remarkable palace with its sumptuous collection of tapestries and other works of art, but it was perhaps in his capacity of Patron of the Viennese Imperial Academy of Arts that Sinzendorf had dealings with various Flemish artists and weavers.[76] The Count met Marlborough on several occasions in the Low Countries.[77]

In addressing the chronological analysis of the Duke's tapestry commissions, the assumption that the final three sets of hangings, including both the *Victories* and *Virtues* sets, were ordered during or after 1710 has been undermined by the discovery of documentary evidence that has been previously overlooked and leads to the probable re-dating of these commissions. In culling data from various archival documents it becomes apparent that the deliberations regarding these commissions had begun either at the end of the 1708 campaign, or at any rate very early in 1709, probably even before the start of that year's campaigning season.

The winter of 1708-1709 was exceptionally severe in Europe. Since the beginning of December 1708 a hard frost had set in throughout the continent which persisted until after Christmas. The Duke arrived in Brussels from England on 23rd January, after a momentary thaw of the ice masses in the Channel had allowed communications to resume for a brief period. The harsh weather conditions had led to widespread famine in France. French troops were left without bread or forage and it was generally considered that King Louis XIV would be incapable of prolonging the war and fighting another campaign, especially after the numerous defeats his army had suffered in the actions of 1708. The Duke remained in Flanders for about a month

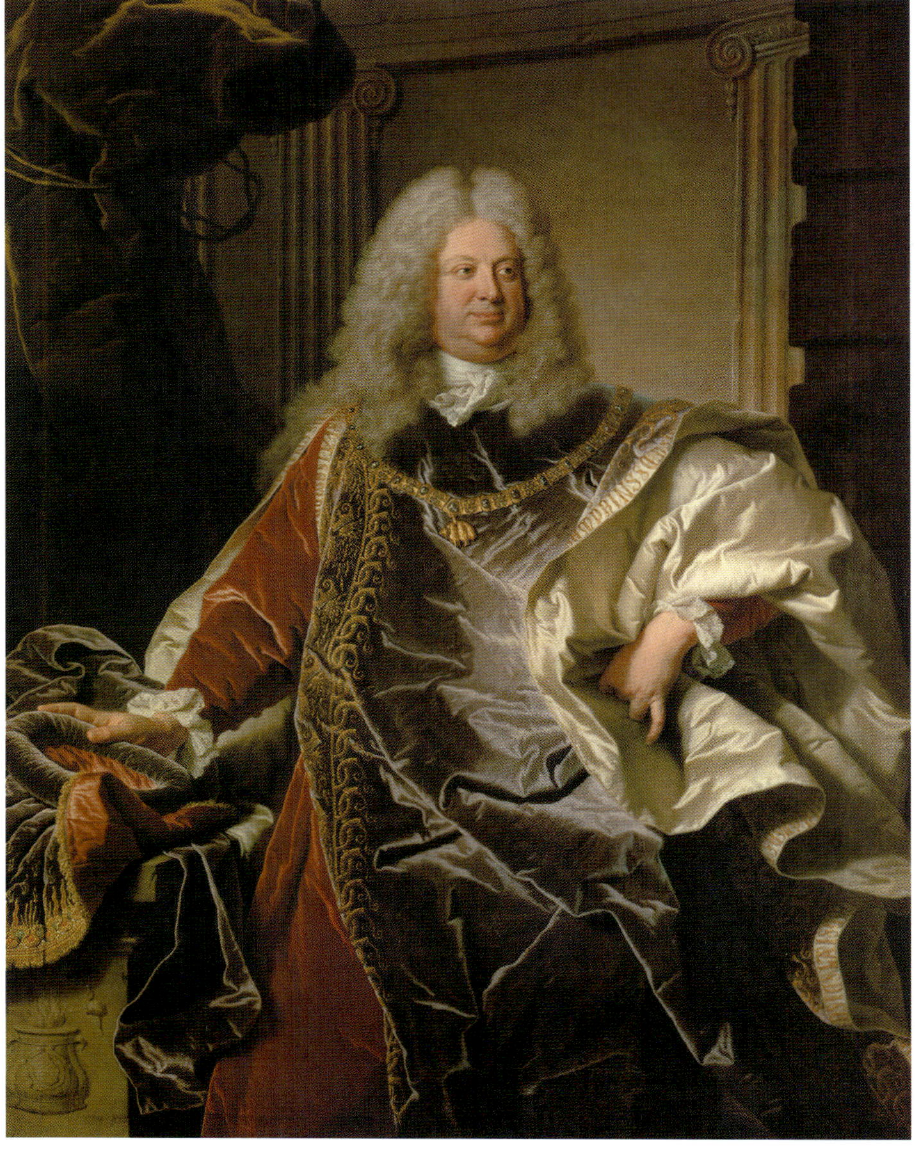

Count Sinzendorf by Hyacinthe Rigaud

on what was mainly a diplomatic mission: although still preparing for war, the Allies in 1709 were actively seeking a peaceful settlement to the hostilities. It was probably during this visit, when Count Sinzendorf was also present in Flanders, that the notion of commissioning a set of tapestries to celebrate his own victories was considered by John Churchill and the Naulaerts firm was asked, by February 1709, to send to Judocus de Vos the border designs which had been specially painted by Jan Van Orley for the Duke's *Art of War* tapestries.[78]

In his final account to the Duke, Judocus de Vos acknowledges receiving a substantial payment of 33,853 florins from Count Sinzendorf in connection with the Duke's tapestry commissions[79] and in an undated and frustratingly incomplete memorandum, Sinzendorf mentions various rooms within Blenheim Palace for which he says tapestry panels were ordered through him: the Bow Window Room, the Duchess's bedchamber, and an unspecified "*grande salle*".[80]

A further document throws more light on the matter and evidences that the last four tapestries of the *Alexander* set, commissioned directly from de Vos, were seemingly undertaken on Sinzendorf's recommendation and that the panels from the *Alexander* series, originally intended to be hung in only two rooms of the Duke's apartments, namely his bedchamber and drawing room, were now additionally to be hung in a third room – the Bow Window Room. The *Pleasures of the Gods* were destined for the Duchess's bedchamber and the *Virtues* were intended to be hung in the "*grande salle*".[81]

Although there were three possible large rooms that might have been alluded to as the "*grande salle*", Sinzendorf is likely to be referring to a scheme planned for the Great Hall rather than for the Grand Cabinet or the Long Gallery. As far as the Grand Cabinet was concerned, even though Vanbrugh had envisaged this room to be wainscoted for hangings[82] in 1707, the plan

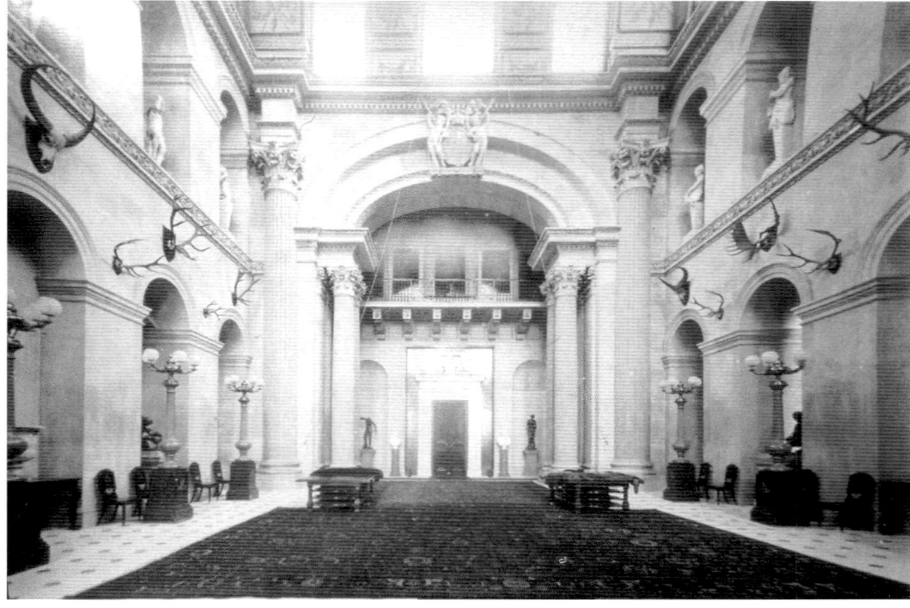

The Great Hall c. 1890

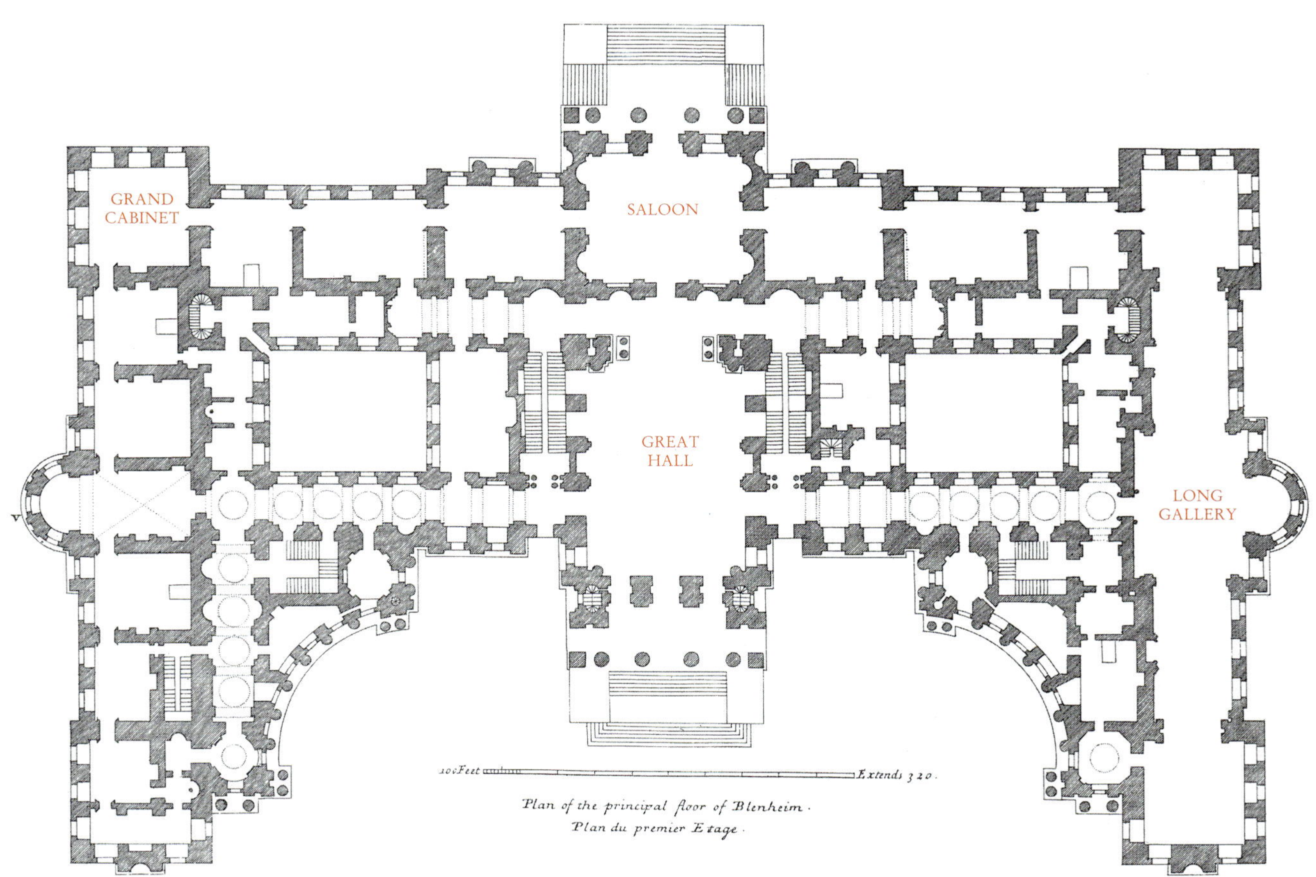

Blenheim Floor plan circa 1725.

had clearly been revised by May 1708 when the Duke revealed his intention to furnish it with the finest pictures he could obtain[83] and no tapestries of any description featured in the final fitting out of this room, where 31 of his best paintings were ultimately displayed. Likewise, the Long Gallery was destined to receive further pictures, mirrors and statues. Moreover, in several other documents also written to the Duke in French at this time, the Great Hall is referred to as the "*grande salle*" and so there is no reason to believe that Sinzendorf would not have used the same terminology. However, it seems that by July 1709 the scheme for tapestries to be hung in the Great Hall was abandoned in favour of a more conventional hanging proposal for the *Virtues* set, which was to perhaps display them in "*the room next to the Sallon*".[84]

Sinzendorf goes on to state that the order for the tapestries of "*the battles won by My Lord Duke*" was contracted with Judocus de Vos "*at the Hague on 19th November*". Regrettably, the year has not been mentioned. However, two letters in the Blenheim Papers allow further confirmation of the dating. On July 4th 1709 the Count writes from Brussels reporting that he has "*finalised the design*" for the tapestries and hopes they will satisfy the Duke.

He informs John Churchill that de Vos will bring these designs as soon as they are completed to the Hague and that from there they would be sent on to his army camp.[85] The second document is a letter written by the Duke on 30th July 1709 to Charles Viscount Townshend, Plenipotentiary at the Hague, in which he adds this postscript: "*My compliments to Count Sinzendorff, and pray lett him know that I have receiv'd from England the measures for the Hangins, and if the designe be finish'd I shou'd be glad the man att Bruxelles [Judocus de Vos] might have orders to lett me see them*".[86] It is not entirely clear whether the design referred to was for the *Virtues* set or the *Victories* set, or both.

However, as we now know that some form of design had been finalised for the tapestries by July 1709 and that the Duke, impatient to see them, had already taken steps to obtain from his wife in England the exact dimensions of the rooms destined to receive the hangings, then it is fairly likely that preliminary discussions for the commissioning of these sets had already begun at the start of that year (when the Van Orly borders were sent to de Vos), if not earlier. It is also reasonable to assume that the idea for this commission was conceived soon after the victories in the campaign of 1708, the year in which the Allies had triumphantly concluded no less than three highly successful actions (Oudenarde, Wynendael and Lille) where Louis XIV's armies had been comprehensively defeated and John Churchill was at the summit of his power and achievement.

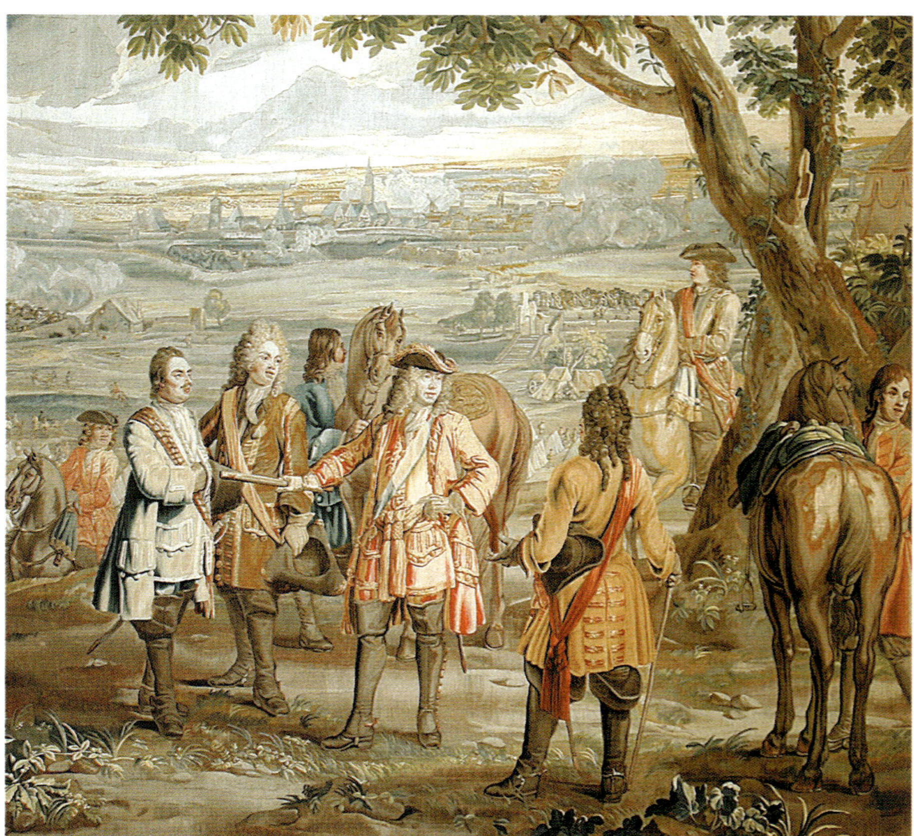

The *Lille* tapestry.

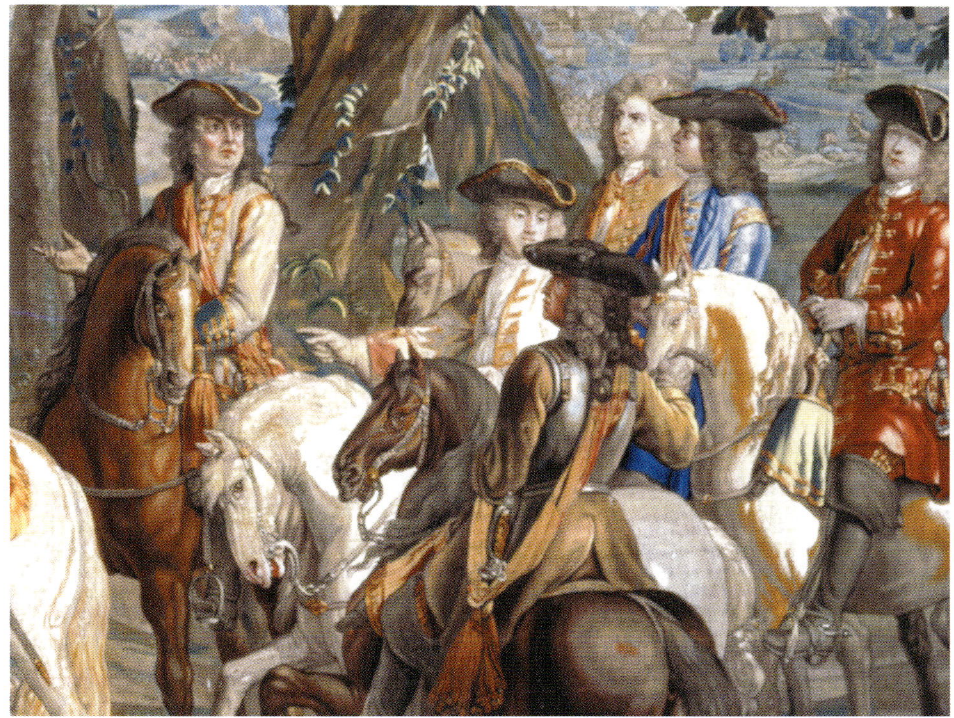

Detail from the *Battle of Blenheim* tapestry. William Cadogan is the figure between the trees, extreme left.

On the other hand, history reveals that in 1710 the Marlboroughs no longer exerted the influence they had previously enjoyed and they were soon to be removed from their positions, their enemies at court having successfully plotted against them. To silence their critics, the Duchess had wanted to put a stop to the construction work at Woodstock and the completion of the entire building project was in jeopardy.[87] It seems highly unlikely that a major order for several sets of tapestries would have been placed in these circumstances. In view of these facts and the archival evidence discovered, it is extremely probable that these significant commissions were made in the winter of 1708-1709 rather than later, and both sets of tapestries – the *Victories* and the *Virtues* – were, in the months that followed, individually designed and made up as newly commissioned work for which John Churchill was charged the premium rate of 45 florins per ell by Judocus de Vos.

The correspondence between the Duke and the weaver was, more often than not, addressed either through Adam Cardonnel, the Duke's army secretary, or through one of his most trusted officers and Chief of Staff, William Cadogan. These two men were also responsible for the writing up and dispatch of orders and instructions to the weaver, as well as the receipt of the finished items when they were delivered to camp headquarters. Payments on account or on completion were authorised by them and were usually paid either through Benjamin Sweet, the deputy-paymaster for the English army in Flanders or sometimes through Henry Cartwright, army treasurer. Some administrative instructions, especially concerning deliveries, were conveyed by them through John Laws, Her Majesty's Secretary at Brussels.

The designer of the *Victories* tapestries has long been thought to be Lambert de Hondt, a Flemish artist admitted to the painters guild on 10th March 1679.[88] Born in Malines (Mechelen) he is reputed to have learnt his trade from Teniers[89] and is listed as an artist making cartoons for weavers at Oudenarde.[90] In 1696 he was commissioned by Max Emmanuel, Elector of Bavaria, to produce designs for the tapestry series called the 'first version' *Art of War*,[91] which were woven by Jaspar and Jacob Van der Borcht from 1700 to 1705. Apart from his work on this set, Lambert de Hondt is known to have specialised in both landscapes and military art, successfully combining both narrative and decorative qualities, and so his studio may have been chosen for this reason alone to produce the designs for the *Victories* panels.

De Hondt had set up his business in Brussels where he was married and had two sons. He was 'privileged' in 1709 which indicates an increase in his business activity at around this time. His older son, Ignatius died in about 1710, but his second son, Philippe is known to have worked with him.[92]

It seems likely that both Lambert and Philippe de Hondt were involved in designing the *Victories* tapestries. Philippe de Hondt is widely regarded as being the artist responsible for the 'second version' *Art of War* series.[93] A comparison of the *Victories* tapestries at Blenheim with a set of 'second version' *Art of War* tapestries, commissioned for the Elector of Bavaria at Schleissheim, demonstrates that four panels are virtually identical in their detail and one other is loosely adopted, seeming to confirm that the artist of the *Victories* set must also have been responsible for the design of the 'second'

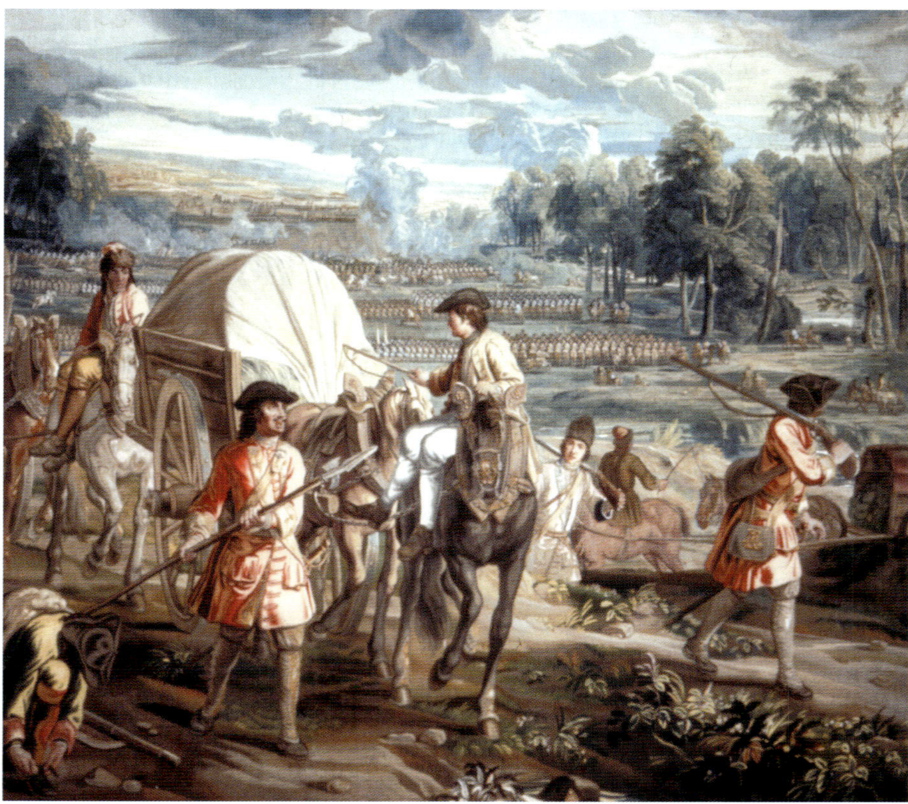

The *Wynendael* tapestry.

Art of War series. It would therefore appear that Philippe de Hondt was also in some substantial way involved in producing the designs of the *Victories* for the Duke of Marlborough.

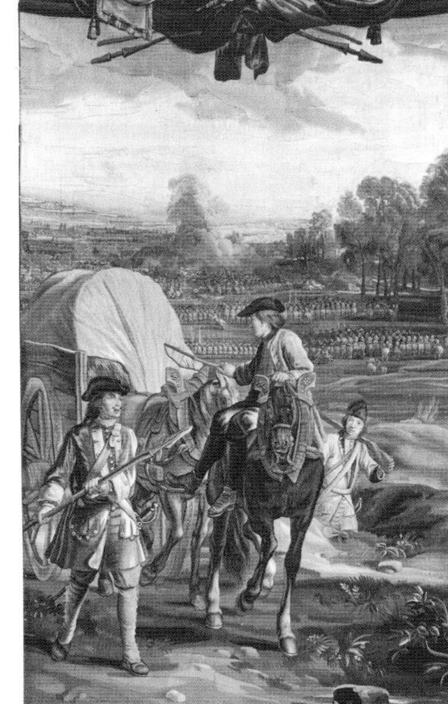

Right: *Wagon with foot soldiers*, a tapestry from the 'second version' *Art of War* set at Schloss Schleissheim. This panel is based on the cartoon for the *Wynendael* tapestry.

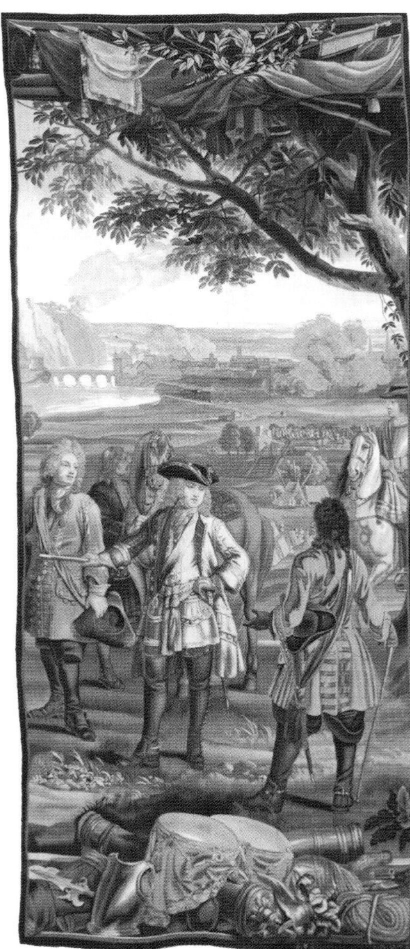

Far right: *Maximilian Emanuel with two officers*, a tapestry from the 'second version' *Art of War* set at Schloss Schleissheim. This panel is based on the cartoon for the *Lille* tapestry.

Philippe de Hondt was 'privileged' on 15th April 1711. Judocus de Vos was one of the signatories on his application for privileges, a sign that the two men already knew each other well.[94] In his application he was acclaimed as Jan Van Orley's successor and attention was drawn to the fact that he also designed tapestry sets and borders for other workshops.[95] It is likely that privileges were granted when Philippe took over his father's business, indicating that Lambert de Hondt was already dead by that date.[96] Therefore, the assumption that Philippe de Hondt may have been engaged in the designs of the *Victories* set along with his father from the very start seems more than possible. This is not only because of the iconographic and stylistic similarity of all the panels in the set but, more importantly, since Lambert de Hondt had died by mid April 1711, that is to say before the siege of Bouchain, one of Marlborough's last and highly successful encounters against the French and around which no less than three *Victories* tapestry panels are based.

Although no documentation survives with details of any contractual obligations, a memorandum written by Count Sinzendorf [97] indicates that a set of twelve panels of equal size was to be commissioned to furnish three rooms at Blenheim Palace. Eleven panels of the set were each to describe a different battle or military engagement in which the Duke and his allies had been victorious over the armies of the French King Louis XIV and the final panel would depict '*Peace*'. The twelve tapestries together were to measure 472 square ells for a total consideration of 21,240 florins. At the rate of 45 florins per ell, this was to prove by far the largest and most expensive set of tapestries made for John Churchill.

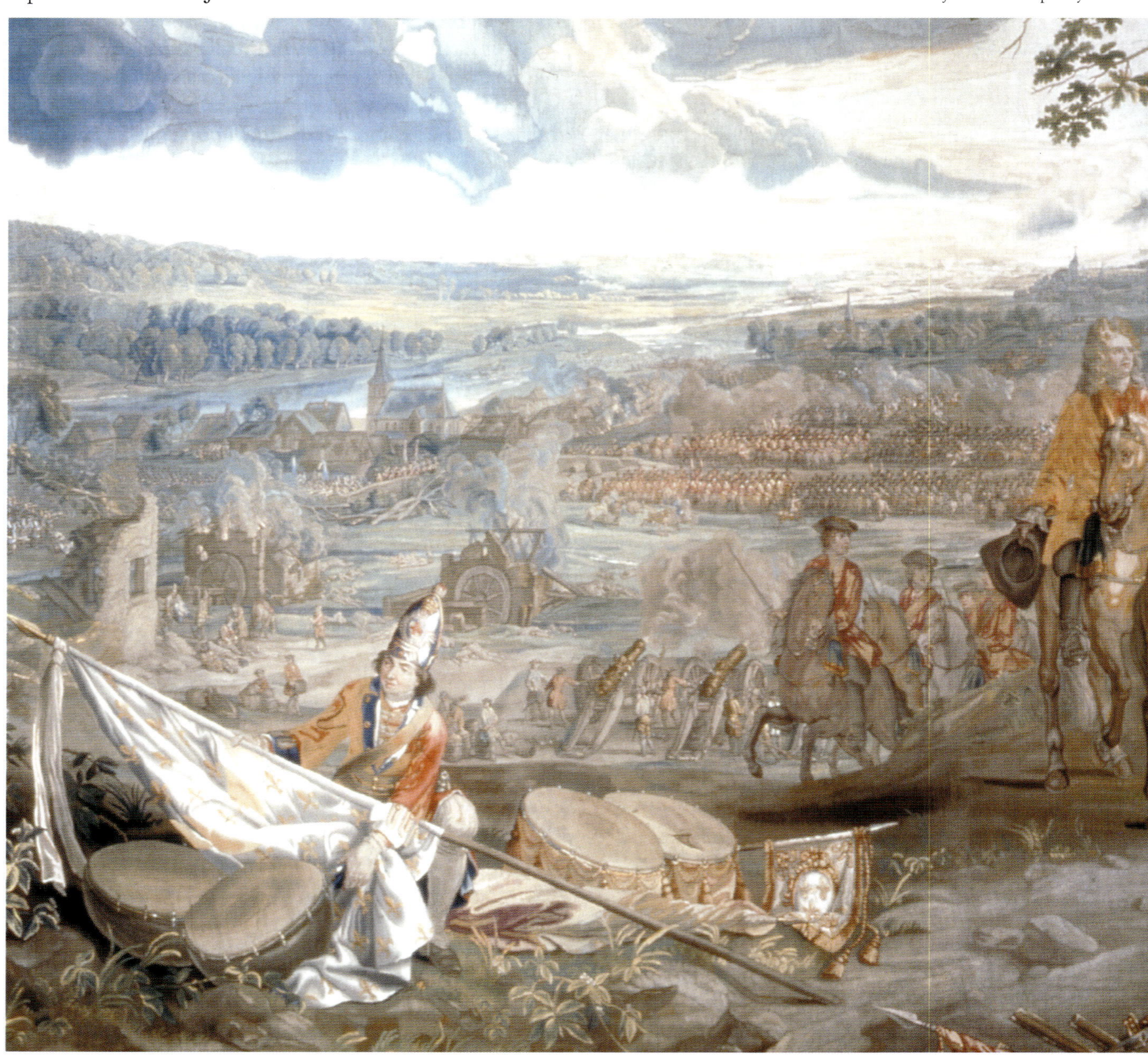

The *Battle of Blenheim* tapestry.

Early in 1710 weaving was already under way on some *Virtues* tapestries and cartoons were being prepared for some of the *Victories* panels, when de Vos wrote regarding difficulties he had encountered and on which he needed instructions. "*I cannot represent the Battle of Hooghstedt [Blenheim] or Ramillies on a piece of only 6¹/₂ ells with the borders, they need 8, 9 or 10 ells at least to execute them according to the design. Enclosed are the arms of your Highness with the crown of the Princes of the Empire; I await your orders before carying out the work…*"[98] He also stated that the work on the other battle hangings was progressing as fast as possible. Attached to his letter was a drawing of the Duke's coat of arms as prince of the Holy Roman Empire, for approval.

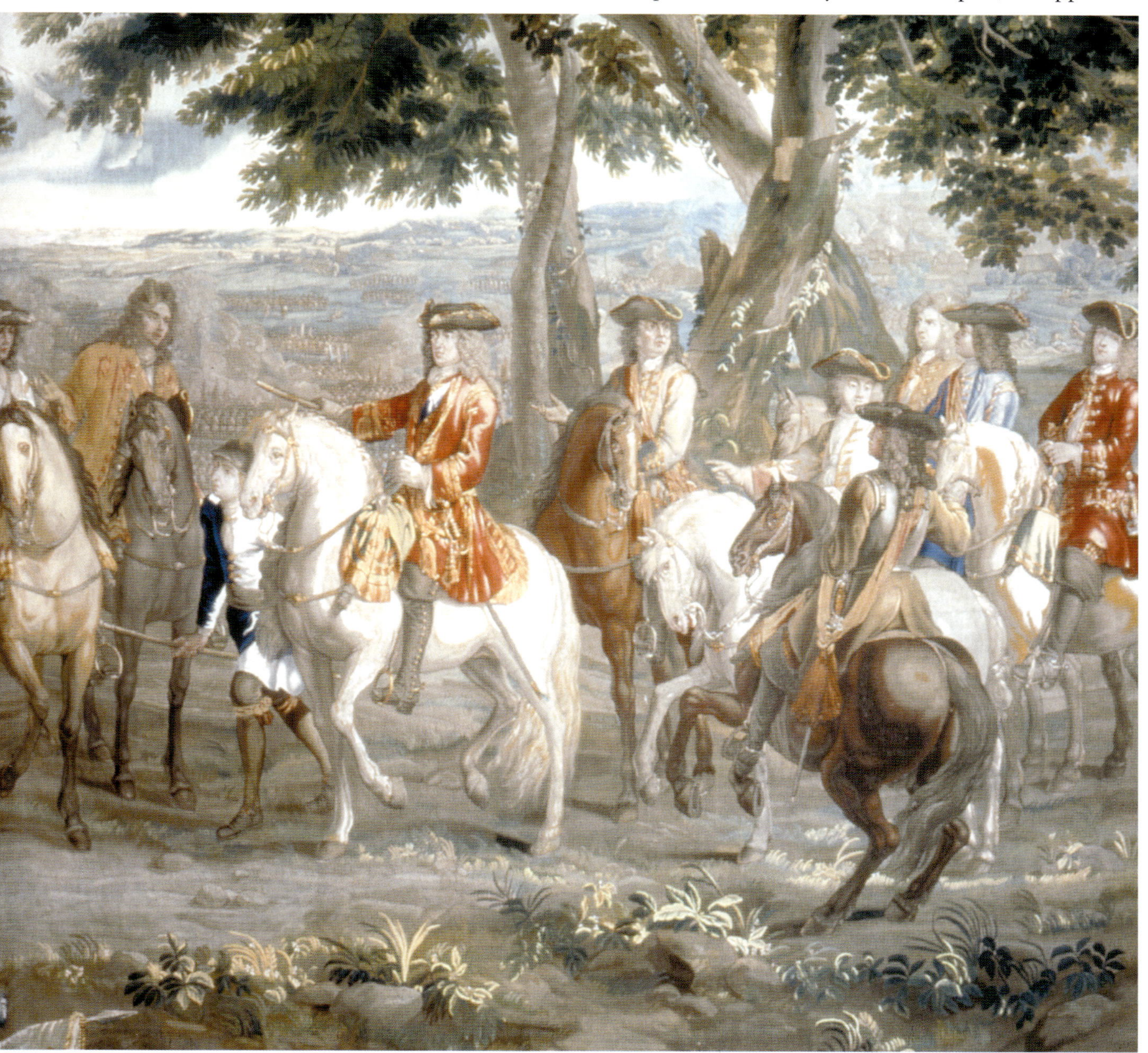

The coat of arms referred to was the focal point for the design of the set of four tapestries called the *Virtues*, still a part of the collection at Blenheim today. Signs of ownership in the form of heraldic arms were a particular feature of tapestries commissioned by both royalty and the nobility. In these exceptional tapestries, the virtues of *Temperance*, *Fortitude*, *Justice* and *Prudence* were allegorically represented around a large, centrally placed ducal coat of arms. The four cardinal virtues were civilizing influences and

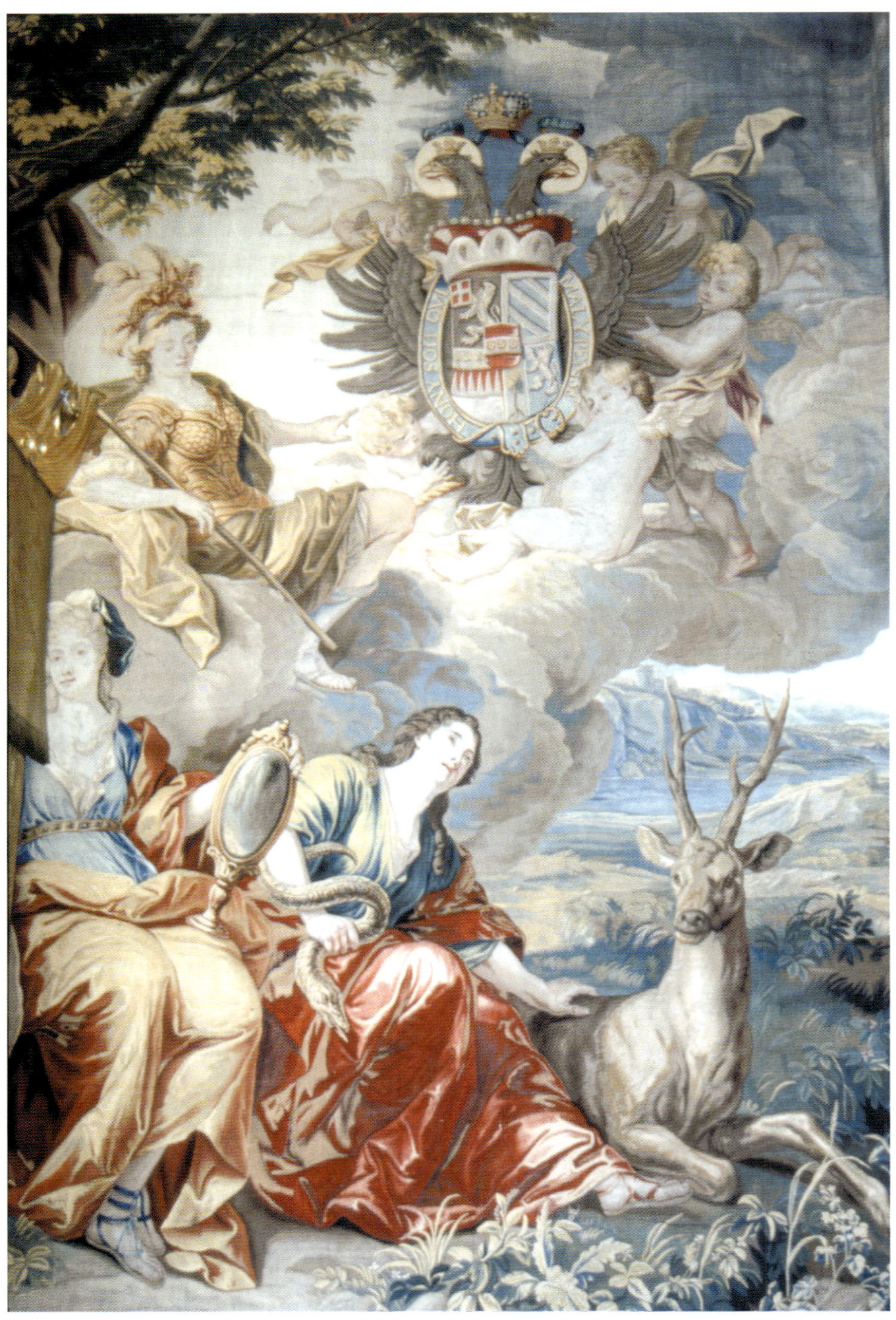

Detail from the *Prudence* tapestry. Two allegorical figures of Prudence are shown. One is holding a mirror in her left hand (viewing the actions of others to enable her to better regulate her own). The other is shown with a snake entwined around her arm (a reference to *Matthew 10:16 – Be wise as ye serpents*) and her hand is resting on the back of a stag (prudent in evading pursuit).

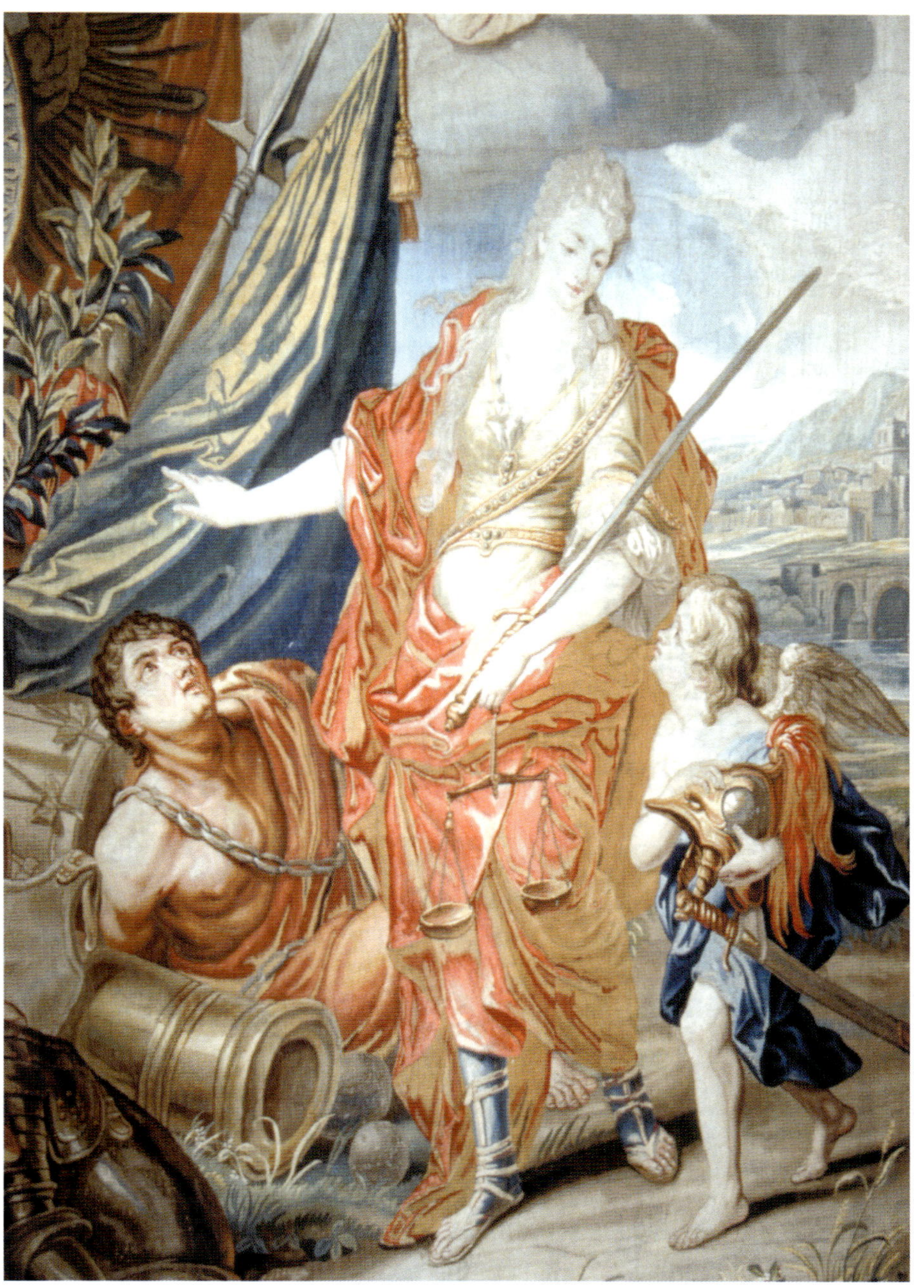

manifestations of moral worth. The emblematic associations made were: for *Temperance* the bridle, for *Justice* the scales, for *Fortitude* Hercules[99] and for *Prudence* the mirror. That Marlborough set particular store in incorporating them in his tapestries is obvious since we also find the same four virtues included, once again, in the medallions in the four corners of the decorative border surrounding the *Victories* panels. The figurative details vary only slightly in the *Victories* medallions where *Fortitude* is represented carrying a sword.

The *Virtues* tapestries were to be of the finest quality, made from specially commissioned designs. Specific details are provided by William Cadogan in a memorandum: *"the area surrounding the arms will be decorated with figures representing the Virtues…who will hold up the arms and carry trophies which will correspond to the nature of the Virtue represented by the figure. The Border will be a simple square one on a blue background"*.[100]

It is likely that this set was ordered to celebrate the elevation of John Churchill, Duke of Marlborough, as Prince of the Holy Roman Empire. This had been suggested as early as June 1704 to the Emperor Leopold I by Count Wratislaw, the Imperial Ambassador at the English Court. This great honour, the closest a person of common birth could get to royal status, was bestowed not only for Marlborough's past achievements in the War of the Spanish Succession, but more crucially to maintain his future support. It was to prove a timely proposal, as the Allied victory at the Battle of Blenheim in August 1704 secured Vienna and saved the Holy Roman Empire from a possible French invasion.

When the Emperor Joseph acceded to the throne in May 1705, the Princedom of Mindelheim was offered to the Duke and his creation as a new Prince was registered in November. Count Sinzendorf played a decisive role in these negotiations. The formalities for taking possession of Mindelheim, which was a small territory in Bavaria captured by the Austrians from the defeated Elector of that state after the Battle of Blenheim in 1704, occurred on 24th May 1706. Marlborough, who must have been flattered on receiving this distinction, used his new status primarily to enhance his

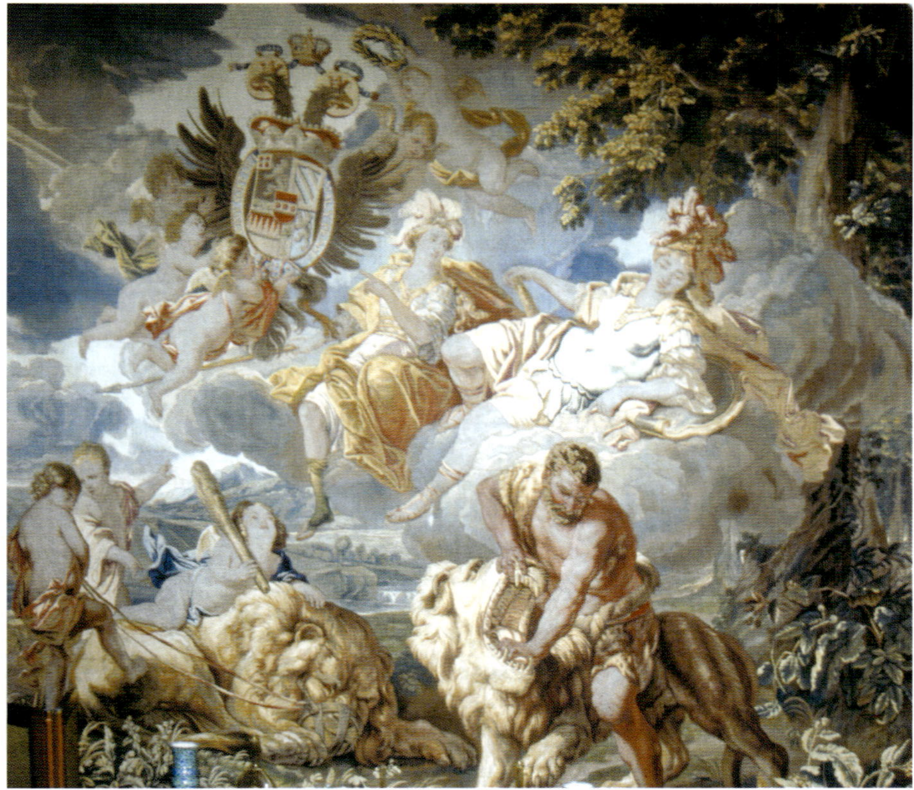

The *Fortitude* tapestry shows an allegorical figure of Hercules forcing apart the jaws of a lion. Fortitude signifies courage, strength and endurance; the lion was considered the bravest of all animals.

The *Temperance* tapestry shows a cloud-borne allegorical figure of Temperance holding her attribute of a bridle. The Winds overlook a marine Triumph, a merman and a sea nymph display the ducal arms and a river god is visible in the right foreground.

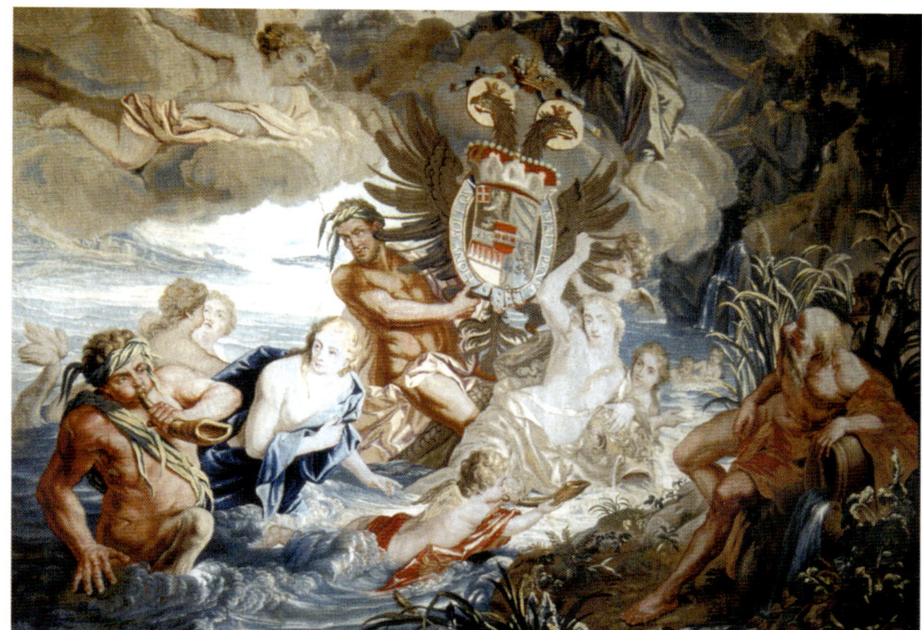

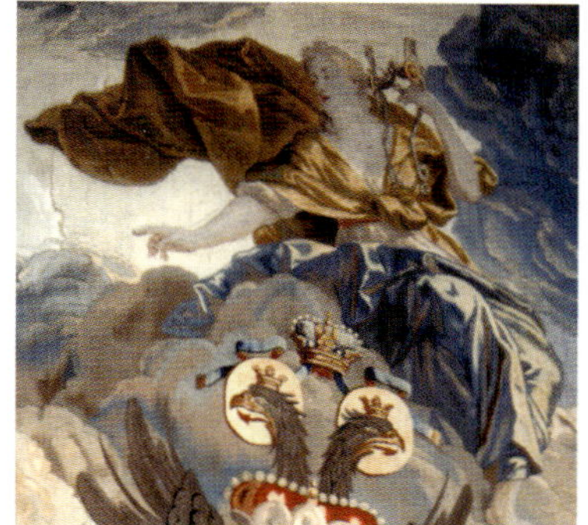

Detail of *Temperance*.

Detail of the river god in the *Temperance* tapestry.

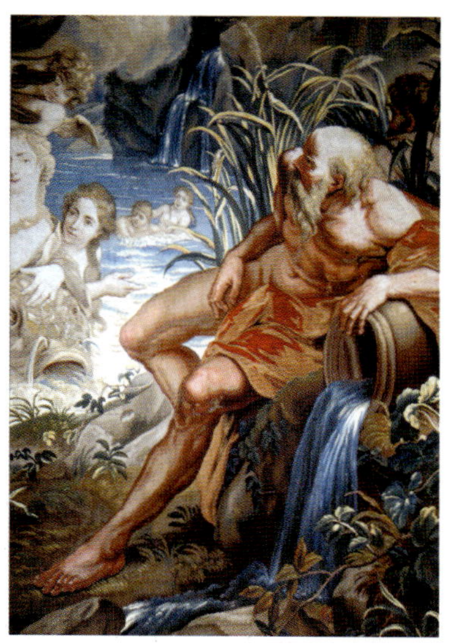

authority in his diplomatic dealings with England's multinational allies. He governed Mindelheim for eight and a half years[101] through appointed agents, raising fairly substantial annual revenues from taxation and customs levies, adding to his numerous other sources of wealth. His coat of arms from 1706 onwards reflected his newly elevated status as Prince of the Holy Roman Empire.

As it turned out, Marlborough did not commission his set of heraldic tapestries immediately because the protracted discussions with the Austrian Habsburgs still continued beyond 1706. Contrary to previous assurances, Mindelheim had been conferred on the Duke as a male sub-fief, entirely disregarding the fact that in the past female succession had prevailed. In addition, the new Prince, who was a Protestant, was disallowed from influencing the rights and position of the Catholic church in Mindelheim. While the religious restrictions did not seem to cause him concern, Marlborough anxiously desired a resolution of the uncertainty regarding the female succession. Both his sons had died young and with only daughters to succeed him, the continuing tenure of the principality was in question. The Emperor played for time by dangling a carrot, promising Marlborough the governor-generalship of the southern Netherlands when the Habsburg claimant, his brother the Archduke Charles, attained the Spanish throne.

Therefore, while the seal used by the Duke's administrators in Mindelheim displayed his new coat of arms incorporating the heraldic bell of the principality, the coat of arms he eventually chose to have woven into his tapestries replaced this detail with the marital shield and was therefore identical to the version which had already been included in the *Art of War* and *Alexander* sets. He confirms this in a letter written to Sarah on 8th March 1709/10 from the Hague: "*I also send you my coat of Armes as they are to be on the hangings now making att Bruxelles, so that I desire you will send for Vandenberg, and that he shou'd take care that the Crown and Armes in the hangings already come over be exact as this is".*[102]

The four *Virtues* panels were ordered at around the same time as the *Victories* set and their weaving was undertaken simultaneously by Judocus de Vos. However, there had obviously been a problem with either the drawing or the final form of the ducal coat of arms, as a few weeks earlier, on the 19th of February 1710, Judocus de Vos had written to His Grace enclosing a revised version.[103] In this letter he also apologised for the delay in sending the new drawing to the Duke, explaining that there was only one painter in Brussels able to execute armorial bearings and that the man had been ill. This is an interesting insight into the availability of labour in the trades associated with tapestry weaving. It is generally considered that only one third of the total number of workmen employed in tapestry production consisted of weavers, while the majority two thirds were more indirectly connected, such as the dyers, the wool and silk merchants, and the various types of painters and cartoon artists.

Map of the Principality of Mindelheim as delineated in 1706.

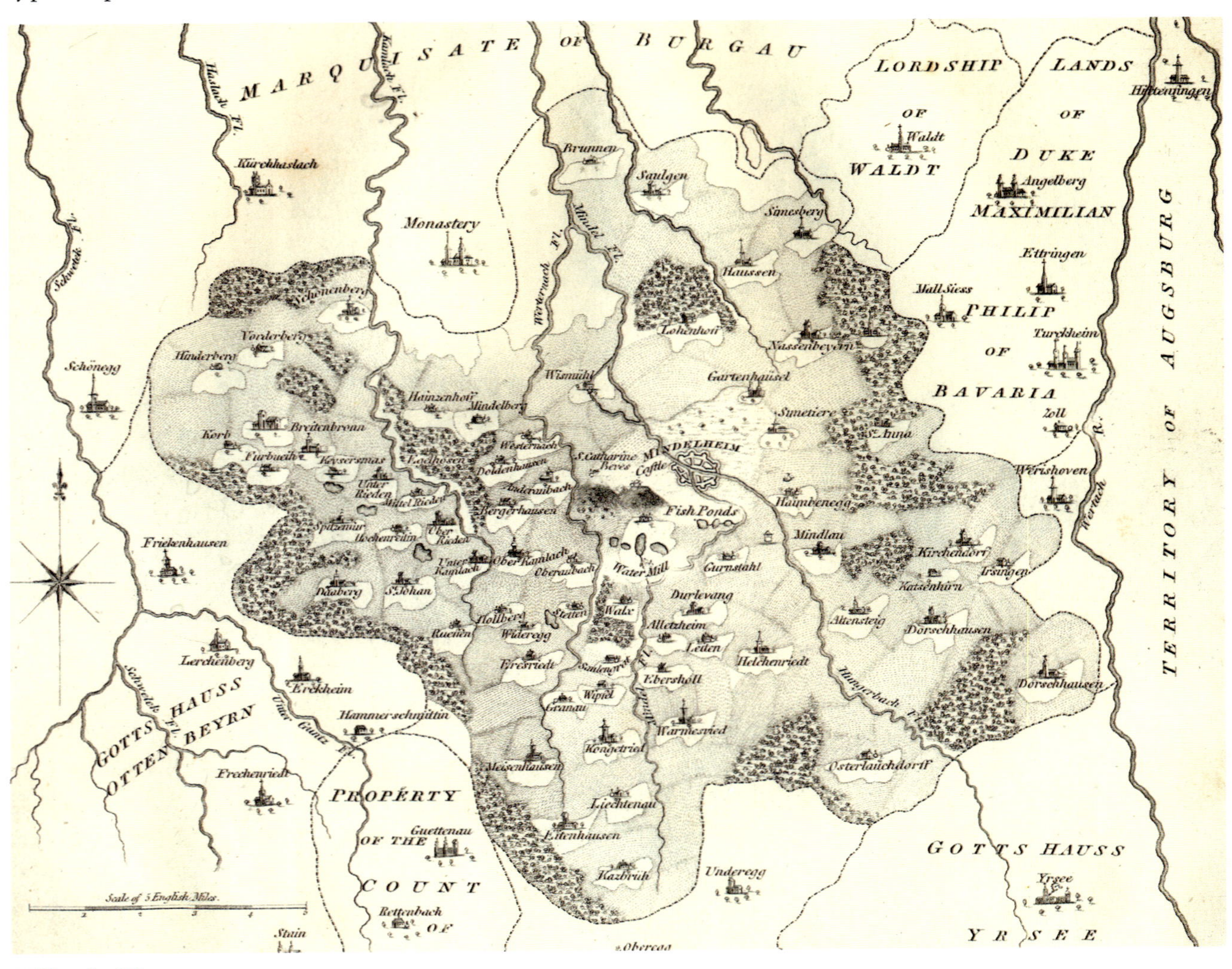

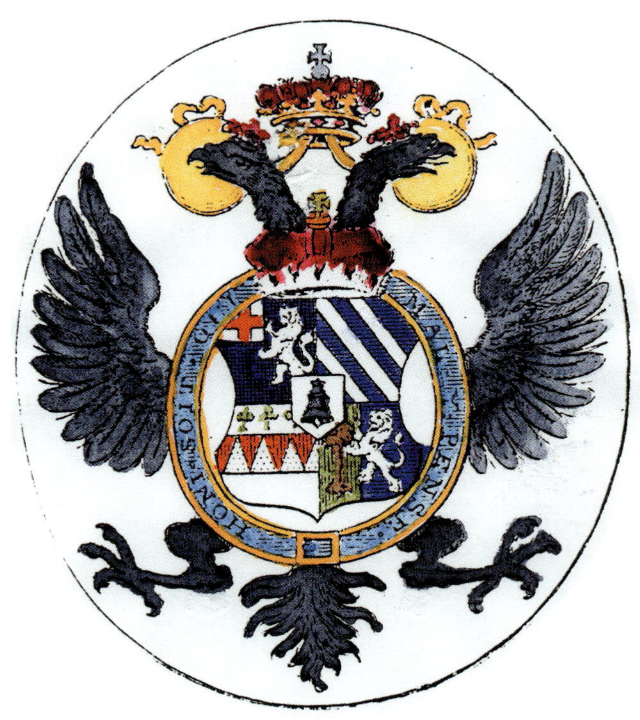

Marlborough actually visited Mindelheim just once, in the second week of June 1713, when he spent a few days there during his travels on the continent in self-imposed exile in 1712 -1713, after he was stripped of all his offices on 31st December 1711 and faced impeachment on the trumped up charge of peculation of army funds. He was joined by his wife for a short while only in 1713 although she had fallen from the Queen's favour and had been dismissed from her royal duties almost a year before her husband. In a touching letter from Maastricht he wrote to her "... *I am extremely sensible of the obligation I have to you for the resolution you have taken of leaving your friends and country for my sake, I am very sure if there be anything in my power that may make it easy to you, I shou'd do it with al[l] imaginable pleasure. In this place you will have very litel conveniences so that we must get to Frankford as soon as wee can, I wish we may be better there, but I fear you will not be easy til wee get to some place where we may settel for some time, so that we may be in a methode and orderly way of living, and if you are then contented I shall have nothing to trouble me. When you go to Bruxelles I desire you wou'd give yourself the trouble of going to see the Hangings at Mons[ieur] de Vost, you may do it in half an hour whicht they get the diner ready*".[104]

As to the weaving of these final tapestry commissions, 1710 saw the completion of the *Pleasures of the Gods* set (which is no longer in the Blenheim collection). This series could comprise up to six panels representing Apollo, Neptune, Ceres, Flora, Vulcan and Bacchus surrounded by their attributes. Also sometimes known as the *Triumphs of the Gods*, the set had first been designed by Noel Coypel (1628-1707) in the late 1680s and was subsequently successfully produced again in the early eighteenth century by the recently reopened Gobelins factory using the contemporary artwork of Claude III Audran.[105] Victor Janssens (1658-1736) also produced designs of this tapestry series which were woven from 1700 onwards by the Auwercx and Judocus de Vos workshops in Brussels.[106] Janssens' designs may well have been used to produce the Duke of Marlborough's set.

Documentary evidence reveals that the Duke only ordered four of these tapestries, two large panels depicting *Apollo* and *Neptune,* and two smaller ones depicting *Ceres* and *Flora.* In July that year the Duke confirmed to Sarah that "*... the tapestry man of Bruxelles has been with me and assures me that I shall bring you over the hangings for your bedchamber and the room before itt, but between this and the month of November*".[107] This set, intended to be hung in the Duchess's bedchamber, was charged at the rate of 22 florins

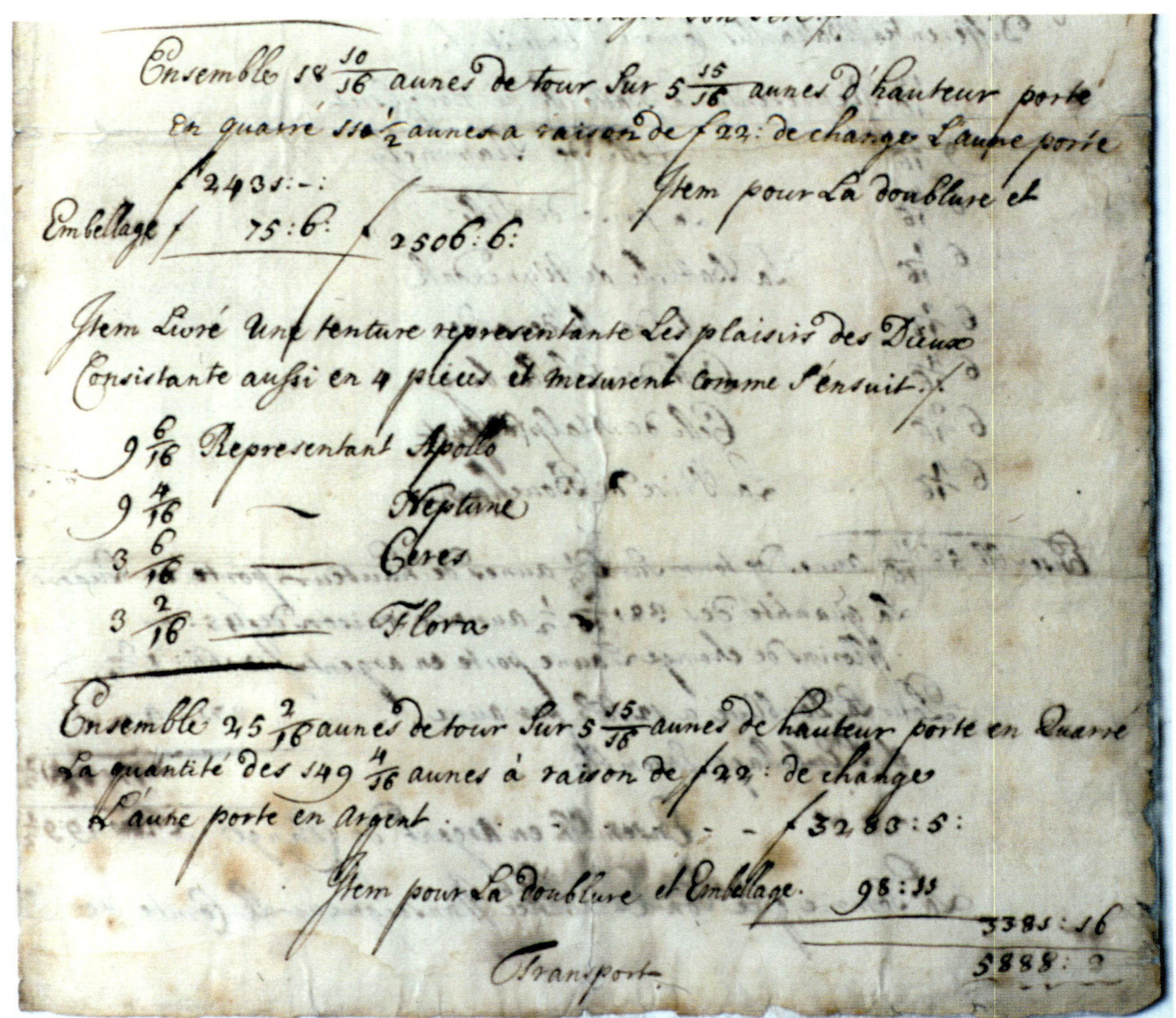

A portion of a document relating to the *Pleasures of the Gods* set of tapestries commissioned by Marlborough.

per ell, being made to designs or cartoons already in existence.

The *Virtues* tapestries were made in 1710-11, each panel with the Duke's coat of arms beautifully rendered figuring prominently within the design, along with complex symbolic and allegorical components around it. Although virtually similar in size to the *Pleasures of the Gods*, the *Virtues* cost more than double the amount paid for the *Pleasures* set because they were a special one-off commission and no other set like it is known to exist.

The delivery of the various sets was not as straightforward as it might seem. Since the Duke was involved in military engagements in various places at different times, delivery of the completed work was more often than not organised through friends or officials based in Flanders. On the 21st of November 1711, Adam Cardonnel wrote to Henry Watkins, the deputy judge advocate of the British forces based at the Hague "*... my Lord Duke desires the three pieces with the arms may be sent immediately to Mrs. Cadogan at the Hague*".[108] Mrs. Cadogan, the wife of Marlborough's trusted Chief of Staff and Quartermaster General William Cadogan, was Margaretta Munter, the daughter of a court councillor at the Hague. Her home was Raaphorst Castle, set in over 500 acres of parkland about ten miles from the Hague, which was often used as a depository for the numerous and various works of art Marlborough collected while on campaign.

Additional details on the transportation of the tapestries and the manner by which they left the weaver's workshop are summarised in a statement of account prepared by John Henley, one of the Duke's footmen who accompanied his master abroad on almost every campaign.[109] Both he and George Collins, the Duke's private messenger, were often asked to render special additional services in the transportation of his personal property. Henley's account runs through the journey he made with the *Pleasures of the Gods* tapestries from Brussels via Antwerp and Rotterdam to the Hague.

Nov. 1710		*florins-styvers*
20th	*Paid for a waggon to carry the baggage to Genll Cadogans*	*5-05*
24th	*Portridge [porterage] at Brussels*	*1-10*
	Carrying the Tapestry to Mr. Cadogan's	*1-08*
	Paid for rope to ty the tapestry	*1-01*
25th	*Portridge at Antwerp*	*1-01*
	Given to the Waggonner that brought the tapestry	*2-16*
27th	*Waggons at Rotterdam*	*3-12*
	A boat to the Hague	*12-12*

Presumably from the Hague the hangings were eventually sent on to England by packet boat across the Channel.

It has already been mentioned that the *Pleasures of the Gods* were made for the Duchess's bedchamber at Blenheim Palace. The height of these tapestries was identical to the four additional *Alexander* tapestries which we know were also made by de Vos.[110] The Duchess and the architect Vanbrugh had had several discussions regarding the design of the cornicing on the ceiling of her bedchamber[111] and there is little doubt that these panels hung in that room, along with a portrait of the Duke by Kneller over the marble fireplace, the design of which lent itself to the display of 13 pieces of Chinese porcelain. Two paintings of '*Madonnas*', one by Rubens and the other by Van Dyke, were hung over the doors.[112]

The *Teniers* set made earlier, also for the Duchess's apartments, was either hung in the Long Closet at Blenheim or else removed to her apartments in one of her numerous other homes – Marlborough House in London, Holywell House in St. Alban's or the Keeper's Lodge in Windsor Great Park. It seems from an inventory of goods made in 1740 that this set was not at Blenheim then.[113]

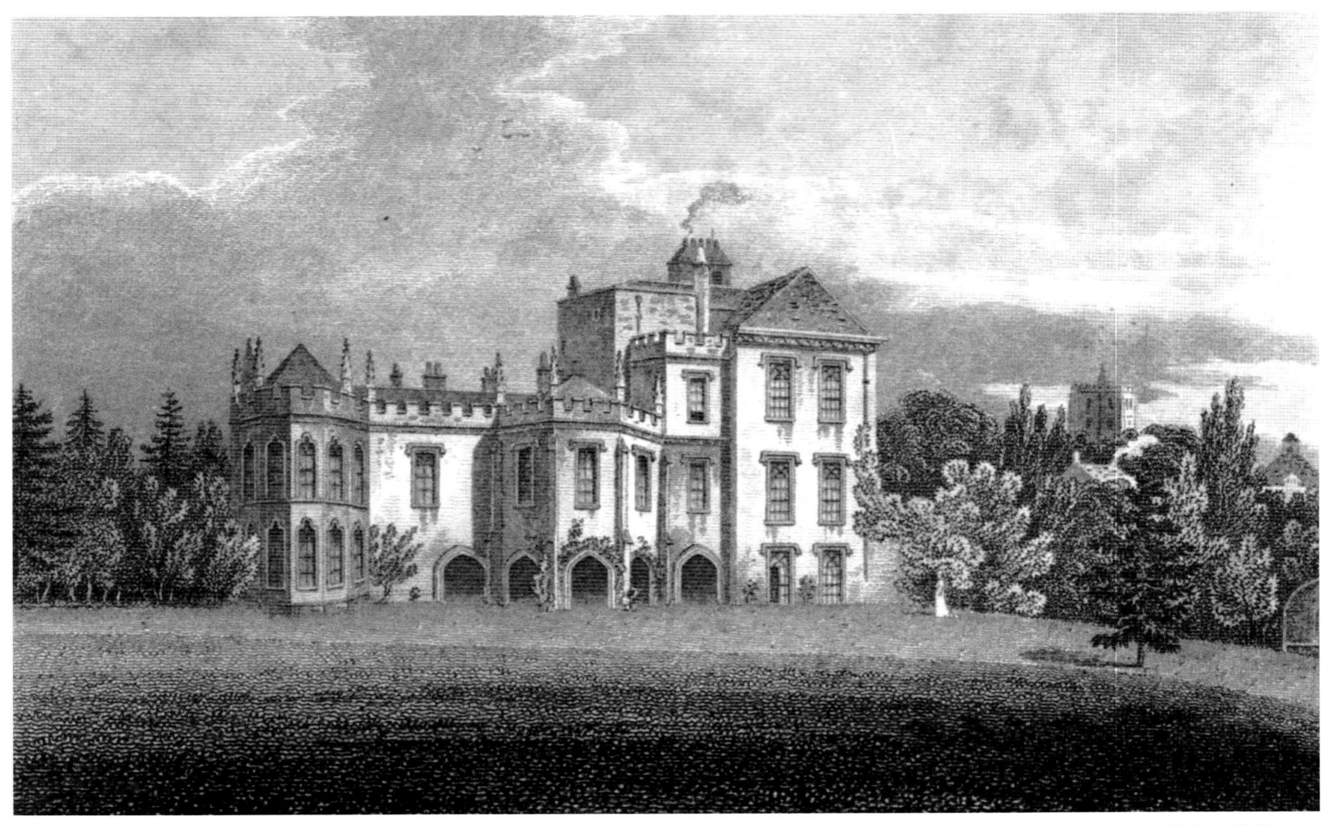

Holywell House.

As for the *Virtues*, it is uncertain exactly where these tapestries were eventually hung although it is possible that they may indeed have either decorated the State Room east of the Saloon or the East State Bedchamber. However, given that their overall dimensions were so similar to the panels of the *Victories* series, and since both these sets were special commissions comprising singular works of very high quality, along with their iconographic importance vis-à-vis the Duke's international reputation, it is unlikely that they were originally intended for any other house but Blenheim Palace.

Tapestries would have been found in all the principal rooms of most important houses. The domestic part of the house, which was normally lived in by the family, was separated from the ceremonial State Apartments.

The latter were decorated as sumptuously and impressively as possible and the finest hangings were always reserved for the most significant rooms there. So, it is more than likely that the *Virtues* tapestries were hung in one of the state rooms at Blenheim. However, we already know that for a family as important, status conscious and wealthy as the Churchills, even their private apartments were furnished with many expensive, inspiring and significant works of art.

Weaving was well under way by November 1711 on the *Blenheim, Ramillies, Schellenburg, Lille, Oudenarde* and *Wynendael* panels of the *Victories* set, (according to a letter written by de Vos to the Duke) and the master weaver had just begun work on the small *Bouchain* panel.[114] In the same letter de Vos also reveals the difficulty he faces in finding maps and plans accurately depicting *"the lines near Louvain [the Lines of Brabant]"* as well as plans for *Malplaquet* and he requests the Duke to send these to him. This is an important document for it enables us to draw several conclusions in connection with the ordering and progression of the design and manufacture of the *Victories* set.

First, it further supports the hypothesis that the contract was initiated in the winter of 1708-1709, since the events at Blenheim, Ramillies, Schellenberg, Lille, Oudenarde and Wynendael had all occurred by the end of 1708, and that these were the first batch of six tapestries, comprising half the proposed commission, being worked on together.

Next, it tells us that not all the designs were prepared in advance before the weaving was undertaken but that both the designing and the weaving

Below : The *Schellenberg* tapestry.
Below right : The *Oudenarde* tapestry.

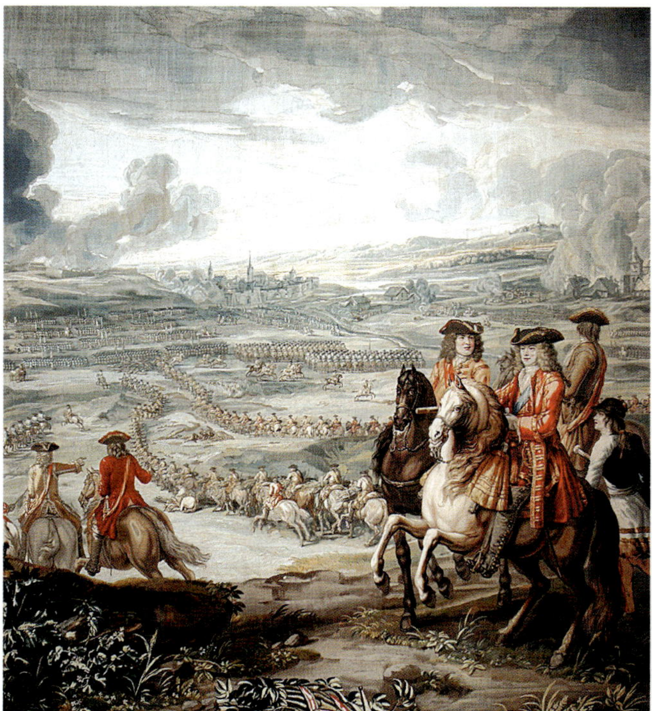

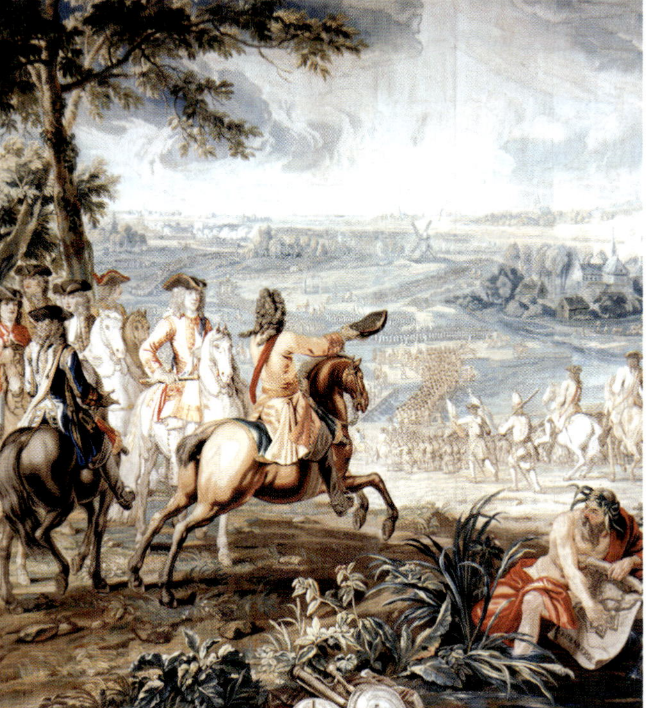

process for the remainder of the *Victories* set was done as a rolling commission, with no specific chronological order, over a period of time. The engagement at Bouchain took place in August-September 1711. This means that the design was certainly produced within a couple of months after the military engagement since de Vos's letter is dated 31st October 1711. However, the design for the Battle of Malplaquet, which was fought on 11th September 1709, was still incomplete two years on. It may have been possible that the *Malplaquet* panel was not ordered immediately after the battle, since it had been Marlborough's most controversial and bloody victory, with the loss of almost 24,000 allied lives and one that resulted in much criticism and reproach in England. Count Sinzendorf had nonetheless suggested to the Duke in a congratulatory letter written two days after the battle, "*Voila une bonne adjonction pour la tapisserie*".[115]

It also indicates that Lambert de Hondt could not have been the artist responsible for the tapestries entitled *Malplaquet*, the *Lines of Brabant* and all of the three *Bouchain* panels. The plans that de Vos required from the Duke were for the use of both the designer of the panel and the cartoon painter, to ensure the accuracy of the topographic details on the tapestries

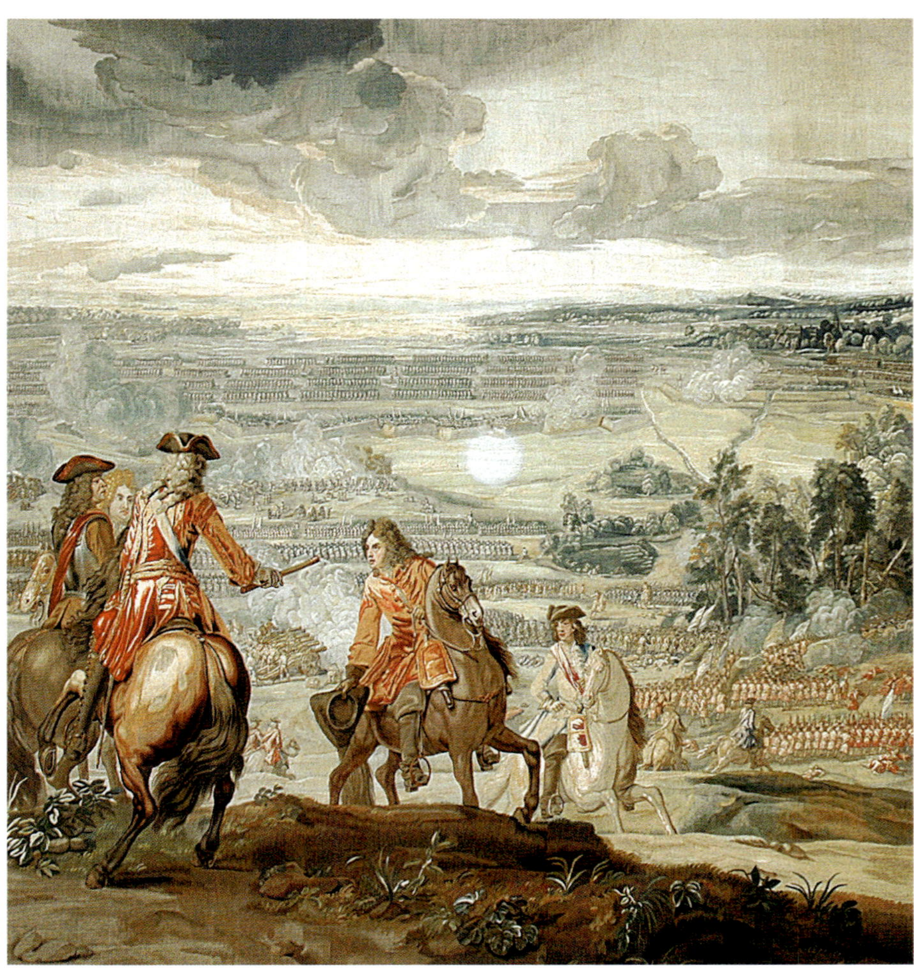

The *Malplaquet* tapestry.

A document relating to the delivery of the first eight tapestries of the *Victories* set and the four *Virtues* panels.

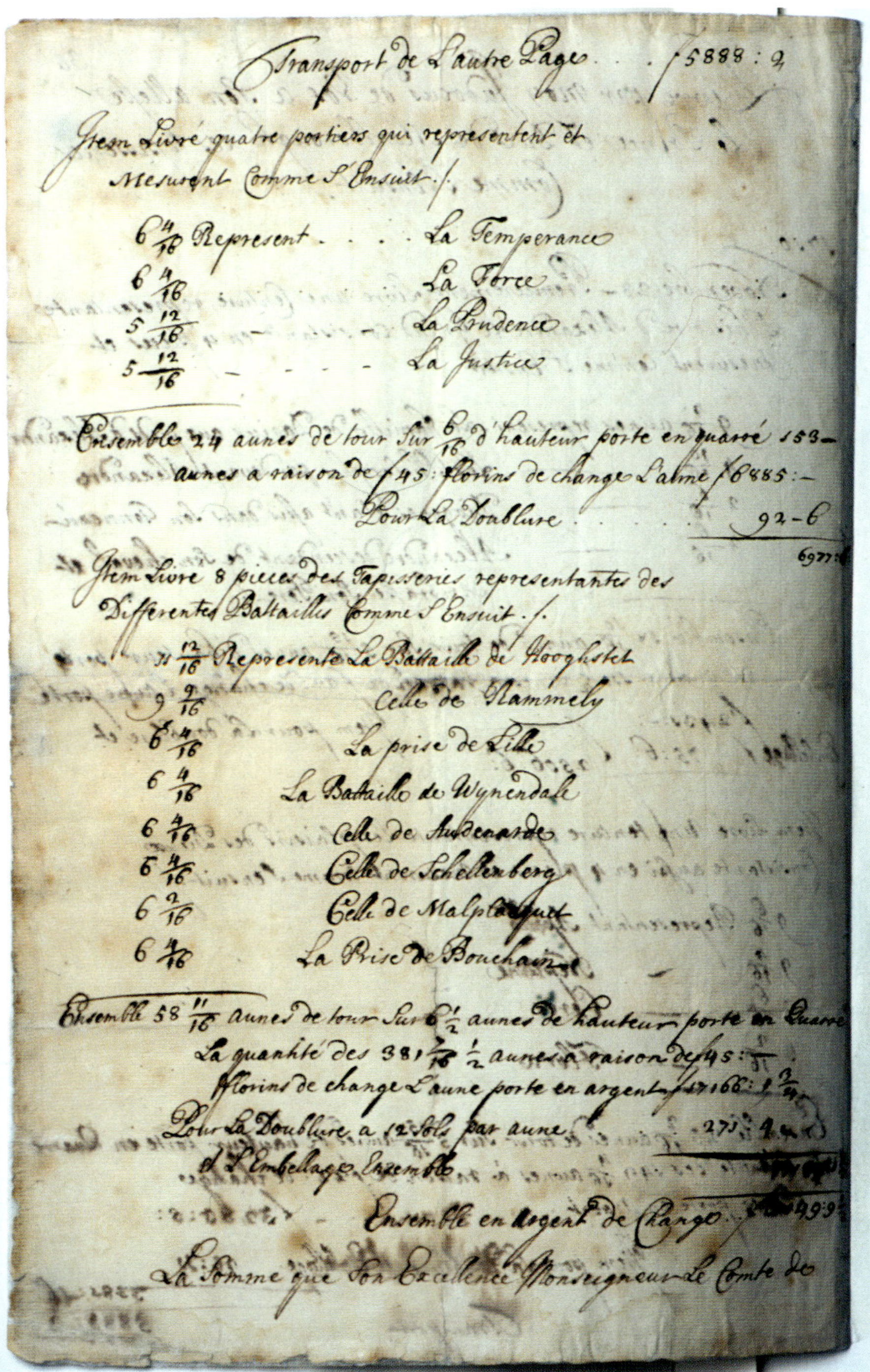

Transport de l'autre Page . . . . 5888 : 9

Item Livré quatre portiers qui representent et
Mesurent Comme S'Ensuit :/.

$6\frac{4}{16}$ Represent . . . . La Temperance
$6\frac{4}{16}$ . . . . La Force
$5\frac{12}{16}$ . . . . La Prudence
$5\frac{12}{16}$ . . . . La Justice

Ensemble 24 aunes de tour Sur $6\frac{6}{16}$ d'hauteur porte en quarré 153
aunes a raison de f45: florins de change L'aune f 6885 :—
Pour La Doublure . . . . 92 - 6

6977 :

Item Livré 8 pieces des Tapisseries representantes des
Differentes Battailles Comme S'Ensuit :/.

$11\frac{12}{16}$ Represente La Bataille de Hooghstet
$9\frac{9}{16}$ Celle de Rammeley
$6\frac{4}{16}$ La prise de Lille
$6\frac{4}{16}$ La Bataille de Wynendale
$6\frac{4}{16}$ Celle de Audenaarde
$6\frac{4}{16}$ Celle de Schellenberg
$6\frac{9}{16}$ Celle de Malplaquet
$6\frac{4}{16}$ La Prise de Bouchain

Ensemble 58 $\frac{11}{16}$ aunes de tour Sur $6\frac{1}{2}$ aunes de hauteur porte en Quarré
La quantité des 381 $\frac{1}{2}$ aunes a raison de f45:—
florins de change L'aune porte en argent f 17166 : 1
Pour La Doublure a 12 Sols par aune . . . 275 : 4
et L'Embellage Ensemble

Ensemble en argent de change . . . .

La Somme que Son Excellence Monseigneur Le Comte de

in question. Therefore, we may presume that Philippe de Hondt was responsible at least for the design of these five panels, if not as well for some of the others in the series, in view of the general stylistic similarity between all the tapestries.

And finally, this letter also indicates that Judocus de Vos oversaw, coordinated and financed the entire production process.

The documentary information on the *Victories* set identifies beyond doubt all the tapestries ordered: eight panels (*Blenheim, Ramillies, Schellenburg, Lille, Oudenarde, Wynendael,* the small *Bouchain* and *Malplaquet)* were delivered to the Duke in 1713,[116] roughly four years after the commission was conceived (presuming that this was done in 1709). Bearing in mind the length of time taken for the process of designing each panel and preparing the corresponding cartoon, this was entirely feasible as Judocus de Vos had a thriving business with 12 looms and up to 35 weavers, so several weavers would have been able to work on different panels at the same time. We also know from a statement of account that de Vos was allowed to extend the *Blenheim* and the *Ramillies* tapestry panels to 11¾ ells (25ft 3in. / 770cms) and to 9½ ells (20ft 4in. / 620cms) respectively. (The *Ramillies* panel is the only one in the *Victories* set which no longer exists at Blenheim Palace. Its fate is unknown). This set was charged at 45 florins per ell, suggesting not only high quality weaving but also specially commissioned artwork, although no mention is made of what portion of this was paid to the artists.

A special commission was the most uncommon method of purchasing tapestries and certainly also the most expensive. On the basis that de Vos

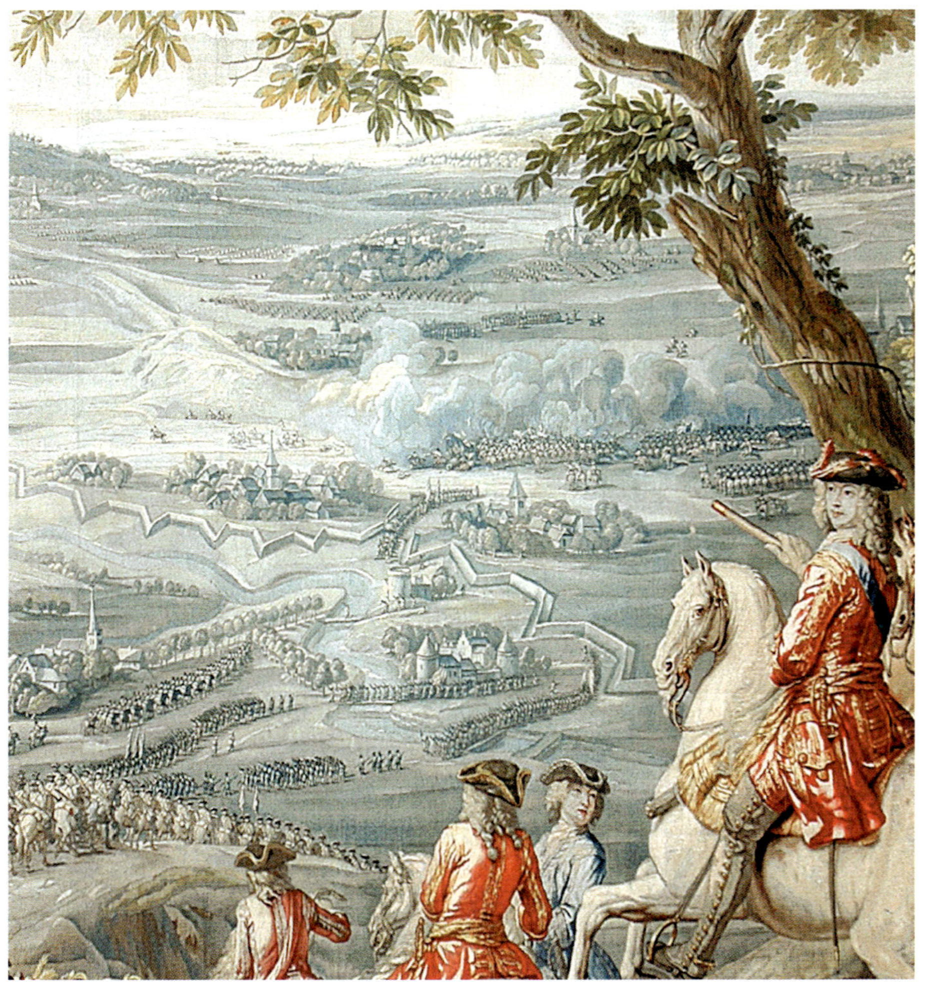

The *Lines of Brabant* tapestry.

charged 22 florins per ell for the weaving of other panels that he supplied to the Duke from cartoons already in existence, it seems that the additional cost of 23 florins per ell would have depended on several factors in the commissioning of new work. These would necessarily include the payments made to the artists for the design and the cartoon (thought to have been roughly 10 florins per square ell in the early 1700s);[117] the size of the tapestries and consequently of the cartoons, as well as supplementary cartoons if any had to be made of portraits, coats of arms and of borders; the speed of weaving dependent on the level of complexity of the design and the density of the weave, the additional daily wages for the different types of skilled weavers depending on how many faces, hands and bodies were to be included in each panel; the cost of stocking raw materials like silks and wools and dyestuffs, as well as the proportion of silk in each panel and the quality of wool used overall and last but not least, the substantial capital outlay required to finance the project up front, perhaps including a calculation of the loss of interest depending on roughly how many years it would take to recoup the money.

The last of the small panels to be woven as part of the *Victories* commission was the tapestry known today as *The Lines of Brabant* and referred to in the documentation as "*the lines near Louvain*". This tapestry was ordered along with the *Malplaquet* panel but it seems that for some reason there was an extraordinary delay in the weaver being sent the plans for the military action which he had requested from the Duke three years earlier, on 31st October 1711.[118]

The delay may also have been caused by the need for a suitable coat of arms to be found for representation in the centre of the top border. This had been a decorative and revealing feature of the entire *Victories* set, as each panel was distinguished by the location of the action being included in a centrally placed medallion at the top of the tapestry. The *Lines of Brabant* panel, which illustrated Marlborough's bold and imaginative attack at three different places along the enemy's highly proclaimed fortified lines, had no single specific location to which a coat of arms could be attributed. A decision must finally have been made to incorporate the ducal coat of arms instead which makes it the only panel in the series with this marked difference.

The time required to complete the weaving of this tapestry is explained by Judocus de Vos: "*On my arrival home I did not fail to look into when Your Highness will have the two tapestries, that is to say one of the large ones and the one representing the crossing of the lines above Louvain. This will take another five months. And for the last of the large ones eight [months]*".[119]

The two large tapestries he refers to are a pair of large *Bouchain* panels, the last two hangings ordered as part of the *Victories* set. A statement describes these panels as being made "*according to the Duke's design*" and they are also referred to in an undated order signed by William Cadogan as "*two more tapestries representing the action of the campaign of 1711, these pieces will be 24 ells in length*[120] *and of the same fine quality of those others which cost 45 florins per ell and the said de Vos will receive the same price for them*".[121] The first panel is described in the statement of accounts as representing "*the taking of the lines above Bouchain*" and cost 4,168 florins and 3 stivers, while the second

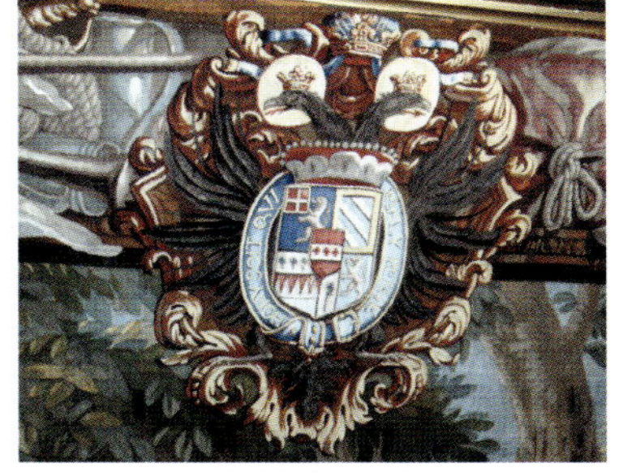

The ducal coat of arms as represented in the top border of the *Lines of Brabant* tapestry.

one, representing "*the figurative map of all the towns around Bouchain*" was just slightly larger and cost 4,200 florins and 6 stivers.

This may also explain why there are three panels for *Bouchain*, Marlborough's last campaign. At the contract date, twelve panels were commissioned totalling 472 square ells, eleven for unspecified battles plus one hanging representing peace. When the first eight were completed,[122] and bearing in mind the adjustments which were made in the course of production in 1710 to the eventual sizes of the *Blenheim* and *Ramillies* panels, which, based on the cartoons supplied to the weavers, ended up being larger in size than was originally provided for, these eight panels together measured

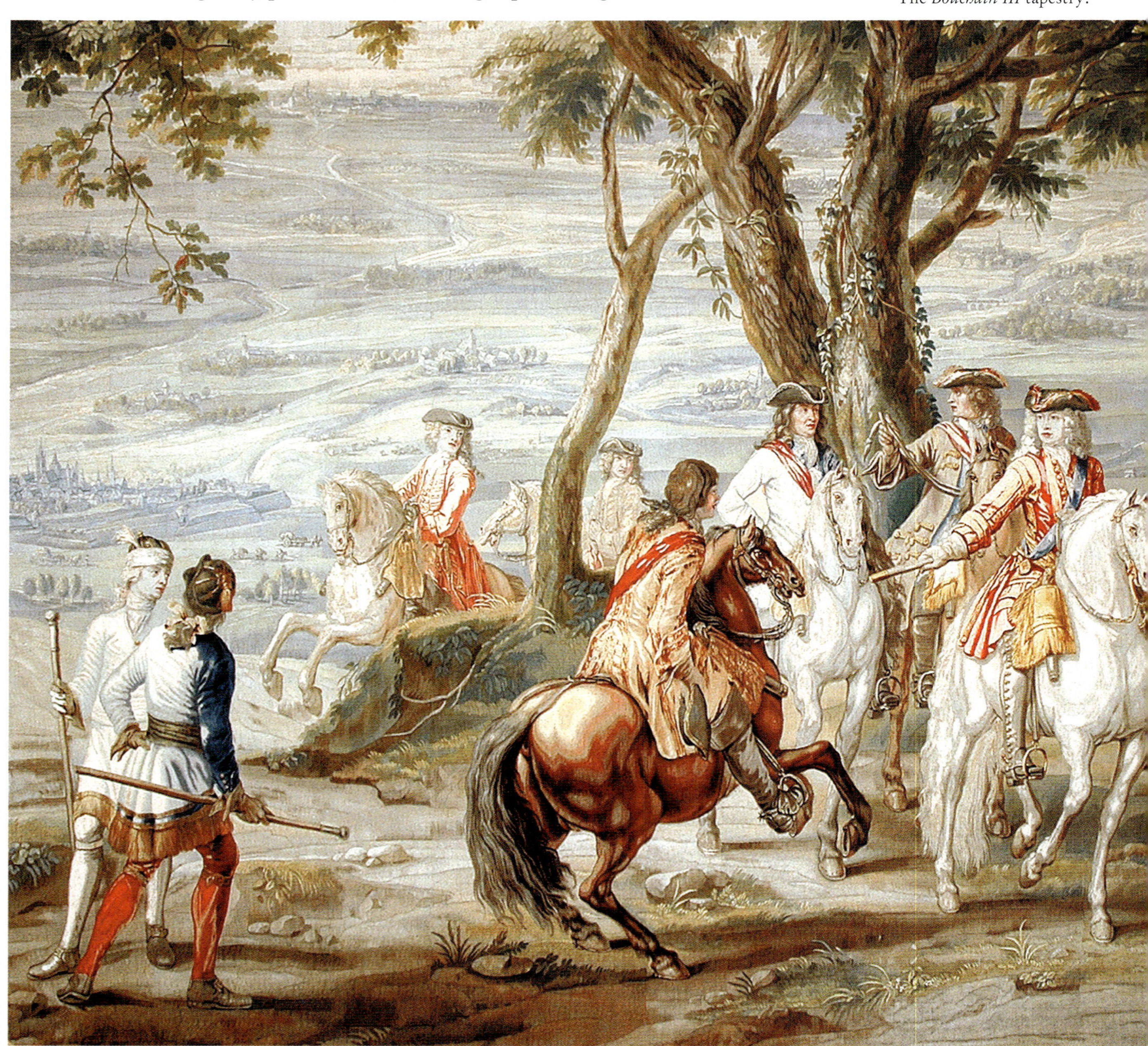

The *Bouchain III* tapestry.

roughly 381 square ells. It is therefore clear that only two further small panels could be made within the contract rather than four. The *Lines above Louvain* had already been ordered measuring around 45 square ells and a further order was necessary to make up the contractual difference to the weaver – 472 square ells having been ordered and only 426 (381 + 45) square ells having been concluded. This should have resulted in one last panel representing peace being ordered as had originally been intended.

However, the war had ended with a negotiated settlement expediently arranged by Marlborough's political enemies in England, under terms he found objectionable.[123] His dismissal from his posts at the age of 61, after ten long

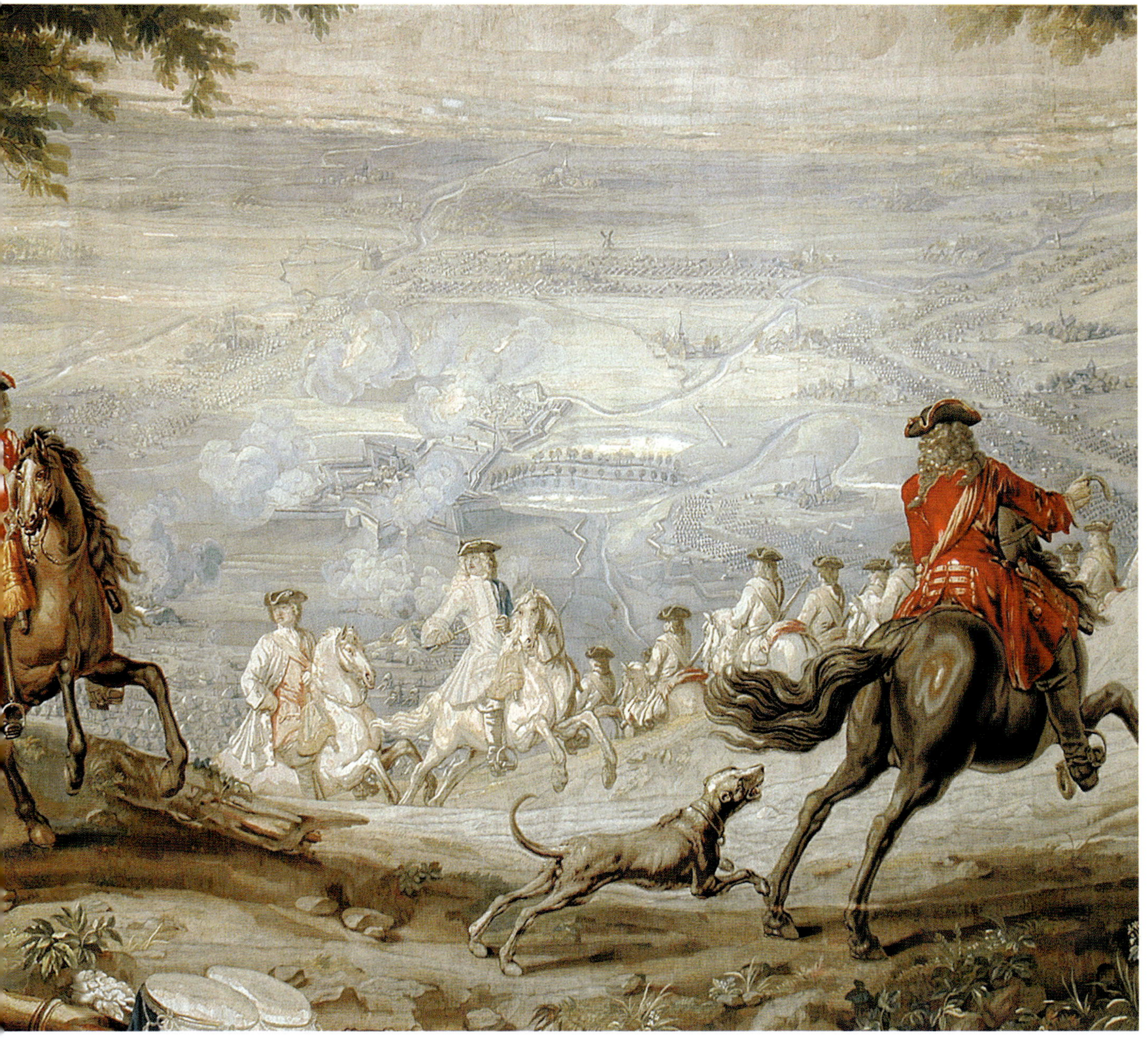

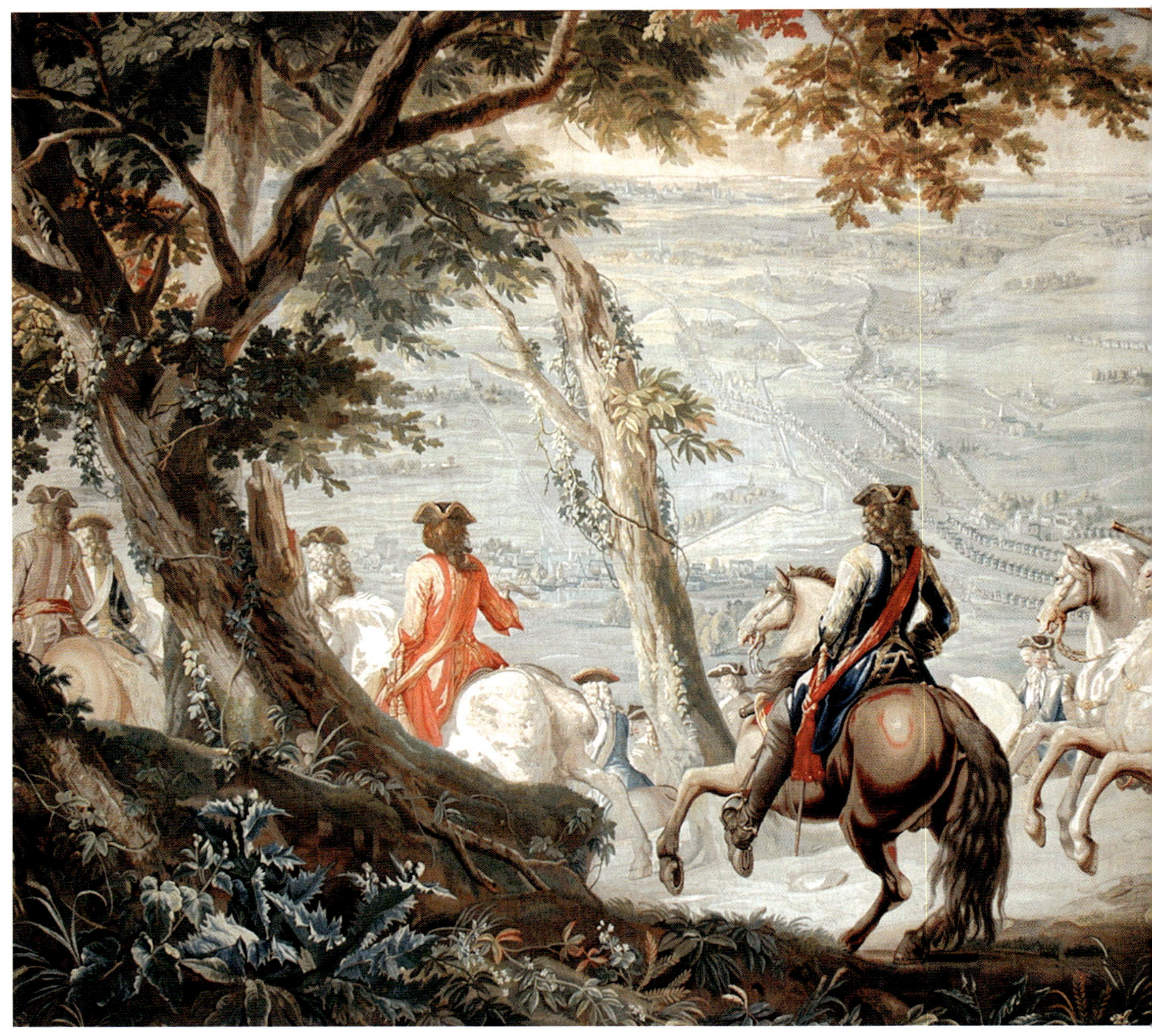

The *Bouchain I* tapestry.

years of waging war and loyally safeguarding British interests abroad, as well as his entire family's removal from Queen Anne's service, might therefore have led John Churchill to abandon his original plan of commissioning a tapestry representing peace. While he stalled the delivery on the "*Lines of Louvain*" panel, he ordered separately, through William Cadogan, two further *Bouchain* tapestries measuring roughly 92 square ells each. This, perhaps, was also to be his emphatic answer to the malice of his enemies at home and his critics' accusations with regard to his conduct in the war. Bouchain was a prized fortress which was taken from the French after cunning tactical manoeuvring as well as a formidable march under cover of darkness had enabled Marlborough's army once again to

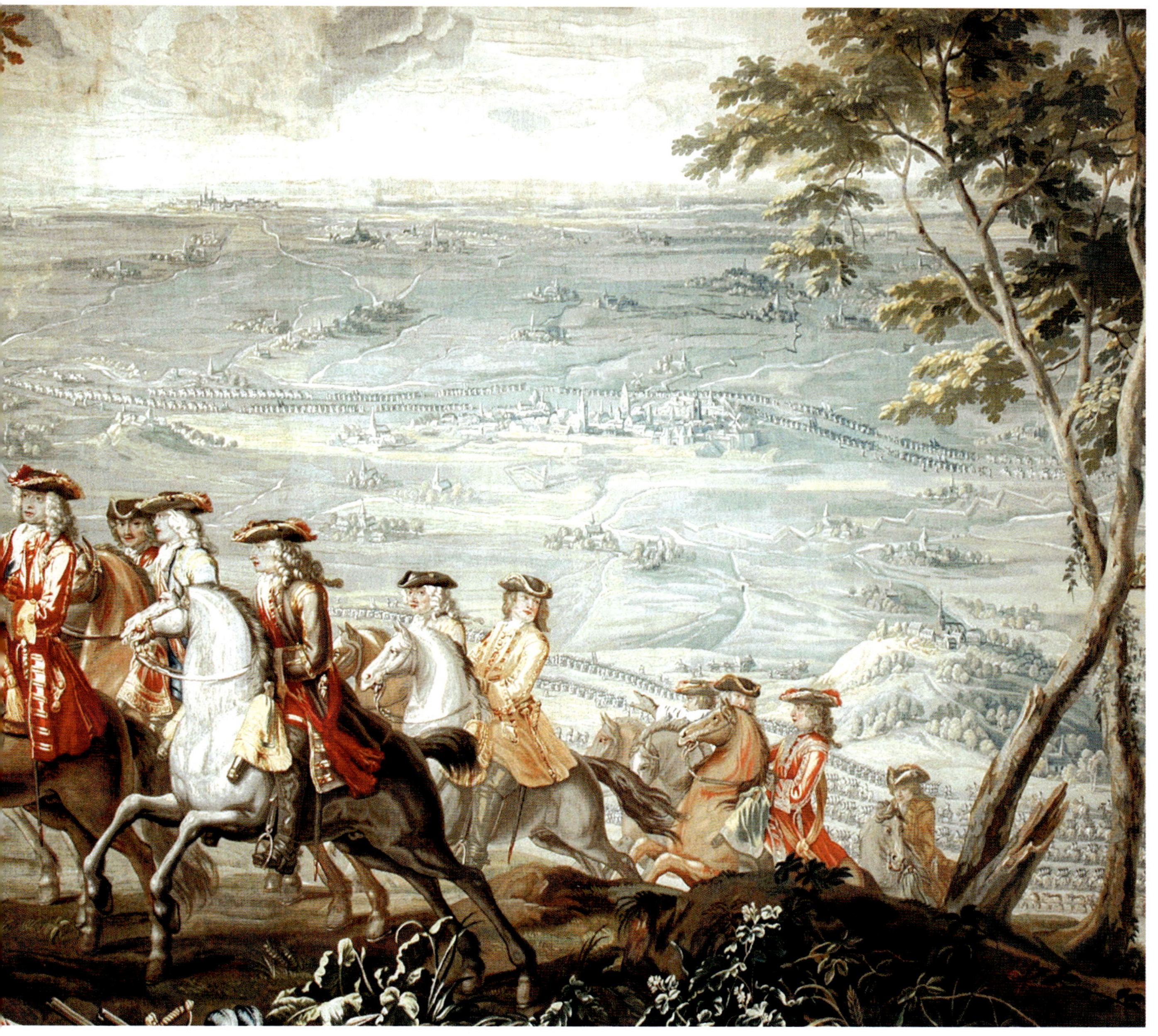

cross the enemy's lines. Furthermore, it was a victory gained with virtually no allied casualties to speak of. It was in fact, John Churchill's final great military triumph.

The last of the *Bouchain* panels was completed by December 1715 and on the 4th of that month the tapestry weaver sent word from Brussels, "*My Lord, I am honoured to report to Your Highness that your tapestries have all been perfectly completed to the great astonishment and satisfaction of all those in the profession who have seen them. [It] is a figurative map from where the landscape and the towns can be viewed from all sides. As these are much more beautiful than those tapestries which I have had the Honour to deliver to Your*

Highness before, I am convinced that you will be very pleased with them. I have also enclosed my account and hope that your Grace will be good enough to pay me the balance".[124]

Letter from Judocus de Vos to the Duke of Marlborough regarding the completion of the pair of large *Bouchain* tapestries.

This last pair of large tapestries was delivered to Mr. Leathes, the British Resident at Brussels, just over a year later, in mid January 1717 and the account was also settled through him. The ten panels had cost the Duke 25,797 florins.[125]

The tapestry representing "*the taking of the lines above Louvain*" though also finished and costing just over 1,828 florins, had not yet been paid for or delivered at this time.[126] It is unclear why this tapestry seemed to be surplus to requirements. Perhaps, because with it, the set would comprise an uneven number of eleven panels. Whatever the reason, it was eventually delivered and would be the final tapestry the Duke received from de Vos's workshop.

Despite the vast sums of money he had already spent on commissioning tapestries, Marlborough actually considered placing further orders with Judocus de Vos. This was probably because building work at Woodstock had resumed in 1716 at the family's own expense. In spite of his failing health, the Duke had hoped to see the project through, as above all, his one unfaltering desire had always been to live at Blenheim in retirement. Severely incapacitated by a stroke after the death of his daughter Anne, John Churchill was effectively removed from any political or other official sphere. He now conducted his personal

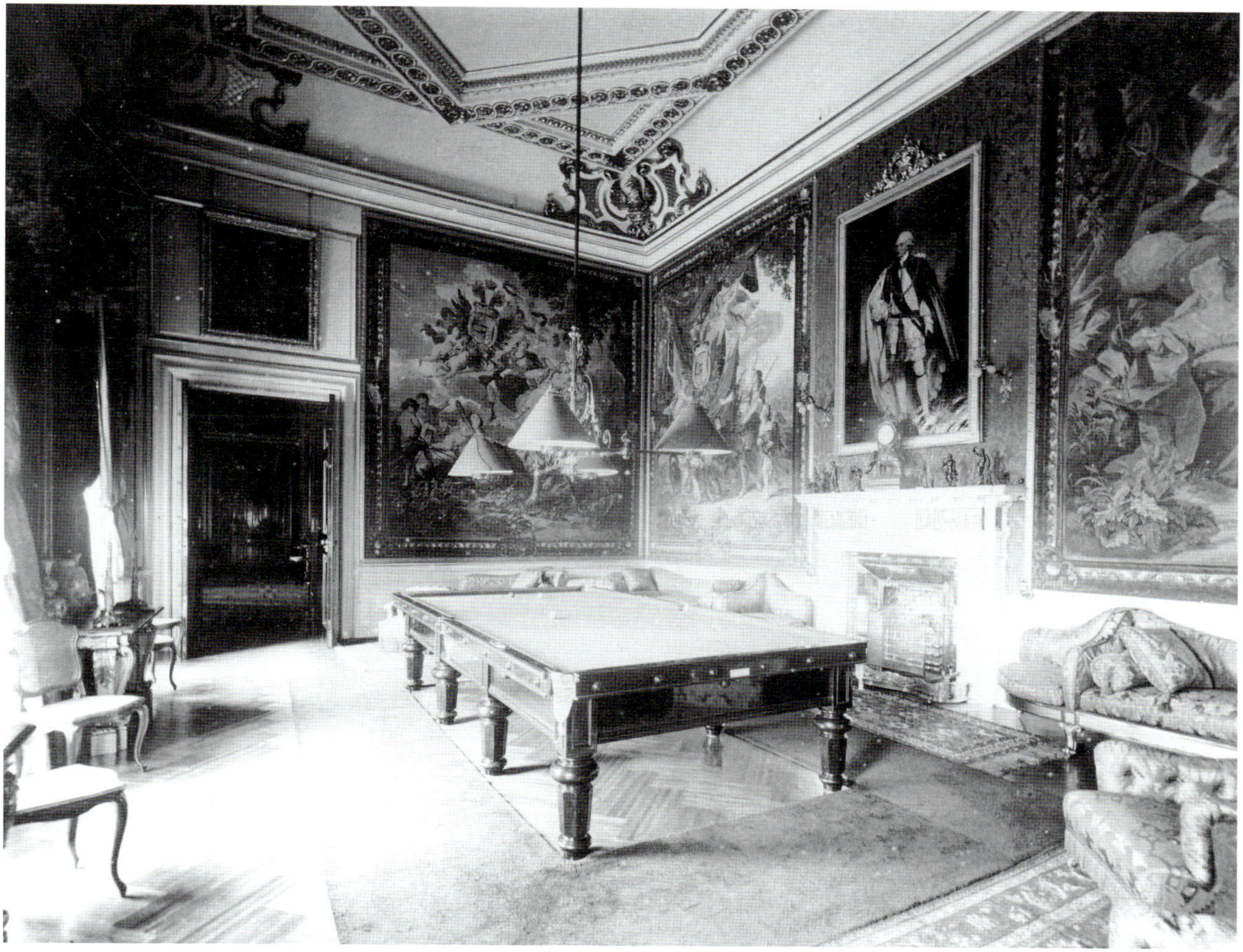

Photograph c. 1890 showing the *Virtues* tapestries hung in the present Red Drawing Room.

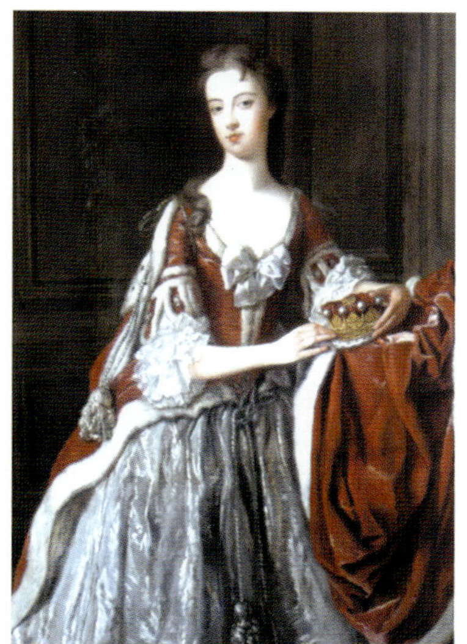

Lady Anne Churchill (the Marlborough's second daughter) by Kneller.

business relying heavily on his wife Sarah's assistance. On 2nd November 1717, the Duchess wrote to de Vos, *"I am commanded by his grace the Duke of Marlborough to thank you for the care you took in doing his last two pieces of hangings, which for want of a good conveyence hee has but just received. Hee likes them so well that hee has a mind to put more in hand, but before hee gives particular derections hee desires to know if you will not take less than you had formerly, because hee is told that the expence of the designs being over, that you now do them cheaper and hee promises that you shall have ready mony for what hee agrees with you for, and without any deductions. His grace desires your answer to this by the first post, and that you will allso send him with it, your last account to him, because my Lord Cadogan left it in Holland coming away in a hurry"*.[127]

A month later, a successful conclusion was reached and the weaver agreed to reduce his rate by 2 florins per ell for any future work. However, there is no documentary or other evidence that any further commissions were made.

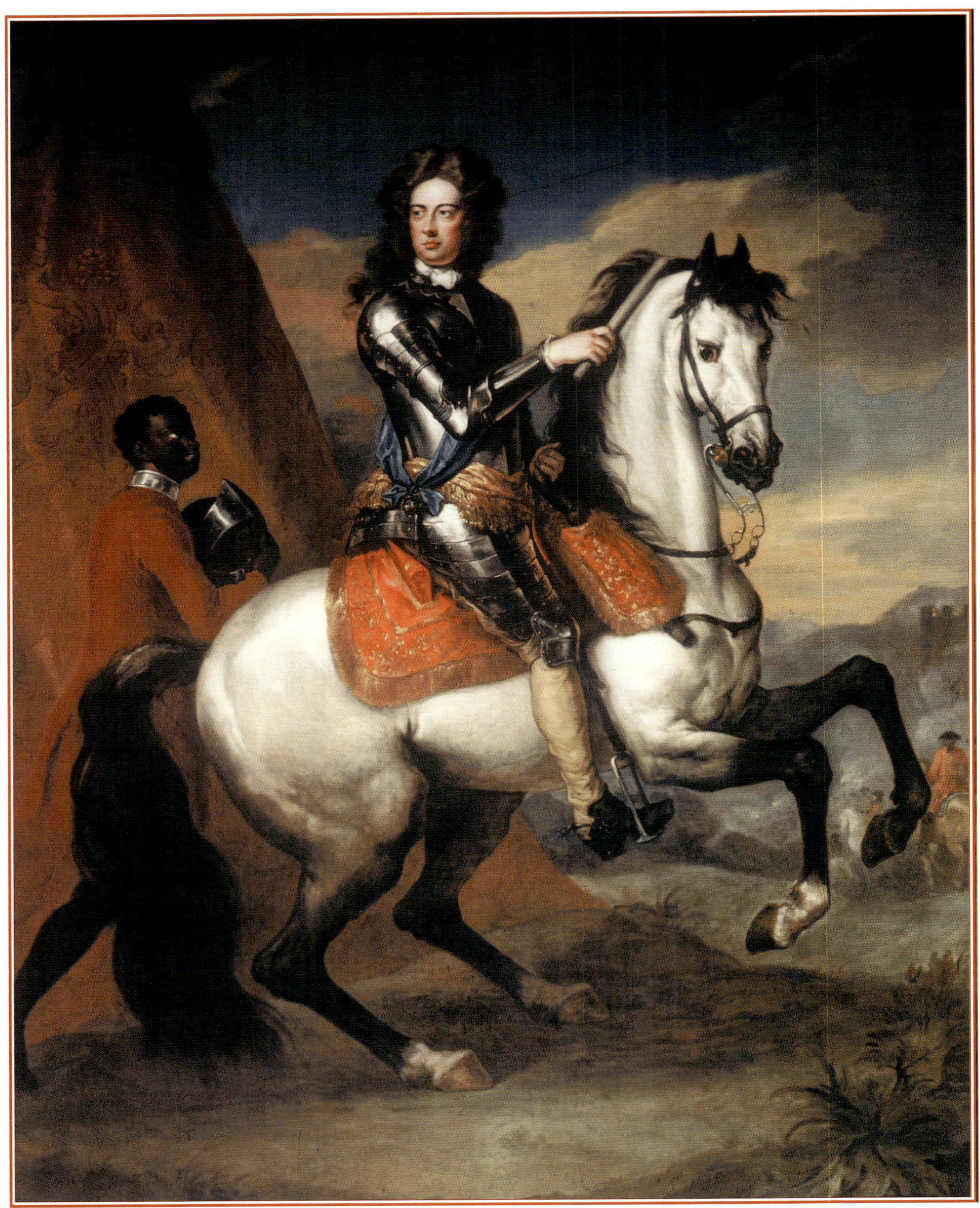

Chapter Six

IMAGERY AND THE PICTORIAL SPACE IN THE *VICTORIES* SET

CEREMONIAL battle portraits were often commissioned as the celebration of a commander's military triumphs. Generally speaking, there were two distinct styles of martial paintings. One, where the scene portrayed reduced the entire conflict into either a single event or a multiple narrative of events which had contributed to the commander's victory and epitomised his glorification, and the other where he was portrayed in full-length and usually on horseback, on rising ground overlooking a distant battle scene.

Officially appointed artists sometimes accompanied their patrons on the battlefield before producing drawings and paintings of their victories. In July 1690 at the Boyne, William III was accompanied by Dirck Maas (1656-1717), his official battle painter. Pieter Snayers (1592-c.1667) was the appointed artist to the Spanish Habsburgs in Flanders. His pupil Adam Frans van der Meulen (1632-1690) accompanied King Louis XIV in the Dutch Wars (1672-1678) as the *peintre des conquetes du Roi*.[128] However, these panoramic depictions paid greater attention to the imagery of the King rather than the battle scenes, once again placing emphasis on the true purpose of the work – the glorification of the commander.

Prince Eugene of Savoy, the distinguished Imperialist general who fought alongside the Duke of Marlborough at Blenheim, Oudenarde and Malplaquet, employed the artist Jan Van Hugtenburch (1647-1733) to depict his own military triumphs. When in 1725 Jean Dumont published a collection of engravings of paintings of Eugene's battles, Van Hugtenburch was described as *"an artist of Battles and of Tapestries"* and was reputed to have worked as a designer at the Gobelins under Le Brun and Van der Meulen in the late 1660s.[129] He is interestingly referred to again in 1763 by Horace Walpole: *"John Van Hugtenburch of Harlem, was employed by Prince Eugene to paint his battles and had a share in the designs for the triumphal tapestry at Blenheim"*.[130]

It is unclear what role Van Hugtenburch played in collaborating with the de Hondts in the design of the Duke's *Victories* but it is entirely possible that Prince Eugene's official artist was consulted in the artistic creation of an important new commission of tapestries in which his patron was also one of the principal protagonists.

What is certain however, is that the Duke did not employ an artist to accompany him on the battlefield. The designs for the *Victories* tapestries were prepared from contemporary accounts of the battles, and the topography was rendered either from local knowledge or from plans and maps made available of each required area.[131] As has already been mentioned, portraits of the principal characters depicted in some panels were provided by the Duke. Lambert and Philippe de Hondt, the designers of these

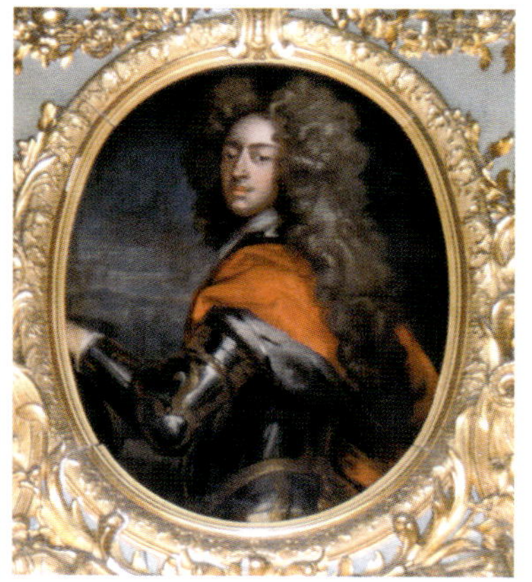

Prince Eugene of Savoy.

Facing page :
The Duke of Marlborough with his Black Page by Kneller.

tapestries, were merely visually confirming what was already known from other sources. The tapestries themselves were more a representation of the battles reflecting Marlborough's specific interests rather than the artist's personal conception of the subject matter.

In all but one of the *Victories* tapestries,[132] the Duke and his generals occupy a prominent position while the action of the military encounter is visible around them. The artist's pictorial strategy was to include precise topographical detail of distant landscapes which would have been recognisable and which were not entirely occluded by the individuals portrayed. However, the grouped figures have often been placed on imaginary hilly outcrops in the foreground from which the panoramic background is viewed, although in reality all of the action illustrated in the panels took place in virtually flat countryside. Trees generally frame the arrangement of figures on one side, adding depth to the spatial composition as the viewer's eye is drawn across to the more distant scene in the background. There is also the uniform use of a high viewpoint in all the panels, the horizon line being so high as to be a veritable bird's eye view.

All the panels have wide decorative borders filled with guns, quivers, saddles, trumpets, drums, trophies, plate, cannonballs, arms, armour and

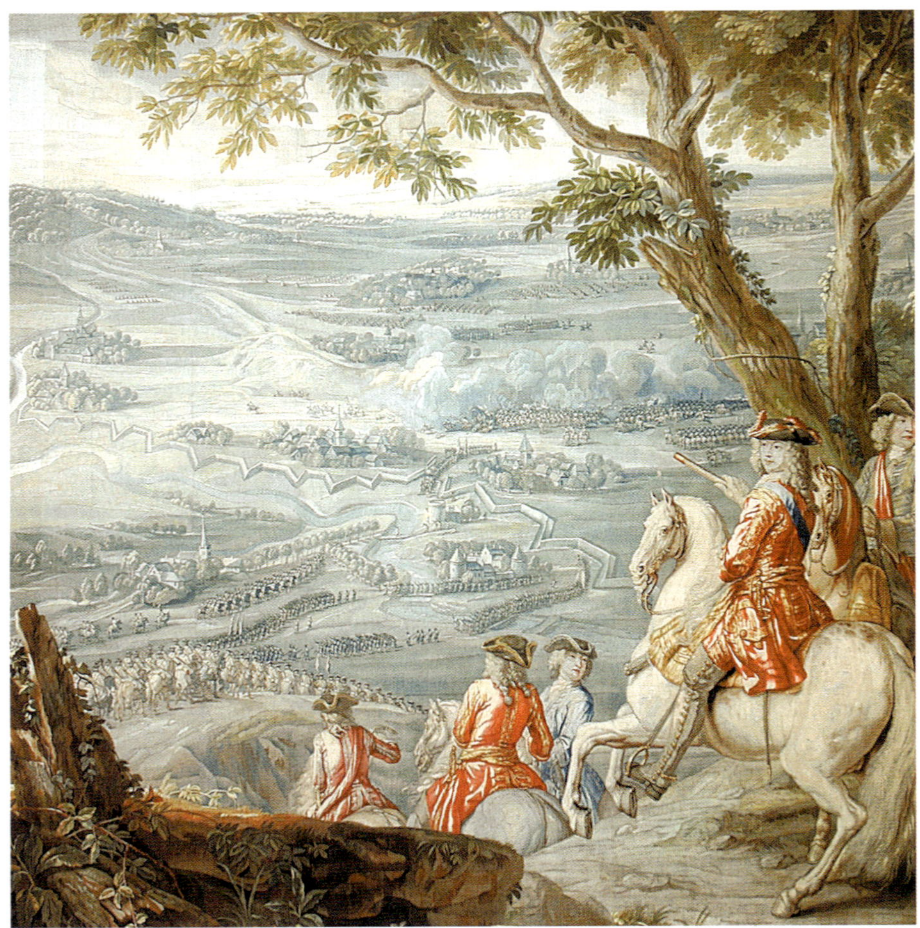

The *Lines of Brabant* tapestry which clearly illustrates every aspect of the artist's pictorial strategy.

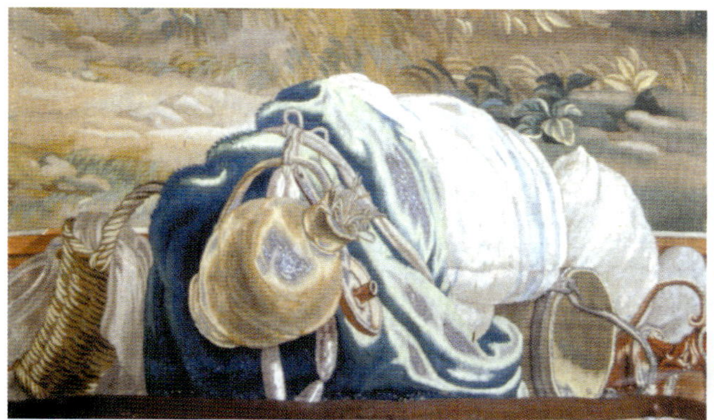
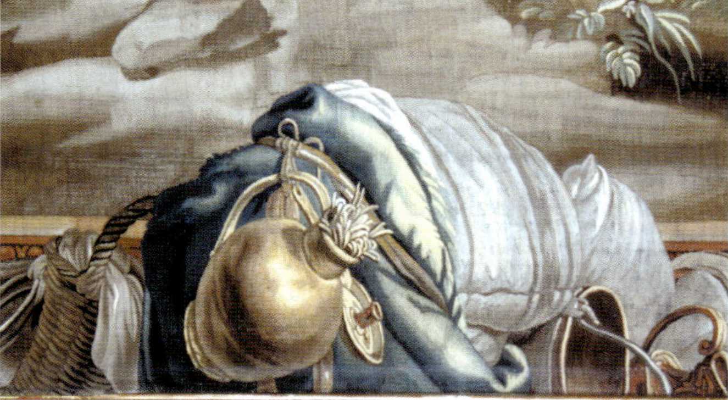

Above left : *Pillage* central border, designed by Van Orly.

Above right : *Bouchain II* central border, copied from Van Orly's design.

other usual impedimenta of battle. The lower borders spill into the central space, a familiar feature of baroque art. Some of the central lower border details are directly taken and duplicated from Van Orly's designs made for the Duke's *Art of War* set.

The idea of setting four round medallions in the corners of the border of each tapestry was perhaps inspired by the model of a series of tapestries called *the Elements*, which had been designed for Louis XIV by Charles Le Brun. In this series, the medallions represented the King's chosen attributes: Piety, Magnanimity, Righteousness and Valour.[133] The Duke of Marlborough chose to depict the four virtues of Fortitude, Prudence, Temperance and Justice in the corner medallions of his tapestries, with the exception of the *Blenheim* panel where they are replaced by a series of coats of arms of captured towns.

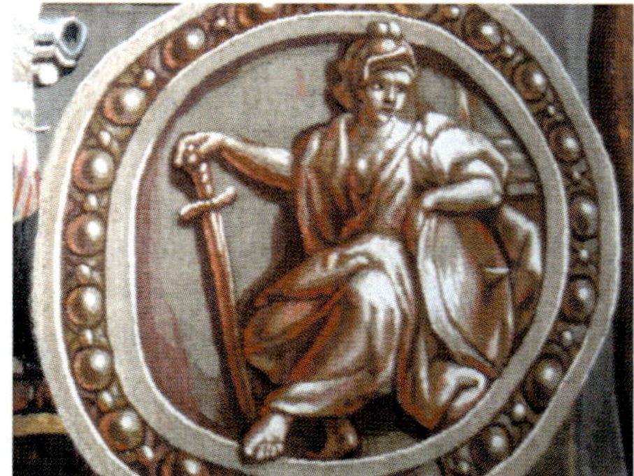

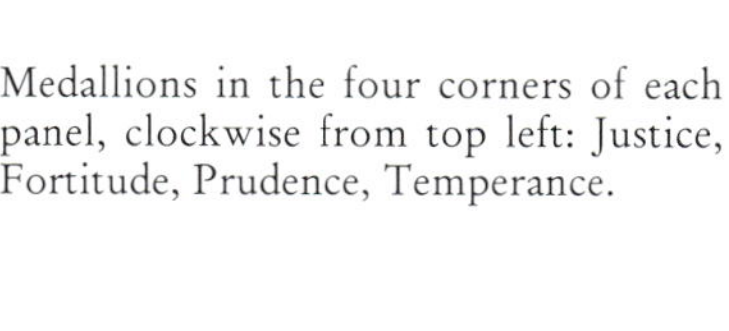

Medallions in the four corners of each panel, clockwise from top left: Justice, Fortitude, Prudence, Temperance.

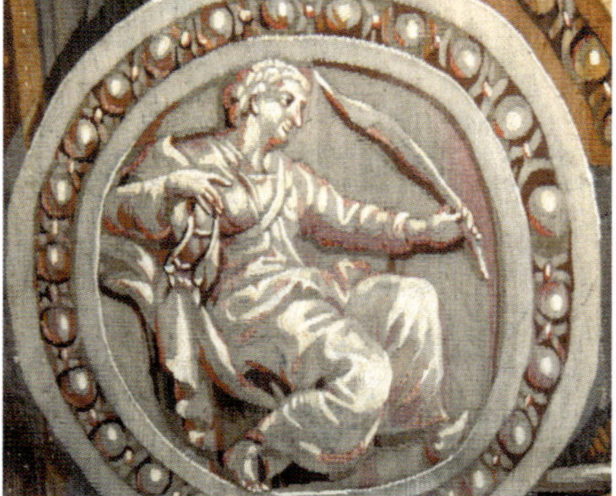
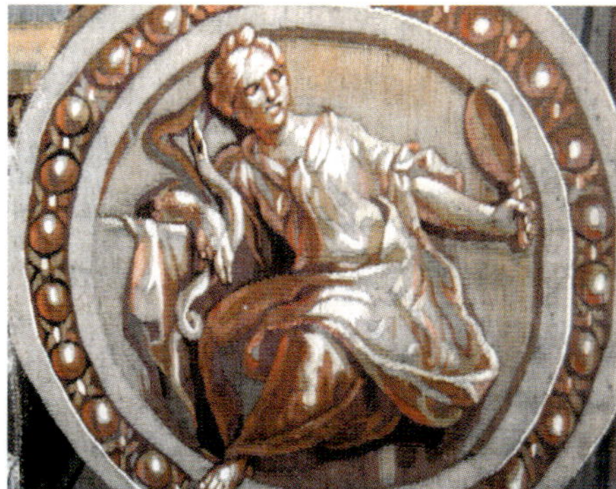

In the centre of the side borders on each tapestry (again with the exception of *Blenheim*), are featured, this time in oval medallions, two images from ancient mythology. These include the Greek winged horse Pegasus on the left hand side and Jupiter's thunderbolt on the right. In Greek legend, Pegasus served Zeus, the supreme God, fetching for him both thunder and lightning. Zeus was the Greek forebear of the Roman God Jupiter. The Romans worshiped Jupiter not only as the supreme God but also as the special protector of the state, his temple was the primary sanctuary in Rome and the hub of political life. Jupiter's attribute was the thunderbolt. So for the original viewers of these tapestries, as for us today, the allegorical elements contained within the borders convey their own iconographic story, associating Marlborough with the power and glory of these classical deities.

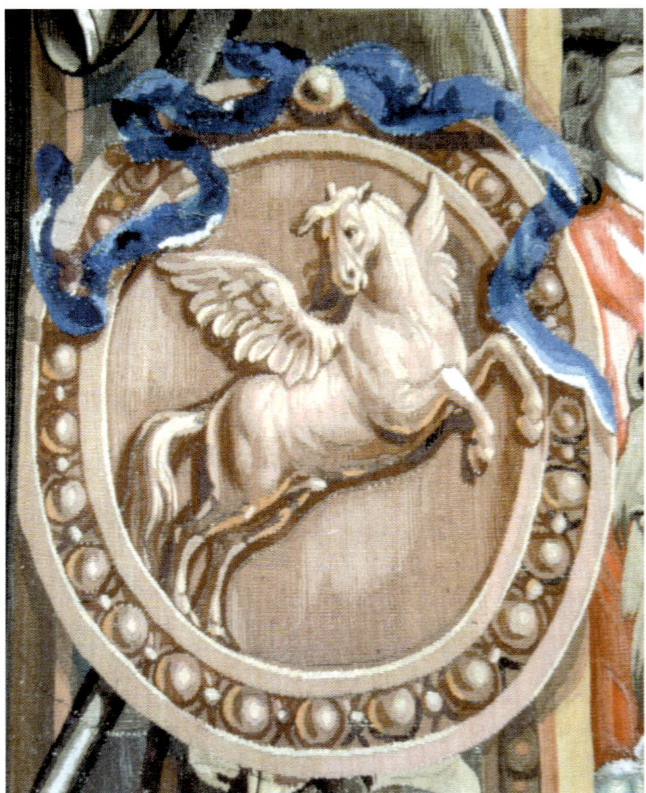

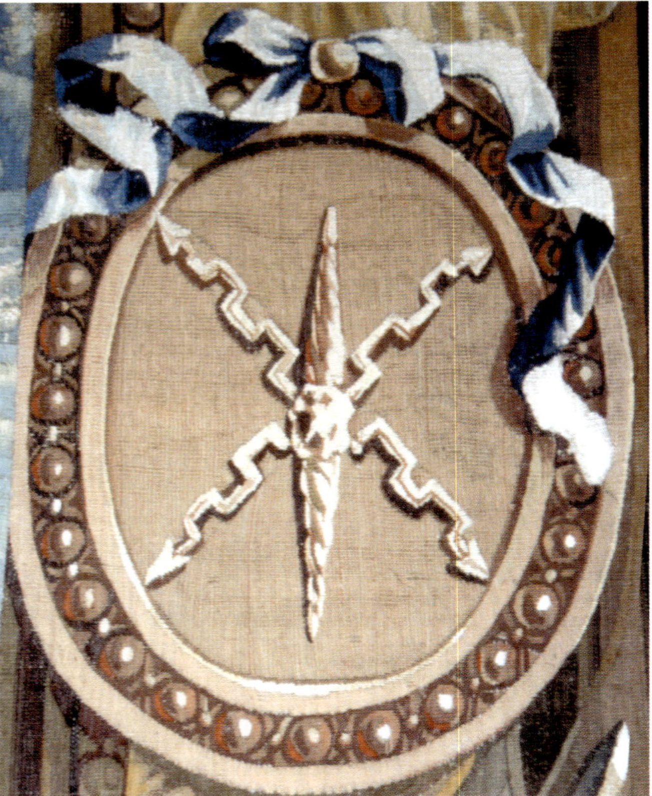

Above Left : Pegasus.
Above Right : Jupiter's Thunderbolt.

Marlborough's personal image is relatively unvarying in both pose and setting. The representation of the uniformed figures display the external signs of social rank, providing to the viewer a clear distinction between higher and lower social orders and class. The immaculate costume also affirms the dignity of the composition and preserves a sense of order. The scale of the figures is accurate, and the profusion of detail in the final composition renders each tapestry visually sumptuous. The tapestries are a rendering of 'elite' male portraiture linked with the narratives of war, that is to say the individuality of the subject was harnessed to his accomplishments on the battlefield.

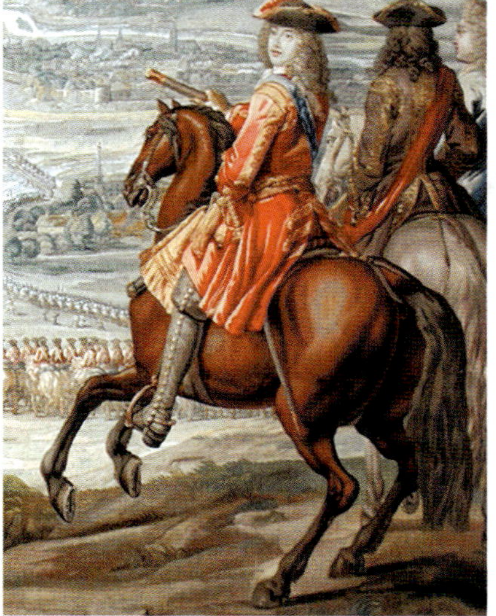

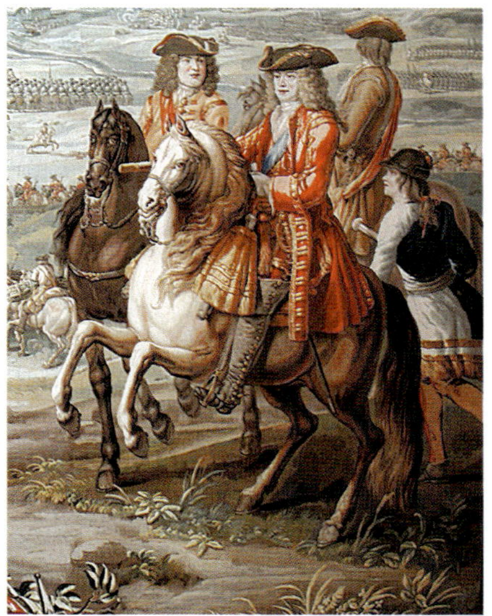

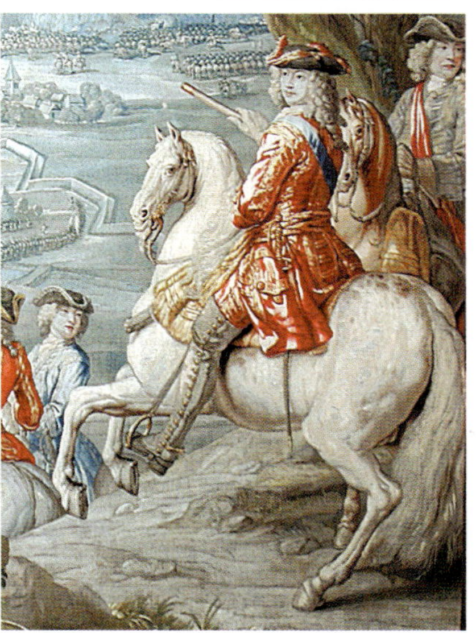

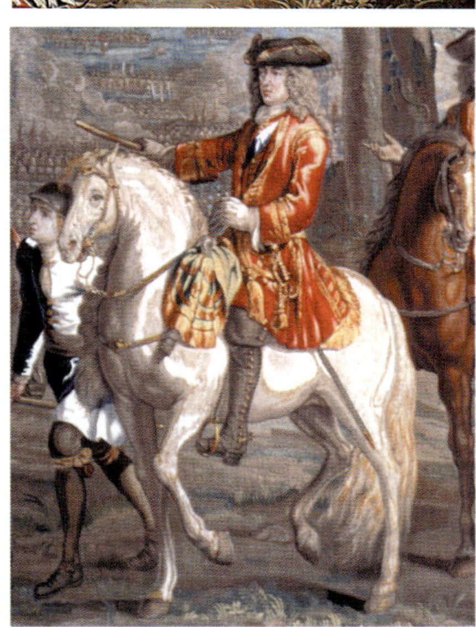

Detail of the Duke of Marlborough in the *Malplaquet* tapestry.

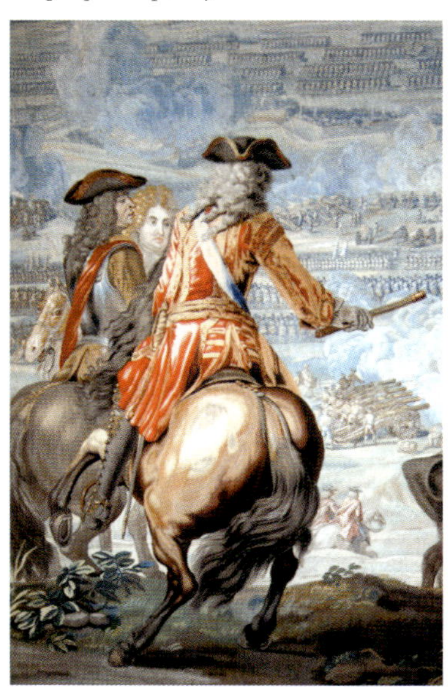

A small detail worth mentioning at this point is the interesting treatment of Marlborough's image in the *Malplaquet* tapestry. This is the only panel where the Duke's face is not visible and he has his back to the viewer. The only recognisable feature that identifies him is his commander's baton. The battle of Malplaquet was the bloodiest battle in the war. At Blenheim 12,000 Allied soldiers were killed or wounded; at Ramillies roughly 4,000; at Oudenarde under 3,000; but at Malplaquet the figure rose to 24,000 men which was a shocking statistic, understandably not well received in England at the time. Perhaps because his victory at Malplaquet was not the usual unqualified success, the imagery in the panel is a reflection of a somewhat subdued achievement compared with the more overt handling of his glorification in the other tapestries.

The viewer is acknowledged by some of the figures looking out of the picture creating a dynamic between the spectator and the spectacle. However, it is a cleansed, polite spectacle and the environment represented is almost totally rid of any bleakness, when in reality, life on the battlefield would necessarily have been uncertain, brutish and often short. The Duke would actually have been in the midst of his troops, rallying them and encouraging them forward into the heat of the battle. At Blenheim he spent 17 hours in the saddle and at Ramillies he led two charges. The contemporary eyewitness account of Captain Robert Parker of the Royal Regiment of Foot of Ireland testifies to his conduct.

"The Duke was in all places where his presence was requisite and in the hurry of the action happened to be unhorsed and in great danger of his life but was remounted by Captain Molesworth, one of his Aides de Camp, the only person of his retinue then near him, who seeing him in manifest danger of falling into the hands of the pursuing enemy, suddenly threw himself from his horse and helped the Duke to mount him. His Grace by this means got off between our lines...His Grace, about an hour later, had another narrow escape, when in shifting back from Captain Molesworth's horse to his own, Colonel Bringfield (his first equerry) holding the stirrup, was killed by a canon shot from the village of Ramillies.

Notwithstanding which, the Duke immediately rode up to the head of his troops and his presence animated them to that degree that they pressed home upon the enemy and made them shrink and give back".[134]

The murals at the Marlboroughs' London home treat the battle scenes in a different manner. Not only is the bloody and brutal nature of each

Two of the murals at Marlborough House depicting scenes from the Battle of Malplaquet were painted by Louis Laguerre based on these designs prepared on canvas.

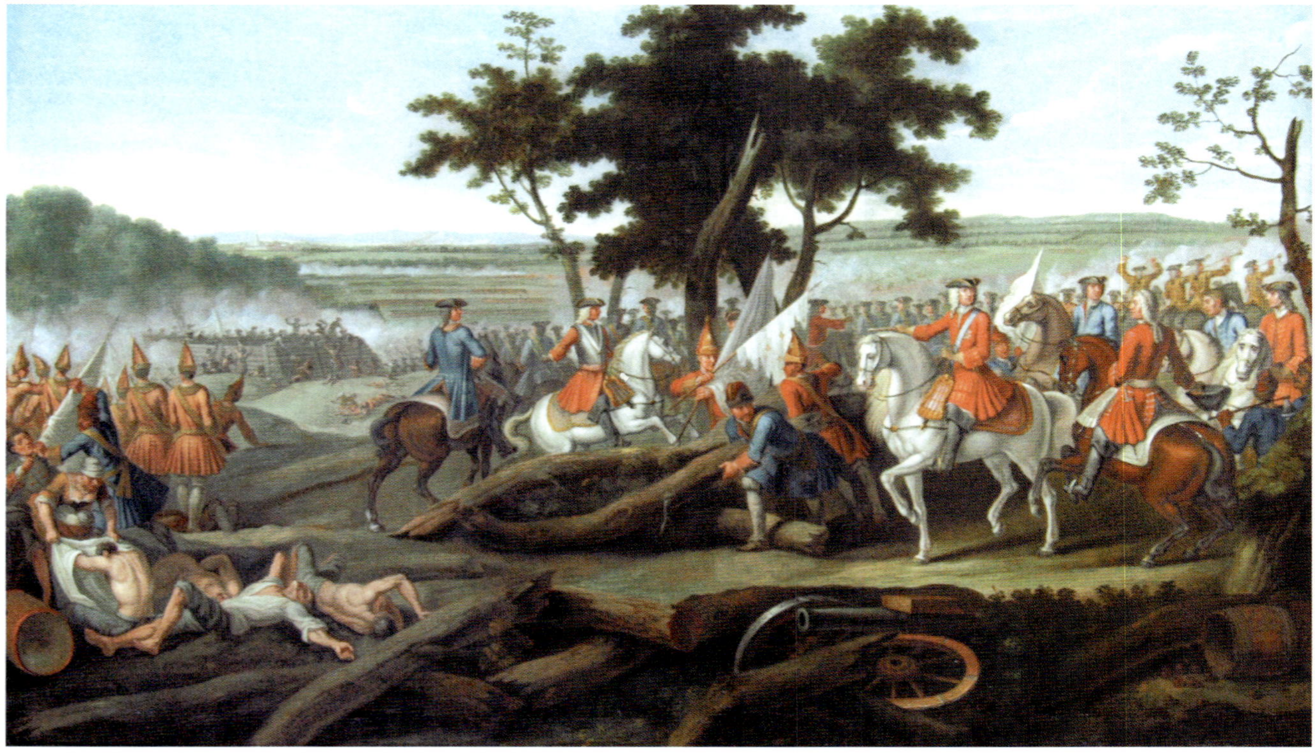

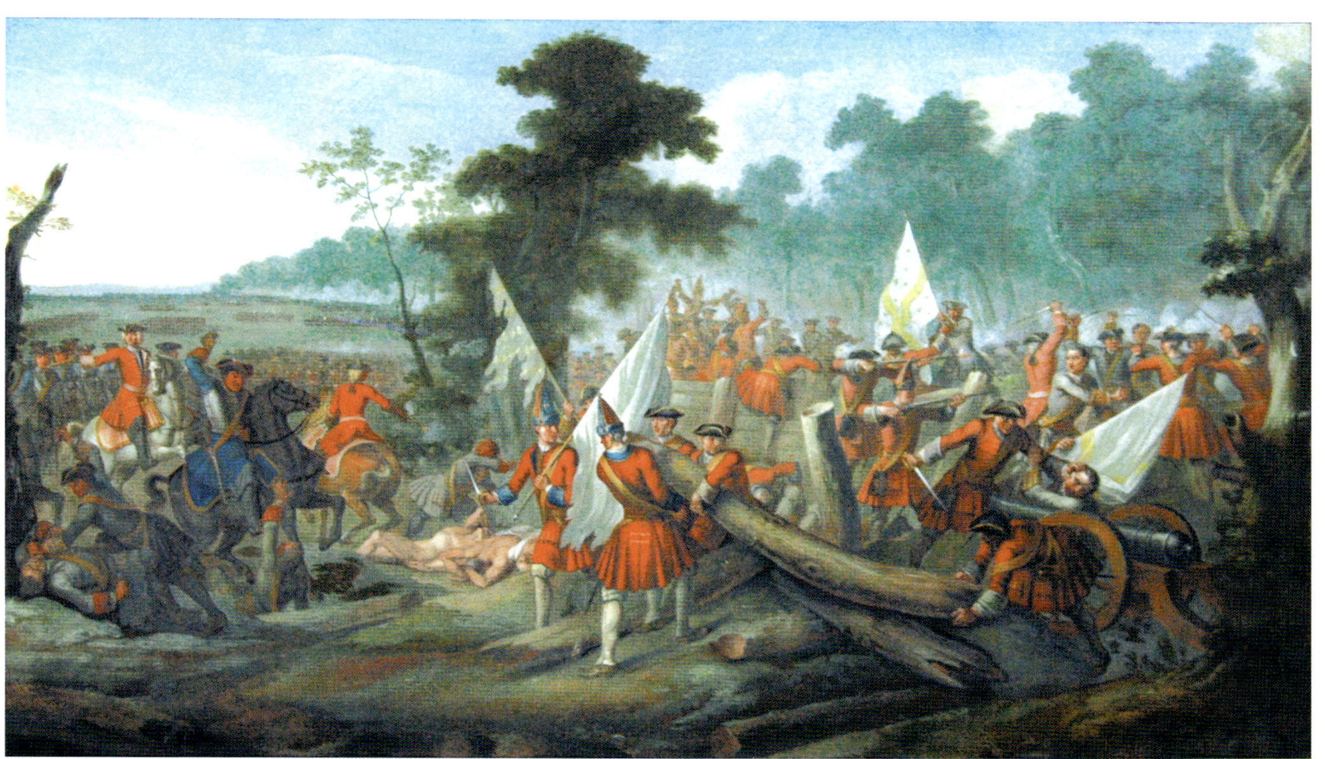

encounter graphically displayed, but the artist at Marlborough House, Louis Laguerre, uses multiple surfaces in which the story unfolds and the action is thus shown at varying points in time on each wall.

As far as the *Victories* tapestries at Blenheim Palace are concerned, each scene depicted is a simultaneous sequence of events. The artists have subtly combined elements of creativity and factual reality in the design of the tapestries. This conforms with Le Brun's view that the artist having only one panel in which to situate all that he wishes to depict must bring together many incidents *"so that his subject will be understandable. Without this, those looking at his work would be no more informed than if an historian, instead of telling the whole story, told only its ending"*.[135] The narrative composition of each tapestry forms a rich assemblage of facts as the story unfolds with the Duke almost always shown (except in the *Wynendael* panel) as the principal figure dominating the events portrayed.

The artists have depicted the Duke in a series of images that clearly satisfied him, for these tapestries, when they were commissioned, were not open to general public display and were hung to impress the visitor privileged enough to be able to progress through the grandest rooms of Blenheim Palace, the State Apartments. Each tapestry has a similar composition, style and design as well as a high degree of perfection in the manufacture of the panels producing a series of panoramic views which are an extraordinary artistic achievement.

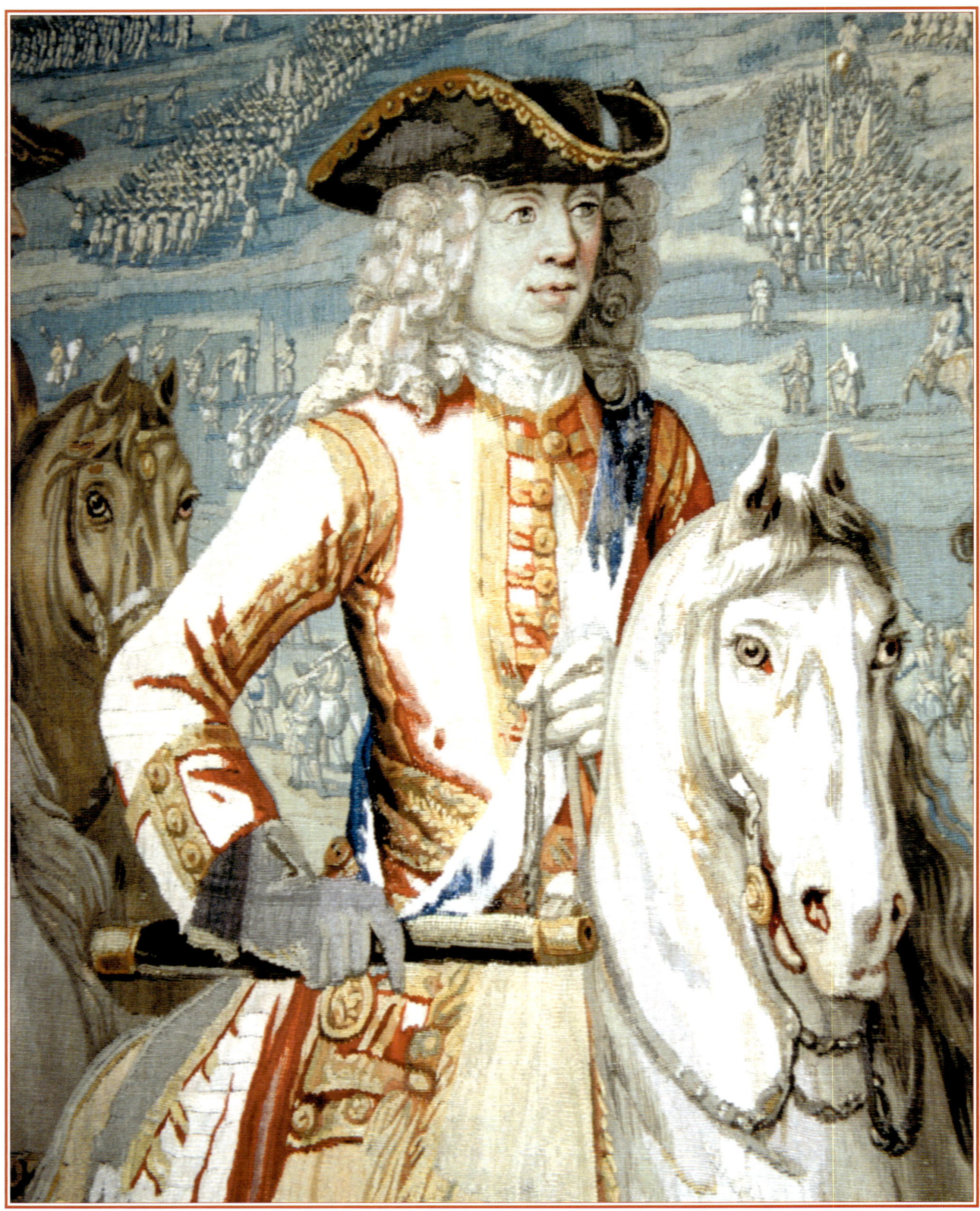

Chapter Seven

THE *VICTORIES*: MARLBOROUGH'S CAMPAIGNS (1702-1711)

WHILE this book deals essentially with the tapestries at Blenheim Palace, they cannot be fully understood or appreciated without some knowledge of the historic events they portray. This is especially true of the *Victories* set where the designer often interlaces, within a single panel, events which actually occurred at different moments in the encounter. The aim of this chapter is therefore, to outline as much of the action that occurred in the War of the Spanish Succession as is necessary to understand the history woven into these tapestries.

In the early eighteenth century, campaigns were usually fought only between April and October, the few months in the year when the primitive roads were passable and food and fodder available, before the army was sent into camp for the winter months. The tendency was to shy away from major battles which were very costly in terms of men and money and to engage in a more defensive type of warfare consisting of sieges, marches and other tactical manoeuvres to gain control of fortresses, key towns and foraging areas.

In the War of the Spanish Succession, Marlborough's initial operations had limited success due to excessive interference from the Dutch. Although he was the Captain General of the Allied forces, every action needed the approval of two Dutch deputies who were reluctant to engage with the enemy in outright battles, preferring tactical manoeuvring or static warfare with a minimum loss of life.

Consequently, the only gains made by the Allies in 1702 were the siege and capture of Venloo, Stevenswaert, Ruremonde and Liege. These modest achievements allowed them to win control of the entire line along the River Meuse from Liege to the sea and cleared the French from the region between the Meuse and the Rhine. This was a vital step in leaving the road to Vienna open to receive the help needed to combat a recently combined Franco-Bavarian enemy. On his return to England that winter, Queen Anne created John Churchill Duke of Marlborough.

1703 was another year of frustration for Marlborough although he successfully besieged Bonn and captured Huy. He also took Limburg to the east of Liege but apart from these limited campaigns the Dutch again thwarted his desire for bold action against the French.

This was all to change in 1704. Louis XIV was suspected of planning a strike on the Danube valley which would have threatened Vienna. Marlborough met the Habsburg Archduke Charles in October and December of 1703 and he spent the winter months planning what would become his most legendary military manoeuvre and battle.

He made careful and secret preparations beforehand, ensuring that his

Facing page :
Detail of the Duke of Marlborough from the *Oudenarde* tapestry.

route was fully reconnoitred, that depots for food and fodder, uniforms and other supplies were set up in advance and most importantly, that funds were freely available. His plan could not have been carried out without the co-operation and assistance of one of his closest friends at court, Sidney Godolphin.

As Queen Anne's Lord Treasurer, Godolphin was under particular strain that year as England had committed troops on active duty not only in Flanders but also in Gibraltar and Portugal. The Navy was commanded to increase its attacks in the Mediterranean as well as on the south coast of Spain so as to induce King Louis XIV to draw his troops away from the north and east of France down into the south. Marlborough let it be known that he would be engaging in operations along the river Moselle. This diverted the troublesome Dutch deputies who would never have agreed to such a bold scheme and allowed Marlborough to set off on his long march to the Danube unopposed.

All along the route, Marlborough disguised his intentions and created several diversions to mask his true objective from the French and Bavarians. Two French marshals, Villeroy (who shadowed his initial movements) and Tallard (who covered from Alsace), hesitated in moving their armies and awaited instructions from Versailles. The rigidity of the highly centralised French command system proved a major disadvantage to them and repeatedly allowed Marlborough to retain the upper hand. Making the most of the situation, Marlborough was unimpeded in crossing the river Main and the Neckar, moving eastwards heading for the Danube.

It was only towards the end of his march that the French realised Marlborough's destination. He had not only managed to keep the initiative but through his attention to logistics had also allowed his troops to arrive in high spirits and good physical condition, having established a very careful and efficient system of administration of supplies and provisions at every camp throughout the march, with the financial base for the entire operation set up at Frankfurt.

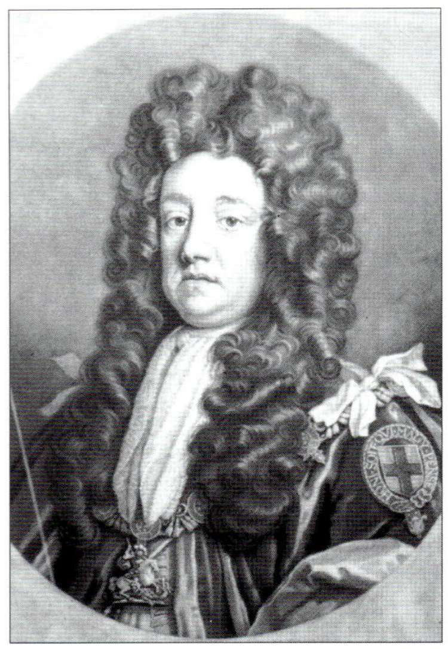

Sidney Godolphin.

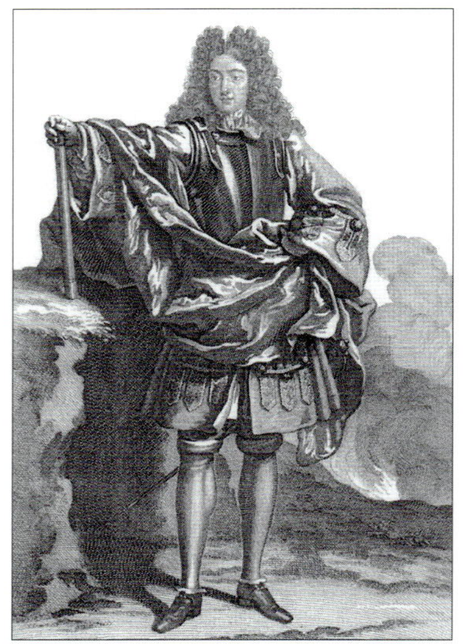

Marshal Villeroy.

Marlborough's March to the Danube

Captain Robert Parker of the Royal Regiment of Foot of Ireland described the march to the Danube in his memoirs. The cavalry marched a day or two ahead of the infantry, the guns lagged several days behind. *"We frequently marched three, sometimes four days successively and halted one day. We generally began our march about three in the morning, proceeded about four leagues or four and a half by day, and reached our camping ground by nine. As we marched through the country of our Allies, commissars were appointed to furnish us with all manner of necessaries for man and horse; these were brought to the ground before we arrived, and the soldiers had nothing to do but pitch their tents, boil their kettles and lie down to rest. Surely never was such a march carried on with more order and regularity and with less fatigue to man and horse."*

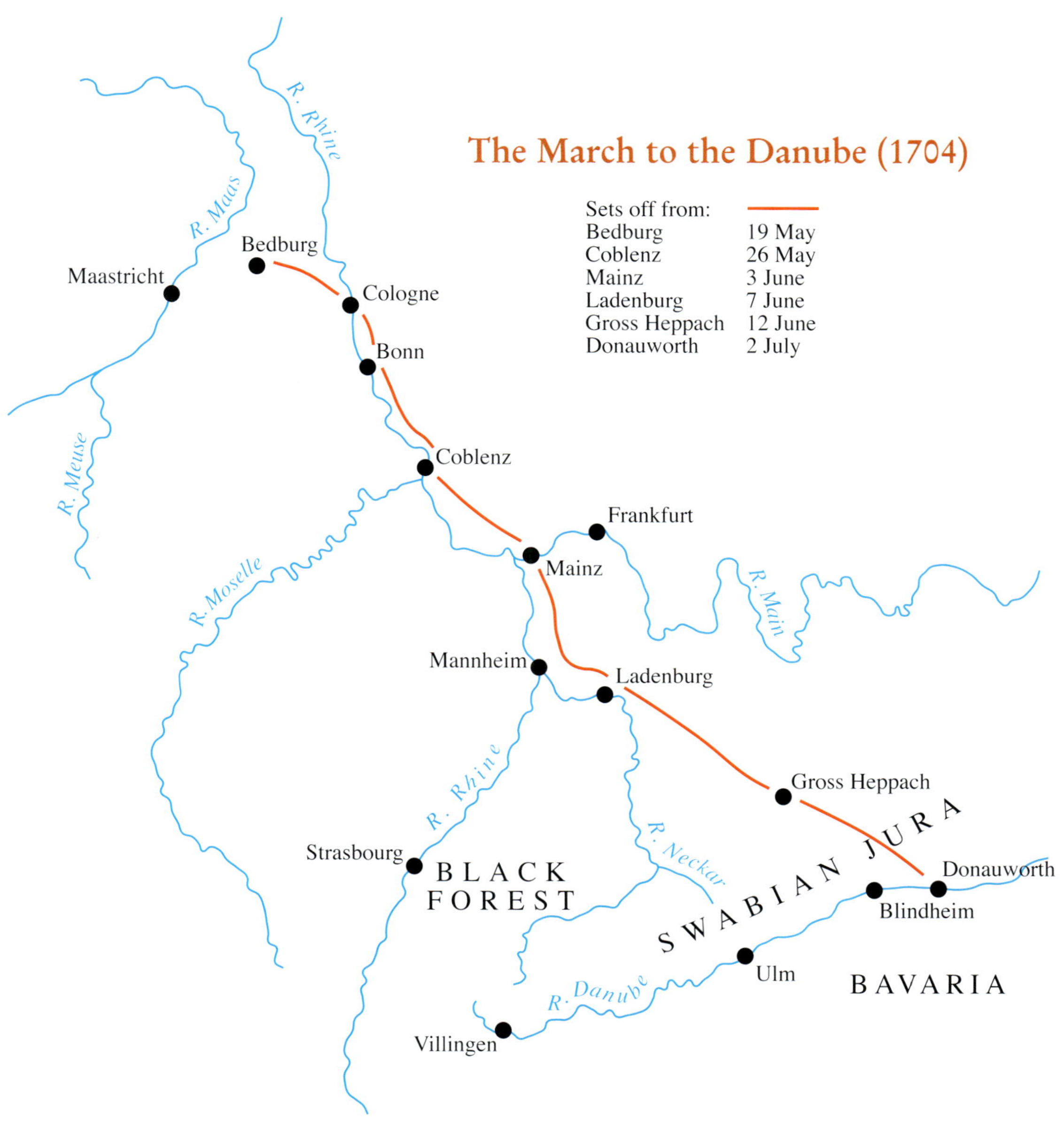

The first sign of French resistance was at Donauworth on 2nd July 1704. The Schellenberg, a 17th century hilltop fortress, dominated the village of Donauworth which was under French-Bavarian control and had to be taken in order to cross the Danube. With only one approachable side to this fortress, there was only one point of attack. In their advance, the Allied armies first had to cross a stream called the Wernitz. Dragoons with fascines (bundles of branches) were sent ahead to prepare the crossing. The enemy in the meantime had abandoned the town of Berg and had set their depots there alight. Count D'Arco, the Bavarian commander, regrouped his troops on the top of the hill and awaited the approaching Allied armies. At 5 p.m. the Allied dragoons rode forward and dropped their fascines in order to facilitate the infantry's advance. The cavalry were then sent in to support the infantry who were engaged in fierce fighting at the top, suffering many casualties. The Allies kept up the pressure for over two hours, when Marlborough received vital information through his system of 'runners'. These running footmen were able to move fast without being easily targeted and were employed to carry messages between the Captain General and his supporting officers. Thus, newly informed of a lightly defended section further along the enemy lines near the village of Donauworth, Marlborough launched his assault and outflanked the Bavarians who finally retreated in panic.

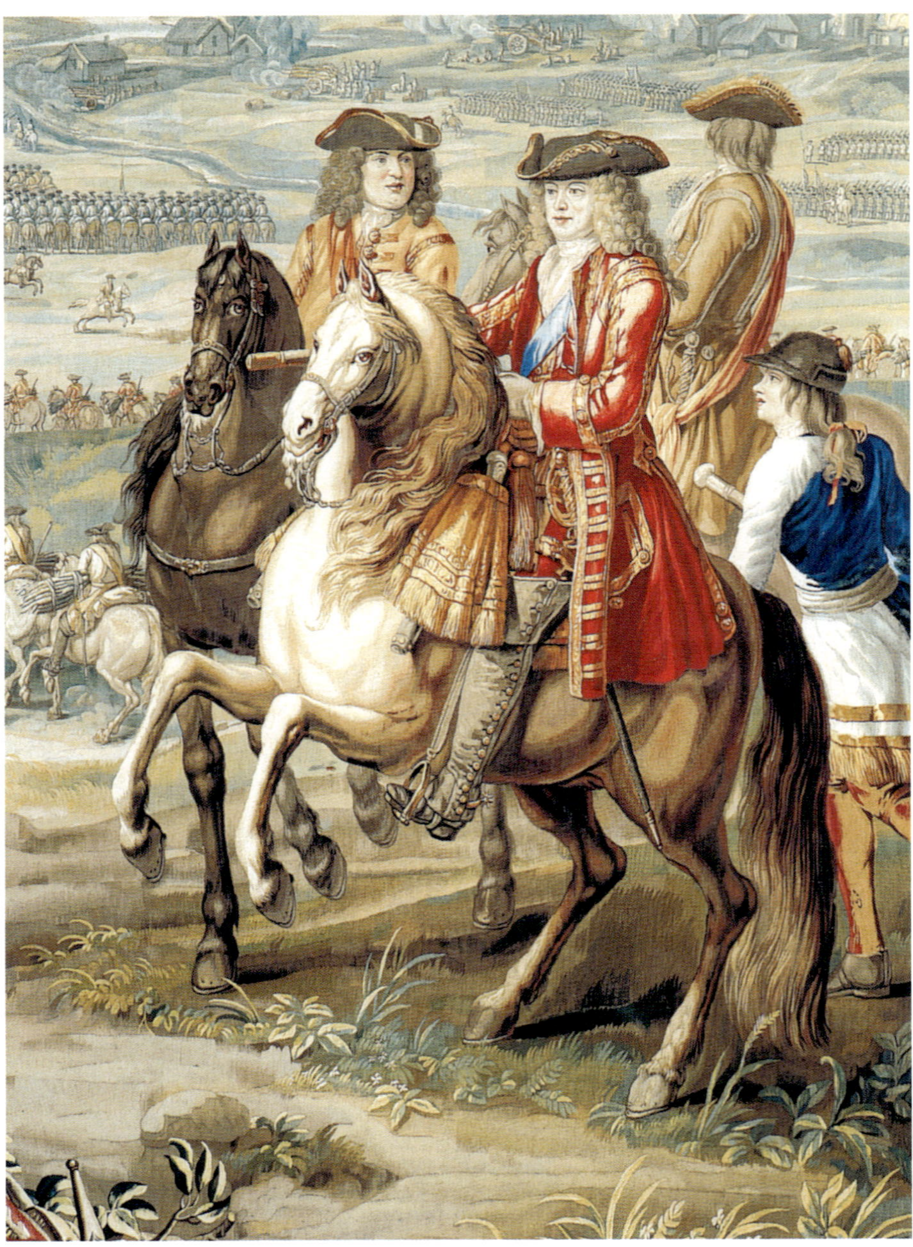

Detail of the Duke with one of his running footmen. These 'runners' wore distinctive caps and short coats which allowed freedom of movement. They also carried a staff (which was sometimes silver or gold topped to denote their rank).

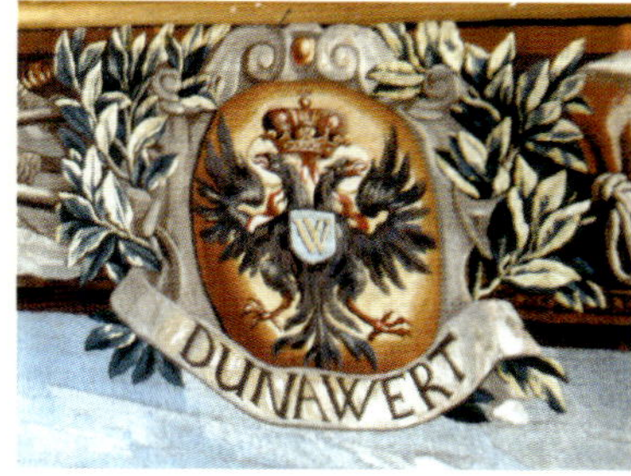

DONAUWORTH: 2 JULY 1704

14ft 6in. (H) x 13ft 4in. (W) / 4.42m (H) x 4.06m (W)

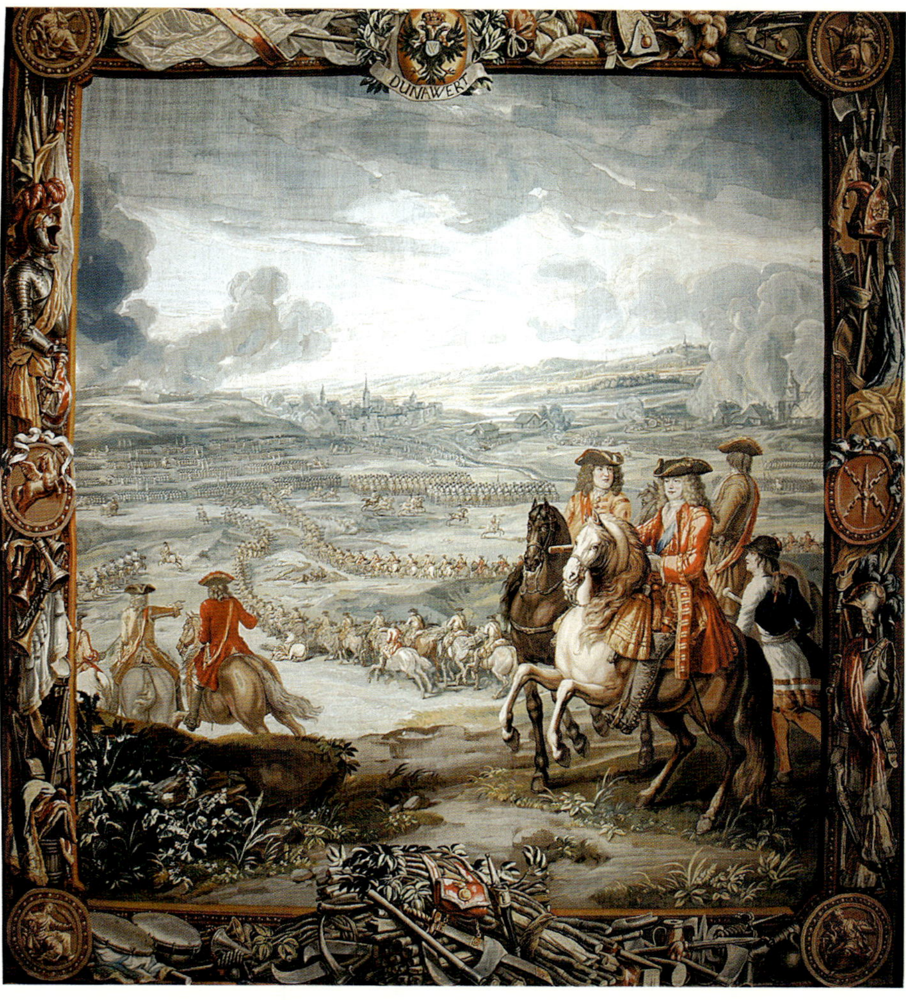

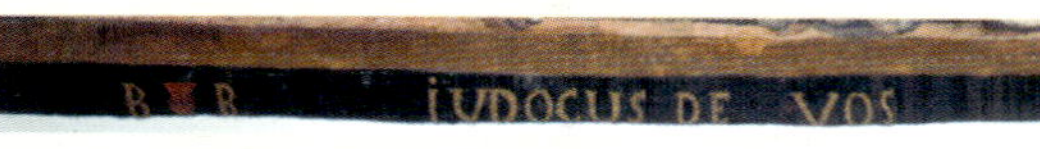

Judocus de Vos's maker's mark and the Brussels-Brabant mark are both clearly visible in the selvedge of this panel.

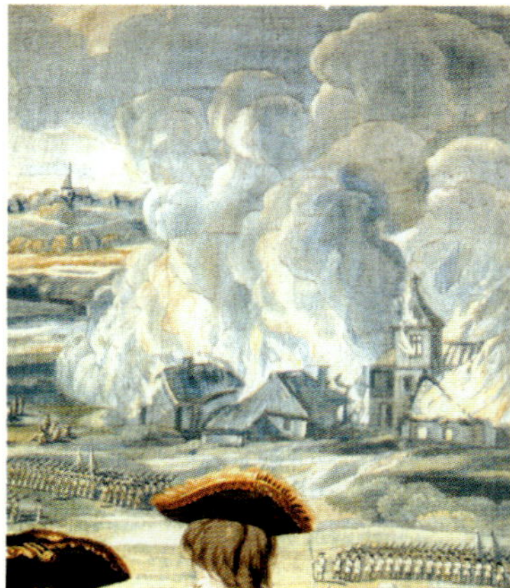

Detail of the town of Berg where the French set their magazines on fire to prevent the Allied army from capturing them.

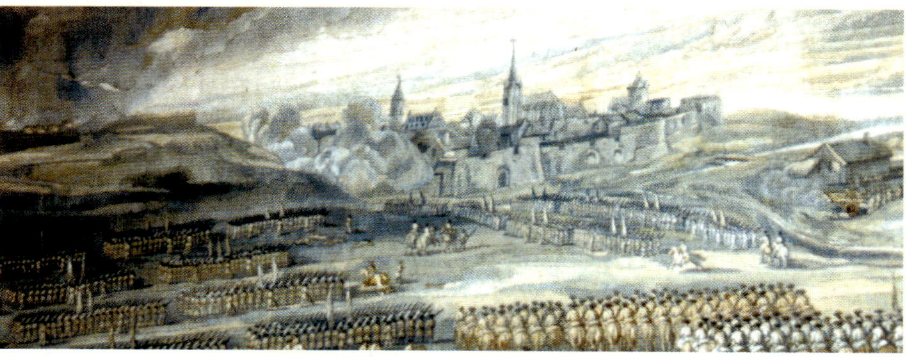

Detail of the Schellenberg fortress and the village of Donauworth.

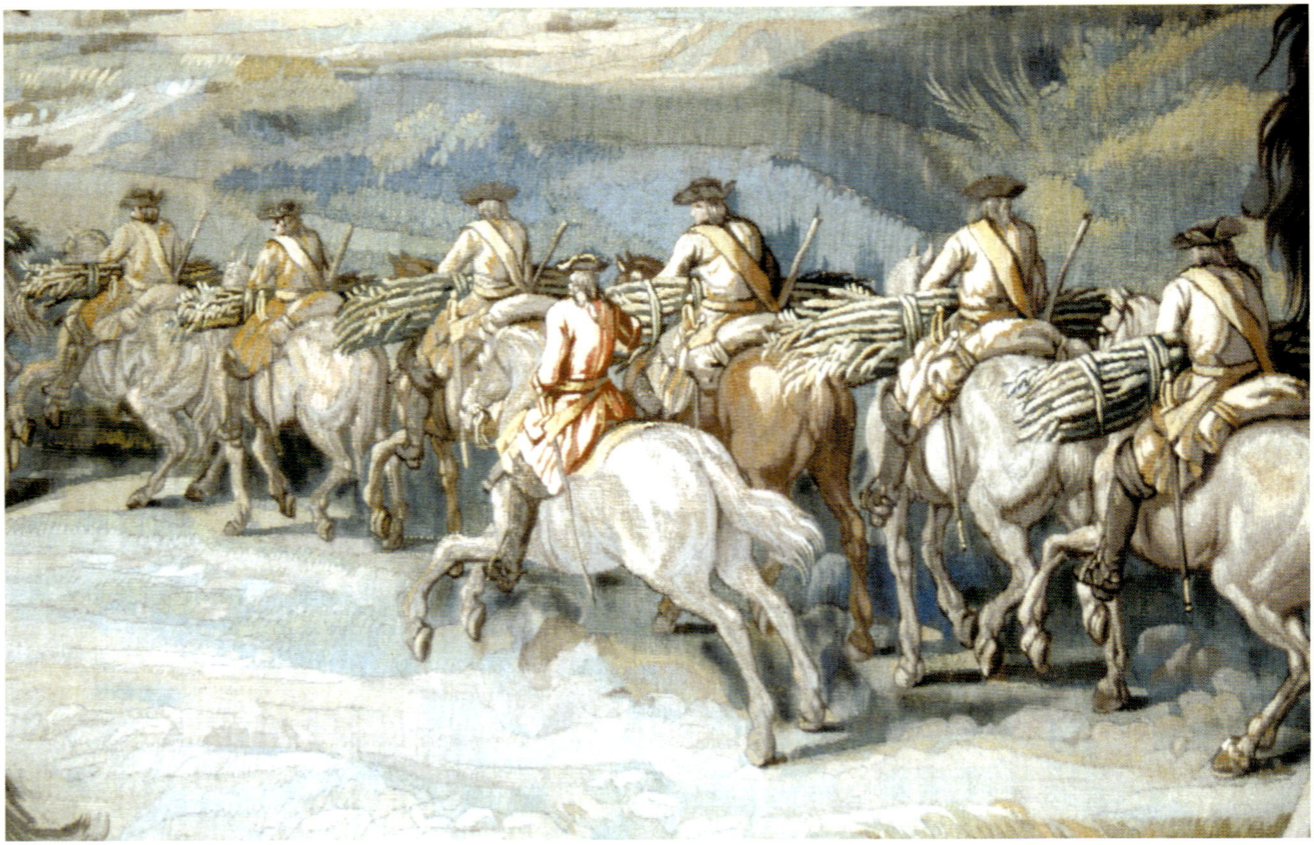

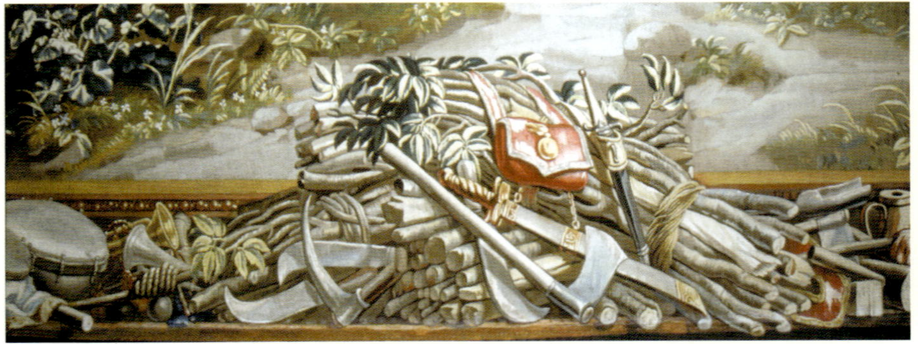
Detail of the advancing dragoons carrying fascines.

Dragoons were a versatile part of the cavalry capable of serving on horse or on foot. They assisted in clearing obstacles, filling trenches with fascines (bundles of branches) and were sometimes used in general reconnaissance duties along with locally hired scouts. They were armed with a short musket or carbine, a bayonet, a long handled hatchet and a small straight sword (called a hanger) which was used either to clear paths or to cut fascines. They were paid less than the elite horsemen but more than foot soldiers. Their tools and fascines are visible in the lower central border.

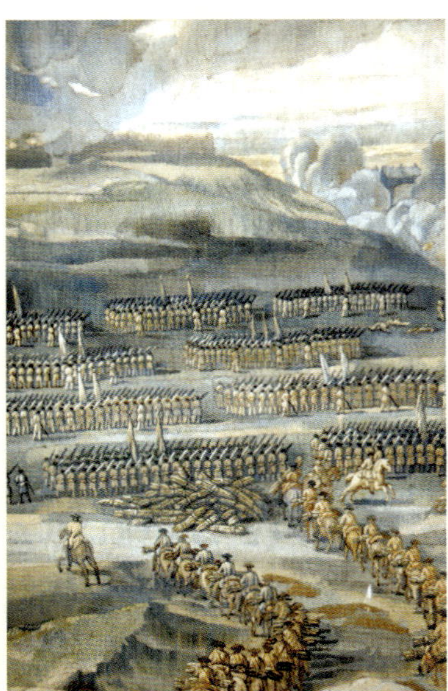
Detail of allied army at the foot of the Schellenberg fortress, preparing to attack.

Lower border of the tapestry with details of fascines and tools used by the dragoons.

Marlborough's 250 mile (400 km) march to the Danube was undertaken in just 6 weeks and the action was to culminate in a head to head encounter with the enemy on the 13th of August 1704.

After the storming of the Schellenberg, the French army commanded by Marshal Tallard swiftly made its way into Bavaria. A few days later, the Duke was joined by the greatest of his allies, the 41 year old Prince Eugene of Savoy.

On 12th August, Marlborough and Eugene rode out to survey the land for a suitable camp for their armies. They found the enemy already in possession of the plain near the village of Blindheim (which the English called Blenheim), holding a position stretching from the Danube to the rough country around Lutzingen about four miles away. In front of their position was the Nebel, a stream with marshy banks. The two commanders decided to attack the enemy the next day.

By daybreak on the 13th of August, the Allies had advanced over the Nebel through the thick morning fog. The French, psychologically as well as numerically superior, never expected for a moment to come under attack. Once over their initial shock, they tumbled out of their tents and hurried into battle formation. Marshal Tallard found himself up against the Allied left and centre under Marlborough, while Marshal Marsin joined with the Elector of Bavaria in contending with the Allied right flank under Prince Eugene.

The battle commenced around mid-day, once both armies were in place. At one end of the four-mile battle line, the village of Blindheim, strongly reinforced by the French, was surrounded and held by General Cutts who had been dispatched there by the Duke. This containing action proved to be crucial to the Allied victory as several thousands of elite French soldiers were effectively cut off here, hemmed in to such a degree that they were prevented from fighting. Marlborough also oversaw the fierce action in the centre around the village of Oberglau, while the forces of Prince Eugene attacked the stronghold of Lutzingen at the other end of the battle line.

As the day wore on, the outcome of the battle was far from certain, until the French, having so reinforced their positions on both flanks, dangerously weakened their centre where Marlborough's brother, General Charles Churchill, led in a combined infantry and cavalry assault. The final fatal blow was delivered to the French after 5 p.m. when Marlborough brought in the 8,000 cavalry he had held in reserve and supported by guns and infantry, stormed through the French centre.

Later that evening, the captured French Marshal Tallard surrendered and so in a day ended over 50 years of French military supremacy in Europe. Marlborough's bold offensive action, his use of surprise and speed along with the excellent support and co-operation he received from Prince Eugene during the battle itself, cleared the Danube of French forces, allowed the Allies to occupy Bavaria and dealt a mighty blow to French prestige.

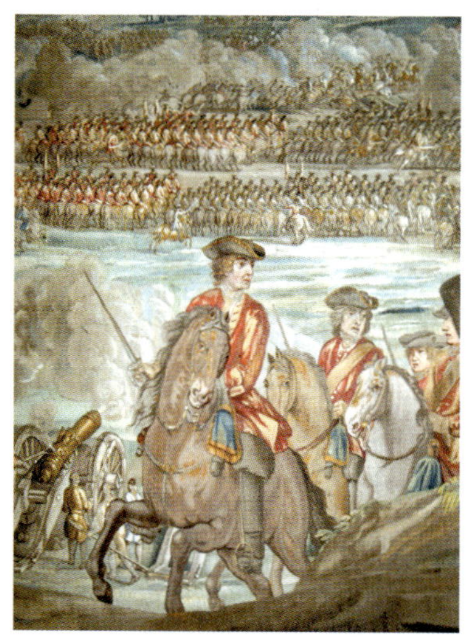

Detail of the final cavalry attack from the *Blenheim* tapestry.

BLENHEIM: 13 AUGUST 1704

14ft 6in. (H) x 25ft 3in. (W) / 4.42m (H) x 7.69m (W)

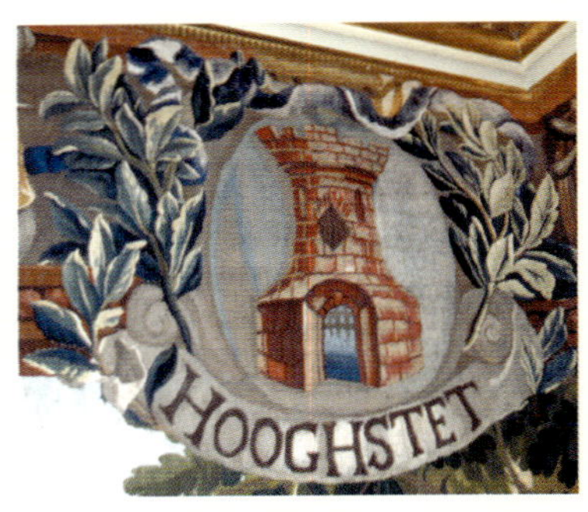

The cartouche in the top border describes this panel as 'Hoogstet'. On the
continent, the Battle was named after Hochstadt, the Bavarian town where
the action concluded, but in England it was called the Battle of Blenheim to
distinguish it from the earlier battle of Hochstadt in which the French under
Marshal Villars and the Elector of Bavaria had defeated the Imperialists under
Count Styrum on 20th September 1703.

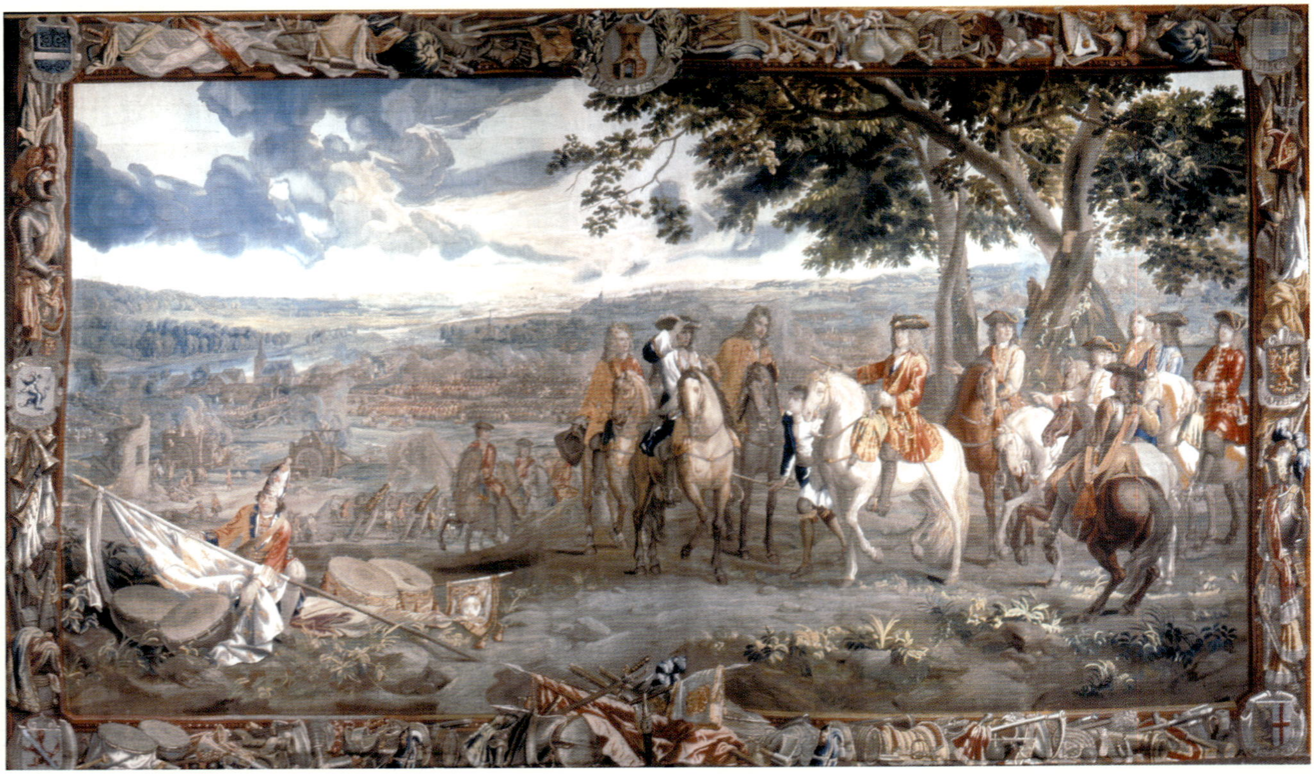

This tapestry shows a decisive moment in British history. In the centre of
the panel the defeated French Marshal Tallard surrenders to Marlborough,
clearly visible in his red coat on a white horse with his commander's baton
held aloft.

The Duke is accompanied by several of his officers, of which General
Cadogan, and Prince Eugene are recognisable. Lord George Hamilton, Earl
of Orkney (possibly one of the figures behind Eugene) persuaded the French
garrisons at the village of Blindheim (Blenheim) to lay down their arms and
surrender, playing a significant part in the Allied victory.

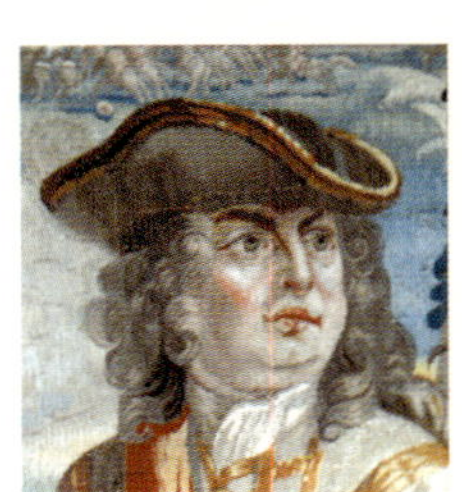

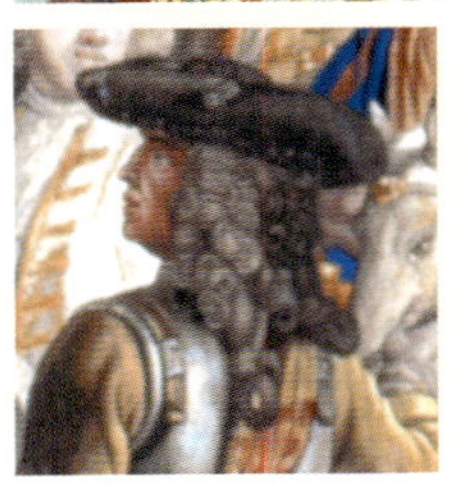

Above right : General Cadogan.
Right : Prince Eugene of Savoy.

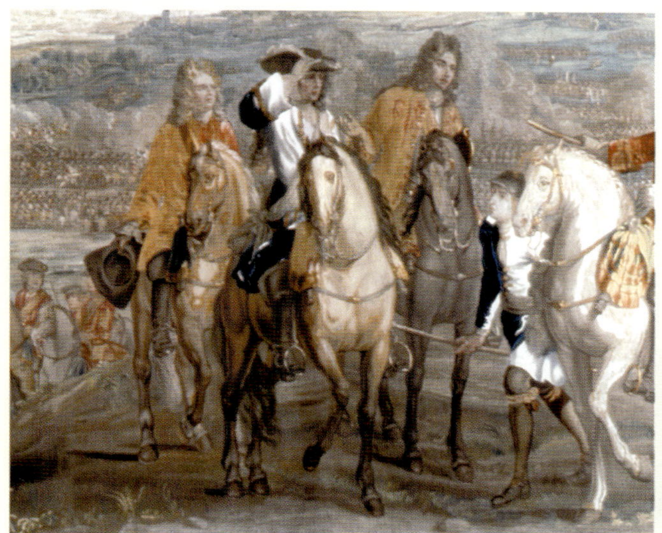

Above : Detail of the defeated French Marshal Tallard who is about to doff his hat in a gesture of surrender.

Above right : The capture of Marshal Tallard by Jean-Baptiste Martin the Elder (called Martin des Batailles). Tallard is being driven away in Marlborough's coach.

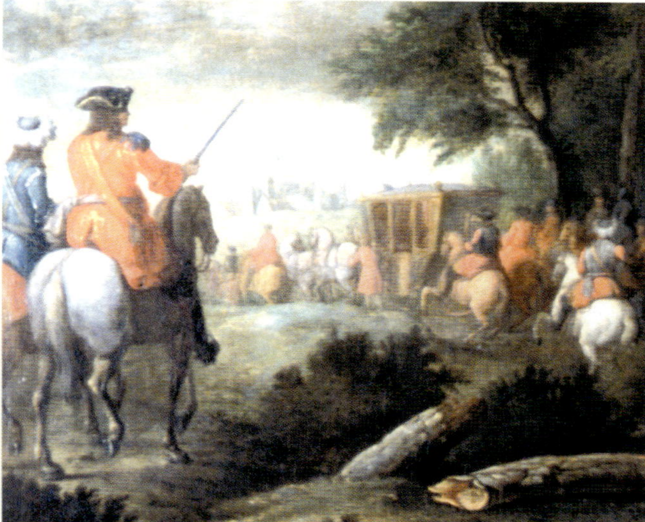

Marshal Tallard was captured by Hessian cavalry officers. He was taken as prisoner in Marlborough's own coach before being transported to England where he languished for seven years under house arrest in Nottingham. His release under parole was arranged in 1711 when secret negotiations were begun to end the hostilities.[136] He returned to Versailles in November that year where King Louis XIV received him with kindness. His freedom was made formal under the Peace of Utrecht in 1713.

The town of Blindheim (Blenheim) was barricaded with cut down trees and hedges, palisades and carts. The French soldiers were so closely packed behind the barricades that their manoeuvrability was seriously affected.

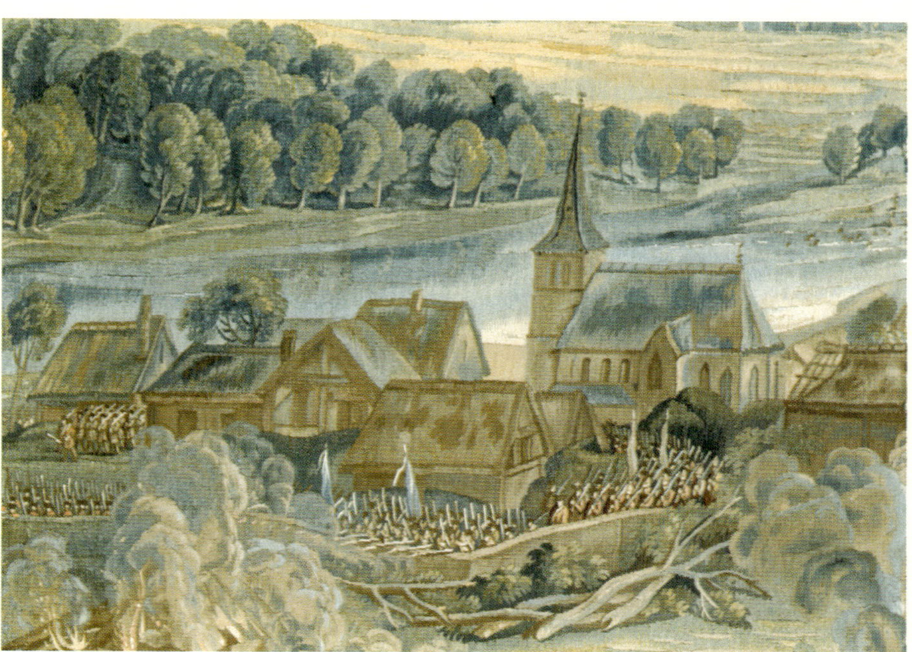

Detail of the village of Blindheim showing French troops hemmed in.

The flintlock musket was the customary firearm during this period and Marlborough's army was well trained in the drill of platoon firing. This innovation allowed English soldiers continuous, controlled and accurate fire on the battlefield. The infantry fired by platoons, a coded system of rolling fire. At any one time one third of the battalion was loaded and ready to fire, a further advantage over the enemy who had yet to adopt this procedure.

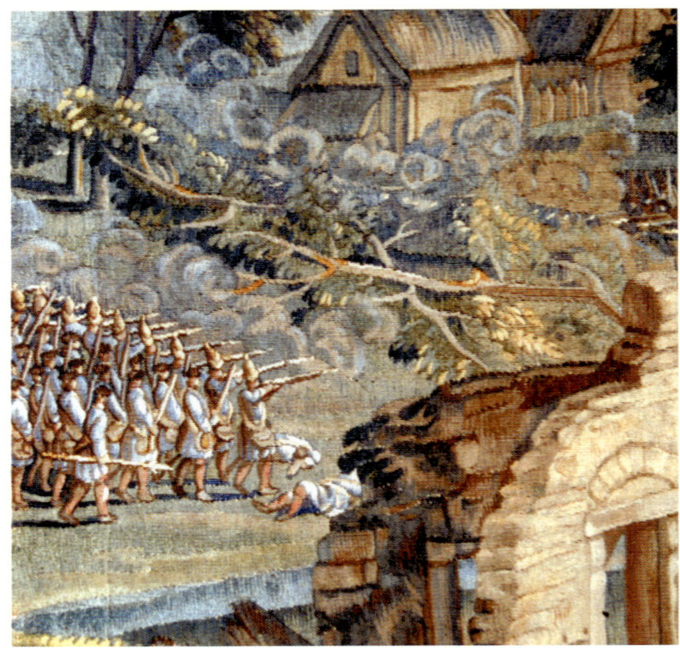

Detail of platoon firing.

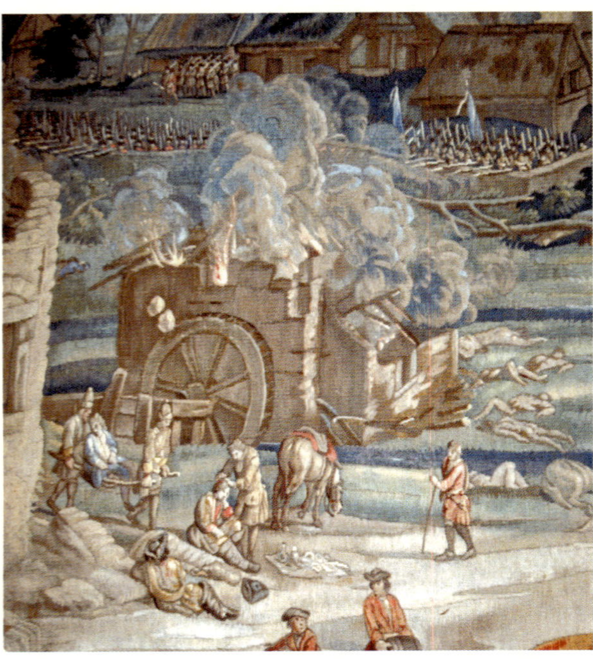

Water mills were set alight by the French to restrict the Allies' room to manoeuvre. A field dressing station tends to the injured on the battlefield.

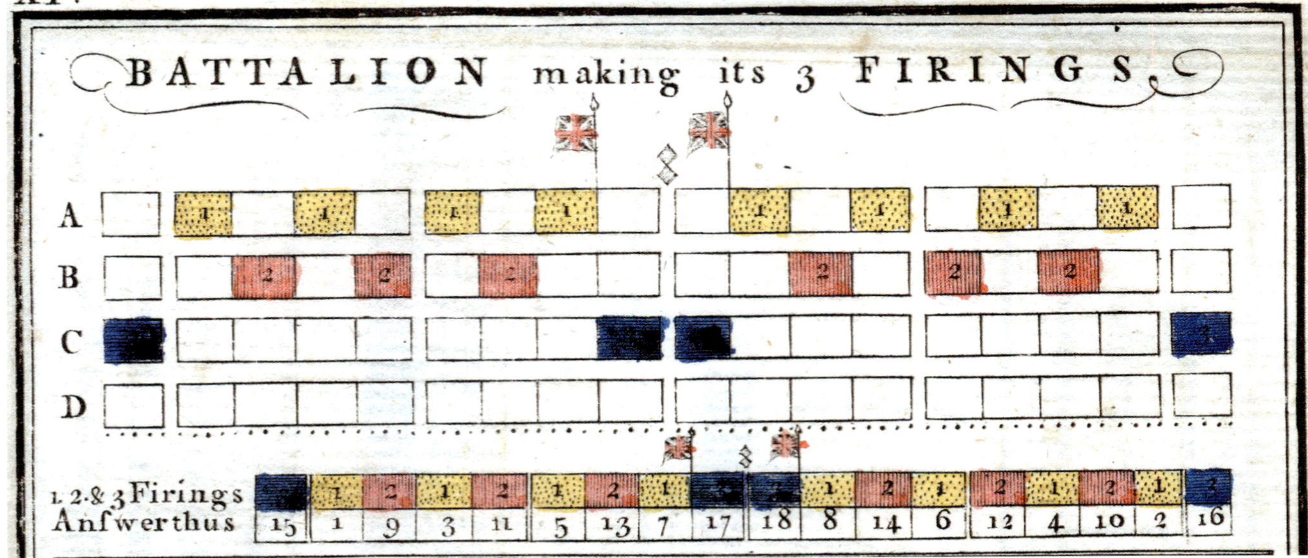

A pamphlet illustrating the discipline of platoon firing.

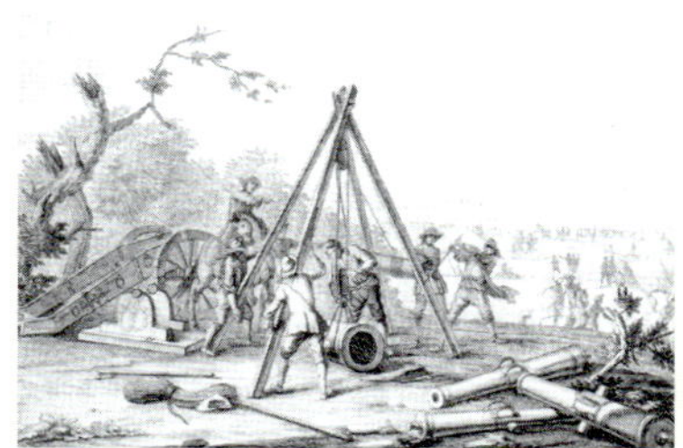

A barrel being lifted onto a gun carriage.

Guns during this period were made of brass or iron. Alongside the gunners who charged and fired the guns, are their assistants called matrosses. The Duke often paid personal attention to the placing of guns on the battlefield and relocated them to new positions in the course of an engagement which was highly unusual for the time but proved to be very successful.

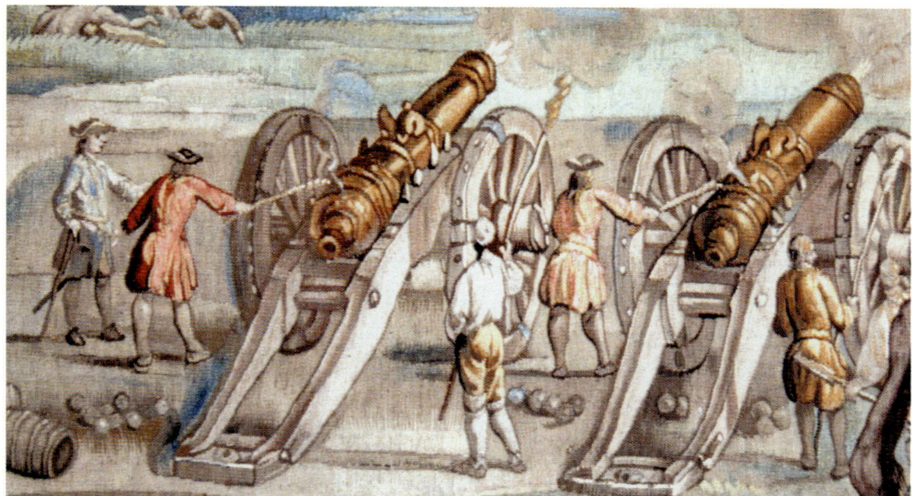

Detail of guns in action.

The final cavalry charge is visible in the centre. The English cavalry charged at a fast trot, in two ranks, in a close knee to knee formation and used the sword as their main weapon. The resulting relentless momentum of advance and attack proved very effective against the French horsemen who used pistols and repeatedly stopped to reload and fire.

The detail shows reserves going in and the French fleeing in the background. Over 3,000 French horsemen drowned in the Danube that evening.

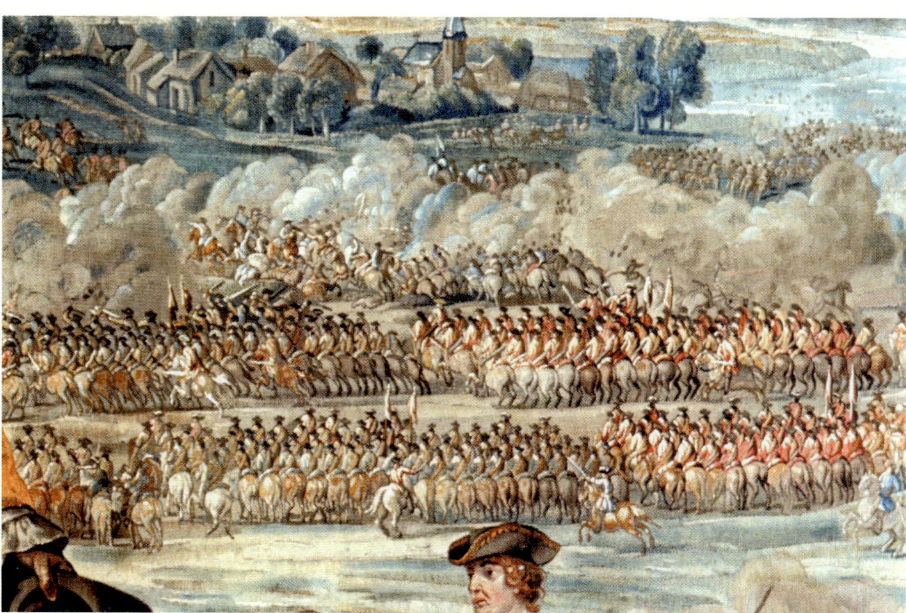

Detail showing the final cavalry charge.

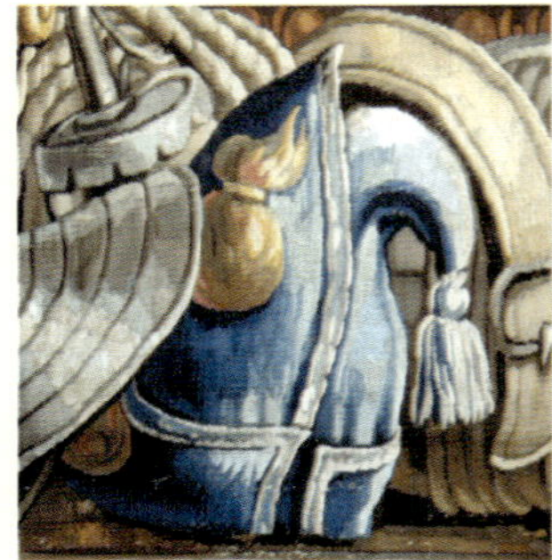
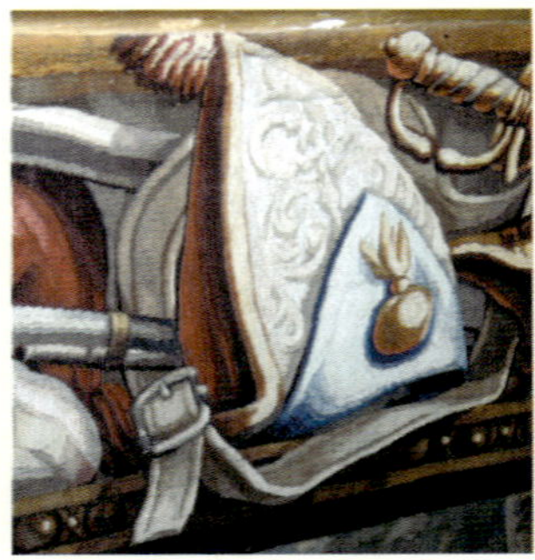
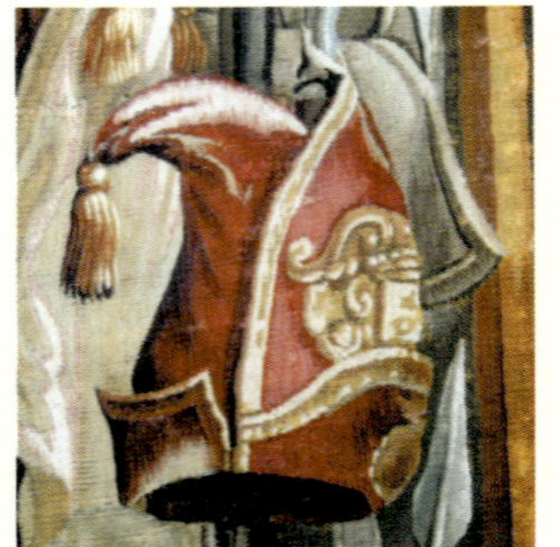
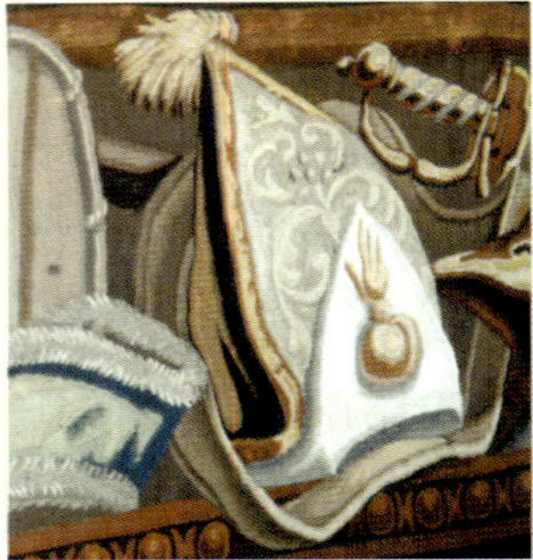

Tapestry border details showing a variety of grenadier caps.

The English grenadier guard wore a brimless mitre cap rather than the tricorn shaped hat worn by other officers and soldiers as he needed his hands free to ignite and throw the grenade after having slung his musket over his shoulder and back. Other tapestry images show various designs from a fur lined bag cap favoured by the Austrians to a cap with a stiffened high upright front as worn by British, Danish and Prussian grenadiers.

The grenadier guard in the left foreground of the tapestry has three trophies of war laid out in front of him. The white standard with gold fleurs de lys of the Regiment du Roi (King's regiment) marks the defeat of the French infantry (the Blenheim Quit Rent Standard is based on this flag). The guidon (dragoon flag) indicates the defeat of the dragoon regiments. The kettledrums symbolise the defeat of the acclaimed French cavalry – the *Gens d'armerie* and the elite *Maison du Roi* (King's troopers).

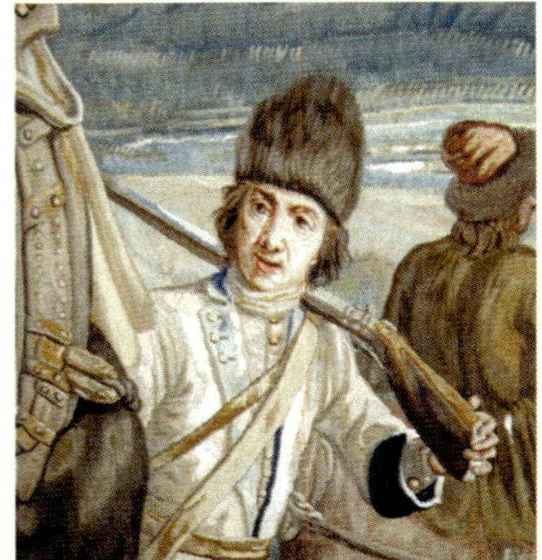

An Austrian grenadier's fur lined cap (detail from the *Wynendael* panel).

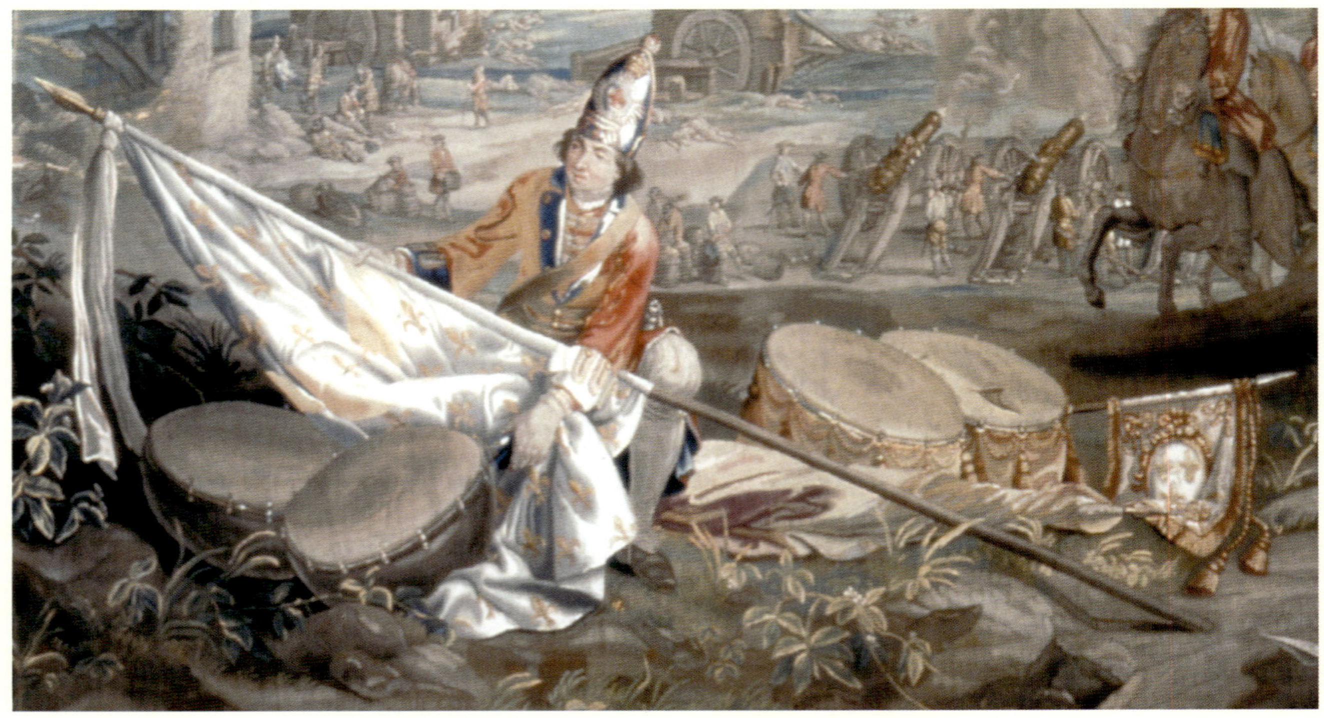

An English grenadier guard with the captured trophies of war.

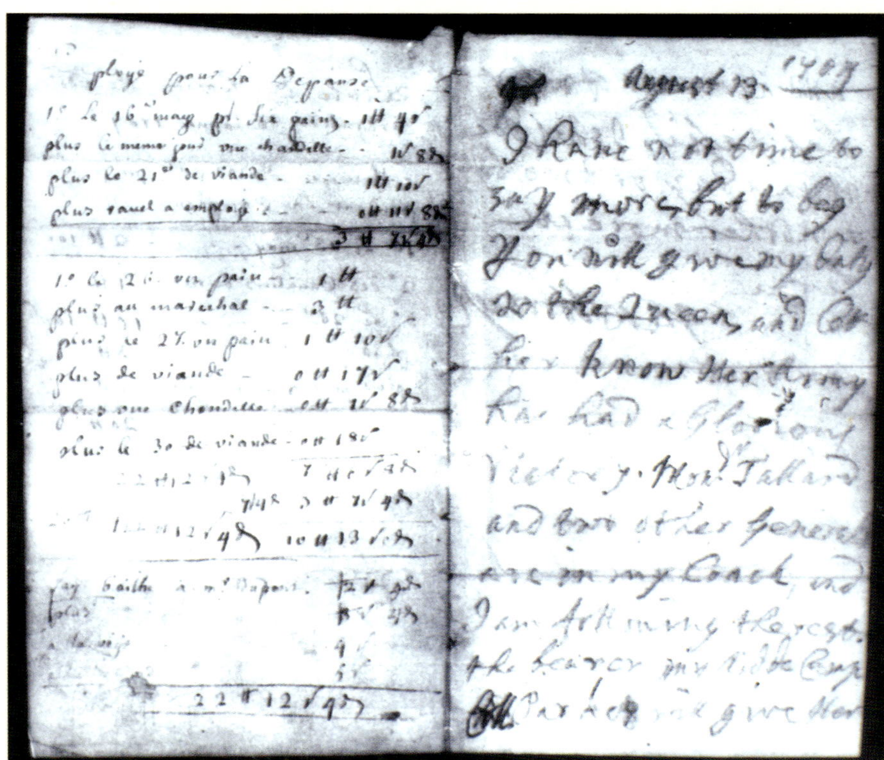

The Blenheim dispatch.

I have not time to say more but to beg you will give my duty to the Queen and let her know that her Army has had a glorious victory. Monsieur Tallard and two other generals are in my coach and I am following the rest. The bearer, Colonel Parke, will give her an account of what has passed. I shall doe it in a day or two by another more at large.

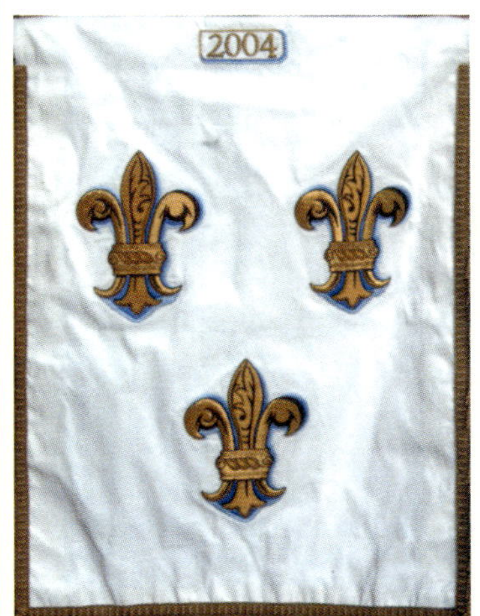

The Blenheim Quit Rent Standard for 2004, the tercentenary of the Battle of Blenheim.

The Blenheim dispatch was hurriedly pencilled by Marlborough (on the back of a bill for provisions) in the evening of 13th August 1704, while he was still on the battlefield of Blenheim. In this short letter he announced his *"glorious victory"* to the Queen who received the news at Windsor Castle eight days later when the letter was brought to her by Colonel Daniel Parke, one of the Duke's aides-de-camp. Great celebrations took place in England and on his return John Churchill was fêted as a national hero. A most generous reward was made by Queen Anne when she gifted the ancient royal manor of Woodstock to the Duke. An Act of Parliament was passed formalising the Queen's grant, where it was also stipulated that every year, on the anniversary of the battle, *"a flag or standard with three fleur de luces"* should be presented to the Sovereign. This token payment of 'rent' is still made when a new Quit Rent Standard is presented to the reigning monarch at Windsor Castle on 13th August every year.

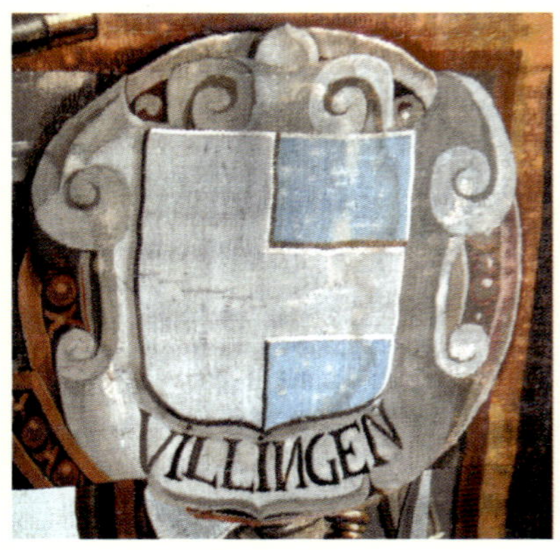

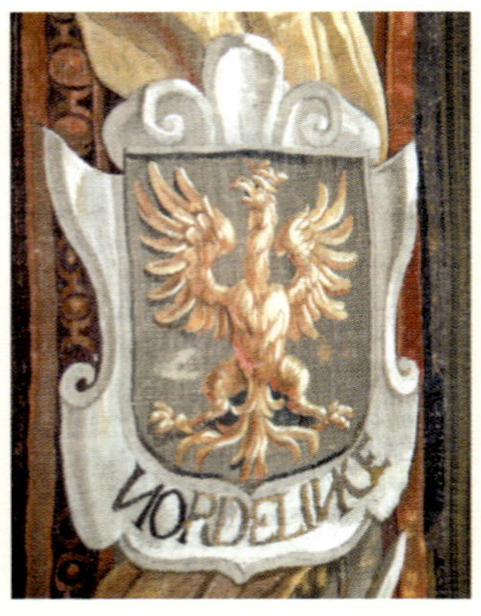

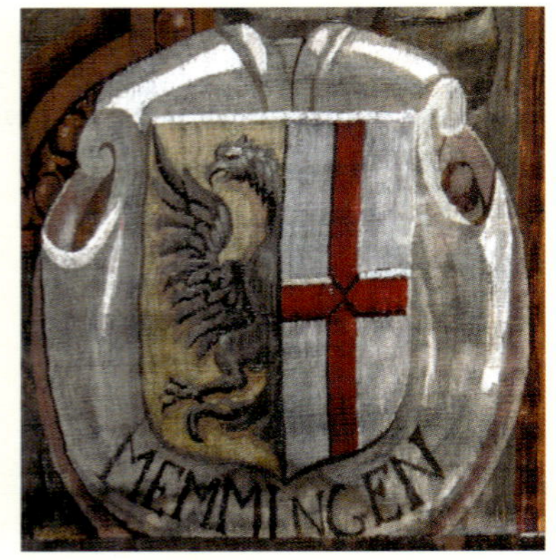

The six medallions in the border of this tapestry, unlike the others in the series, show the coats of arms of towns captured in the course of this campaign. They represent Ulm, Ingolstat, Passau, Villingen, Nordelinke and Memmingen. Had Marlborough and his troops not been so very exhausted, the pursuit of the enemy would have resulted in a greater number of spoils. As it was, the allies were left with two serious problems. First, a field hospital was set up at Nordlingen to tend the large numbers of their own wounded. The other, which they had never encountered before on such a vast scale, was the problem of dealing with the many thousands of captured enemy soldiers, including a whole host of officers, each with a substantial amount of baggage. Prisoners of war were normally exchanged for one's own soldiers of similar rank who had fallen to the enemy.

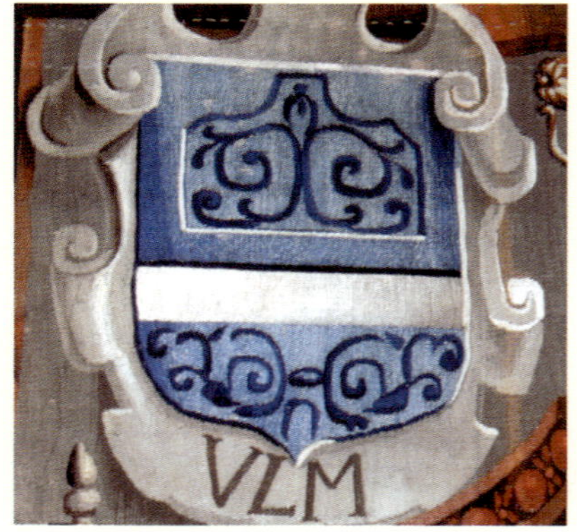

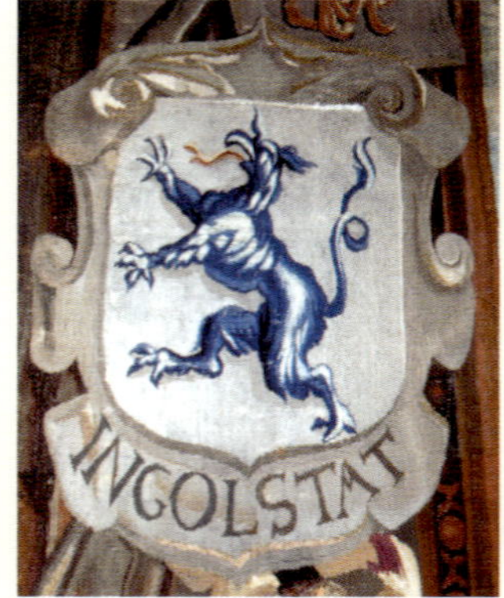

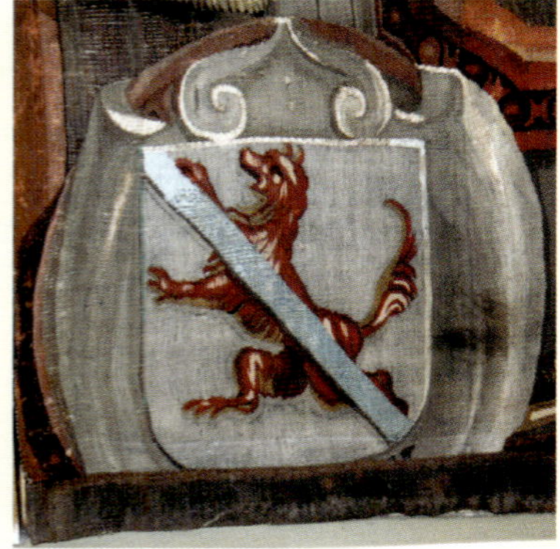

CARTEL to EXCHANGE PRISONERS of WAR
In 14 Days Officers &c of = Rank 1 for 1 or Pay for.

	Livres	L.	s.	d		Livres	L.	s.	d
Mareschal or Comander	50000				Wagon Master Gen.l	150			
Capt. Gen.l	40000				His Lieut.	80			
Gen. & Lt. Gen.l	20000				Comiſsary Gen.l Transports	150			
Great Mr. Ordnance					Lieut.	50			
Mareschal de Camp	4000				Conductors	10			
Colonel {Horse					Judge	25			
General {Dragoons					Capt.s {Guides	80			
Mr. de Camp {Horse	3500				{Lieut.	50			
General {Dragoons					{Cornet	35			
Comiſsary Gen.l Horse	3000				Horse Guides *as* Troopers	20			
Intend.t Armies or Provinc.	5000				Chief Ingineers	500			
Comiſsioners under them	1500				*Months Pay for others*				
Lt. Gen.ls {Ordnance	1000				ORDNANCE				
	1500				Col.o or Partic.r Lieut.	400			
Maj. Gen.l {Horse or Foot	800				Provinc.l Comiſsary }	250			
Brigad.rs }	600				or Lieut. Col.o				
Major Brigad	300				Comiſsary {Ord.ry or Major	150			

Tariffs were set out for the exchange of prisoners of war.

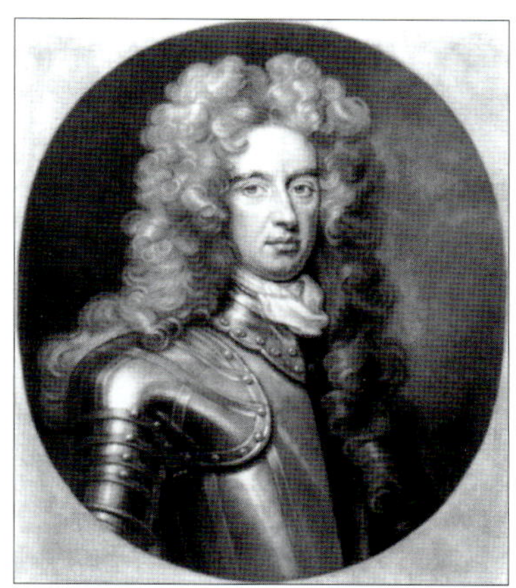

Overkirk.

Marlborough aimed to try and bring the enemy to battle as often as he could. The French had fortified their lines in Brabant along a 70-mile stretch from the sea at Antwerp to the river Meuse at Namur. They considered these lines to be impassable. In 1705, Marlborough conceived an ingenious plan which he carried out with the Dutch Lieutenant Overkirk's assistance. He decided to use Overkirk to make a feint by arranging to build pontoon bridges (a floating bridge which was formed by linking a series of flat bottomed boats) over the river Mehaigne at a weak point in the French defensive lines. When the French Marshal Villeroy received news of this he dispatched large numbers of troops to cover the area he believed to be under threat.

On July 18th 1705 at 4 a.m. having made a 15-mile night march to the north, Marlborough's advance guard was within a mile of the French lines at Orsemall. Overkirk reversed his troops and marched north as well, forming up with the rear of Marlborough's army. Pontoon bridges were quickly laid across the river Gheet and the Allies then breached the French lines in three places along a $3^{1}/_{2}$-mile front close to the village of Elixheim. At dawn, the now lightly manned French posts near Ober Hespen, Wanghe and Elixheim were captured with little resistance and a substantial stretch of the vaunted lines was soon under Allied control.

Marlborough wanted to retain the advantage and take the town of Louvain, 7 miles away, but Overkirk refused any further action and the momentum was lost. This was another example of the numerous occasions when the Dutch lack of initiative hindered Marlborough's ambitions. However, the Duke was a patient and far sighted politician and he favoured long term diplomatic gains over short-term military expediency. The remainder of the campaign season produced no further profitable achievements in the field, so Marlborough, as adept a statesman as he was a general, made an extended tour of all the allied headquarters later that year, thereby reinforcing the Grand Alliance for the next campaign.

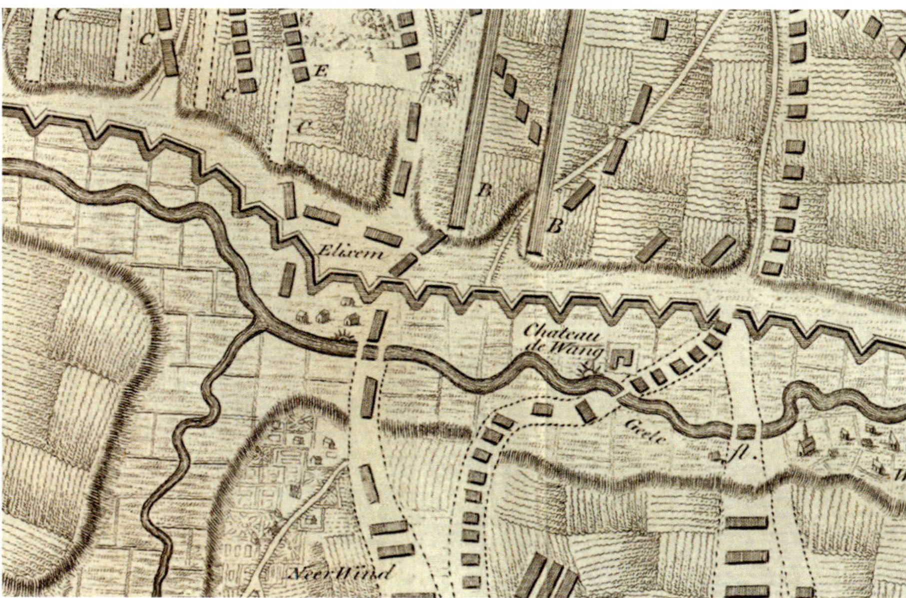

A contemporary plan showing the crossing of the lines of Brabant, near the town of Elixheim and the castle of Wanghe.

LINES OF BRABANT: 18 JULY 1705

14ft 6in. (H) x 12ft 6in. (W) / 4.42m (H) x 3.82 m (W)

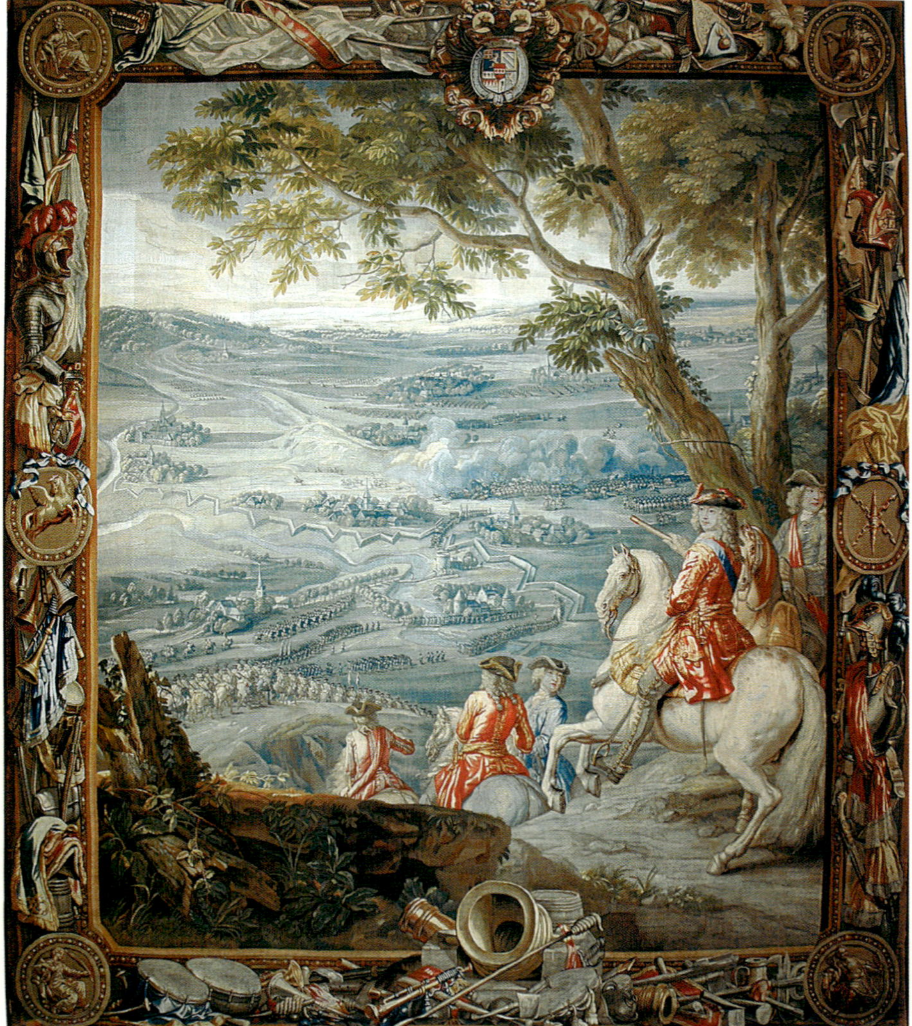

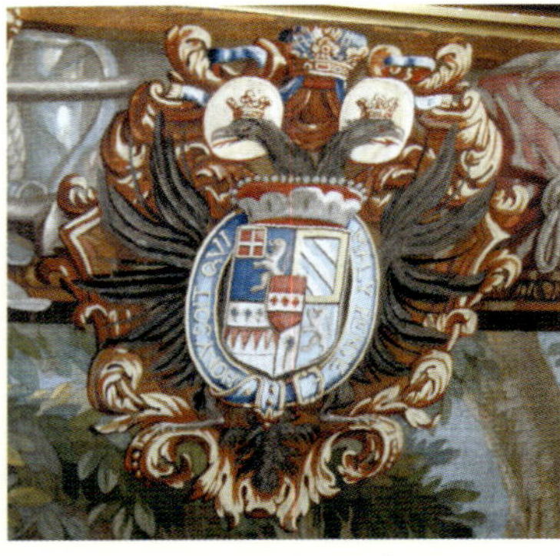

With the action based on a three-pronged attack on enemy lines, this tapestry contains the ducal coat of arms in the central cartouche of the top border rather than a single town's arms.

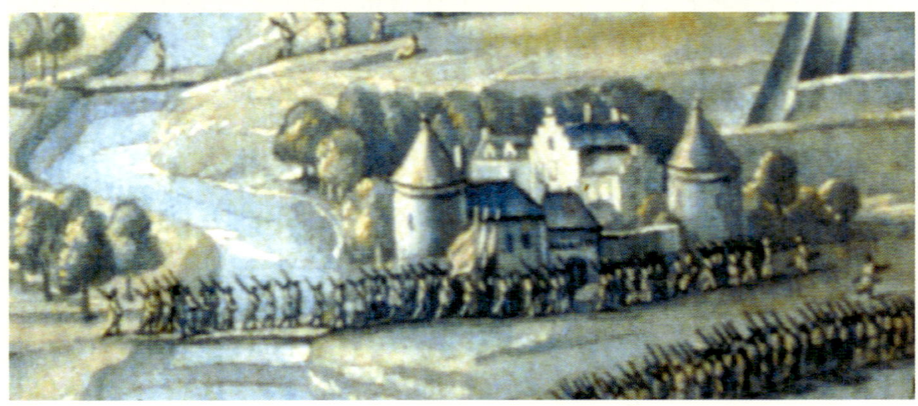

Detail of the Castle of Wanghe near the French fortified lines.

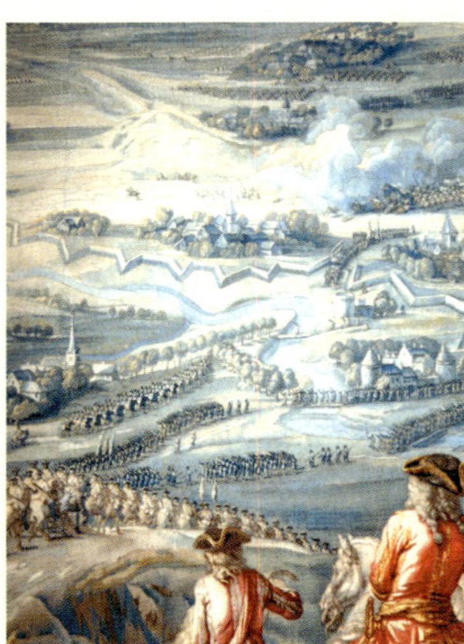

Detail of the allied army crossing the enemy lines.

At the start of the 1706 campaign Marlborough wrote to his trusted friend Sidney Godolphin, *"God knows I go with a heavy heart, for I have no hope of doing anything considerable, unless the French do what I am very confident they will not, namely come out and fight"*. For once, he was wrong. Louis XIV's war machine was seriously in debt: the French campaign of 1705 had been ineffective, his armies had been spread too thinly over too great an area and their morale was at an all time low. Louis now changed tactics and encouraged his generals to act more decisively. Therefore, when Marlborough began to advance on Namur he was surprised to learn that the French Marshal Villeroy was already on the move and so decided to march towards him. Villeroy had received a message from Louis *"Do not expose yourself to a general engagement without need, but do not avoid it with too much precaution"*. He interpreted this fairly ambiguous statement as being an instruction to actively seek battle.

The two armies met and occupied the level ground near the village of Ramillies. At dawn on 23rd May 1706, the French deployed in battle readiness along a stretch of open ground from Taviers on their right to Autre-Eglise on their left. But Villeroy had already committed mistakes which Marlborough would use to his advantage. The French right flank was invisible to their commander as they stood in dead ground. Furthermore, their overall battle line formed a very large concave arc which would naturally slow down any troop movements.

Marlborough's strategy that day, as at Blenheim two years earlier, was to probe the French left and right, to then charge through the centre, breaking up the French line. The strategy worked very well, the allied cavalry was used to great effect and Villeroy's French army was routed in a matter of hours. While the Allied victory was complete, Marlborough narrowly survived an attempt on his life during the battle. His aide-de-camp, Colonel Bringfield,* who was holding the Duke's stirrup while he mounted a fresh horse, took the shot instead.

Unlike Blenheim, where the Allies had been so exhausted that they were unable to pursue the fleeing enemy, at Ramillies the chase extended over 12 miles until failing light and sheer exhaustion finally forced them to call a halt. Several major towns and fortresses capitulated soon afterwards with little or no resistance and by the end of that year's campaign, Marlborough was in an extremely strong position, controlling a substantial part of the Spanish Netherlands. The inscription on the Column of Victory at Blenheim Palace succinctly sums it up: *"Places which had resisted the greatest generals for months, for years, provinces disputed for ages, were the conquests of a summer"*.

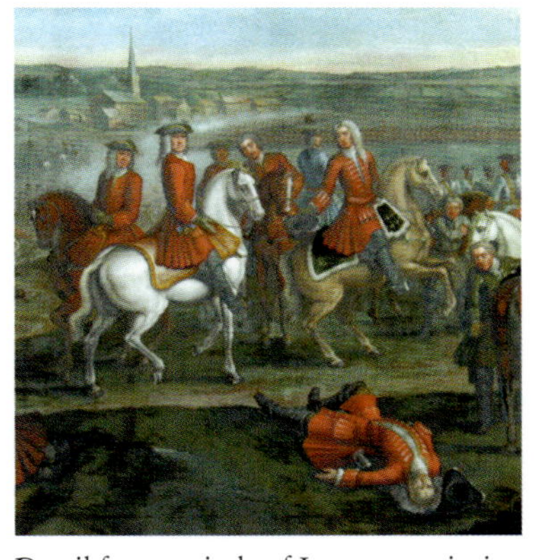

Detail from a circle of Laguerre painting showing Colonel Bringfield lying dead.

* James Bringfield, equerry to Prince George of Denmark was Major of Horse during the War of the Spanish Succession. When he was killed at Ramillies, Marlborough wrote the day after the battle *"Poor Bringfield is killed, and I am told he leaves his wife and mother in a bad condition"*. Sarah paid a visit to Bringfield's widow on 28th May 1706 and arranged for her to receive a pension of £100 per annum for the rest of her life.

RAMILLIES: 23 MAY 1706

(from archival records) 14ft 6in. (H) x 20ft 4in. (W)/4.42m (H) x 6.20m (W)

Tradition has it that the Ramillies tapestry was never woven. However documentary evidence has proven this to be untrue. Ramillies counted as one of the greatest of Marlborough's victories and it would have been inconceivable for it not to have been commemorated. The problem is that the panel no longer exists at Blenheim Palace and there seems to be neither an easy or logical explanation nor a corroborated reason as to why this should be the case: this tapestry is the only one missing from the set today. The last specific reference to it actually being hung at Blenheim Palace is made by Stuart J. Reid in his 1914 publication, *John and Sarah, Duke and Duchess of Marlborough 1660-1744*.[137]

Nevertheless, we know that it was commissioned in the first batch of six panels of the *Victories* series. Sized at 20ft 4in. in width, it was not quite as large as the tapestry depicting the Battle of Blenheim (25ft 3in.) although from documentary evidence it is known that like the Blenheim panel it probably had a highly decorated border with coats of arms of the various towns taken by the Duke immediately after the battle, which may have included Ghent, Antwerp, Ostend, Menin, Dendermonde, Louvain or Ath.

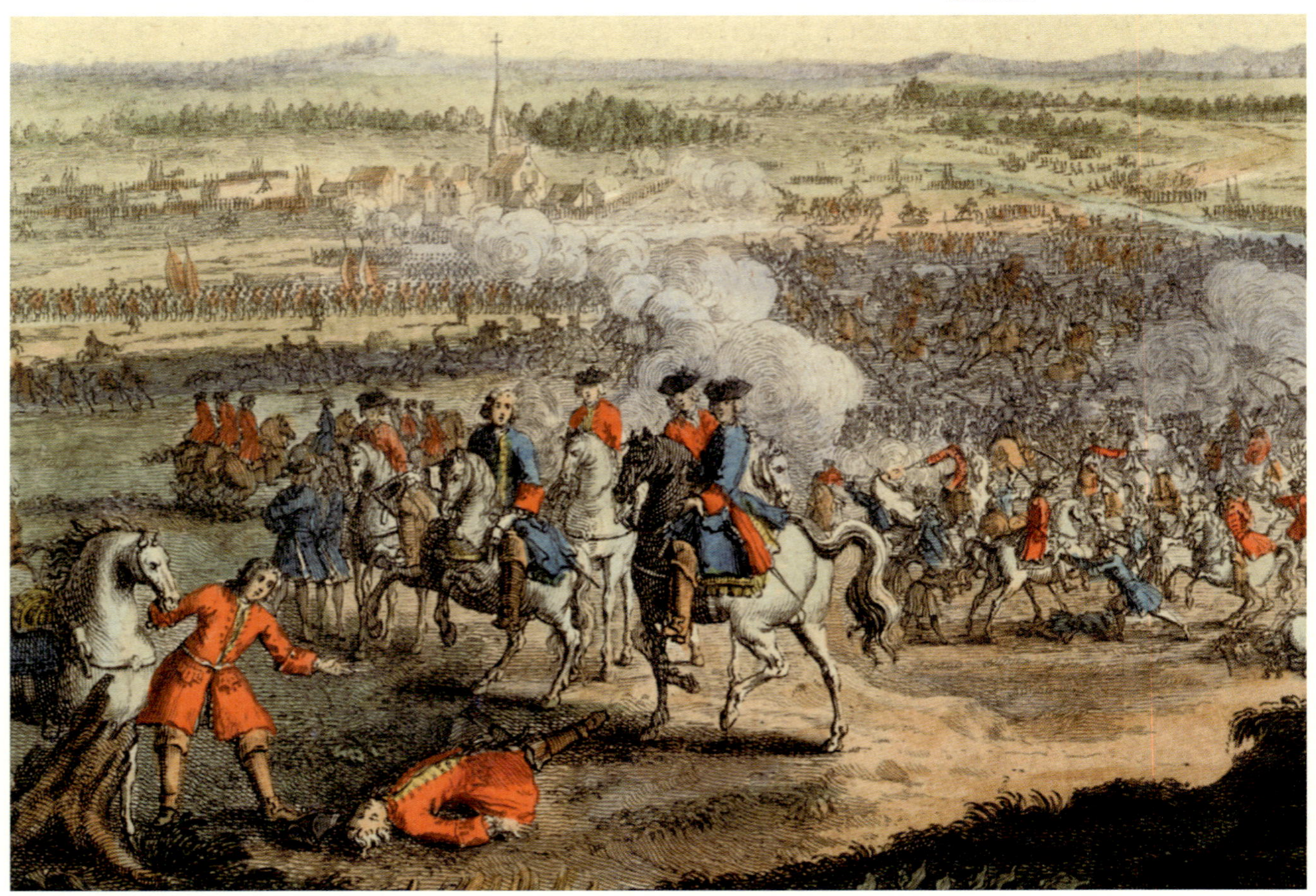

A contemporary print of the Battle of Ramillies.

The pictorial content of the main work is however, unknown as no sketches survive. In his book, *The Marlborough Tapestries at Blenheim Palace* Alan Wace has suggested that if the panel existed it may have been based on a design in the drawings collection of the Kunstindustrimuseet in Oslo.[138] This seems unlikely as the stylistic handling of that image is too disparate from the others in the series, which are consistent in their portrayal of the Duke and his officers within the action.

However, it is a tantalising possibility that one of the panels from the 'second version' *Art of War* series designed by Philippe de Hondt and woven by Judocus de Vos (which are stylistically related to the *Victories*), may have been based on the cartoon made for the *Ramillies* tapestry. The panel in question is entitled *The March*. In this tapestry the near flat landscape of the

La Marche, from the 'second version' *Art of War* tapestry series, designed by Philippe de Hondt.

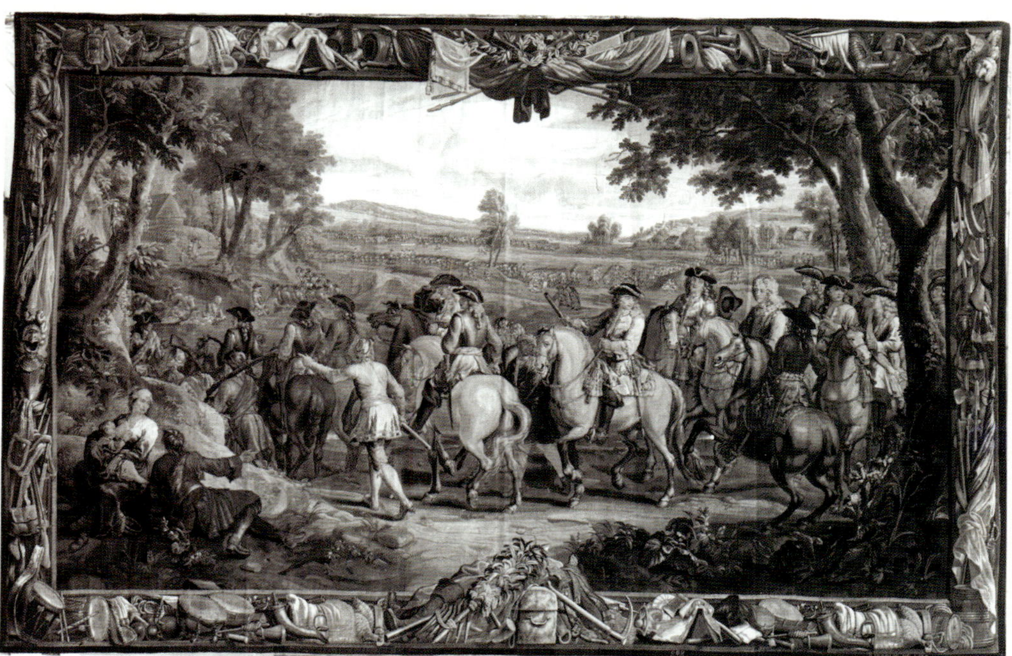

Ramillies battlefield is accurately rendered along with certain other details, such as the Duke's 'runner' and his coloured page. Although the page does not figure in any other of the *Victories* tapestries, he is clearly visible in the murals at Marlborough House in London.

Several walls at Marlborough House are spectacularly painted with images of the Duke's battles. The principal staircase, which is now called the Ramillies staircase, portrays the events of that historic day in quite graphic splendour. In fact, it is ironic that the Duchess not only chose Louis Laguerre, a godson of King Louis XIV to decorate her residence[139] but also that the substance of the decoration bursts with blood-spattered detail, whereas the Duke's tapestries at Blenheim portray his battles virtually sanitised and almost devoid of any gory imagery whatever, although it is well recorded that wars in this period (as in many others) were really a harsh lesson in horror.

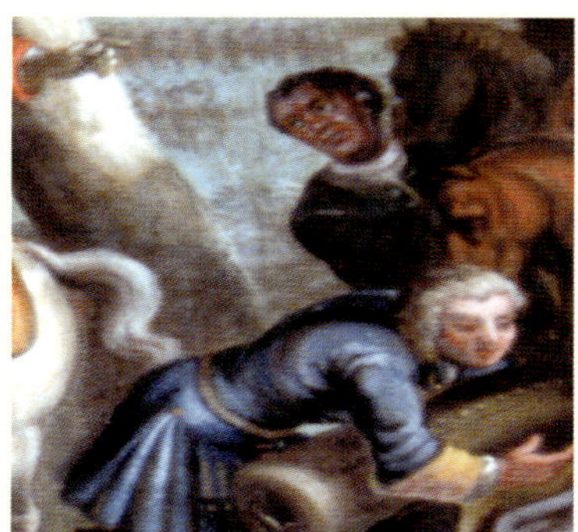

Detail of the Duke's coloured page, from a painting of the Battle of Ramillies after Louis Laguerre.

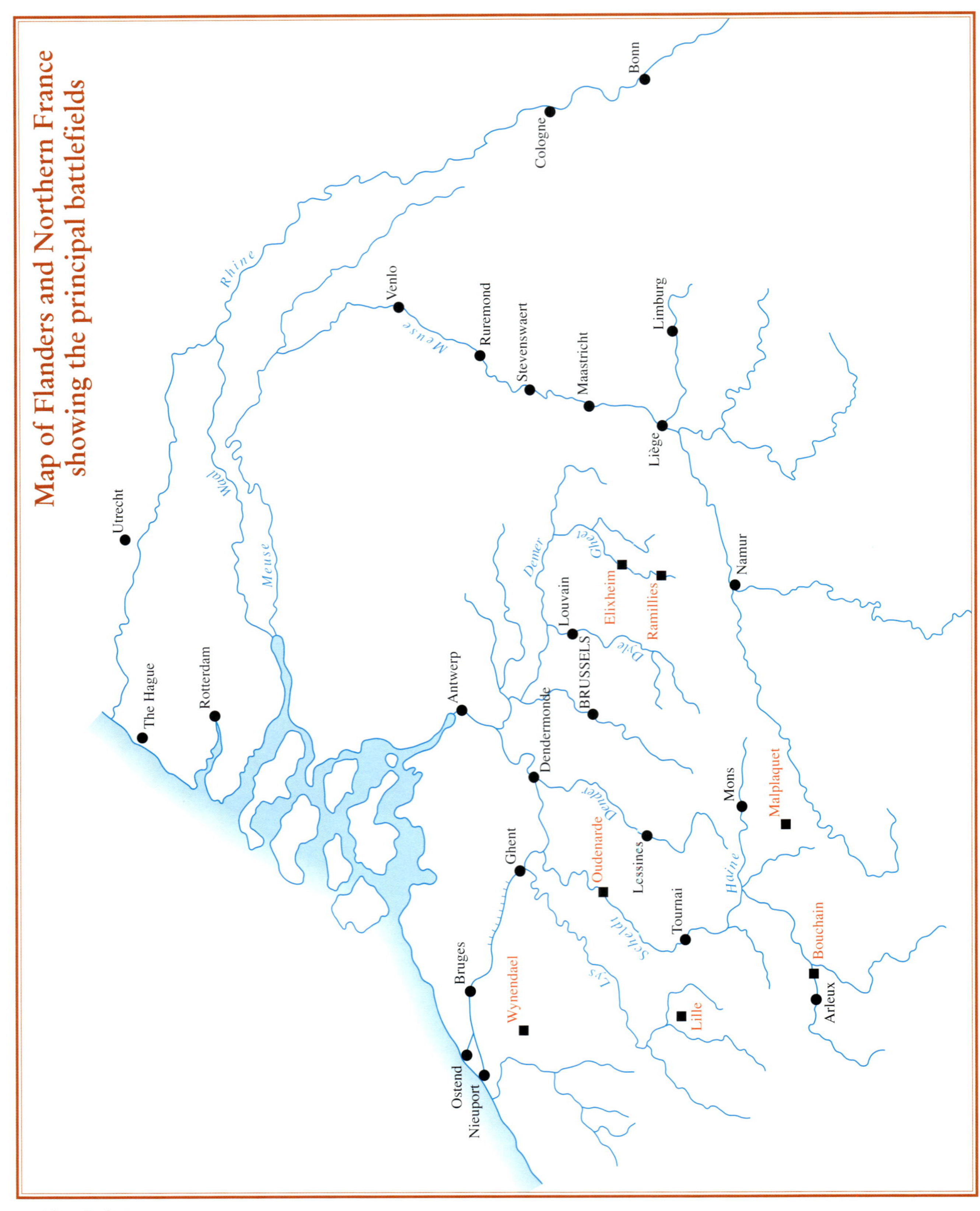

Map of Flanders and Northern France showing the principal battlefields
Bonn
Cologne
Utrecht
Rhine
Venlo
Ruremond
Stevenswaert
Maastricht
Limburg
Meuse
Waal
Meuse
The Hague
Rotterdam
Liège
Namur
Antwerp
Demer
Gheet
Louvain
Elixheim
Ramillies
Dyle
BRUSSELS
Dendermonde
Mons
Malplaquet
Ghent
Dender
Oudenarde
Lessines
Hayne
Tournai
Scheldt
Bouchain
Bruges
Wynendael
Lys
Lille
Arleux
Ostend
Nieuport

After the great successes of 1706, 1707 proved to be one of the most frustrating years of the entire war for Marlborough, being as it was almost totally devoid of any conclusive action. After starting the campaign season on further diplomatic missions, a particularly wet summer put paid to any reasonable chance of engaging the French in a head-on battle. Both armies manoeuvred, marched and camped for prolonged periods of time before retiring into winter quarters by October.

In 1708 the French surprised the Allies by taking Bruges and Ghent early in the campaign and then moved to Lessines with the intention of taking Oudenarde in order to improve their lines of communication. Marlborough, not one to let an opportunity pass, lost no time in force-marching his army to Lessines. This near 50-mile march was accomplished within two days and was a real feat of endurance, without precedent, which prompted the French Marshal Vendome to remark *"If they are there, the devil must have carried them. Such marching is impossible"*. The Allied advance guard under General Cadogan secured the passage of the River Scheldt at Oudenarde and by 2 p.m. on 11th July 1708, Allied troops poured across the river.

The French command that day was jointly held by Marshal Vendome and the Duke of Burgundy[140] but each of them wanted to carry out a different plan, Vendome wanting to attack the Allies as they crossed, Burgundy wanting to occupy the higher ground to the north. Vendome sent a part of his army forward, but they were repulsed by the Allies. The French then ordered a general advance but they had crucially lost valuable time while they had been numerically superior and had carelessly allowed the main body of the Allied army through. The conflict that day was a bold and daring action on Marlborough's part, and displayed the high morale and physical condition of his troops, who after a long and physically demanding march, went straight into battle.

By 6 p.m. the French were being driven back on their left but held the rest of their front. The climacteric moment of the battle was reached when Marlborough decided to take a hill called the Boser Couter which dominated the whole of the French right flank. Overkirk and his Dutch troops occupied the hill without opposition and then launched their attack into the French flank. The French were thus surprised and routed. By 9 p.m. panic had set in and they were in full retreat, only darkness saving them from complete disaster when a cease fire was called by Marlborough, concerned that the Allied troops encircling the French would end up killing their own men.

The next day the French were pursued towards Ghent. French lines between Ypres and the River Lys were also destroyed. Vendome retreated behind the Bruges-Ghent canal, leaving the way to the French capital open. While Marlborough considered it viable, the Dutch deputies and Prince Eugene opposed this scheme. They considered that Lille, the capital of French Flanders should be taken first.

OUDENARDE: 11 JULY 1708

14ft 6in. (H) x 13ft 3in. (W) / 4.42m (H) x 4.04m (W)

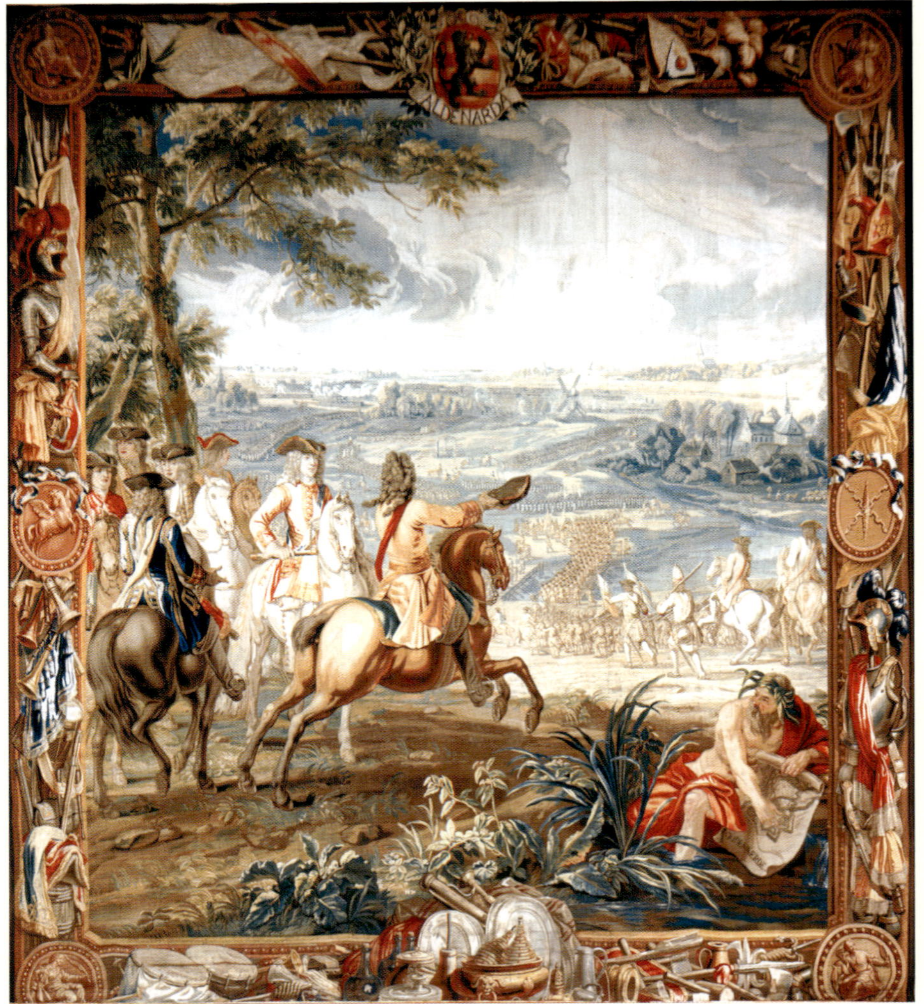

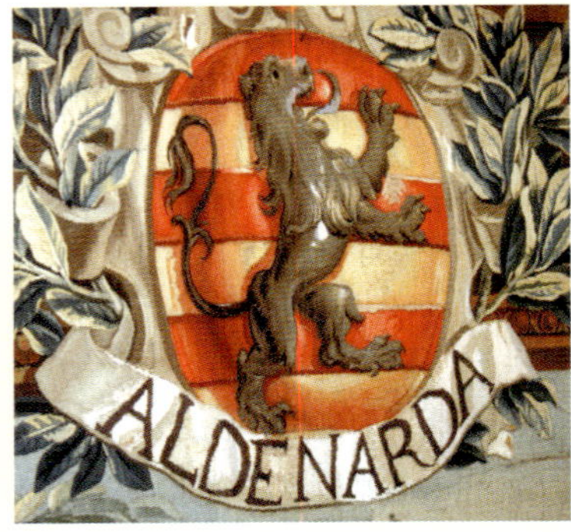

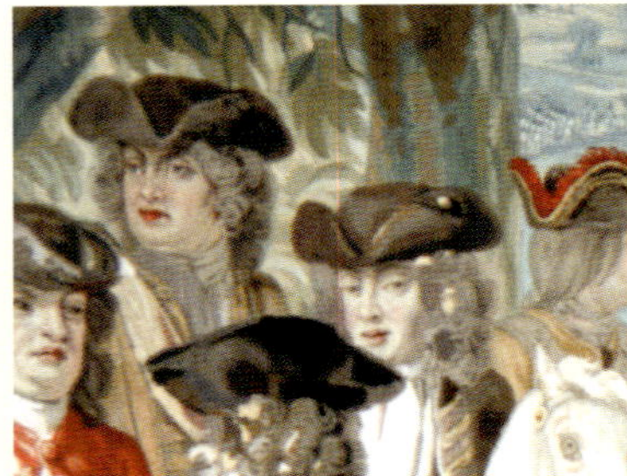

Detail of Cadogan and Armstrong.

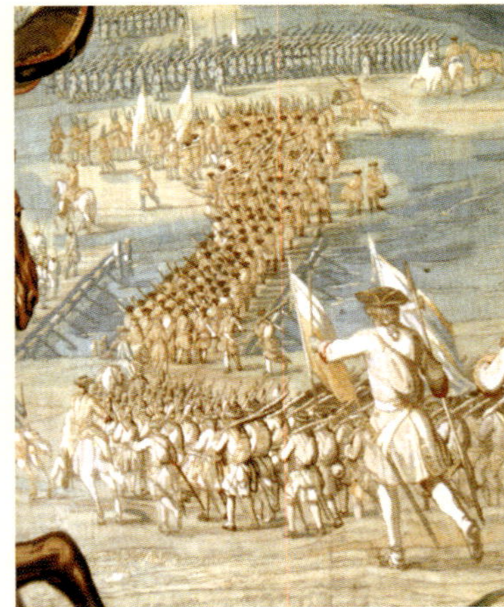

Detail of troops crossing pontoon bridges.

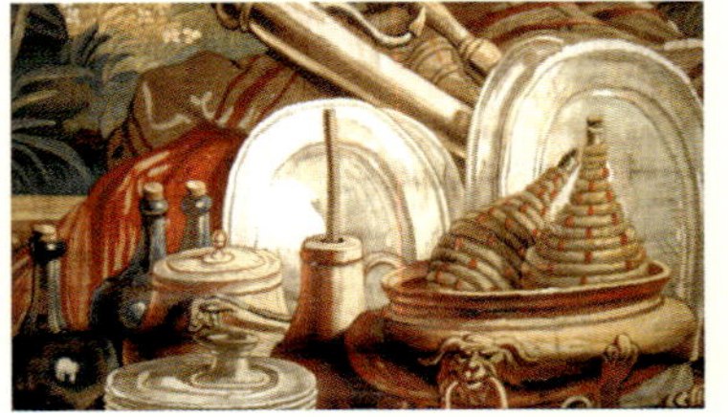

Detail of lower border.

The landscape is very well rendered and may have been drawn from local knowledge. The army is shown going over pontoon bridges on the river Scheldt forming into their battle lines as they march across. On the right of the panel is the farm at Diepenbeeke, a hamlet south of the open plain stretching to Oudenarde. William Cadogan (Quartermaster General) and John Armstrong (Chief Engineer) are visible amongst the officers alongside the Duke. The inclusion of a symbolic mythological river god in the bottom right corner of the tapestry follows a Netherlandish tradition showing the importance of the river in the action and the greatness of Marlborough's achievement. The central portion of the lower border shows plate captured from the French Marshal Vendome in the action.

After the success at Oudenarde in July 1708, Marlborough and Prince Eugene made a quick tactical decision in early August to attack Lille in an attempt to open up the road to Paris itself. Lille was a strongly fortified place, an important road centre and army magazine, on the banks of the River Deule. This stronghold in northern France had a fortress designed by Vauban, the greatest French engineer of his day.

The decision astonished the French as they expected the Allies to take the towns of Tournai or Mons rather than converge on Lille where large numbers of French troops were already encamped in fairly close proximity. Marlborough with the main army accompanied the 'Great Convoy' on its last stages to Lille. This convoy or siege train, with 3,000 wagons and 100 cannon, along with ammunition, provisions and other baggage, extended 15 miles along the road. It had left Brussels in July under the command of William Cadogan, the Duke's Quartermaster General, taking 7 days to travel a distance of 75 miles to Menin. Each of the heavy guns (there were 80 of them) was drawn by 20 horses, and the mortars by 16 horses apiece. Nine thousand men were deployed in the protection of the convoy under a strict rota system so that it was never left open to French raids as Cadogan had instructions to ensure that there was no risk to the cannon, a vital element of any siege operation.

By the evening of 11th August 1708, the investment of the town (cutting off lines of communication and supply) was complete. Within the fortifications, Marshal Bouffleurs commanded the French army and he ordered all the buildings near the outer fortifications be burnt down to improve the French field of fire and observation. Marlborough and Eugene decided to split their forces, Prince Eugene taking charge of the siege operations with a small army of men and Marlborough commanding the larger covering force, which would hopefully intercept and head off any external attack on the besieging army.

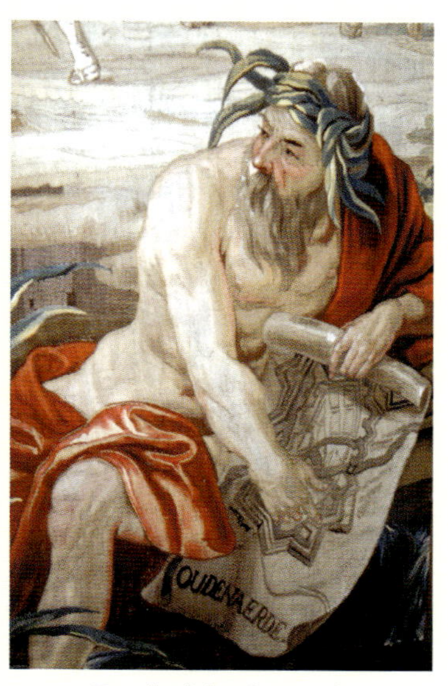

Detail of the river god.

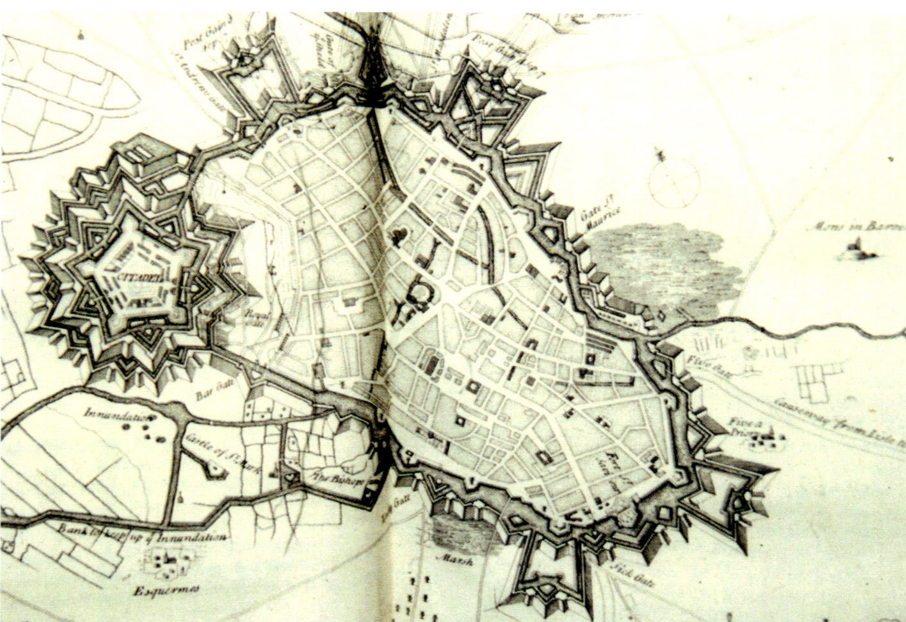

Contemporary plan of the fortified town of Lille with the citadel.

The Allied troops secured their lines and the French inside Lille were now totally isolated. Marlborough and Eugene decided to bombard the town from the north and once the 'Great Convoy' under Cadogan arrived on the 17th of August, all the siege guns and mortars were put into action. Unfortunately, Eugene's engineers miscalculated the operational range of their guns and sited them too far back to have the immediate impact Marlborough required. Encouraged by the ineffective allied attack, Boufflers led a sortie out into enemy lines but was unsuccessful.

By early September, the French under Marshal Vendome and the Duke of Burgundy moved to confront Marlborough and his covering force near Ennetieres. Despite having greater numbers of men in the field and direct instructions from Versailles to attack, the French generals hesitated, perhaps on account of Marlborough's awesome reputation and his string of recent victories. Their delay was long enough to permit Marlborough to draw on reserves from Eugene's besieging army and to successfully head off the French external forces. Boufflers, within Lille, also acting on instructions from Versailles, attacked the allied entrenchments once Eugene's reserves had been drawn off, but this second sortie also proved to be a failure.

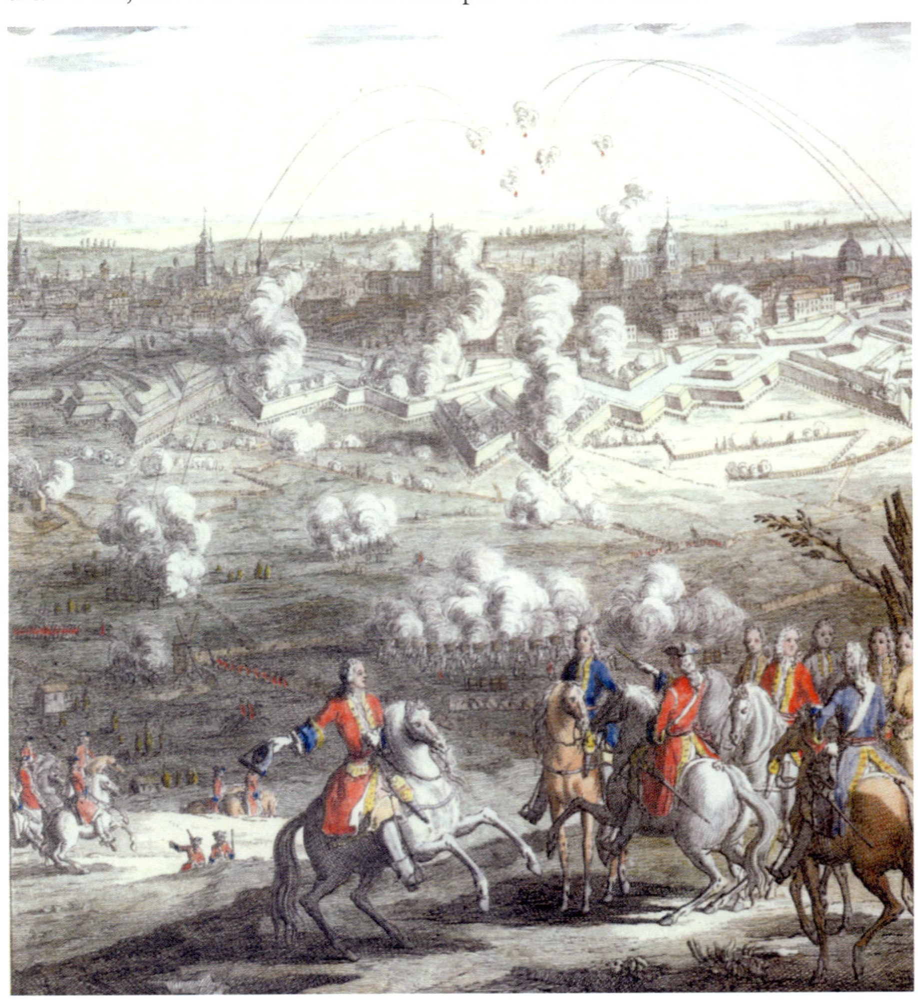

Engraving of the siege of Lille, by Claude du Bosc.

The French now changed tactics. Rather than confront Marlborough again, they decided to intercept the allied lines of communication and seized several crossings along the River Scheldt. Marlborough frustrated the French by opening Ostend as a sea-borne supply depot, from where convoys of wagons transported the stores required by the allied armies at Lille. The French tried to sever this new supply route as well. On 27th September, a crucial convoy of 700 wagons loaded with munitions and other supplies started out from Ostend to join Marlborough's army. The next day, Vendome sent out a French army of 22,000 men from Bruges under General de la Motte to intercept this convoy which was accompanied by an allied force of just 7,000 men under General Webb.

At Wynendael, on 28th September 1708, General Webb took up a position on a narrow front with both flanks resting on woods in which two battalions of his men were hidden. When the French attacked, they could not profit from their superior numbers due to the limited frontage and the fact that they were being fired on simultaneously from the flank as well as from the front. Having been defeated once again, the French retreated with a loss of 4,000 casualties and all their artillery. The convoy proceeded safely, with its load unharmed, to its destination at Lille.

By the end of September Prince Eugene's forces captured the outworks. In October, to prevent a second convoy of supplies reaching the allies, Vendome decided to open the dykes between Bruges and Nieuport and flood the country around Ostend and Oudenburg. Marlborough, the master of flexibility in action, got around this new obstacle by providing for his supplies to be taken out in flat bottomed boats to Leffinghen and then out of the flooded area in specially commissioned carts (referred to as 'Marlbrouks') made with very high wheels, carrying lighter loads, and so a further convoy of 900 wagons with 1700 barrels of gunpowder reached the besieging army.

On 21st October Prince Eugene made a final attack on Lille after which a *parley* was held on the 24th when it was agreed that the French would surrender the town of Lille and in return be allowed to remove their remaining soldiers into the citadel of Lille and their injured to Douai.

After having allowed him the surrender of the town, the French now tried to draw Marlborough away from Lille by launching an attack on Brussels. Instead of marching to Brussels and responding predictably as the French had hoped, Marlborough once again surprised them by counter attacking five of their positions along the River Scheldt in a synchronised dawn raid on 26th November, taking 1,000 prisoners and all their baggage. Two weeks later, on 9th December, the French surrendered the citadel of Lille and Eugene now joined Marlborough in order to recapture Ghent and Bruges before the army was sent off, much later than usual, to winter quarters.

WYNENDAEL: 28 SEPTEMBER 1708

14ft 6in. (H) x 13ft 6in. (W) / 4.42m (H) x 4.11 m (W)

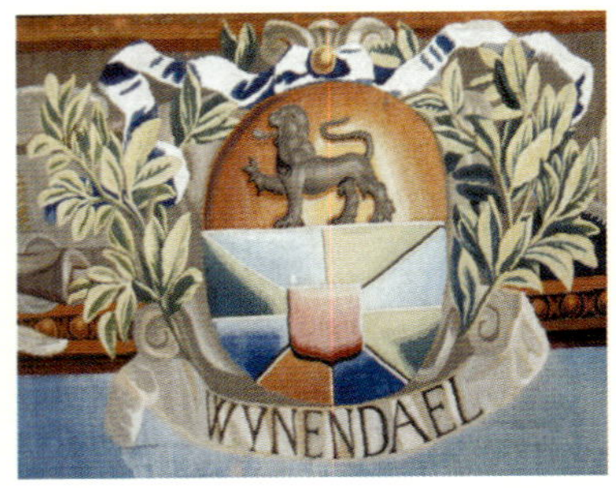

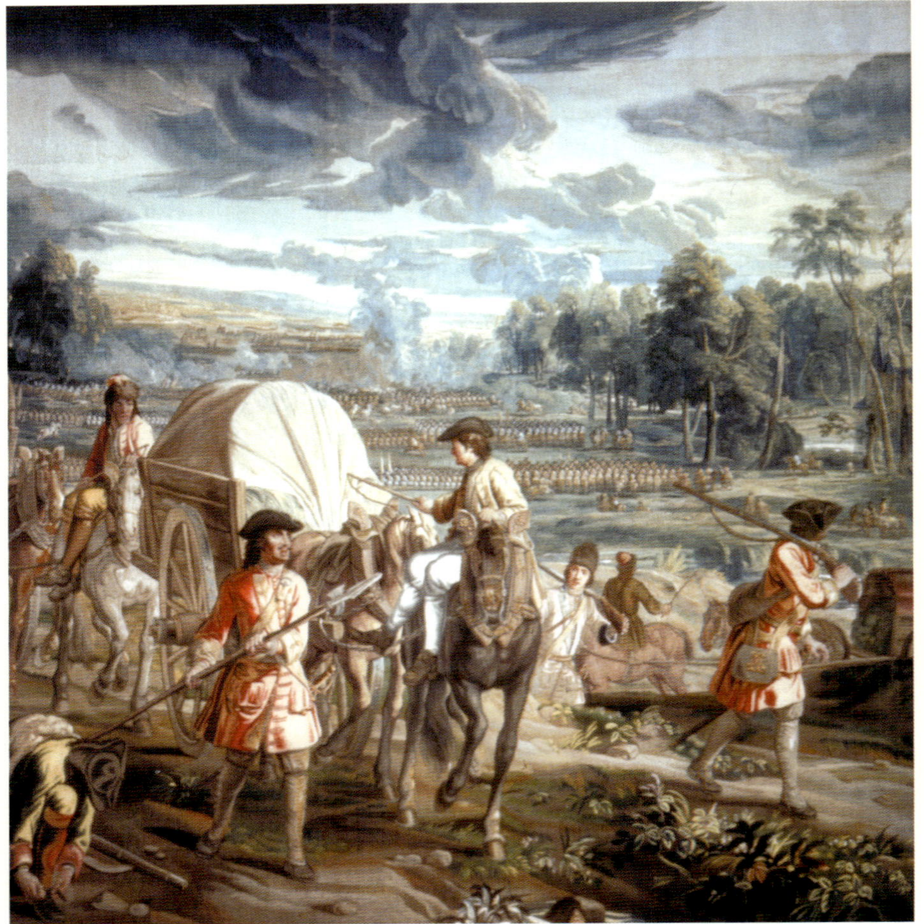

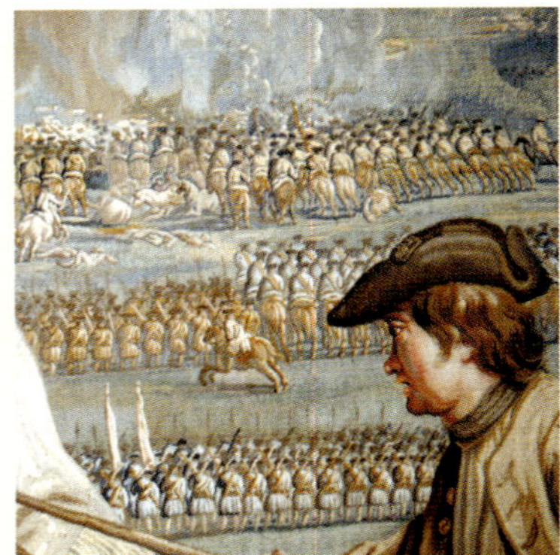

Detail of troops in action.

This tapestry centres around a convoy of supplies which is on its way to the Allied armies besieging Lille. This is the only tapestry in the series in which Marlborough and his generals do not figure at all. Ordinary soldiers are the focus of attention but they are treated as a social group rather than as individuals.

Notice the rough, primitive road. The action visible in the background of the tapestry shows General Webb's forces ambushing the French. In the rear, Cadogan's supporting cavalry arrives which prompts the French to surrender very rapidly. Webb retired after this campaign as he felt credit had wrongly been given to Cadogan who arrived with the cavalry after Webb's infantry had already saved the day.

The forest and chateau of Wynendael are portrayed on the extreme right of the panel.

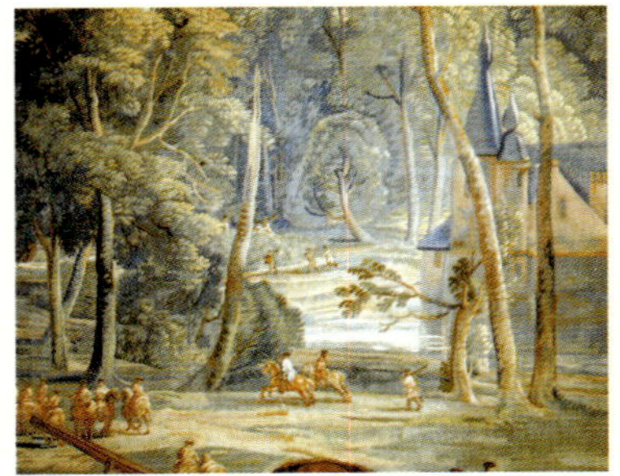

Detail of the chateau of Wynendael.

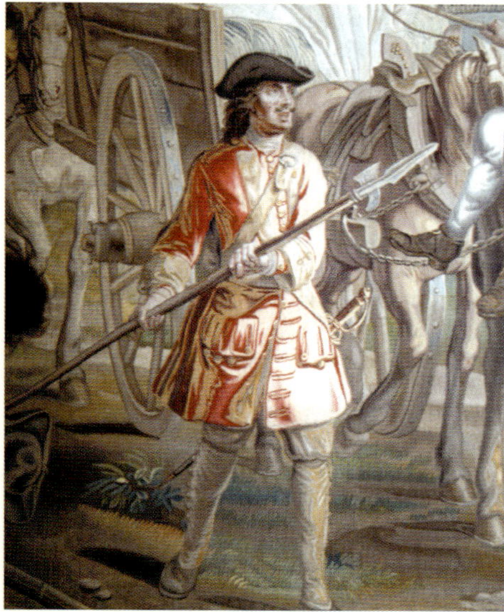

Sergeant with spontoon.

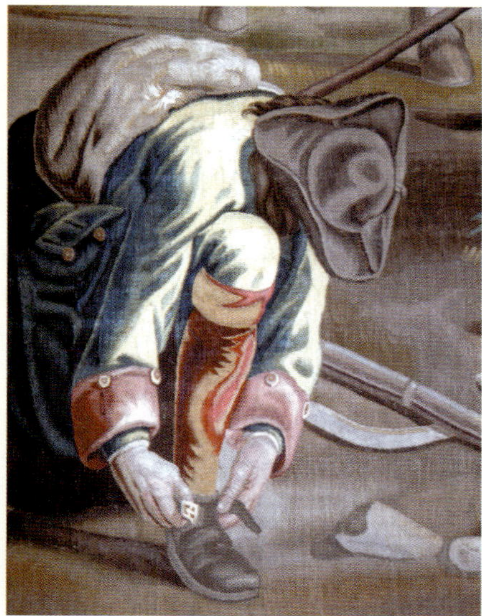

Soldier tying his shoes.

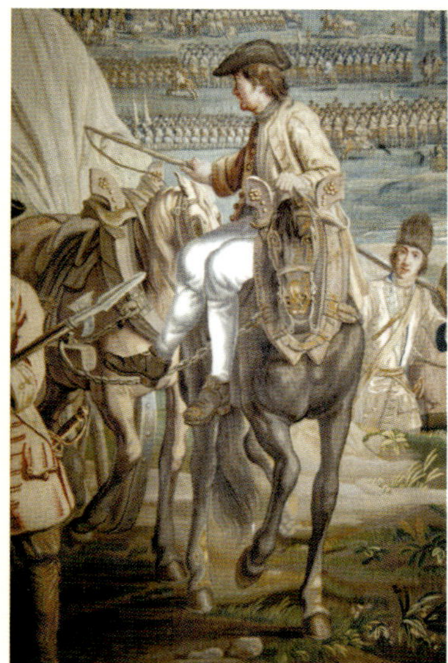

Horses harnessed one behind the other.

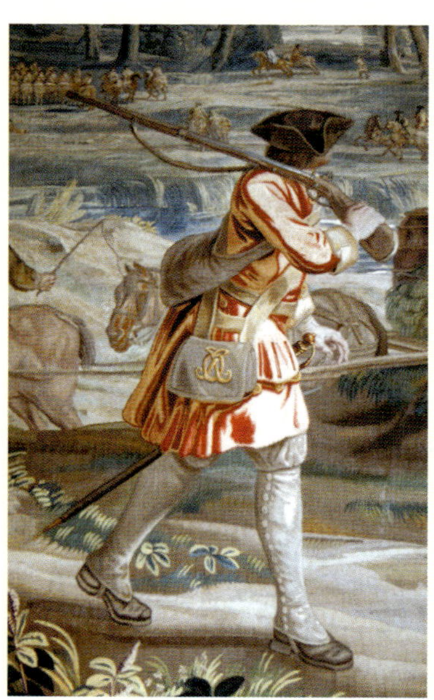

An ordinary foot soldier.

In the foreground of the tapestry is a series of carts with very large wheels. These carts were called 'Marlbrouks'. The Duke was credited with their invention and they were alleged to have been specially designed with large wheels for travel through flooded areas. They were usually drawn by two horses not harnessed in tandem but one behind the other.

The Sergeant is carrying a spontoon. In earlier times this was called a half pike. It was not used as a fighting weapon but only to control the line of fire when muskets were discharged.

The soldier tying his shoe is perhaps a reference to Marlborough's concern for his army. He kept them well fed and regularly supplied with new shoes and blankets.

The ordinary soldier carried a weight of almost 50lbs which consisted of a flintlock over his shoulder, a cartridge pouch with 60 musket balls, a 'snapsack' containing a spare shirt, his rations and sometimes also his cooking pots. His uniform consisted of a shirt, coat and waistcoat, breeches and gaiters (or 'spatterdashes') to keep the mud off the breeches. Old coats were cut up and made into the next year's waistcoat. When marching, coats were worn inside out so that the colours would not fade and the clean side could be presented when soldiers were asked to turn out. Uniform had only just begun to be adopted in armies and the red coat was worn by English, Hanoverian, Saxon and some Danish troops. The Bavarians wore sky blue, the Swedes and Prussians dark blue. Some Austrian, Danish and Dutch troops wore shades of grey to white which was basically undyed woollen cloth. The similarity of uniform styles and colours made it difficult to distinguish not only the enemy, but also between the various troops within a large multi-national Allied force. This is why cockades or field symbols were also sometimes worn in hats.

THE SURRENDER OF LILLE: 9 DECEMBER 1708

14ft 6in. (H) x 12ft 4in. (W) / 4.42m (H) x 3.76m (W)

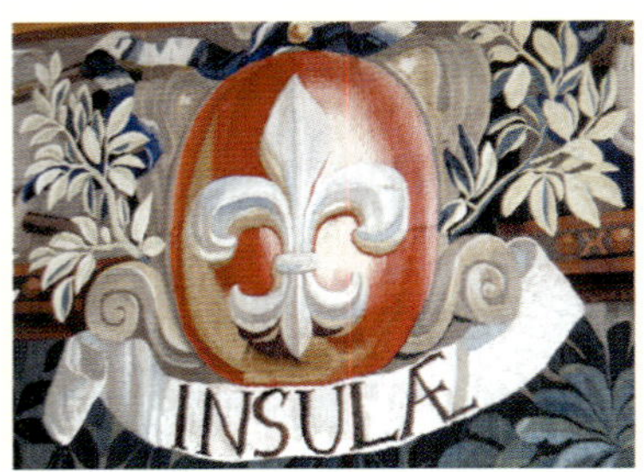

The cartouche in the top border describes this panel as *Insulae* which is the Latin word for island and the French equivalent is l'ile. More than just a clever play on words, L'ile was actually the name the town was known by from the 11th century onwards until the standardisation of its modern spelling.

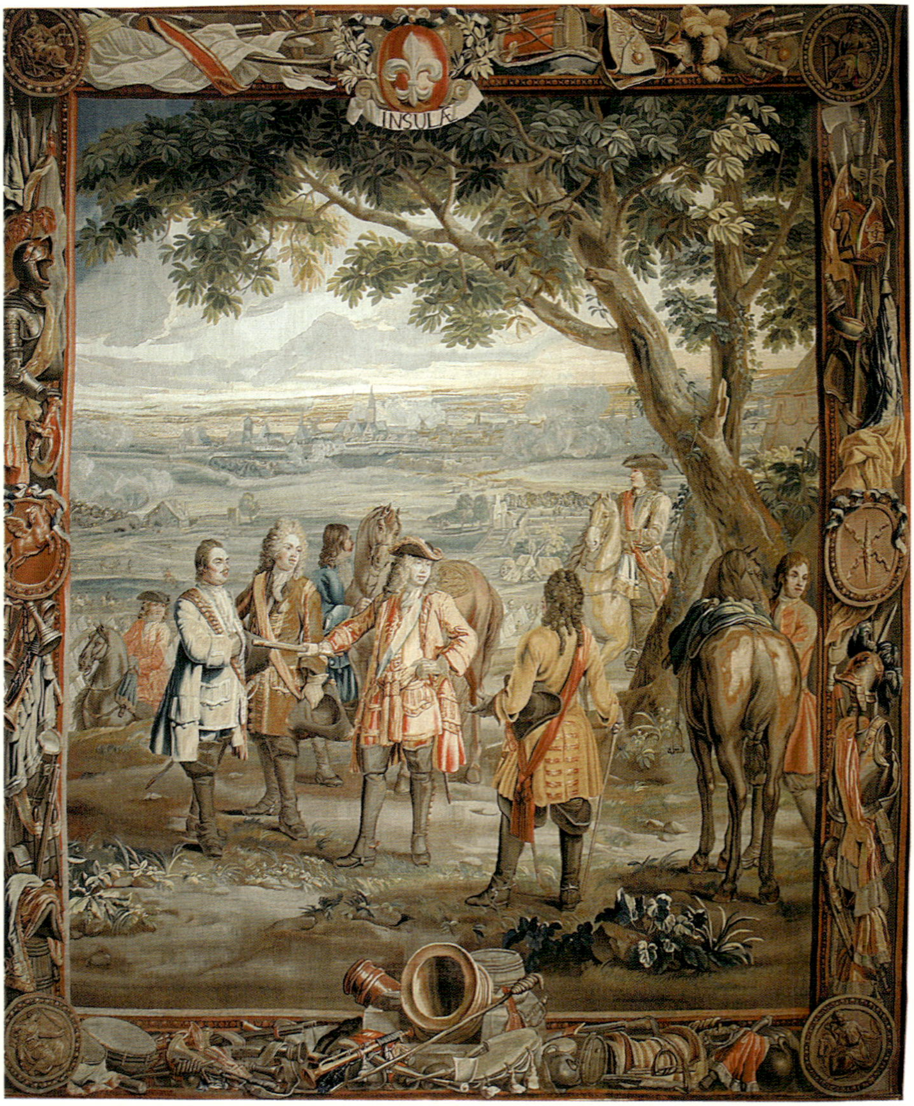

The Lille tapestry shows the town in the distance with Marlborough in discussions with two men in the foreground. This is the only tapestry where the Duke is shown standing rather than on horseback although the two horses being held by staff suggests that two of the four men in the group have only just ridden up to the meeting. The town is drawn without any clearly marked features. Only the enceinte or outer defences are discernible, but it is likely that this is a view of Lille from the north-east from where the citadel would not be seen. The men are apparently near an Allied camp and soldier's ridge tents along with a general's field tent are clearly visible.

It has been suggested that Prince Eugene of Savoy who commanded the siege operations may be the man with his back to us. This is unlikely, because in several contemporary images where Eugene is represented, (including two other *Victories* tapestries and in the Marlborough House murals), he is shown with a metal breast and back plate typically worn by the Imperialists and not in the ordinary uniform worn by this officer. Moreover, Eugene being of equal if not higher social rank would not have needed to remove his hat in Marlborough's presence. Furthermore, the surrender of the citadel of Lille, (a masterpiece of military architecture designed by Vauban in the shape of a regular pentagon and built on Louis XIV's instructions in 1667), was Eugene's achievement and this feature is noticeable by its absence since it would not have specifically glorified Marlborough in this action.

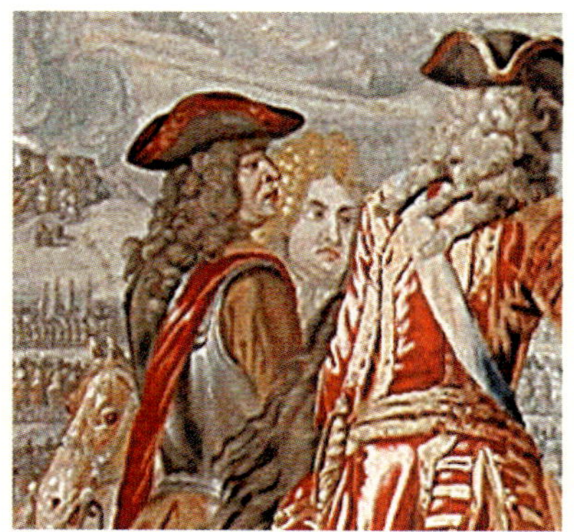
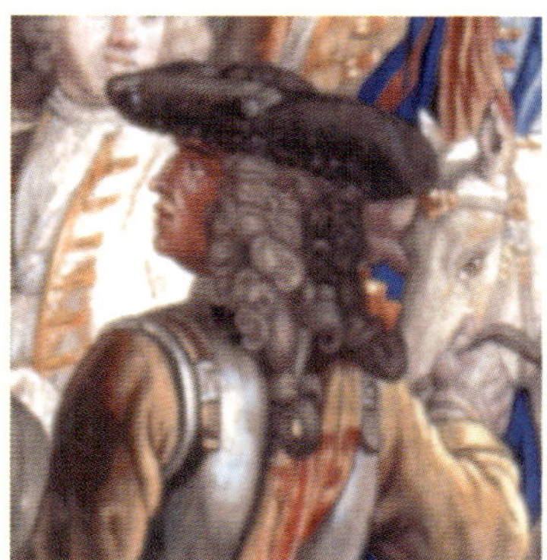

Detail of Prince Eugene from the *Malplaquet* tapestry on the left and from the *Blenheim* tapestry on the right.

It is therefore more likely that the tapestry shows the famous *parley* between Marlborough and the French Marshal Bouffleurs which took place on 24th October 1708, and Marlborough is instructing one of his officers of the terms of surrender that have been agreed.

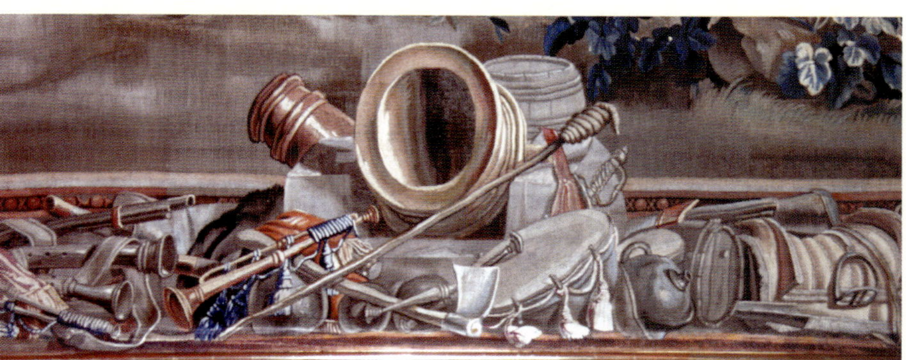

The lower border incorporates cannon and mortar, the use of which were vital to this operation.

In 1709 the Allies took Tournai and advanced to besiege and capture Mons, which was the last French stronghold on the road to Paris. On 6th September 1709 the two armies approached each other in a largely forested area south of Mons. The allies seized the passage of Jemmappes on 7th September but were confronted by Marshal Villars at Malplaquet, impeding their investment of Mons. Marlborough wanted to attack the French there the very next day but was prevented from doing so by Prince Eugene who believed that Villars would move away and not stop to fight. The Dutch too supported Eugene's view and opted to wait for the last detachments of their armies and artillery to arrive from Tournai.

Malplaquet was to be Marlborough's last pitched battle. The French had begun to recognise and anticipate his tactics and at Malplaquet they were well prepared. Villars, arguably the most able of all the French commanders, had reinforced his position by gaining control of two gaps between the woods of Taisniers, Lasniers and Sart and had strongly entrenched his army in three lines in front of the village of Malplaquet. He further used the time afforded him by the Allied delay to conceal his flank in the woods, digging trenches, covering them with *abattis* (sharpened stakes) and tree trunks roped together, and also masking a battery of guns, thereby deliberately reinforcing

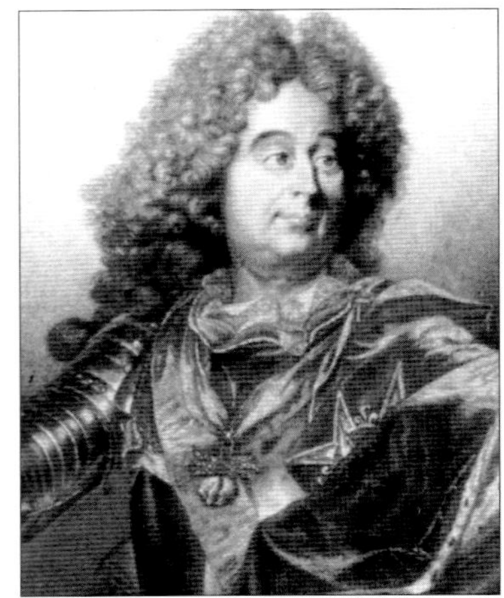

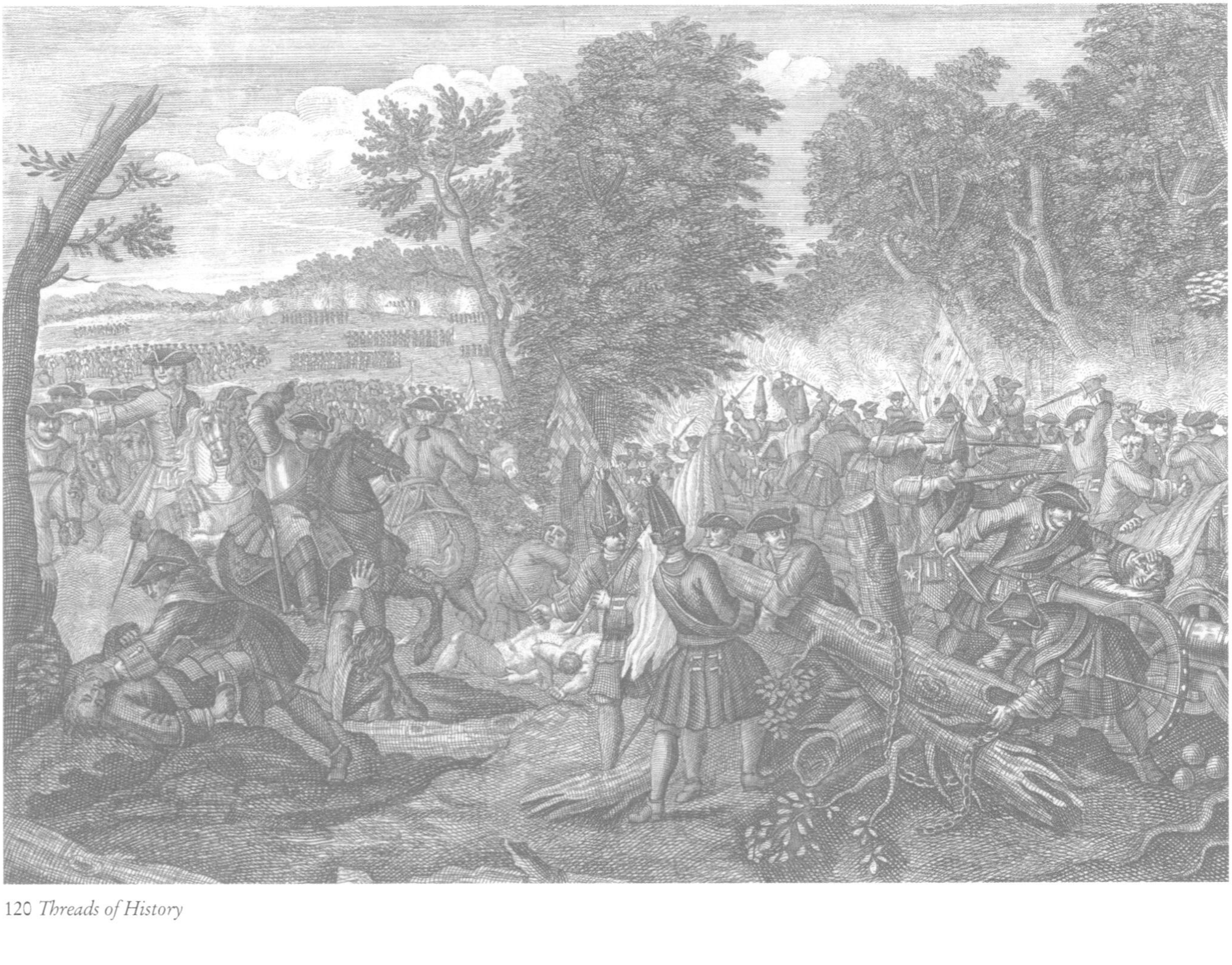

Marshal Villars.

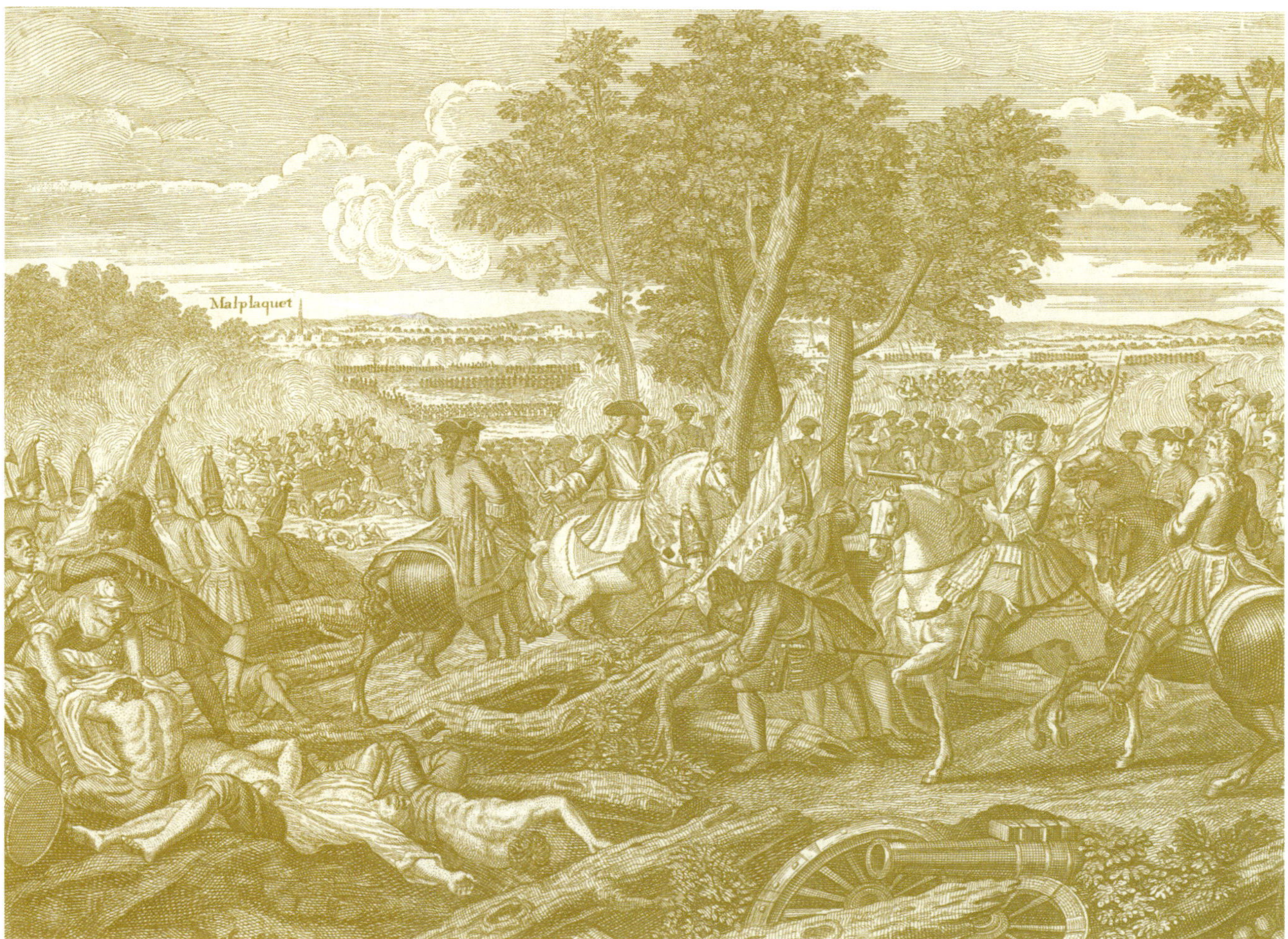

Above and opposite : Two contemporary prints of the Battle of Malplaquet, based on the murals at Marlborough House.

his flank to counter Marlborough's customary method of attack.

For the first time in a long time, the French held the initiative. When the Allied armies arrived to confront them on 11th September, they were unable to measure the strength of the enemy. A preliminary artillery attack started at nine in the morning and the advance of the Allied left wing was halted under fire of the concealed French guns. The Allied advance was further hampered by mounting casualties as they came under fire of the French in the woods. The Allies however, had the advantage of numbers and they forced their way through by the afternoon, when a furious cavalry battle took place. After several hours of fighting, the French were finally overwhelmed and decided to quit the field.

At this battle both sides claimed victory, for although the Allies gained possession of the area, they lost 24,000 men – almost twice the number of French casualties. Malplaquet was without doubt the bloodiest battle of the war. Despite winning an enormously strong entrenched French position which led to the eventual capture of Mons, the carnage at Malplaquet not only severely eroded Marlborough's position of unquestioned dominance in the field but also sullied his reputation at home.

MALPLAQUET : 11 SEPTEMBER 1709

14ft 6in. (H) x 13ft 4in. (W) / 4.42m (H) x 4.06m (W)

Malplaquet had to be taken before the investment of Mons. Mons was the capital city of the county of Hainault. The central cartouche refers to *Montes Hannoniae* which is the Latin for Mons in Hainault.

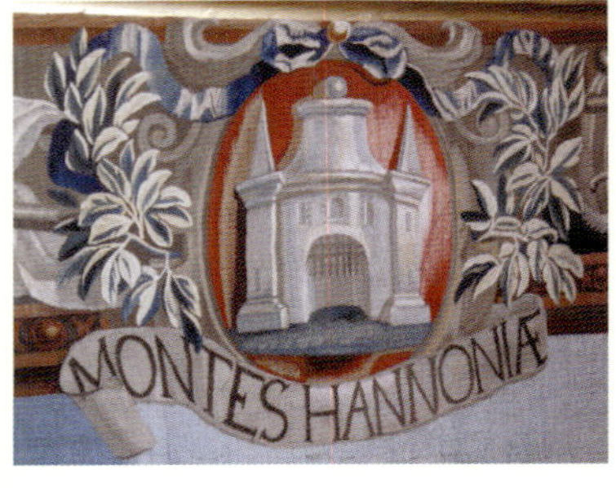

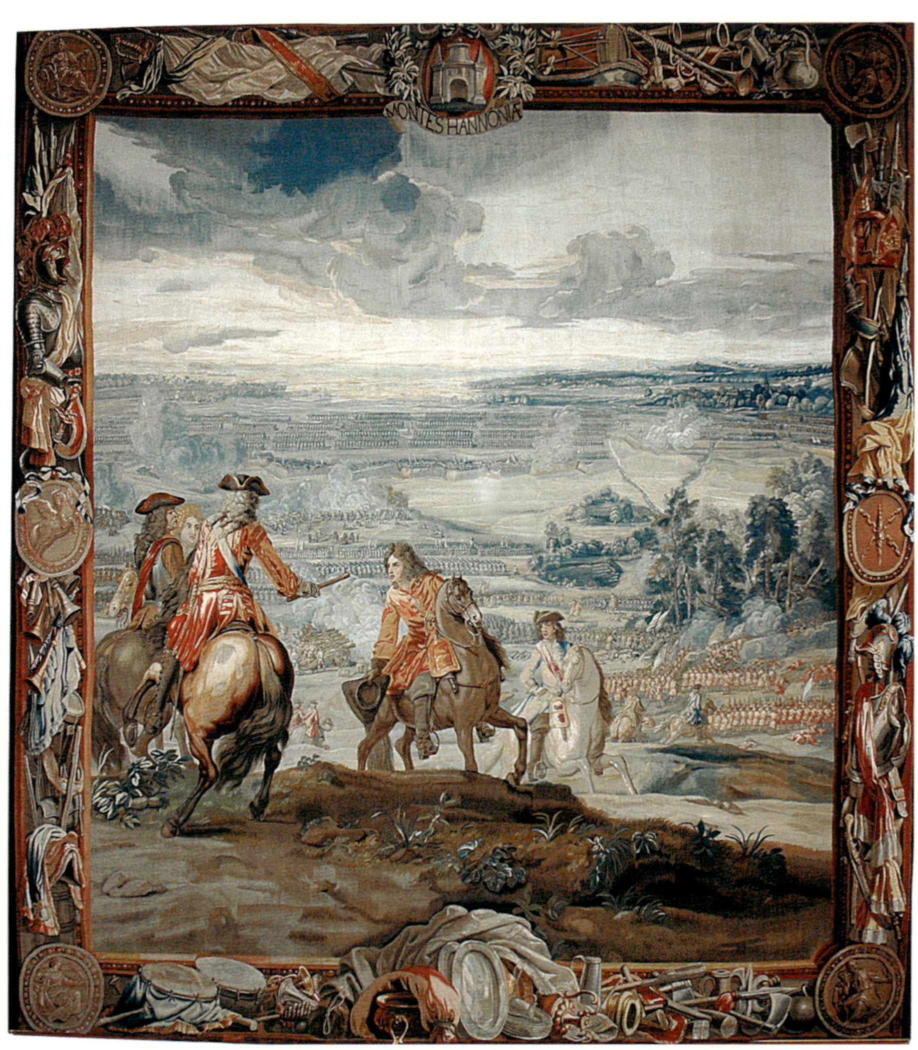

Marlborough (with his back to the viewer) is despatching orders to an officer. Prince Eugene is by his side.

On the extreme right of the panel, the allied attack on Sart wood can be seen. French breastworks projected in front of their left flank and prevented a direct Allied attack.

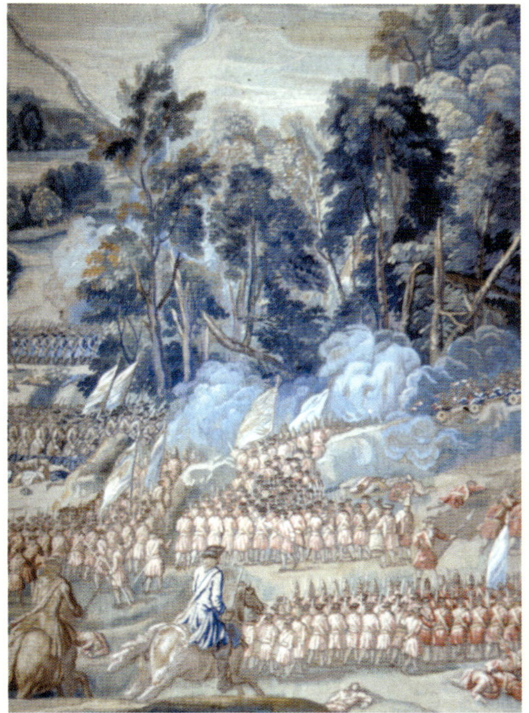

Detail of the action in Sart wood.

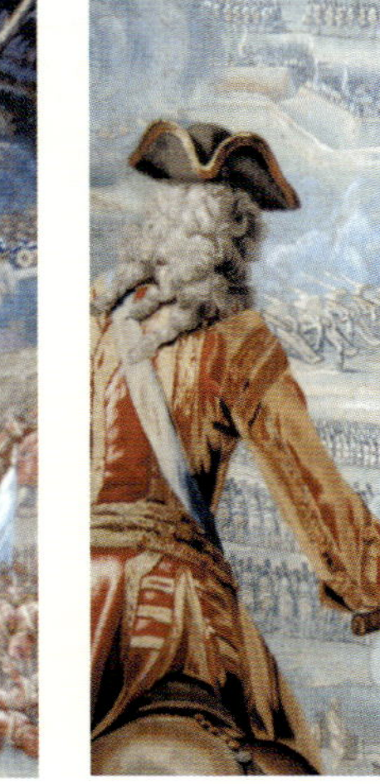

Detail showing the extremely strong French position.

In the background three French lines are visible showing how very strong the French position was, perhaps to justify the great numbers of casualties.

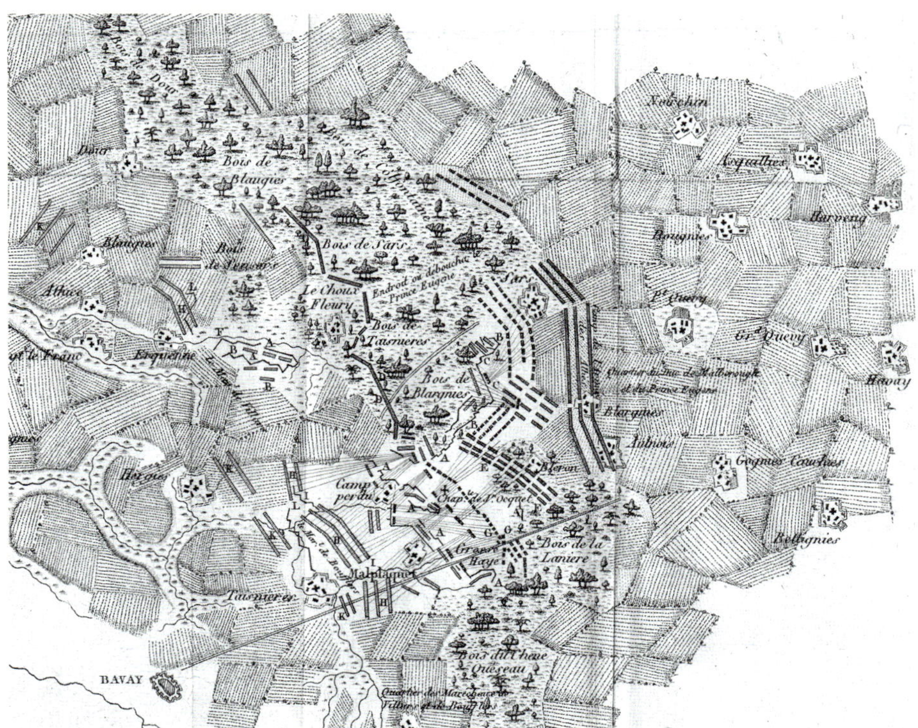

Contemporary plan of the Battle of Malplaquet.

French morale significantly improved after Malplaquet, with a growing sentiment that even if they were unable to win the war against a rival like Marlborough, then at least it was now possible that they would not lose it. With the ground laid for peace negotiations, the French campaign for 1710 was defensive in the extreme and Louis XIV instructed all his generals in no uncertain terms to avoid a battle at any cost. The Allied campaign was based on breaking through the French northern frontier defences. Douai and Bethune were the first of four towns to be besieged and taken, but any satisfaction the Duke might have had from these operations was marred by the news of Godolphin's dismissal in August, removing Marlborough's closest and only remaining friend at court in England. The Duke's own position in fact was fast becoming more precarious with Sarah now publicly in royal disfavour. The key fortresses of Aire and St. Venant were also taken before the end of the campaign, but the writing was now on the wall for Marlborough, who was politically isolated at a time when it was increasingly apparent that no single decisive military action could bring the war to its conclusion.

In April 1711 the Emperor Joseph died and his brother Charles ascended the Imperial throne. This development gave fresh impetus to a push for peace, as it now became just as impossible to allow the new Habsburg ruler to claim the throne of Spain as it had been to accept the Bourbon grandson of Louis XIV. The massive and ever rising cost of the war further spurred the new Tory ministry in England to bring hostilities to an end.

Joseph's sudden death impeded the Allied campaign planned in Flanders for 1711 as Prince Eugene was called away with his army to cover Frankfurt during the Imperial election. This left Marlborough with not only a weakened force but also pitted against the very able Marshal Villars. The French, in

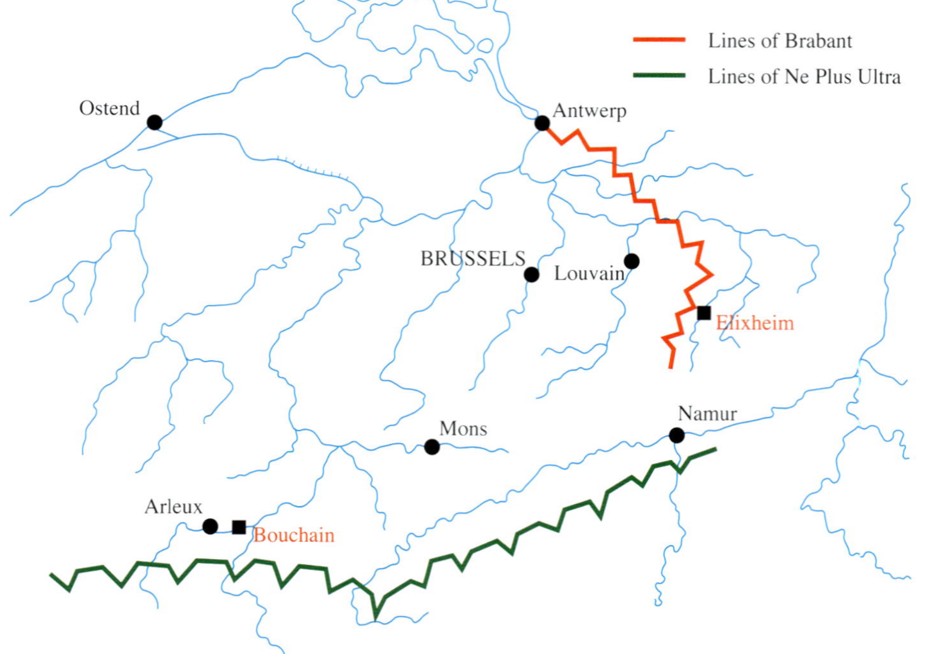

Sketch map showing the Lines of Brabant and the Lines of Ne Plus Ultra.

order to safeguard their northern frontier, had constructed in the winter months of 1710-11, the supposedly impregnable lines called *Ne Plus Ultra* (meaning 'nothing further is possible' and sometimes referred to as *Non Plus Ultra*), reaching from the sea coast across to Namur. Villars refused to be drawn past these lines to engage in battle.

The armies confronted each other for some weeks before Marlborough put into effect what was by far his most cunning plan of tactical manoeuvre. He captured the fort at Arleux on the river Sensee and pretended to strengthen it. He then moved away westwards from Arleux as though intending to drive his army through to Arras. Villars played right into his hands when he destroyed the fort at Arleux on 22nd July and hastened to confront the Allies at Arras which was exactly what the Duke had wanted him to do. Marlborough swiftly force-marched his men back on the night of 4 - 5th August (in an unmatched effort, covering 40 miles in just 18 hours) and pushed across the river at Arleux virtually unopposed. Now inside the vaunted enemy lines, the Duke laid siege to the fortress at Bouchain. Despite every French endeavour to frustrate him, the Duke captured the fortress and town of Bouchain on 13th September.

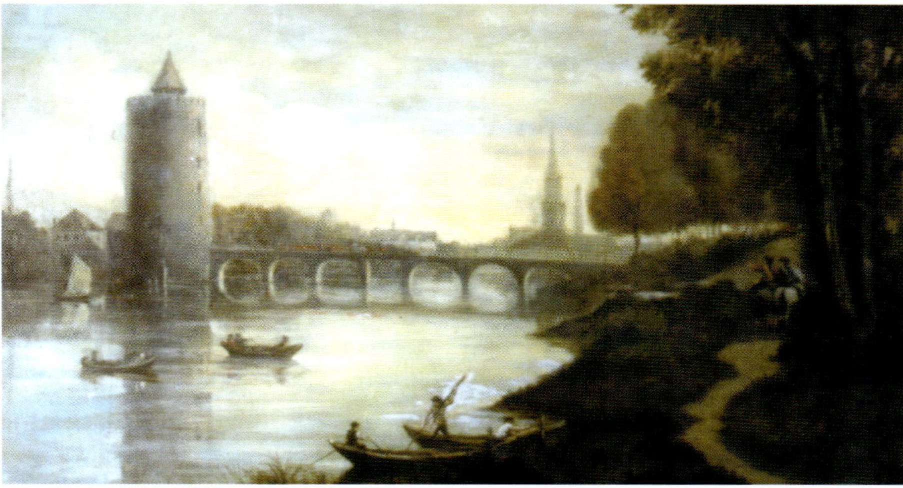

View of Arleux and the river Sensee.

The campaign of 1711 was a supreme demonstration of the Duke's military expertise and tactical astuteness. The Allies had not lost a single man in crossing the lines of *Ne Plus Ultra* and had sustained under 5,000 casualties in the subsequent siege of Bouchain. This was undoubtedly a relief for Marlborough who had been greatly criticised after the carnage at Malplaquet.

The Allies were now well positioned to advance into France, but 1711 was to be Marlborough's last campaign. The Tories had been conducting peace negotiations in secret with the French and on his return from Flanders that winter, the 61 year old Duke was ignominiously dismissed from all his posts. Bouchain remains Marlborough's most significant tactical triumph, but it was a sad end not only to his long and successful career as a soldier but also to his many political achievements as a statesman, his actions in both spheres proving his loyalty to the Allied cause.

14ft 6in. (H) x 28ft 3in. (W) / 4.42 (H) x 8.61 m (W)

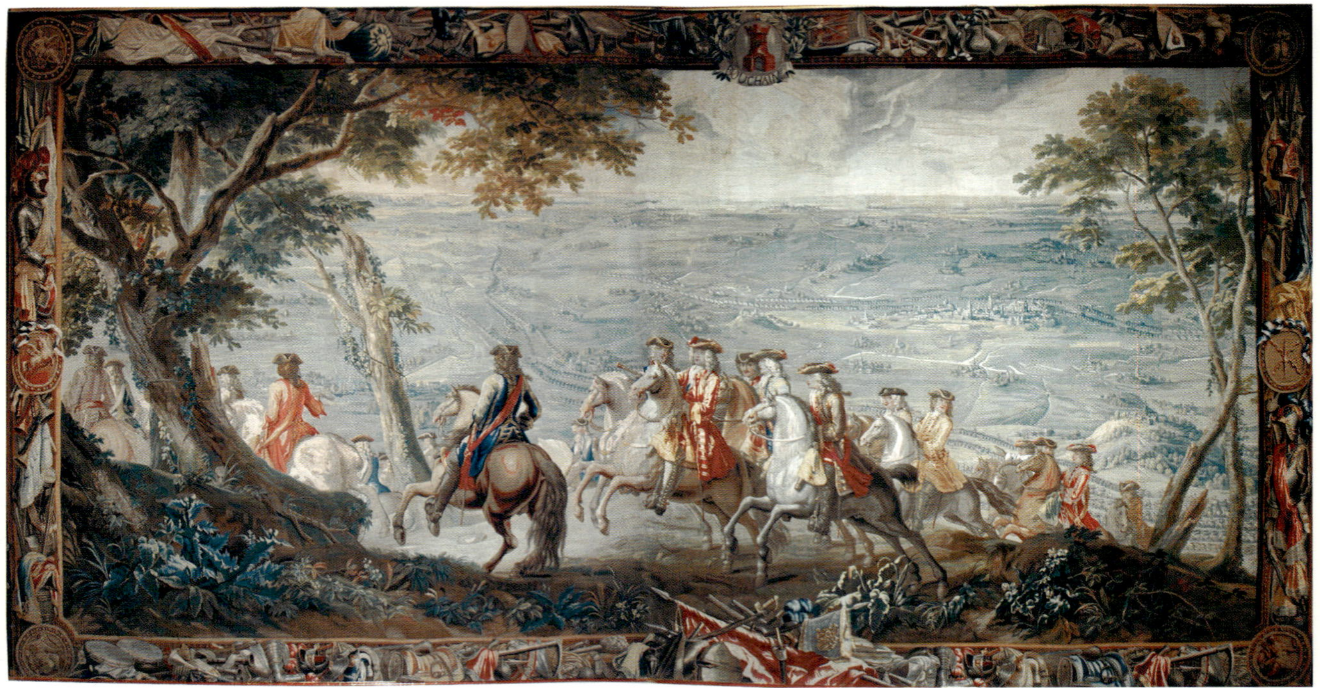

The tapestries provide a visual rendering not only of uniforms and weapons but also of methods of attack and manoeuvre. Armies marched an average of 10 miles a day, either in a line formation or in separated field columns. They spread themselves not only along the available roads, which were often little more than tracks in a dismal state of repair, but also through the countryside. The cavalry normally moved a day or two ahead of the infantry, followed by the guns which lagged 2-3 days behind. They formed up again in battle order when in camp and before engaging to fight the enemy. Pontoon wagons and guns were crucial in their contribution to winning a battle but their weight and the obviously slow rate of progress along inadequate, pitted roads was fatal to any encounter which relied on the rapid deployment and movement of forces. Marlborough is known to have left his heavy guns behind on several occasions thereby allowing himself daring and rule defying marches in the face of his enemy. On his great march to the Danube, he recorded that his guns were six days behind him.

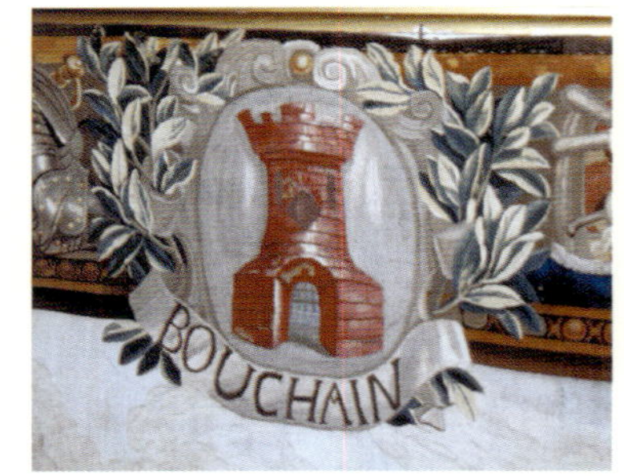

   The other uncertain factor in the moving of armies, of course, was the weather. Roads often became deeply rutted and totally impassable in wet weather, especially for the heavier guns. A three tonne cannon would need six or eight horses to pull it and the heavier guns would need up to twenty horses. Oxen and mules were also used as pack animals to move parts of the

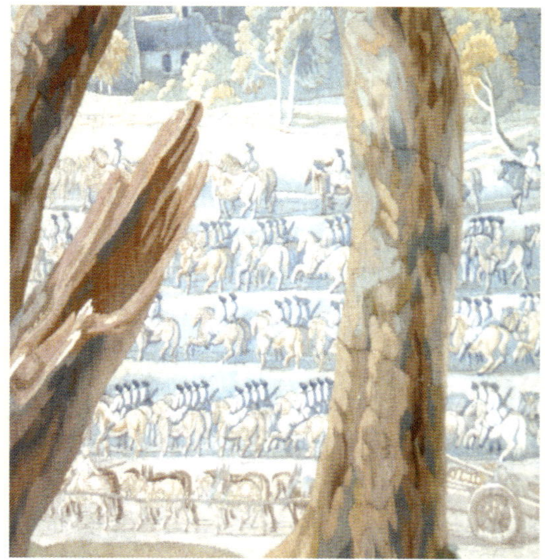

Detail of supply train showing mules pulling a gun carriage.

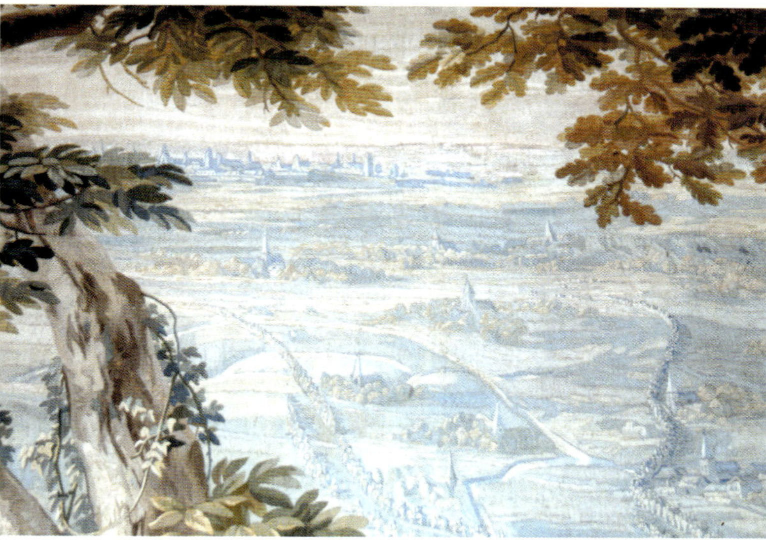

The town of Bouchain is visible on the horizon under the branches of the tree on the left. The allied army is making its way through the countryside towards it in several columns as can be seen in the image *above* and those *below left*.

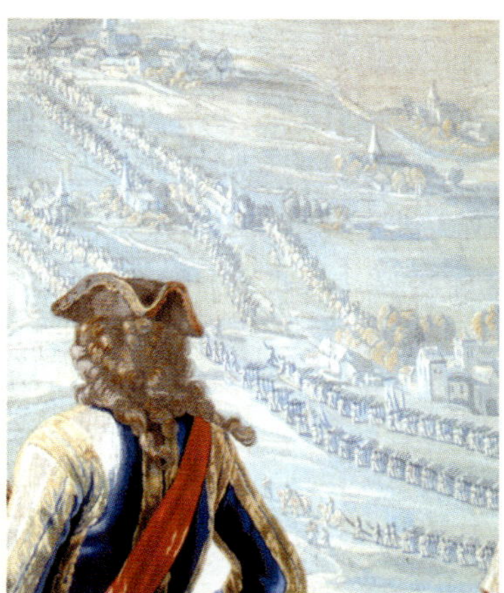

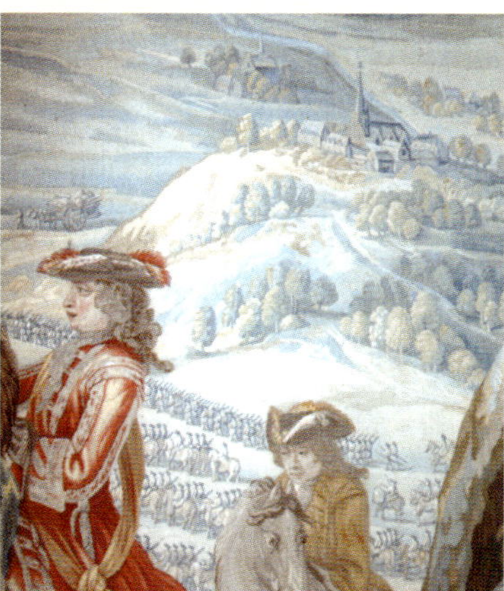

supply train which extended a distance of many miles behind the infantry and cavalry divisions. Winston Churchill likened these troop movements to a "scarlet caterpillar" moving across the landscape.

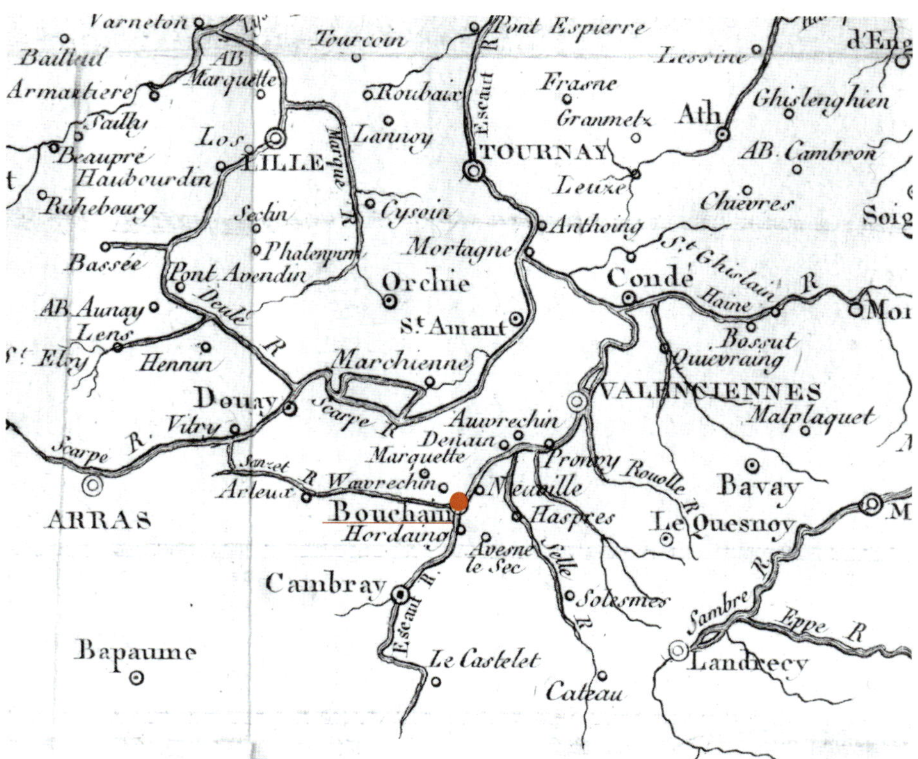

Contemporary map showing Bouchain and the surrounding area.

BOUCHAIN II: LAYING SIEGE, AUGUST 1711

14ft 6in. (H) x 12ft 5in. (W) / 4.42 (H) x 3.78 m (W)

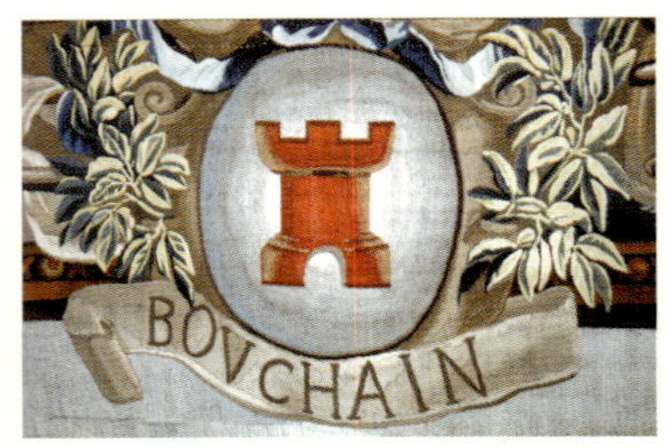

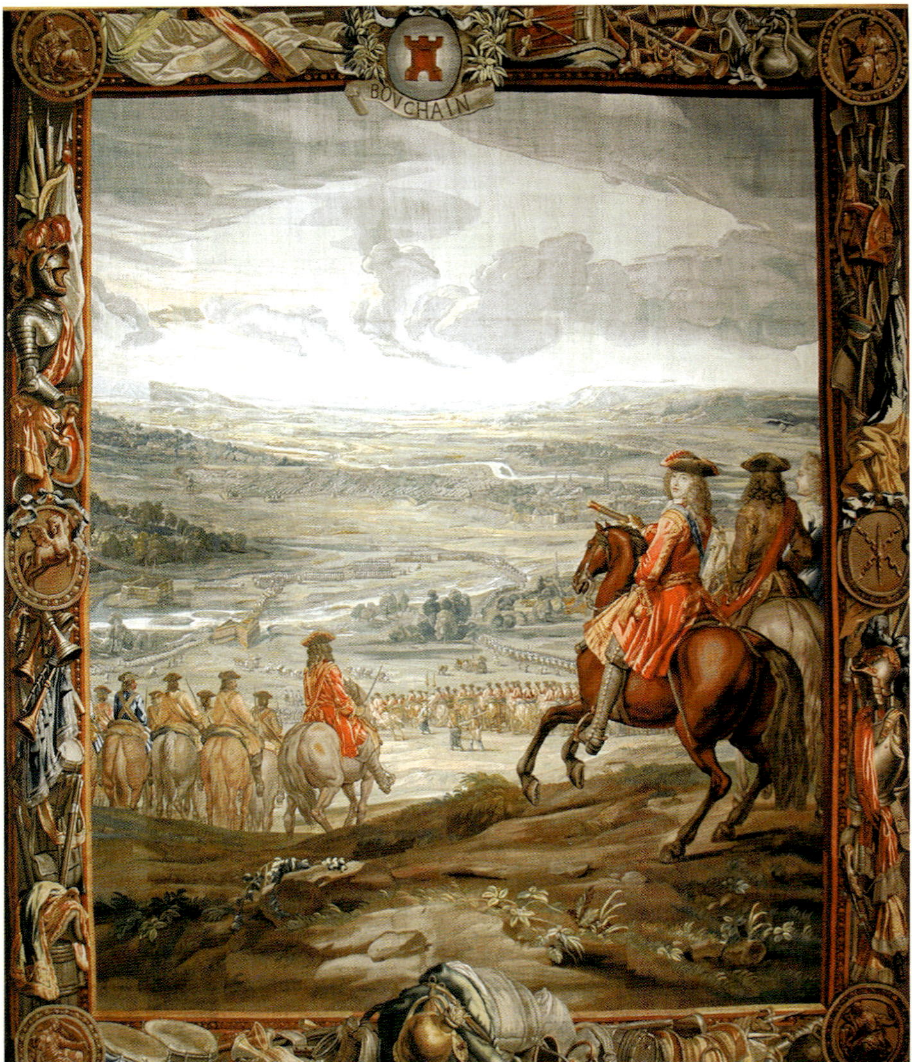

Marlborough crossed the river Scheldt at Etrun. The fortress of Bouchain was located in a flooded plain and consisted of an upper and lower town. Sited at the confluence of the Selle and the Sensee before they ran into the Scheldt, it was naturally protected by marshland. Besides the difficulties caused by the terrain, the French had established a formidable entrenchment, fenced with redoubts. This was protected by 30 battalions and 50 pieces of cannon under the command of Monsieur Albergotti. The French camp lay to the south near the hamlet of Wavrechin.

Marlborough drew up his lines of circumvallation between these entrenchments and the town of Bouchain. This led the French Marshal Villars

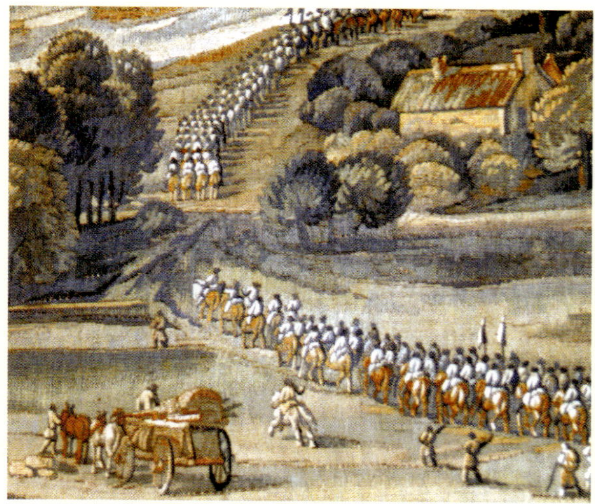

Detail of army crossing.

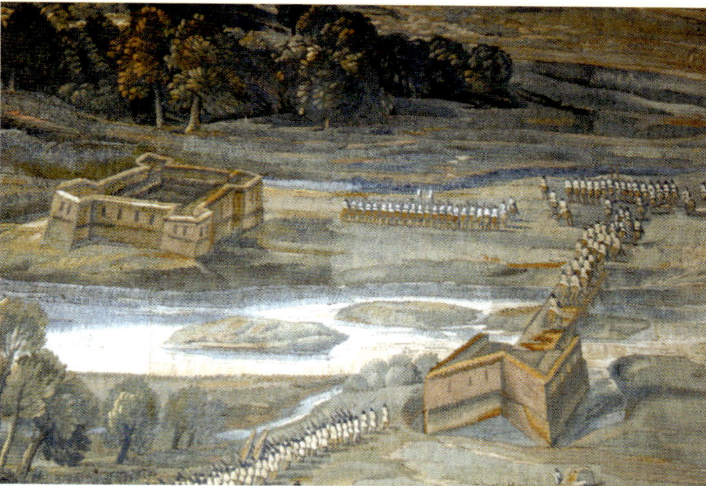

Detail of abandoned fortifications and redoubt.

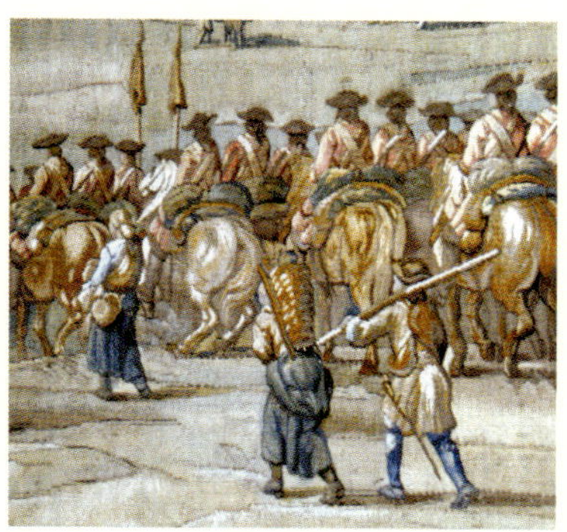

Detail of women.

to attack the Allies but they were seen off in a confrontation led by General Cadogan. The French were forced to surrender their entrenchments and redoubts. The scene in this tapestry shows the Allied armies crossing the flooded plain towards Bouchain as well as the unmanned French fortifications. The town was invested within ten days of this manoeuvre.

Large numbers of women followed a marching army, some selling goods and wares and others cooking and cleaning for the soldiers in return for a small payment. This is the only panel where women can be seen in the detail.

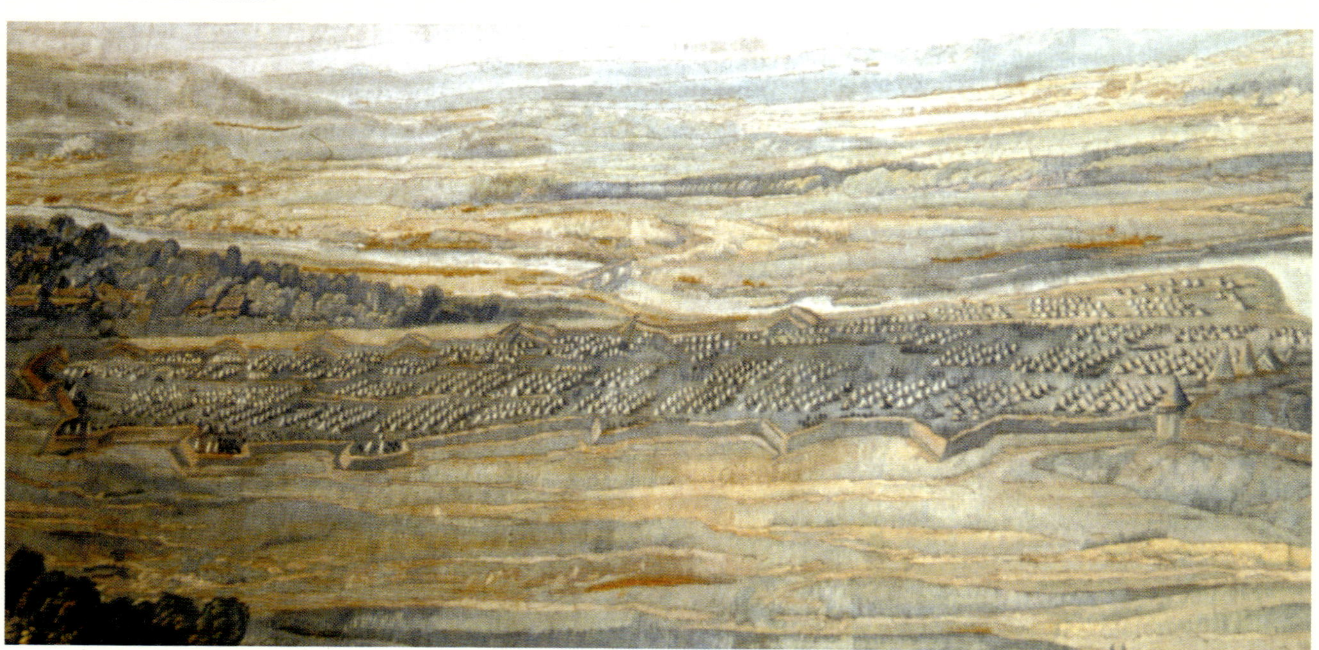

The fortified town of Bouchain in its flooded plain.

BOUCHAIN III: THE SIEGE AND CAPITULATION, 9 AUGUST TO 13 SEPTEMBER 1711

14ft 6in. (H) x 28ft 3in. (W) / 4.42m (H) x 8.61m (W)

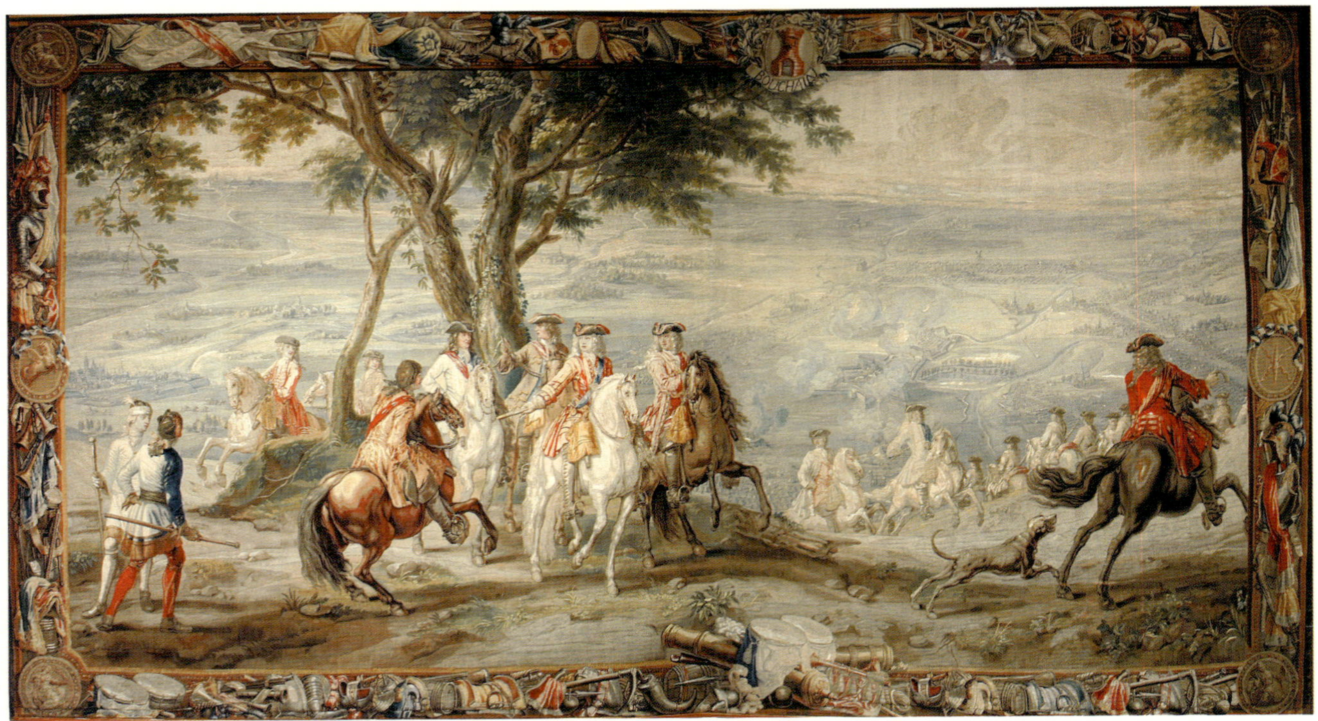

In this tapestry Marlborough receives news of the surrender of Bouchain. The siege was a complete success in which a large part was played by Colonel John Armstrong (1673-1742), chief engineer and Surveyor General of the Ordnance. In the group of officers alongside the Duke under the tree in the centre of the panel, Colonel Armstrong and General Cadogan are clearly recognisable.

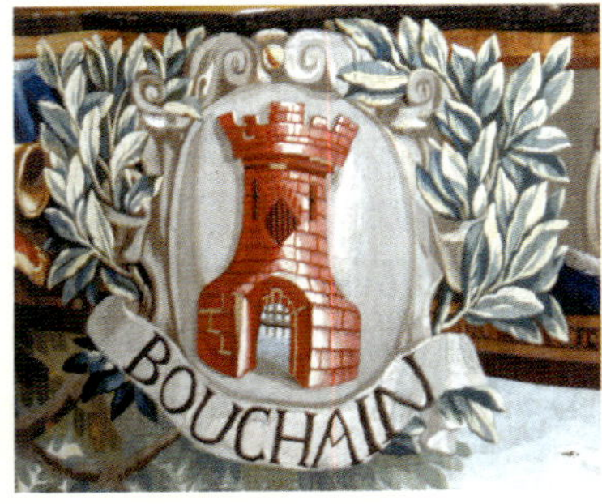

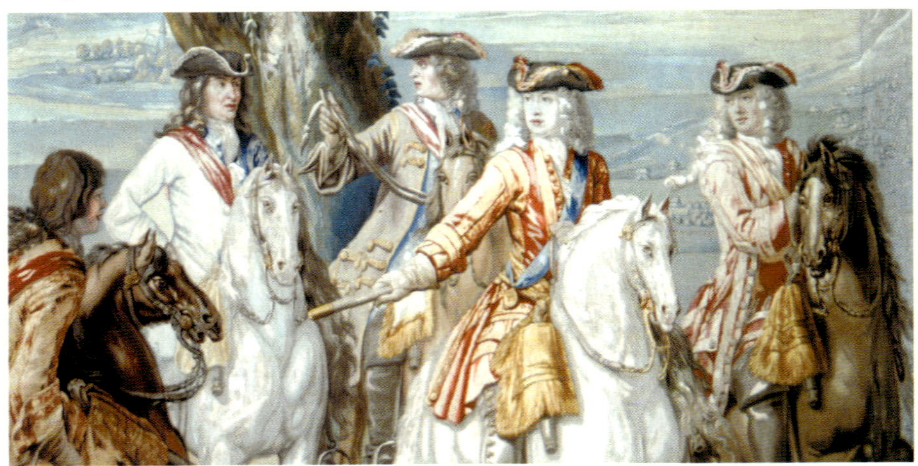

Detail of Armstrong (2nd from left) and Cadogan (3rd from left).

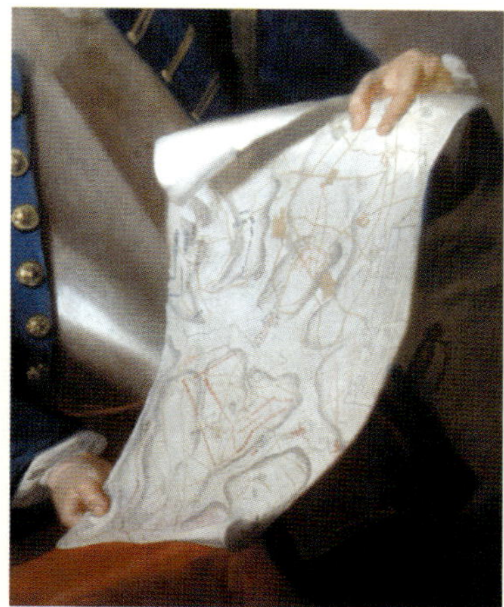

Detail of the plan of the Siege of Bouchain taken from the painting alongside.

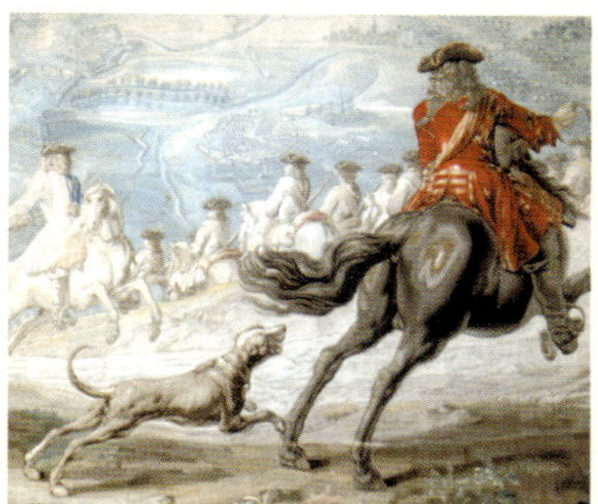

Detail of galloping dog.

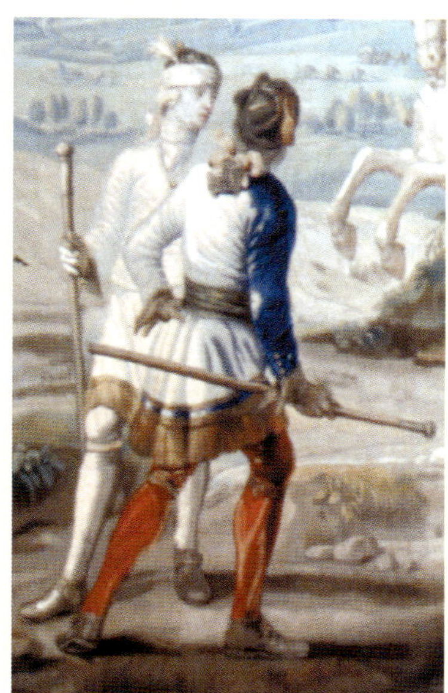

Detail of Marlborough's running footmen. Notice their gold and silver topped staffs.

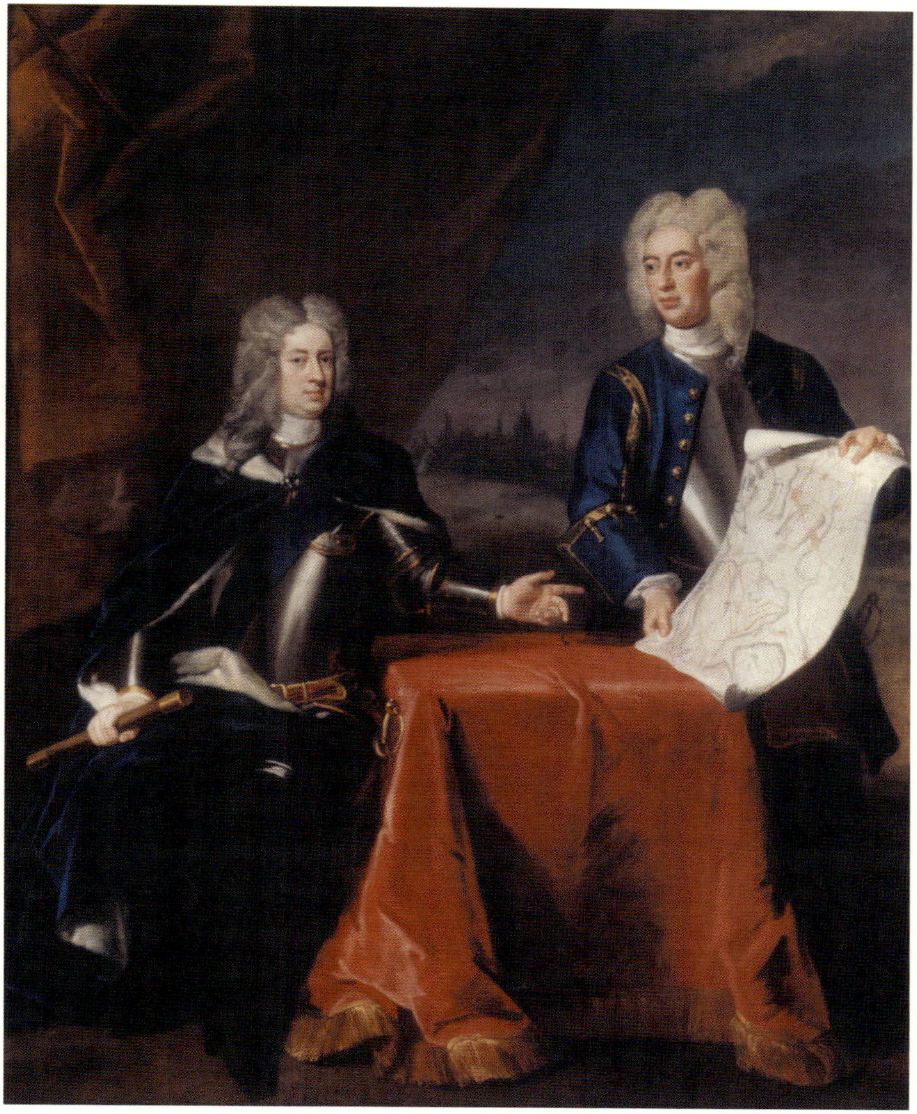

The Duke of Marlborough with Colonel Armstrong by Enoch Seeman.
Armstrong is holding a plan of the Siege of Bouchain.

In the right foreground, an officer is seen galloping away from us with a dog running alongside. The dog has been the subject of much speculation as it is the only one in the entire series of tapestries. Tradition has it that the dog belonged to Cadogan and it is supposed to have followed him on campaign throughout the War of the Spanish succession. While it was not unusual to have dogs in camp, it has also been suggested that this dog symbolises Cadogan, who was known to his troops as 'the dog' (Ca-dog-an). The peculiarity of the dog having horses hooves has already been discussed in Chapter Two.

To the extreme left of the tapestry two 'runners' (messengers and guides on foot) can be seen. They played a crucial role in the siege of Bouchain, bringing back regular reports on the enemy's movements to the Duke.

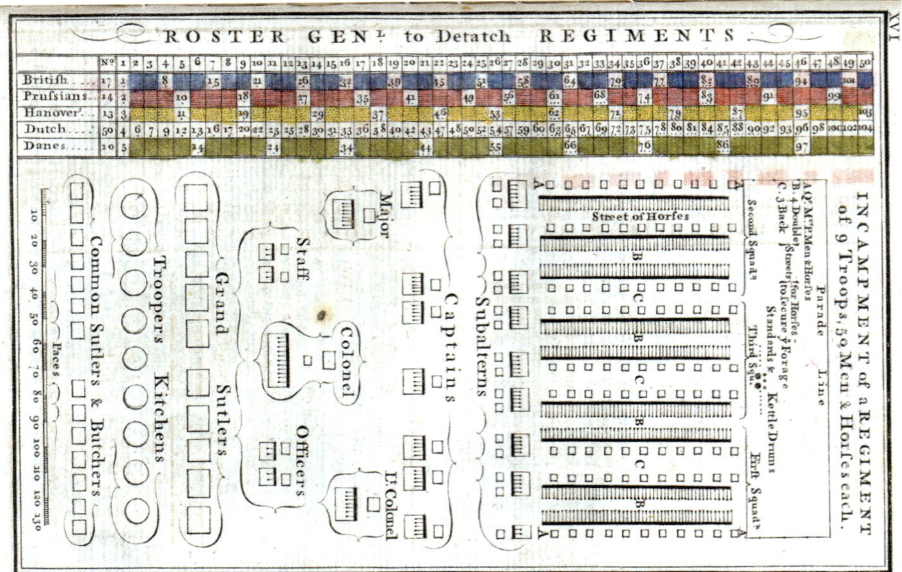

A scheme showing the layout of a regiment in camp.

This tapestry is rich in carefully observed military detail. In the background to the right of the panel, the Allied army is clearly visible in camps encircling the fortified town of Bouchain. Camps were laid out in battle line formation with the horse on the outside and the infantry in the centre. Guns and munitions were generally separated from the main camp for reasons of safety, while the supply or baggage train was camped quite apart from the solciers: both were clearly kept well secured. Sutlers and other peasants following the army in order to sell their wares were able to set up their wagons nearby.

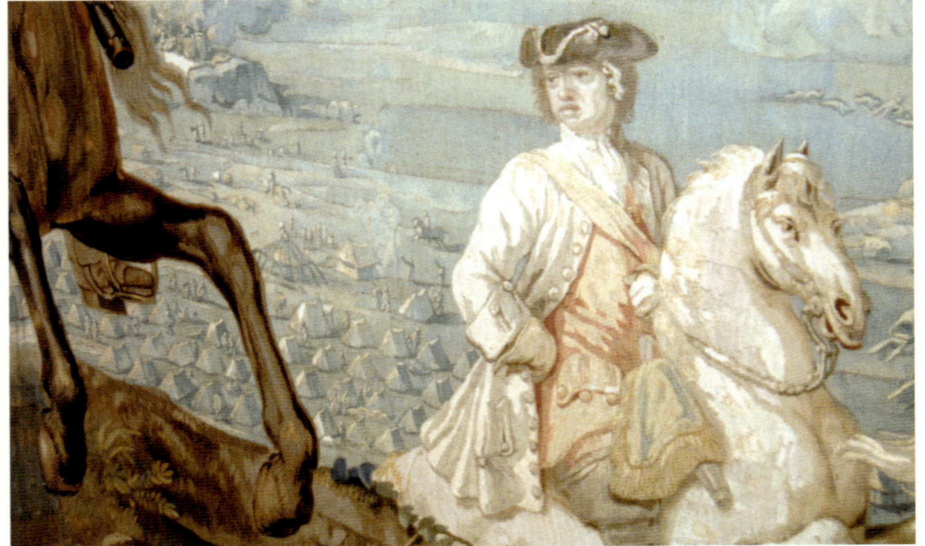

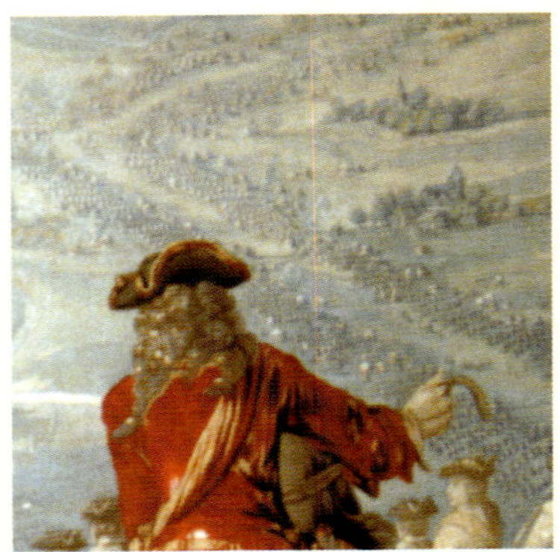

Details of the Allied army camps.

A painting by Sir Winston S. Churchill of the Second State Room at Blenheim Palace, distinctly showing the *Bouchain III* tapestry. Sir Winston was born on 30th November 1874 at Blenheim, the home of his grandfather the 7th Duke of Marlborough. His father, Lord Randolph Spencer-Churchill, was the third born and second surviving son of the 7th Duke and so did not inherit the family title. Throughout his life Sir Winston was a frequent visitor at Blenheim and a fervent admirer of the 1st Duke of Marlborough. He spent many years at the Palace in the 1930s researching archival material for his four volume biography of his great ancestor.

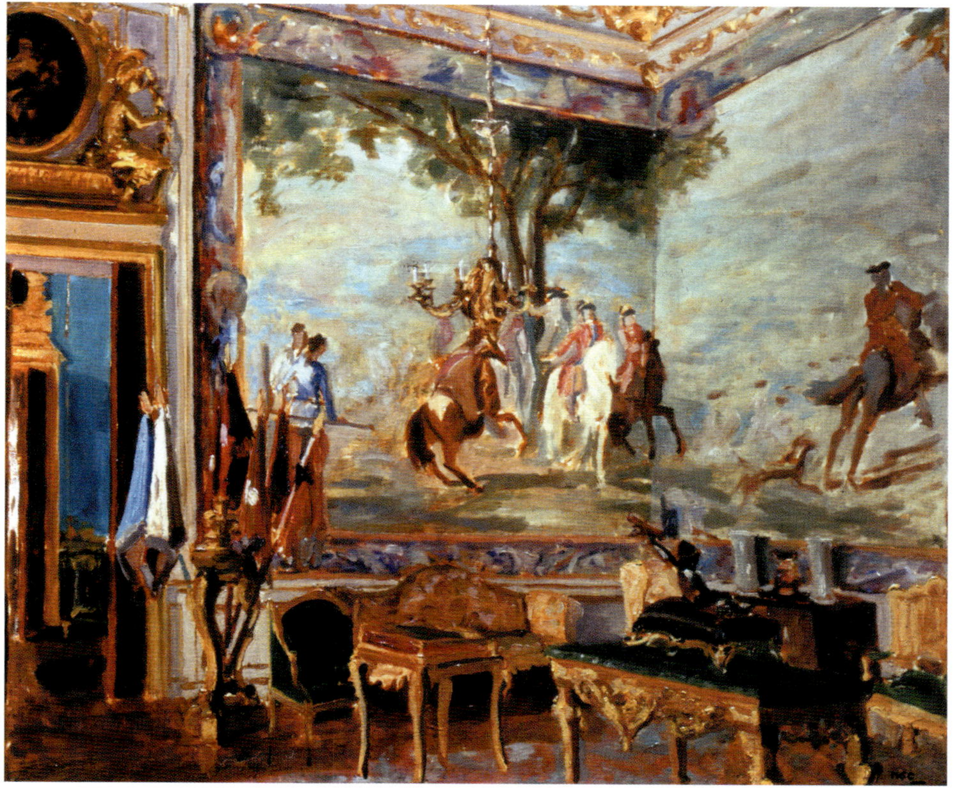

Marlborough's tactical appreciation of any situation had created such a culture of success that after his dismissal, it came as no surprise that the Allies suffered a series of setbacks and defeats without him. The Duke's first biographer, Thomas Lediard, paid a telling tribute when writing that "*he passed all the rivers and lines he attempted, took all the towns he invested, won all the battles he fought (this often with inferior, rarely with superior force) was never surpriz'd by his enemy, nor charg'd with one action of cruelty, was ever beloved by his own soldiers, and dreaded by those of his Enemy*".[141]

John Churchill was one of the greatest leaders the British army has ever produced. He was a humane soldier who had the courage of his convictions, who led by personal example and had the unreserved support of all the men he commanded. He was ambitious and charming, courageous and responsible, competent and far-sighted in his judgement, a supreme strategist, an able statesman, a peerless administrator, a patient and loving husband, a dedicated and loyal subject.

It is proper perhaps to leave the last word to Sarah, who outlived Marlborough by twenty two years and at the age of 84, convincingly acknowledged her husband's military talent when she wrote "*and I think it is more Honour to rise from the lowest Step to the greatest, than as the Fashion is now to be Admirals without ever having seen Water but in a Bason [basin] or to be Generals that never saw any Action of War*".[142]

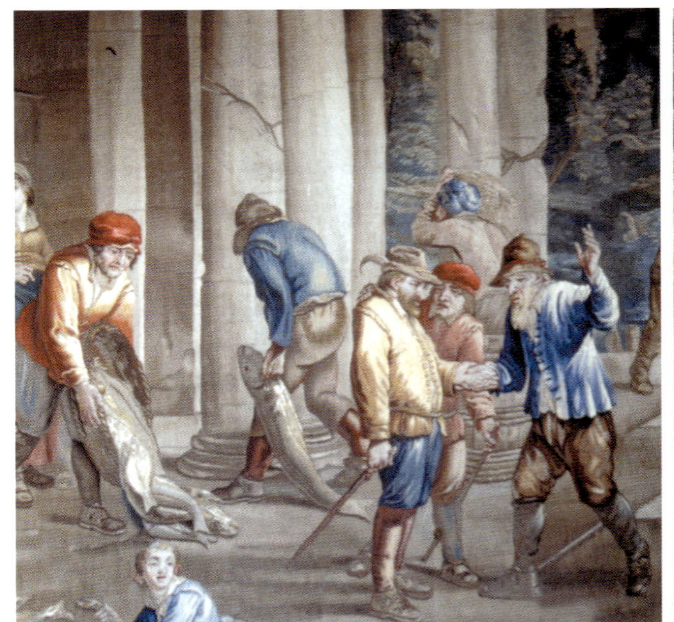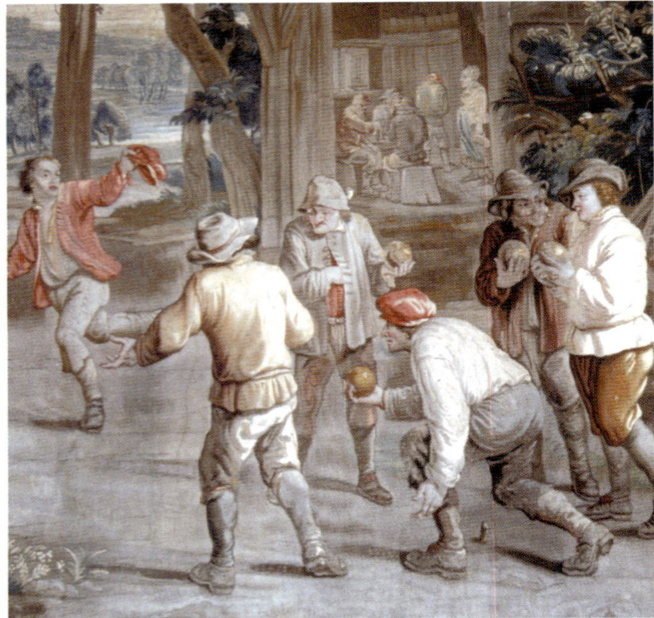

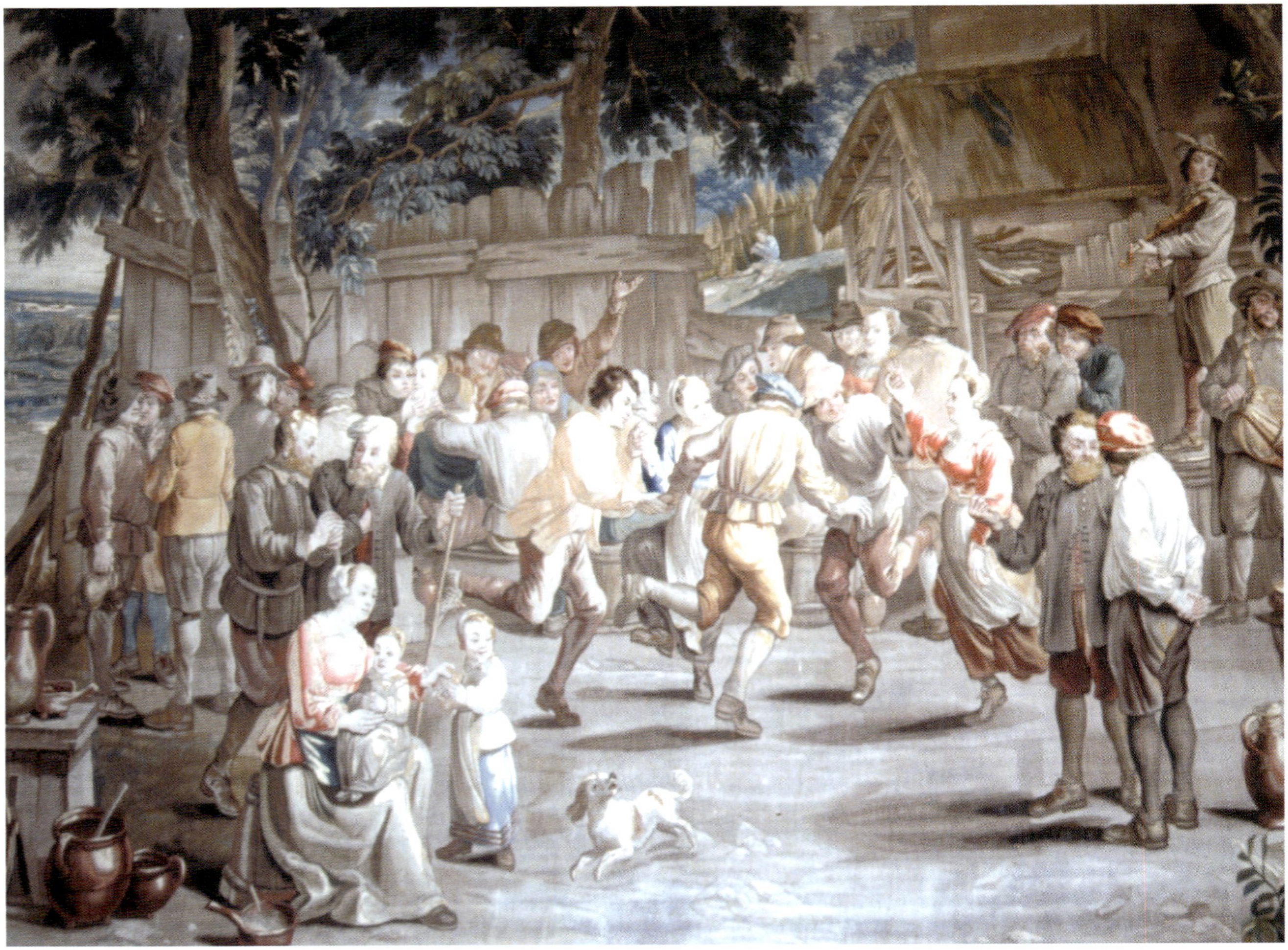

TAPESTRIES GIFTED TO THE DUCHESS OF MARLBOROUGH

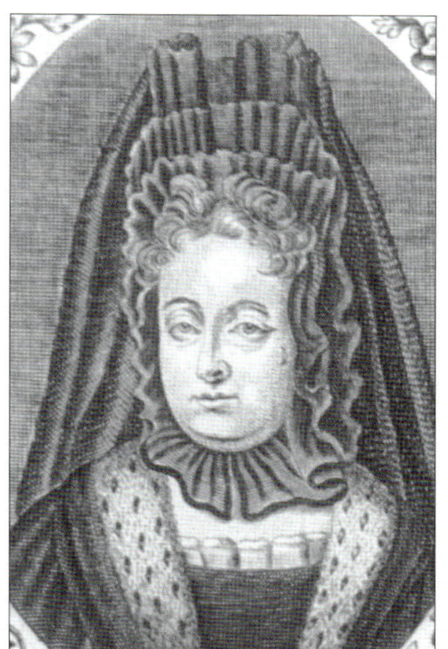

Electress Sophia of Hanover.

Electress Sophia of Hanover (1630-1714) was a granddaughter of James I. She was married to Duke Ernst August, who became Elector of Hanover in 1692. The Act of Succession in 1701 guaranteed a Protestant heir to the throne of England if King William or subsequently Queen Anne were to die without surviving issue. Sophia was thus declared heir to the English throne when all of Queen Anne's children died young. However, her death, a few months prior to Queen Anne's, resulted in her son succeeding to the throne as George I.

In June 1703, Sophia had requested the Duchess of Marlborough to send her a picture of Queen Anne. Sir Godfrey Kneller was commissioned to paint the portrait which was dispatched to Hanover. In return, the Duchess was gifted a set of ten tapestries, which was received by the Duke at his army camp in Flanders before he returned to England in December 1704. The tapestries were stored in canvas bags and carted by wagon to the Hague.

The design of the tapestries is not exactly known, but they are described in letters and documents as having "*little figures*" in them. They were most probably tapestries depicting scenes of country life by Teniers.[143] The panels were rather large as is evident from the Duke's letter to Sarah "...*The weather begins to be very cold, so that I hope by the beginning of the weeke the wind will come so faire, that I may have the happyness of being in a few days after with you. The hangings I bring you having been thrown into a little river, I was obliged to open them, but they received no damadge, they will please you for thay are fine and very agreeable, but thay are too deep for any of your rooms*".[144] She eventually hung them at her London residence, Marlborough House, which was completed in 1711, situated alongside St. James's Palace.

The Duke and Duchess had a particularly unusual domestic arrangement for the time, Sarah being permitted by her husband to keep her own income and properties separate from his. Both John and Sarah Churchill had accumulated vast fortunes during their lifetimes. While the Duke ensured that he left his wife very well off on his death, his will principally provided that his fortune and estate went with the title, to the heir to the Dukedom. The Duchess on the other hand, wrote and rewrote her will more than a few times over, as favourite children and then favoured grandchildren either died or else fell out with her. Sophia's gift of tapestries featured in the amendment the Duchess made to an early version of her will in June 1729, where she stated "...*the ten pieces of Hangings given to me by the Electress of Hannover which are at Marlborough House I give to my lord Sunderland*".[145]

At this point, the Spencers of Althorp bore the title of Earls of Sunderland. The Churchill's second daughter Anne, had married the 3rd Earl of Sunderland, Charles Spencer. The Earl of Sunderland that Sarah refers to in

The Spencer and Churchill Lines of Succession

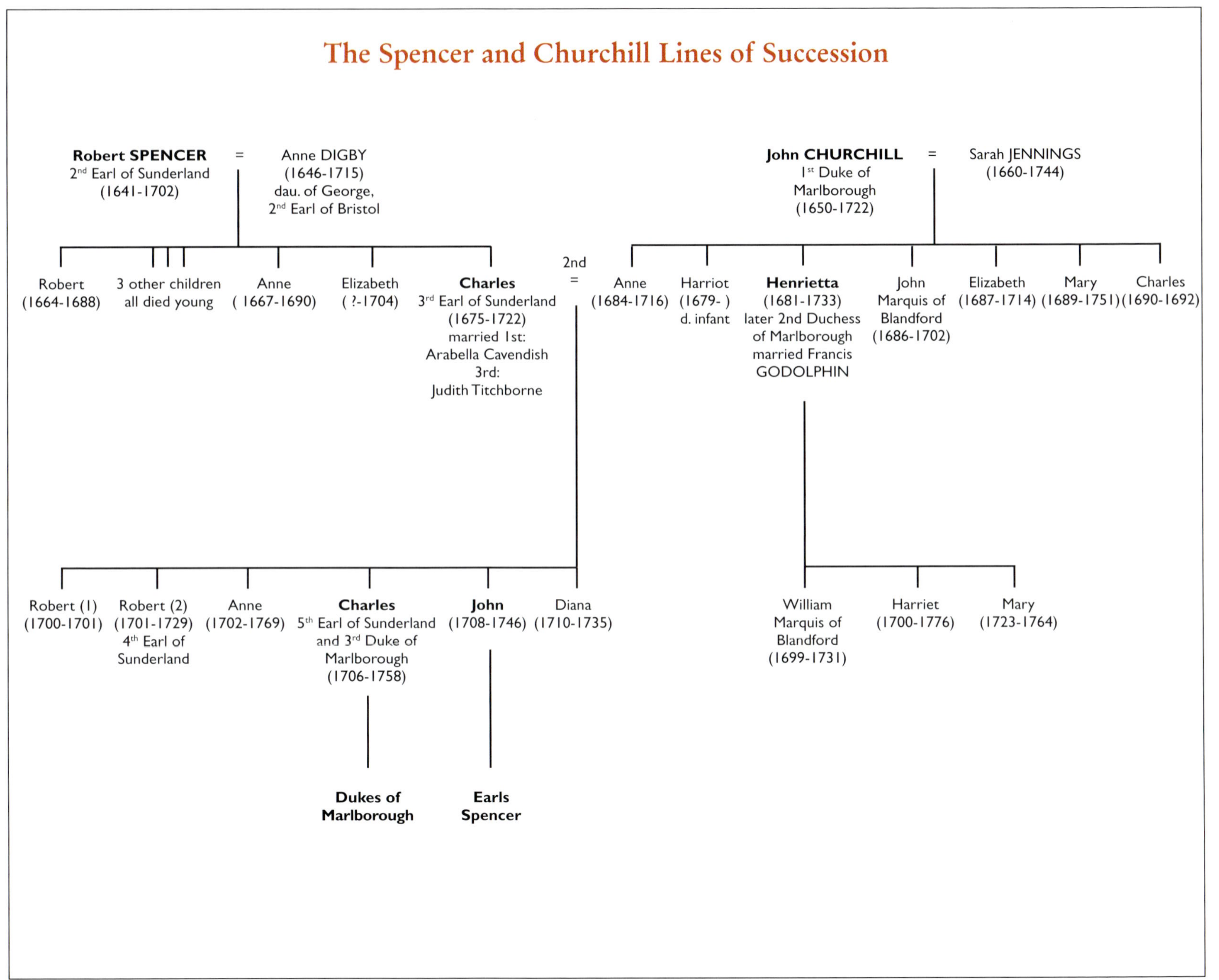

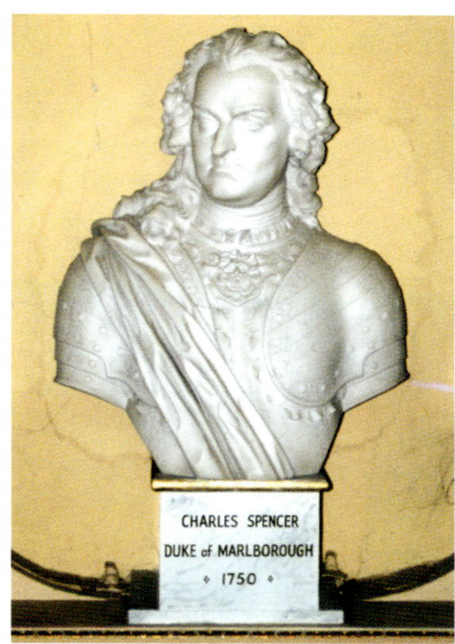

Charles, 5th Earl of Sunderland,
later 3rd Duke of Marlborough.

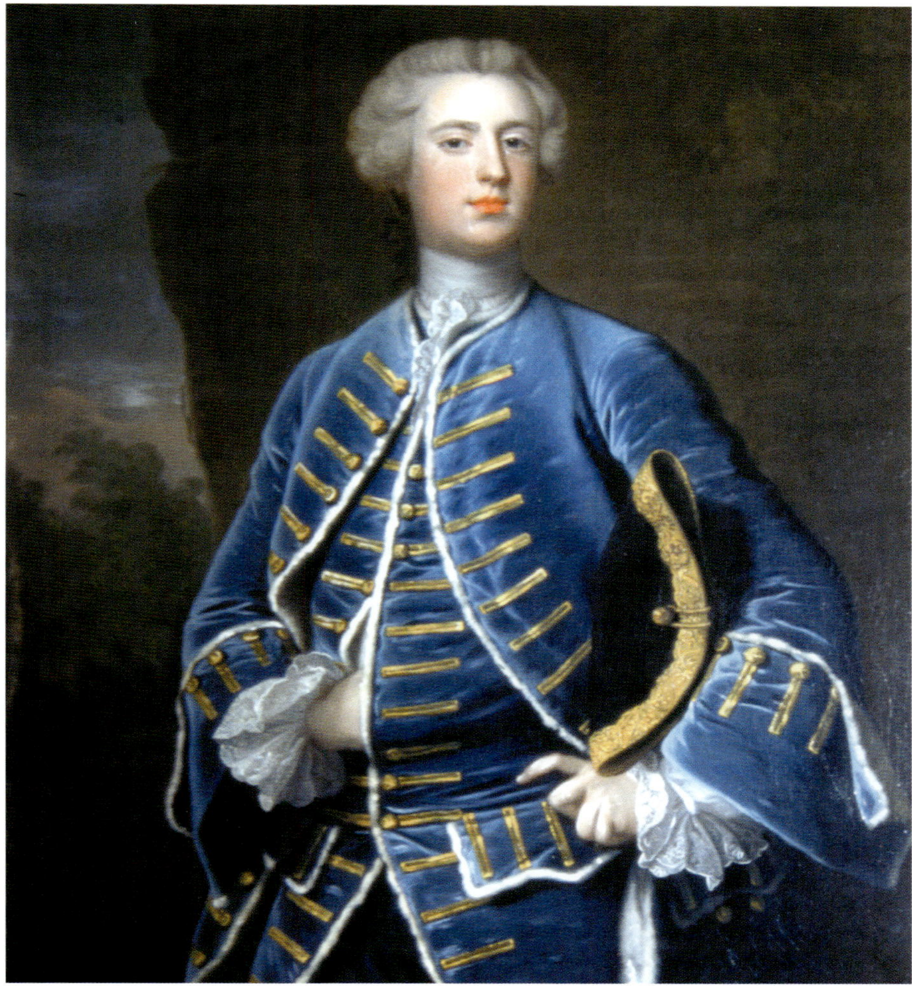

Right : Robert, 4th Earl of Sunderland
attributed to Enoch Seeman.

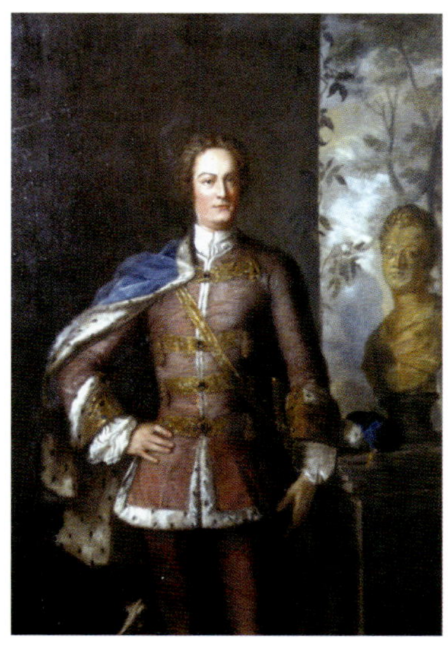

The Hon. John Spencer
by Stephen Slaughter.

this version of her will was the 4th Earl, her grandson Robert Spencer. He tragically died of a fever while visiting Paris in September 1729, unmarried and aged just 28. Robert was succeeded by his brother Charles, the 5th Earl, with whom Sarah initially was on good terms and in a further amendment to her will, she bequeathed to him *the hangings given me by the Electress*. However, the relationship soon soured and Sarah turned her affection and attention to Charles's younger brother, John Spencer. Although these tapestries are not specifically mentioned in her final will, it is quite likely that when the Duchess eventually died in October 1744, she would have left them to "Johnny" as he inherited the lion's share of her considerable personal wealth and possessions, some of which can still be seen at Althorp.

Charles Spencer would not have minded the loss of this one set of tapestries as, in due course, he succeeded to the greater prize of the Dukedom of Marlborough (in October 1733 when his aunt Henrietta, 2nd Duchess, died) and therefore inherited the *Art of War, the Alexander, the Pleasures of the Gods, the Virtues* and the *Victories* sets as well as the innumerable other works of art that then filled Blenheim Palace.

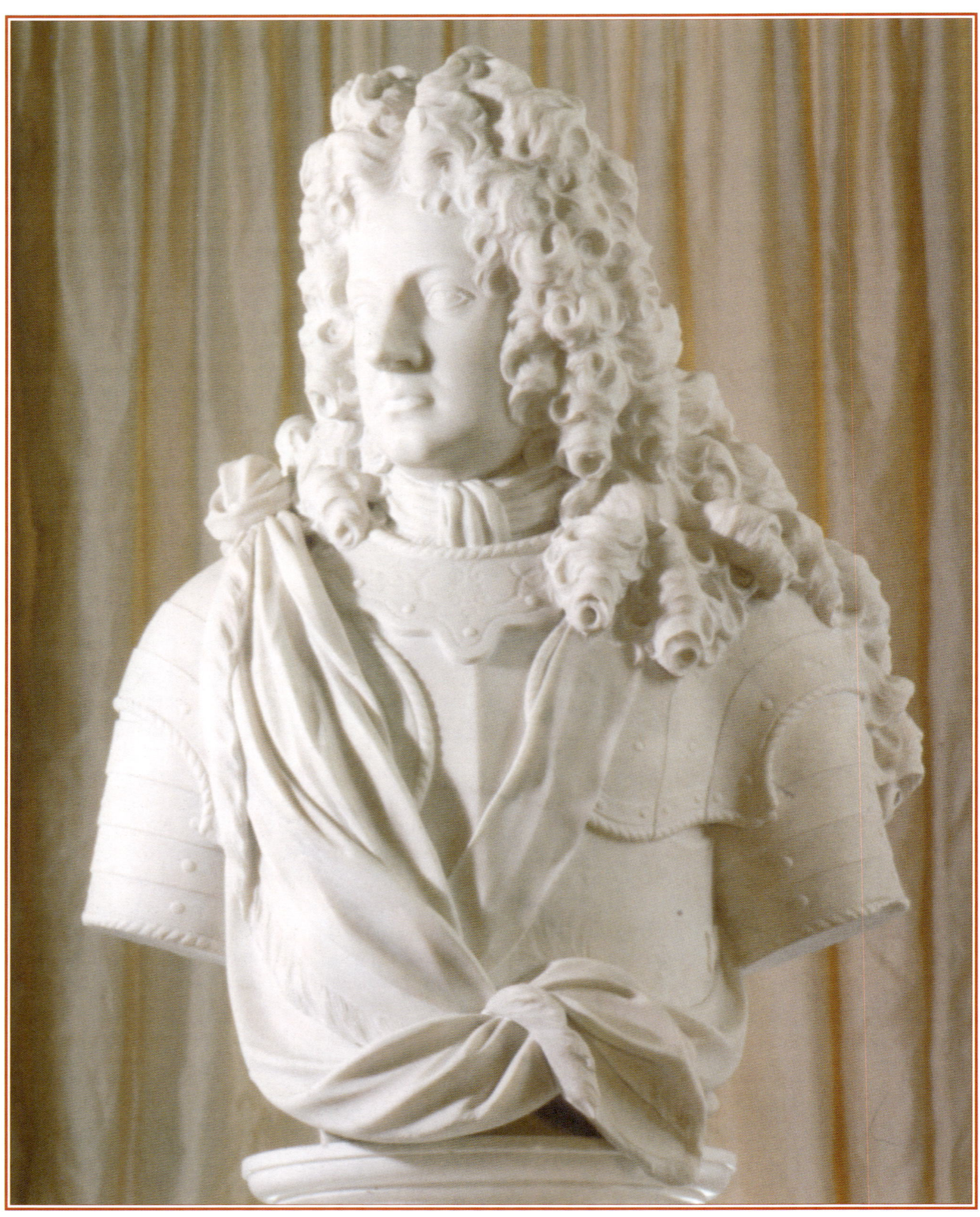

OTHER TAPESTRIES OFFERED FOR SALE TO THE DUKE OF MARLBOROUGH

A.   King William's set

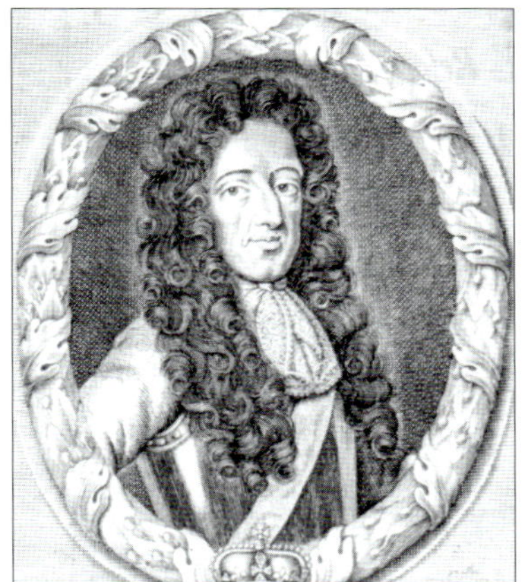

King William III.

When King William III came to the throne in February 1689 he inherited a collection of around 900 tapestries commissioned principally by Henry VIII in the 16th century and the early Stuarts in the 17th century.[146] William commissioned several new sets of tapestries from both English and Flemish workshops (including a set of Teniers peasants)[147] for his homes in Holland as well as for Kensington Palace, which he purchased from the 2nd Earl of Nottingham in 1689, and which Wren was instructed to enlarge. Several pictures and tapestries were also *"carried to Holland"* from England and included:

"[Seven] copies of the cartoons after Raphael in Distemper by Mr. Cook...
Six pieces of Forrest work of the Story of Meleager in His late Majesty's house at the Hague
Six pieces of the Months with Gold and Silver (but tarnished) sent into Holland by Mr Kean, closet keeper
Five pieces of Polidore, sent into Holland by Mr Kean" [148]

The refurbishment of the State Apartments at Hampton Court was still ongoing when King William had three sets of tapestries commissioned in 1700 through the workshops of the best of Brussels' weavers. The Van der Borcht and Le Clerc firms were supposed to have worked together with Judocus de Vos and Jan Cobus in the weaving of these tapestries for the King. Their workshops had previously collaborated in the weaving of a set of heraldic tapestries for William between 1695 and 1700.[149] The new contracts were made through the artist Lottin, who acted as the King's agent.[150] The orders comprised a set of *Art of War* tapestries designed by Lambert de Hondt and three panels to celebrate his own successes at *Bresgate, Torbay* and *the Boyne.* The subject of the third set is unknown. However, there is no evidence to establish which of these tapestries were completed or delivered and it is presumed that work on them must have come to a standstill on William's death in March 1702.

A set of William III's tapestries was offered for sale to the Duke of Marlborough when he was on campaign. On the 11th of August 1706, Charles Montagu, Earl of Halifax, who had just visited the Duke in Flanders wrote from the Hague, *"At Antwerp I saw a great many fine Pictures, particularly one of Lot and his family going out of Sodom, drawn by Rubens: Mons[ieur] de Wit, in whose Cabinet it is told me the City designed to buy it, to make a present of it to your Grace...I saw at the same time a mighty fine set of Tapestry Hangings wh[ich] are said to be bespoke by the King at 36 gs [guineas] an ell, nothing can be nobler, and may be had very cheap for few People can use them. I send your Grace the measures, which perhaps you will transmit to Woodstock."* [151]

About a month later, on September 13th 1706 the Duke wrote to his wife in England with some further details about this set, *"... I am told of a sute of Hangings that is at Antwerp, that may be baught for eightien hundred pounds, and that they are worth much more; wou'd you have me bye them, thay have neither silver nor gold in them, nor were ever us'd, thay were bespoke by the late King..."* [152]

It is not clear what the subject of these tapestries was but in any case the Duke did not purchase them. They might have been the undelivered *Art of War* set which would have been almost identical to the tapestries John Churchill had already ordered for himself a year earlier, but it is equally likely that they were the third, unknown set.

At Hampton Court Palace today, there are seven tapestries of the *History of Alexander* series woven by Judocus de Vos in Brussels from the Gobelins designs of Le Brun. They are reputed to have been purchased by General Cadogan in Flanders in the reign of King George I. [153] It is a tantalising possibility that this was the third set of tapestries commissioned by William III and still in Flanders in 1706. This may also have been the set that was offered to the Duke of Marlborough who perhaps thought £1,800 too high a price to pay, but inspired by it, commissioned his own set of *Alexander* tapestries a year later in 1707.

Cadogan had been Marlborough's Quartermaster-General in the War of the Spanish Succession, but twenty five years younger than the Duke, he went on to serve the new Hanoverian King and was promoted in 1717 by George I to *"General of all and singular the foot forces employed or to be employed in our service"*. [154] He conducted negotiations at the Hague from 1714-1718. It is possible that the set of tapestries in question were purchased by Cadogan for George I during this period.

The lack of documentation renders this theory hypothetical and it would be interesting to discover any evidence which lays to rest the speculation regarding the King William set.

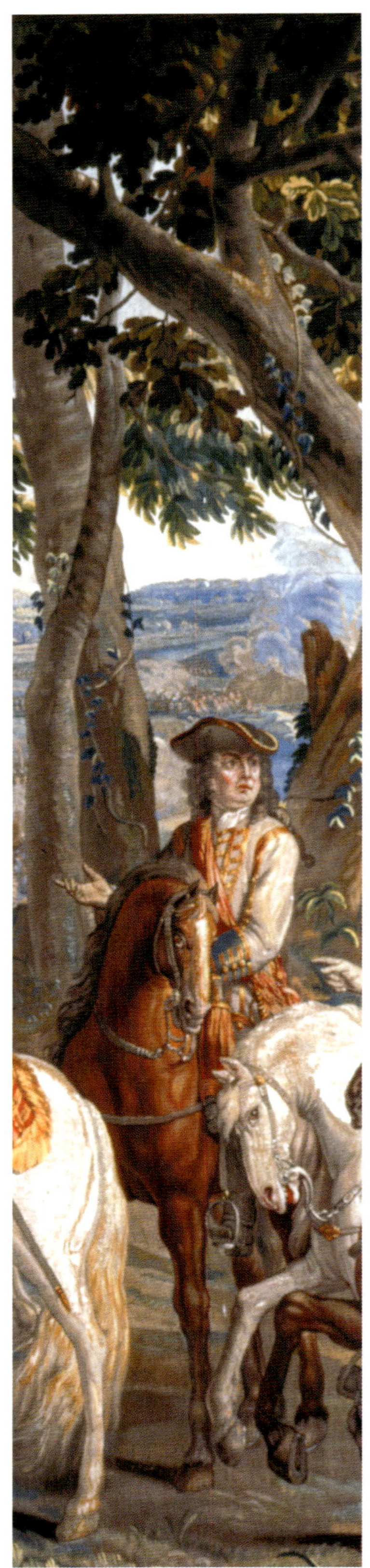

The image of Cadogan taken from the *Blenheim* tapestry.

B.   The *'Old Testament'* or *'Genesis'* set

In the Blenheim Papers there also exists a memorandum of a set of ten tapestries depicting scenes from the Old Testament. The memorandum is undated and states that the tapestries were *"based on designs by Raphael Urbini, famous artist of Rome"*.

The panels are described as:

"a long piece,		
	The creation of the world	*12¹/₂ ells*
	Adam and Eve under the tree	*10*
	The holocaust of Cain and Abel	*10*
	The world of Fire	*11*
	Noah and the Ark	*11¹/₂*
	The Flood begins	*15*
	The Flood ends	*13*
	The making of two columns?	*10*
	Noah's holocaust	*9*
	Noah drunk	*10*

At 6¹/₂ ells in height, a total of 726³/₈ ells, the final price at 24 florins per ell." [155]

A set of tapestries from the book of Genesis exists in Poland at Wawel, a royal castle at Krakow. The King of Poland and Lithuania, Sigismund II Augustus displayed these tapestries in 1553 at his marriage to Catherine Habsburg. The design of the set is attributed to Michiel Coxcie, a Netherlandish artist who worked in Rome from 1529 for about ten years, where he must have studied the renaissance creations of both Michelangelo and Raphael, including the fresco of *The Flood* in the Vatican Loggia executed by artists from the school of Raphael.[156]

The tapestries listed in the Blenheim memorandum were presumably made in Flanders based on the Coxcie designs. It is not known when they were offered for sale to the Duke of Marlborough, but they were not purchased by him.

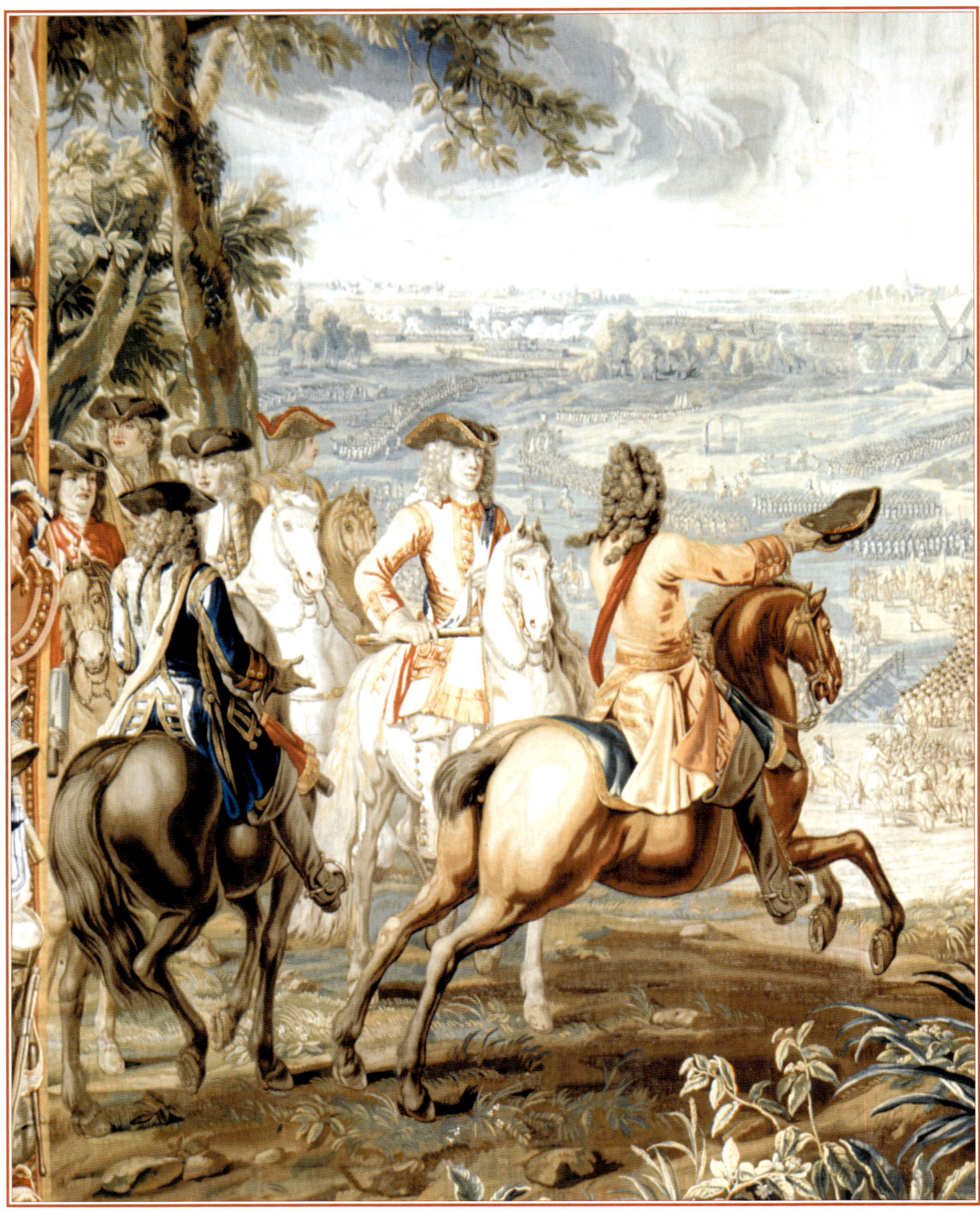

TAPESTRIES MADE FOR MARLBOROUGH'S GENERALS

Six of Marlborough's generals, all of whom were either building, expanding or refurbishing their own houses in the early 18th century, were reputed to have purchased sets of *Art of War* tapestry similar to their commander's prime set.

At Stowe, Sir Richard Temple, Lord Cobham, had ordered John Vanbrugh to make additions to the house between 1719-24 and later in around 1740, the interior of the State Gallery was totally refurbished by Henry Flitcroft. Cobham's set of *Art of War* tapestries comprising four panels (*Campement, Embuscade, Attaque,* and *Fouragement*) was commissioned between 1706 and 1712 and was originally hung in the Great Parlour at Stowe. He also commissioned a *Plaisirs des Dieux* set of tapestries. Sadly, the contents of the house including all these tapestries were sold off in 1921-22.

At Cliveden, Lord George Hamilton, Earl of Orkney had two wings added to the house around 1705 by the architect Thomas Archer. The only survivors of the numerous *Art of War* sets reputed to have been made for Marlborough's generals are to be found here. The tapestries had previously all been disposed of when the estate was bought by the Dukes of Sutherland in 1849, but three

Facing page : Detail of Marlborough with his Generals from the Oudenarde tapestry

The north prospect of Cliveden from Colen Campbell's *Vitruvius Britannicus.*

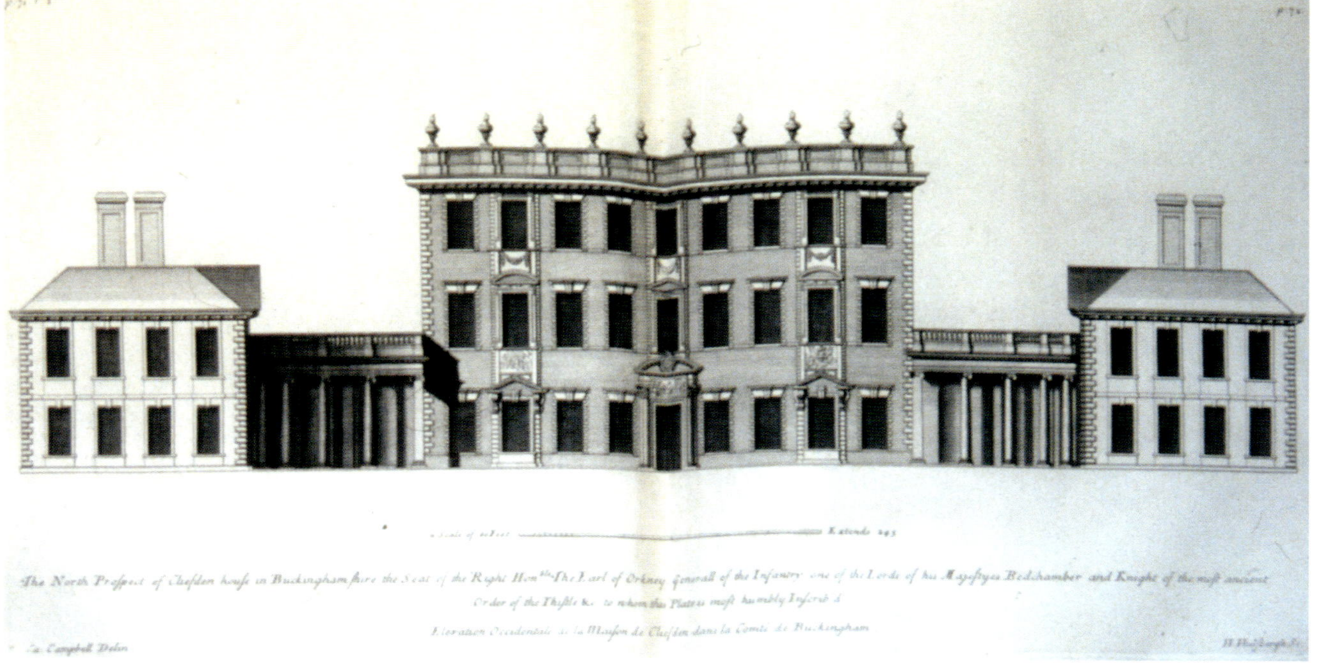

panels (*Campement, Embuscade* and *Rencontre)* were discovered in Paris in the 1890s by Lord Astor (a subsequent owner of Cliveden) who purchased them and brought them back to hang in the house. They were woven by Le Clerc and Van der Borcht and bear Orkney's coat of arms in the top borders. The fourth panel of the Orkney set, entitled *La Marche,* is now to be found in the USA (at Brown University, Providence, Rhode Island). The panels from this set have Van Orley borders similar to the Duke of Marlborough's *Art of War* set at Blenheim and therefore must have been commissioned after his set.

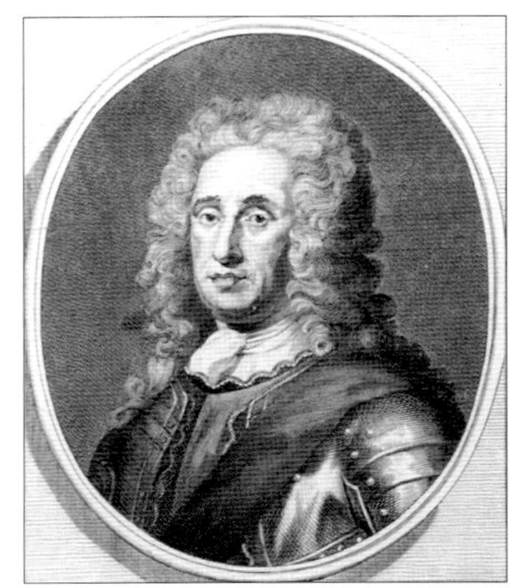

Earl of Orkney.

At Inverary, John Campbell, 2nd Duke of Argyll had a pavilion built in 1720-22. (Inverary Castle itself was rebuilt later in 1746). A descendant, the 9th Duke, mentions the sets of tapestries commissioned for Marlborough's generals (*Priceless Tapestries,* London Magazine XXIII, 1910, 650) but the whereabouts of the Argyll set itself is not known.

At Caversham, the old house purchased by William Cadogan was pulled down in 1718 to rebuild a new one in the latest fashion. Cadogan also enjoyed the use of his wife's home (Raaphorst Castle) in Holland, the likely setting for a set of *Plaisirs des Dieux* tapestries ordered by him before 1711. (Blenheim Archives, Long Library Portfolios Vol. II, f. 33) His set of *Art of War* tapestries is supposed to have perished in the fire that destroyed the house in 1850.

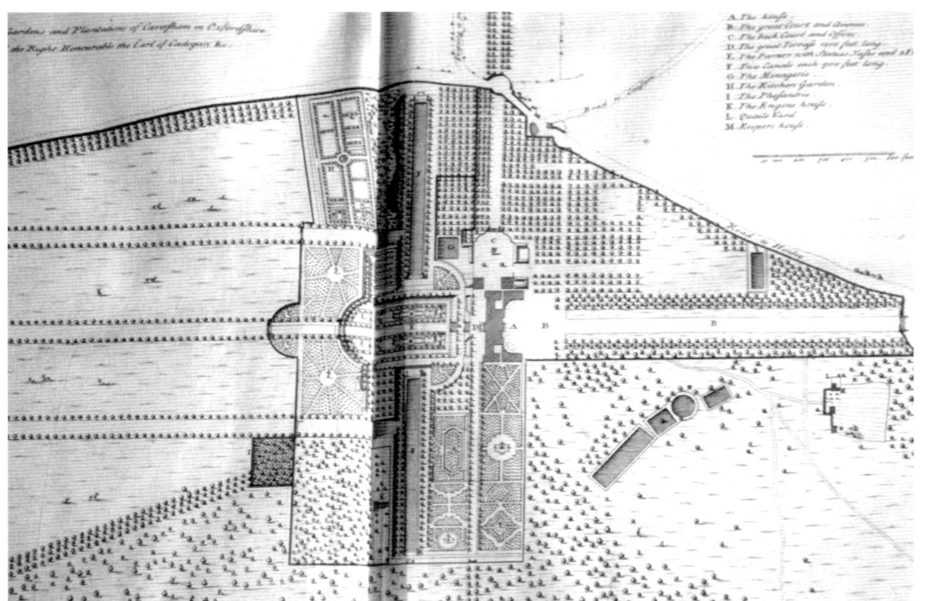

A contemporary plan of Caversham.

At Biddesden, General John Richmond Webb had a red brick mansion built for himself in 1711 on an estate purchased in 1692 from the widow of Sir George Browne. His set of *Art of War* tapestries cannot be traced.

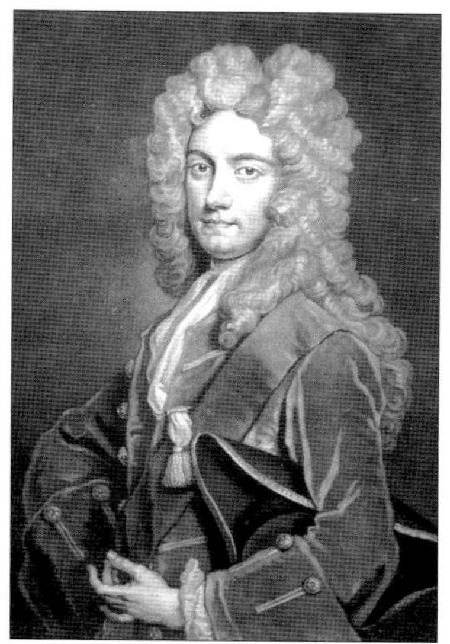

Earl of Scarborough.

Stanstead Park (designed by William Talman in 1686) was the home of Richard Lumley, the 1st Earl of Scarborough. Both he and his younger brother Henry, served in Marlborough's wars. A set of *Plaisirs des Dieux* tapestries is recorded as being made for "*Mons. Lumley commandant de la ville de Gand [Ghent]*" in 1707 (Naulaerts day book, J. Denuce in *Antwerp Art Tapestry & Trade*, Antwerp and The Hague 1936). It is not known whether these were hung at Stanstead or at Lumley Castle in Co. Durham, where Vanbrugh was engaged by the family in 1722 to remodel the entrance front and alter the interiors. Of his *Art of War* set, *Campement, Faschinade, Embuscade, Pillage* (in 2 panels), *La Marche, Fouragement* (in 2 panels) and *Rencontre* were known to have been woven. Consisting of nine panels, it seems to be the largest of the six generals sets. The Lumley set was sold first in 1911 and certain panels were disposed of again at subsequent sales in 1938 and 1961. Three panels, *Embuscade, Campement* and *Faschinade* were repurchased by the family and restored to Stanstead.

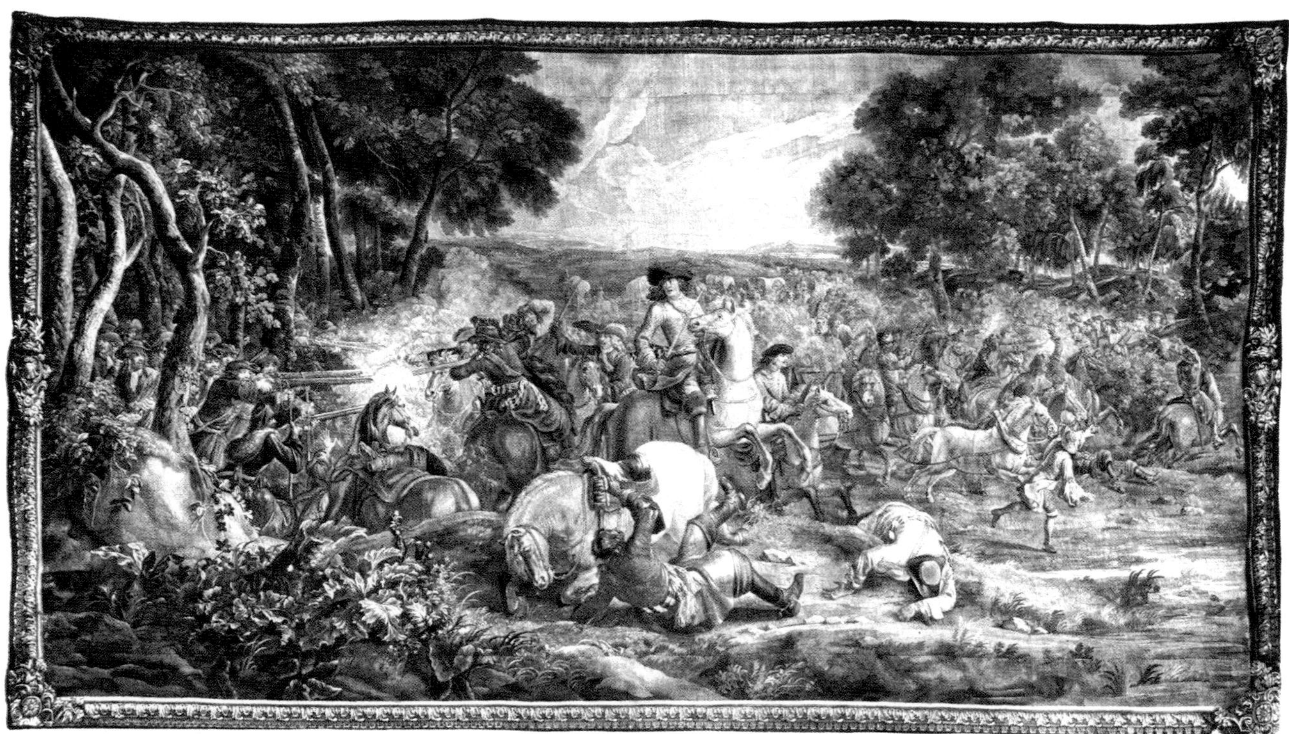

The *Embuscade* panel from the Lumley set.

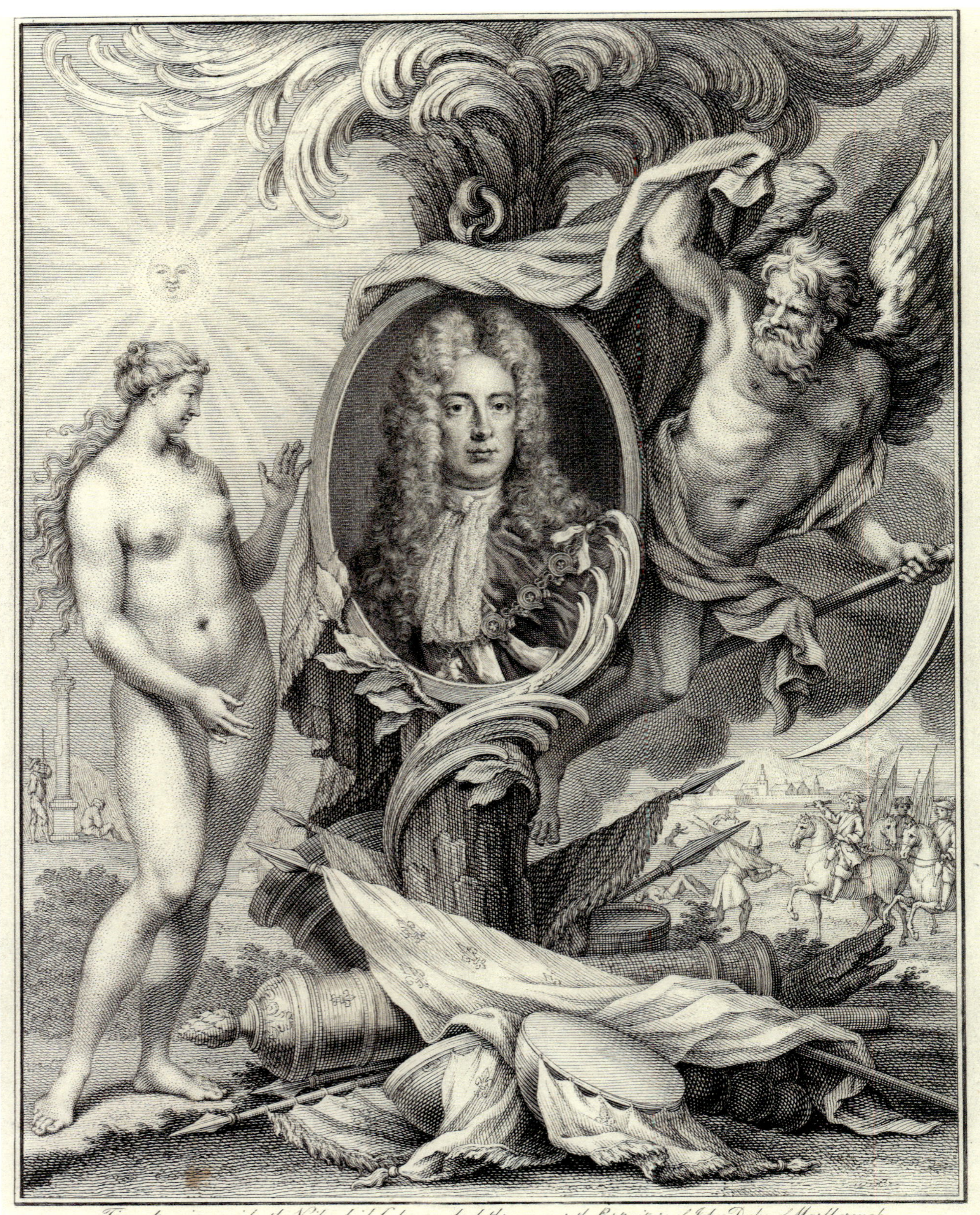

Time drawing aside the Veil which Calumny had thrown over the Portraiture of John Duke of Marlborough, and Truth directing the Brightness and Beauty of her light upon it.

A POEM ON TAPESTRIES FOR THE DUKE OF MARLBOROUGH

Instructions to Vanderbank : A Sequel to the Advice to the Poets,
A Poem occasioned by the Glorious success of Her Majesty's Arms
under the Command of the Duke of Marlborough, the last year in Flanders[157]

Then Artist, who dost Nature's face express,
In Silk and Gold, and Scenes of Action dress;
Dost figur'd Arras animated leave,
Spin a bright Story or a Passion weave
By mingling Threads, canst mingle Shade and Light,
Delineate Triumphs or describe a Fight,
Do thou relate the Hero's toil, record
The Train of new Events that crown'd his hardy Sword.

O Belgian work a piece by this cartone
And be this Picture by thy Art out done.
Show how he flew intrepid on the Foe
Plung'd deep amidst the Files, force'd his Passage thro
How the great youth with veteran Captains vy'd
What trophys crown'd a Sword till then untry'd.
Then show the Conqueror in another Scene
Protecting with his Arms the brave Eugene.

Belgian, attend, and from thy noble Loom,
Let the great Chief August in Triumph come;
For Blenheim's lofty Walls the Work design
In every Piece let Art and Labour shine;
Let glorious deeds, the Britons Palace crown,
Not those of ancient Heroes, but his own.
In the bright Series of his Story show
What Albion, what Mankind to Marlbro owe.

The poem from which the above extracts are taken was published in 1709 by Sir Richard Blackmore. Blackmore had a varied career as a physician and poet. He was born at Corsham, in Wiltshire, in the mid seventeenth century. He held the office of physician in ordinary to King William III and was knighted in 1697. Subsequently, he was physician to Queen Anne but fell from favour when the Queen experienced a number of miscarriages and still-births and some of her children died in infancy.[158]

Facing page : Print showing Time drawing aside the Veil which Calumny had thrown over the Portraiture of John Duke of Marlborough and Truth directing the Brightness and Beauty of her light upon it.

Blackmore had a passion for writing epics. *Prince Arthur, an Heroick Poem in Ten Books* appeared in 1695 and received an extremely favourable reception with three editions in two years. This was followed by other equally long poems: *Alfred*, *Satire upon Wit*, and in 1705, the much criticised *Eliza*. Blackmore then wrote a piece on the Kit-cat Club before publishing *Advice to the Poets how to celebrate the Duke of Marlborough* in 1708. In 1709, joining in the euphoria of a further campaign of Allied military success, Blackmore followed-up his *Advice to the Poets* with a poem verbosely entitled: "*Instructions to Vanderbank: A Sequel to the Advice to the Poets, A Poem occasioned by the Glorious success of Her Majesty's Arms under the Command of the Duke of Marlborough, the last year in Flanders*".

Blackmore's laudatory 517-line poem was essentially advice to a weaver of tapestry instructing him on methods and reasons to glorify the Duke of Marlborough. It was addressed to John Vanderbank who was the chief tapestry worker of the Great Wardrobe in the late seventeenth and early eighteenth century, based in London's Great Queen Street. Amongst other commissions, Vanderbank made tapestries for Queen Mary's apartments at Kensington Palace, as well as for Ralph, Earl of Montagu at Boughton House and for John, Earl of Exeter.[159] Vanderbank is not known to have undertaken any tapestry commissions for the Duke of Marlborough.

A BRIEF CHRONOLOGY OF EVENTS IN FLANDERS IN THE WAR OF THE SPANISH SUCCESSION

1702	May 15	Allies declare war on France
	July 1	Marlborough takes command as Captain General of Allied forces in the Netherlands.
	July 26	Marlborough is made Master General of the Ordinance.
	August	Marlborough is blocked by the Dutch from attacking the French near the Heaths of Peer.
	September 25	Allies besiege (August 29) and capture Venloo
	October 2	Allies besiege (September 26) and take Stevenswaert
	October 6	Allies besiege (September 26) and capture Ruremonde
	October 23	Allies take Liege
	October	Bavaria joins forces with the French
	December 14	Queen Anne confers dukedom on Marlborough

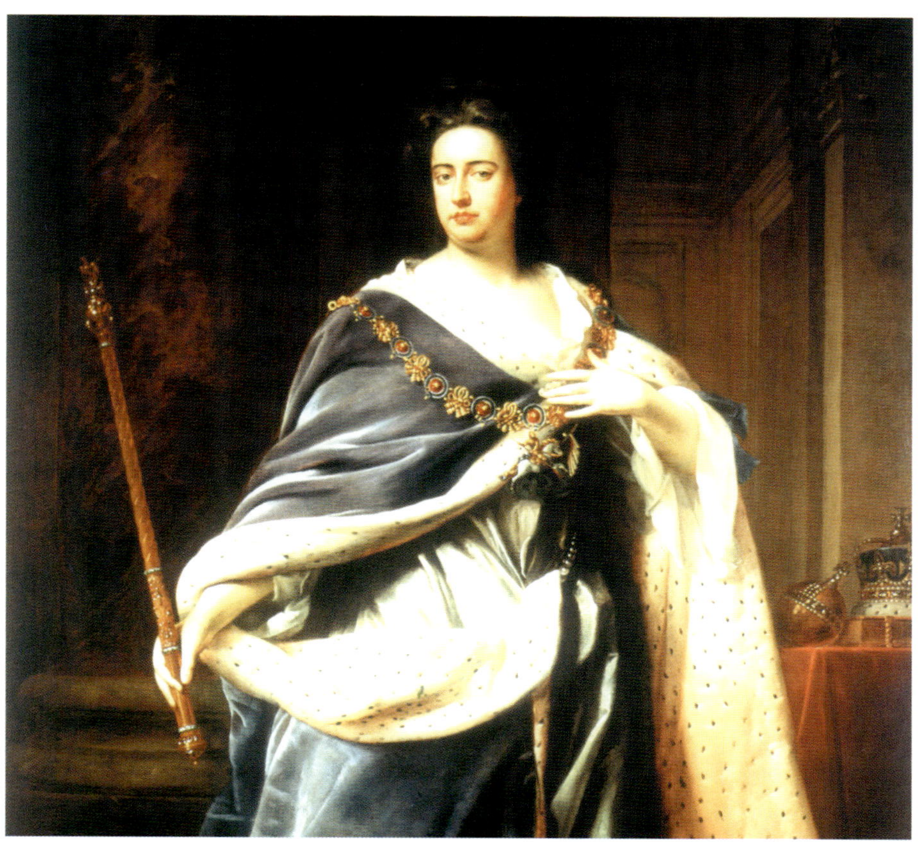

Queen Anne by Edward Lilly (detail).

1703	May 18	Allies besiege (April 27) and capture Bonn
	August 25	Allies besiege (August 14) and capture Huy
	September 27	Allies besiege (September 10) and capture Limburg
	November	Savoy joins the Allies
	December	Portugal joins the Allies
1704	May 19	Marlborough sets out from Bedburg on his epic march to the Danube
	July 2	The storming of the Schellenberg and the capture of Donauworth
	August 13	Allied victory at the Battle of Blenheim
	August 21	Allies besiege (August 11) and capture Ingolstadt
	November 23	Allies besiege (October 24) and capture Landau
	November 26	The Allies take Treves (Trier)
	December 20	Allies besiege (November 4) and capture Trarbach
1705	May 5	Joseph I accedes to the Imperial throne on the death of Leopold I
	June 10	French besiege (May 28) and capture Huy
	July 11	Allies besiege (July 6) and recapture Huy
	July 18	Allies cross the Lines of Brabant
	November	Marlborough visits courts of Vienna, Berlin and Hanover
1706	May 23	Allied victory at the Battle of Ramillies
	May 25	Allies take Louvain
	June 1-3	Allies capture Ghent and Bruges
	June 17	Allies take Antwerp
	July 6	Allies besiege (June 19) and capture Ostend
	August 22	Allies besiege (July 22) and capture Menin
	September 9	Allies besiege (August 27) and capture Dendermonde
	October 2	Allies besiege (September 16) and capture Ath
1707	April 27	Marlborough meets Charles XII of Sweden at Alt Ranstadt
	May 5	Marlborough visits King Frederick of Prussia
	June 1	Marlborough occupies a position at Meldert to cover a possible French advance into Brabant. He remains here for 2 months.
	August 11	Marlborough marches to Nivelles. Forced to remain in the vicinity by unusually wet weather.
	September 1	The Allies cross the River Dendre at Ath, the French retreat towards the Scheldt.
	September 7	The Allies reach Helchin, the French withdraw towards Lille.
	October	Both armies go into winter quarters.

1708	July 5	The French take Bruges
	July 7	The French capture Ghent
	July 11	Allied victory at the Battle of Oudenarde
	August 11	Allies besiege Lille
	September 28	Allies win encounter at Wynendael
	October 24	Marshal Bouffleurs surrenders the town of Lille and withdraws into the Citadel
	December 9	The Citadel of Lille capitulates
	December 29	Allies besiege (December 18) and recapture Ghent
	January 2	Allies recapture Bruges
1709	June 27	Allies besiege Tournai
	July 30	The governor of Tournai surrenders the town and retreats into the Citadel with the garrison
	September 3	Tournai surrenders to the Allies
	September 7	Allies seize the passage near Jemmappes
	September 11	Allied victory at the Battle of Malplaquet
	October 11	Allies besiege (September 7) and capture Mons
1710	March	Abortive peace negotiations held at Gertruydenburg
	June 26	Allies besiege (5 May) and capture Douai
	August 8	Godolphin removed from office, new ministry in England under Harley
	August 28	Allies besiege (15 July) and capture Bethune
	September 29	Allies besiege (September 5) and capture St. Venant
	November 12	Allies besiege (September 12) and capture Aire
1711	April 17	Charles VI accedes to the Imperial throne on the death of Joseph I
	July 6	Allies capture Arleux
	July 22	French retake and raze Arleux
	August 4/5	Allies cross Lines of *Ne Plus Ultra*
	August 9	Allies besiege Bouchain
	September 13	Allies capture Bouchain
	October	Secret Anglo-French peace negotiations begin
	December 31	Dismissal of Marlborough from all his offices. Duke of Ormonde appointed Captain General. Lord Rivers appointed Master General of the Ordinance
1712	July 4	Allies besiege (June 8) and capture Le Quesnoy
	July 16	British forces withdrawn from war
	July 24	French victory at the Battle of Denain
	July 30	French besiege (July 25) and capture Marchiennes
	September 8	French besiege (August 14) and recapture Douai
	October 3	French besiege (September 8) and recapture Le Quesnoy

October 19	French besiege (October 1) and recapture Bouchain

1713 April 11   The Peace of Utrecht signed between France, England, the United Provinces (Holland), Portugal, Savoy and Prussia

        July 13   Peace treaty signed between Spain and England

1714 March 6   The Peace of Rastadt signed between France and Austria

        June 26   Peace treaty signed between Spain and the United Provinces

        August 1   Queen Anne dies, George I accedes to the throne

        August 17   Marlborough reappointed to his posts

        September 7   The Peace of Baden signed between France and states of the Holy Roman Empire (other than Austria)

1715 February 6   Peace treaty signed between Spain and Portugal

        September 15   King Louis XIV dies

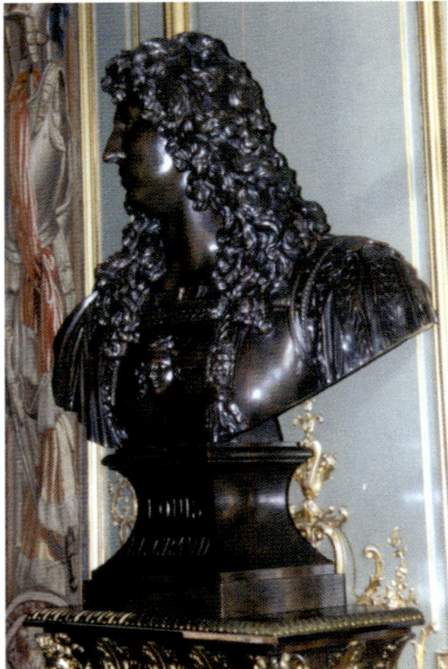

Bronze bust of Louis XIV.

NOTES

1. British Library Add. Mss. 61,429 f. 196
2. Daniel Defoe, *The Duke of Anjou's Succession,* 1701. Also contains an interesting reference to the clause in Louis XIV's Contract of Marriage, renouncing the Spanish throne. Louis's support of his grandson to the Spanish throne was an obvious way to circumvent these restrictions and gain control of the vast wealth of Spanish territories and trade.
3. A. Boyer, *The Life and Reign of Queen Anne,* 1735. Churchill was created a Duke on 14 December 1702.
4. T. Campbell, *Tapestry in the Renaissance: Art and Magnificence,* New York 2002, 13-27
5. M. Fenaille, *Etat general des tapisseries de la manufacture des Gobelins depuis son origine jusqu'a nos jours, 1600-1900,* Paris 1903
6. See Appendix II.
7. G. Delmarcel, *Flemish Tapestry,* Tielt 1999, 228
8. Blenheim Archives, Long Library Portfolios Vol. II, f. 32. There were three battle scenes in the *Alexander* series each of which could be divided into up to three panels. M. Fenaille, *Etat general des tapisseries de la manufacture des Gobelins,* Vol. 1662-1699; and K. Brosens, *A Contextual Study of Brussels Tapestry,* 83
9. GAC acquisition number 13145.
10. M. Fenaille, *Etat general des tapisseries,* Vol. 1662-1699, 99
11. Blenheim Archives, Long Library Portfolios Vol. II, f. 35 - letter dated 11 June 1714 which refers to the Duke's image in the tapestry panel called the *Lines above Louvain [Lines of Brabant].* He is referred to as 'Your Highness' because by this time he was a Prince of the Holy Roman Empire.
12. Blenheim Archives, Long Library Portfolios Vol. II, f. 43.
13. A. Wace, *The Marlborough Tapestries at Blenheim Palace,* London 1968, 132
14. W. Hefford, *Some Problems concerning the* Art of War *Tapestries,* Bulletin de Liaison of the Centre International d'Etude des Textiles Anciens, Lyon (No. 41/42, 1975 - I et II).
15. A. Wace, *Ibid,* 90-108 and W. Hefford, *Ibid,* note 12
16. B. Seeley, *Stowe - A Description of the House and Gardens, 1797,* 59. See Appendix III
17. For an analysis and illustrations of the various sets, see A. Wace, *The Marlborough Tapestries at Blenheim Palace,* London 1968, 49-59 and 124-130.
18. A. Wace, *Ibid,* 103
19. G. Delmarcel, *Flemish Tapestry,* 14
20. K. Brosens, *A Contextual Study of Brussels Tapestry 1670-1770 - The Dye Works and Tapestry Workshop of Urbanus Leyniers (1674-1747),* Brussels 2004, 46
21. J. Denuce, *Antwerp Art Tapestry & Trade,* Antwerp and The Hague, 1936
22. K. Brosens, *Ibid*
23. K. Brosens, *Ibid,* 61-62
24. W. G. Thomson, *A History of Tapestry,* 1973, 375
25. A. Wauters, *Les Tapisseries bruxelloises: Essai Historique sur les Tapisseries de haute et de basse-lice de Bruxelles,* Brussels 1878, 161
26. K. Brosens, *Brussels Tapestry Producer Judocus de Vos (1661/62-1734) - New Data and Design Attributions,* Studies in the Decorative Arts Vol. IX, No. 2 (2002), 59.
27. K. Brosens, *Ibid.* I am indebted to Dr. Brosens for much of what follows on de

Vos's life.

28 A. Wauters, *Les Tapisseries bruxelloises*, 351

29 G. Delmarcel, *Flemish Tapestry*, 285

30 A. Wace, *Ibid*, 29-30

31 W. Hefford, *Ibid*

32 A. Wace, *Ibid*, 124

33 A. Wace, *Ibid*, 122

34 W. Hefford, *Ibid*. The dealer's records, called the *'Memorial Naulaerts'*, covering the period 1699-1709 were published by J. Denuce in *Antwerp Art Tapestry & Trade*, Antwerp and The Hague,1936.

35 J. Denuce, *Antwerp Art Tapestry & Trade*, 279 (f.130)

36 J. Denuce, *Ibid*, 304-5 (ff.159 and 162)

37 In English: *The March, The Ambush, The Siege of a town, Making Fascines, The Skirmish, The Camp, Foraging,* and *Pillage.*

38 British Library, Add. Mss. 61,348 f.83

39 See Appendix I.

40 British Library Add. Mss. 61,429 f.7

41 British Library Add. Mss. 61,429 f.71

42 K. Brosens, *A Contextual Study of Brussels Tapestry*

43 British Library Add. Mss. 61,429 f.75

44 British Library Add. Mss. 19,591 f. 2

45 NG 1172. Bought by the National Gallery in 1885/6 from the 8th Duke of Marlborough for £17,500

46 Calendar of Treasury Books, *Out Letters (General) XVIII.*

47 British Library Add. Mss. 61,429 f. 87

48 British Library Add. Mss. 61,348 ff. 58-59

49 British Library Add. Mss. 61,429 f. 96

50 British Library Add. Mss. 61,354

51 G. Delmarcel, *Ibid*, 250-251

52 K. Brosens, Studies in the Decorative Arts Vol. XI, No. 1 (2003)

53 K. Brosens, *A Contextual Study of Brussels Tapestry*, 83

54 British Library Add. Mss. 61,429 f.124

55 British Library Add. Mss. 61,429 ff.134 - 5

56 British Library Add. Mss. 61,429 f.136

57 British Library Add. Mss. 61,348 f.56. It was signed at the Army's camp at Soignes on 31st August 1707 by Jan-Jozef Naulaerts (the youngest son of Nicholaas Naulaerts), Frans Blommaerts and Judocus de Vos. Note however, that the Duke said he had *"bespoke them"* two months before the contract was officially signed.

58 British Library Add. Mss. 61,348, f. 57

59 British Library Add. Mss. 61,351, ff. 34-35

60 J. Denuce, *Antwerp Art Tapestry & Trade*, 325 (f. 181)

61 J. Denuce, *Ibid.*, 333 (f. 189)

62 K. Brosens *A Contextual Study of Brussels Tapestry*, 95, 99

63 K. Brosens , *Ibid*, 95

64 J. Denuce, *Ibid*, 334 (f. 189)

65 In English: *The Battle with Darius [Battle of Arbella], the Crossing of the River Granicus, the new piece being the Battle of Porus [Battle of Hydaspes], the triumphal entry into Babylon, the gathering of remains, Pillage, taking Prisoners, and the Capture of Porus.*

66 British Library Add. Mss. 61,429 f. 196

67 J. Denuce, *Ibid.* and K. Brosens, Studies in the Decorative Arts Vol. IX, No. 2 (2002), 64

68 British Library Add. Mss. 61,348 f. 83

69 British Library Add. Mss. 61,430 f.146

70 H. Synder (Ed.), *Marlborough Godolphin Correspondence*, 1975, 1315

71 Blenheim Archives, Long Library Portfolios Vol. II, f. 30 In English: *The family of Darius at Alexander's feet, Alexander meets the Philosophers, Diogenes in his tub, and Alexander dismounting to greet his father.*

72 Blenheim Archives, Long Library Portfolios Vol. II, f. 41

73 G. Delmarcel, *Ibid.*

74 British Library Add. Mss. 61,215 f.62. The *'great roome'* mentioned was an unspecified room, but was probably the Great Hall at Blenheim Palace.

75 Blenheim Archives, Long Library Portfolios Vol. II, f. 30v

76 Count Sinzendorf was petitioned in 1715 by tapestry merchants and weavers from Flanders and Brabant to intervene and support their bid for the reduction of tariffs and duties imposed on imports of their goods into England, France and Holland. (A. Wauters, *Essai Historique*, 224). That they felt comfortable in approaching the Imperial State Minister in this way indicates a certain degree of familiarity.

77 British Library Add. Mss. 61,430 f.156

78 British Library Add. Mss. 61,348 f. 83

79 Blenheim Archives, Long Library Portfolios Vol. II, f. 42

80 Blenheim Archives, Long Library Portfolios Vol. II, f. 34

81 Blenheim Archives, Long Library Portfolios Vol. II, ff. 30v, 33-33v

82 British Library Add. Mss. 61,354

83 British Library Add. Mss. 61,429 f. 196

84 H. Synder ed., *Ibid*, 1315

85 British Library Add. Mss. 61,216 ff. 39-40

86 British Library Add. Mss. 41,178 f. 39

87 British Library Add. Mss. 61,355 f. 5 Work on the building was eventually stopped in 1712 after the Queen's relations with the Duke and Duchess had reached its lowest point and both were removed from their posts. Construction only resumed in 1716.

88 A. Wace, *Ibid*, 112 and W. Hefford, *Ibid*, 110.

89 A.J. Wauters, *Essai Historique sur les Tapisseries*

90 Alexandre Pinchart, *Tapisseries Flamandes*, 109-110

91 G. Delmarcel, *Ibid*, 343

92 K. Brosens, *A Contextual Study of Brussels Tapestry 1670-1770* , 309

93 K. Brosens, Studies in the Decorative Arts Vol. IX, No. 2 (2002), 73

94 K. Brosens, *Ibid*, 79

95 G. Delmarcel, *Ibid*, 325

96 K. Brosens, Studies in the Decorative Arts Vol. IX, No. 2 (2002), 72

97 Blenheim Archives, Long Library Portfolios Vol. II, f. 34

98 British Library, Add. Mss. 61,367 f. 104. Letter of 6th January 1710.

99 Hercules was the classical prototype of strength and virtue, a symbol of heroic valour

100 Blenheim Archives, Long Library Portfolios Vol. II, f. 33

101 The territory was restored to the Elector of Bavaria at the end of the war under the terms of the Peace of Rastadt in 1714. See D. Chandler, *Marlborough*

    as Military Commander, 1984, 306-307.
102 British Library Add. Mss. 61, 431 f. 5
103 British Library Add. Mss. 61,367 f. 121
104 British Library Add. Mss. 61,431 f.197, letter dated Feb 5th 1713. These would have been hangings from the *Victories* set.
105 K. Brosens, *A Contextual Study of Brussels Tapestry 1670-1770* , 89
106 K. Brosens, *Ibid* , 101
107 British Library Add. Mss. 61,431 f. 63
108 British Library Add. Mss 42,176 f. 317
109 British Library Add. Mss 61,347 f. 137
110 British Library Add. Mss 61,351 f. 34v
111 British Library Add. Mss 61,353 f. 48 (the plastering was completed by Oct 1708). The original cornicing was modified when the 4th Duke carried out extensive renovations to the interiors.
112 Blenheim Archives, Treasury Box XXII, 74/1, document dated 21 September 1719
113 British Library, Add. Mss. 61,473 and Duveen archives regarding *Pleasures of the Gods*.
114 British Library Add. Mss. 61,368 ff. 73-74, letter dated 31st October 1711.
115 British Library Add. Mss. 61,216 f.46
116 British Library Add. Mss. 61,351 ff. 34-35v
117 K. Brosens, *A Contextual Study of Brussels Tapestry*, 44
118 British Library Add. Mss. 61,368 ff. 73-74
119 Blenheim Archives, Long Library Portfolios Vol. II, f. 35, letter dated 11 June 1714.
120 This dimension is for the two tapestries together, i.e. 12 ells (835 cms) in length each.
121 Blenheim Archives, Long Library Portfolios Vol. II, f. 33v
122 Blenheim Archives, Long Library Portfolios Vol. II, f. 30v. Described as the *Battle of Hooghstet [Blenheim], that of Ramillies, the Taking of Lille, the Battle of Wynendale, that of Oudenarde, that of Schellenberg, that of Malplaquet, the taking of Bouchain* (small panel).
123 Later historians generally concur that the Grand Alliance 'won the war but lost the peace'.
124 Blenheim Archives, Long Library Portfolios Vol. II, f. 37
125 In the currency of the time this amounted to roughly £2,350-2,450. With the *Lines of Louvain [Lines of Brabant]* tapestry added, the commission was worth £2,500-2,600.
126 Blenheim Archives, Long Library Portfolios Vol. II, f. 40v
127 Blenheim Archives, Treasury Box XII (39).
128 J. de Maere & M. Wabbes, *Illustrated Dictionary of 17th century Flemish Painters*, Brussels 1994
129 W. Hefford, *Ibid*, 110
130 Horace Walpole, *Anecdotes of Painting in England*, Strawberry Hill, 1763, collected by the late George Vertue Vol. 3, 158 "*The following slight notices relating to artists who have worked for the English but came not to England*"
131 British Library Add. Mss. 61,368 ff. 73v-74
132 The *Wynendael* panel is the exception.
133 M. Fenaille, *Ibid*, Vol. 1 1662-1699, 54
134 D. Chandler (Ed.), *Military Memoirs of Marlborough's Campaigns 1702-1712*,

1998, 60
135   M. Gareau, *Charles Le Brun First Painter to Louis XIV*, New York, 1992
136   British Library Add. Mss. 22,210 f.25
137   Page 381. I am grateful to Connie Ellis for bringing this to my attention.
138   A. Wace, *Ibid*, 119
139   The work was carried out in 1712-14 under the supervision of Sir Godfrey Kneller.
140   Louis, Duke of Burgundy (1682-1712) was a grandson of King Louis XIV.
141   T. Lediard, *The Life of John, Duke of Marlborough, Prince of the Roman Empire*, London 1743
142   British Library Add. Mss. 75,401 (unbound, Althorp Papers D14)
143   Illustrated examples of Teniers' tapestries can be seen in Guy Delmarcel, *Flemish Tapestries*, 352-360
144   British Library Add. Mss. 61,428 f. 147, letter dated December 8/19 1704.
145   British Library Add. Mss. 38,056 f. 26
146   T. Campbell, *William III and the 'Triumph of Lust'*, Apollo CXLI 1994
147   Guy Delmarcel, *Ibid*, 352
148   British Library Add. Mss. 61,359 f. 80
149   Guy Delmarcel, *Ibid*, 219
150   A. Wace, *Ibid*, 40
151   British Library Add. Mss. 61,134 f.168-169
152   British Library Add. Mss. 61,429 f. 49
153   H.C. Marillier, *The Tapestries at Hampton Court Palace*, London 1931, 28
154   Military Entry Books (Home Office), XI, 219
155   British Library Add. Mss. 61,359 f. 82
156   T. Campbell, *Tapestry in the Renaissance: Art and Magnificence*, 445-447
157   Printed and sold by H. Hills in Black-fryars near the Waterside, 1709
158   Samuel Johnson, *The Works of the English Poets from Chaucer to Cowper*, London, 1810 and E. Sanford, *The Works of the British Poets with Lives of the Authors*, Philadelphia, 1819, Vol XV
159   W. G. Thomson, *A History of Tapestry*, 1973, 361,489

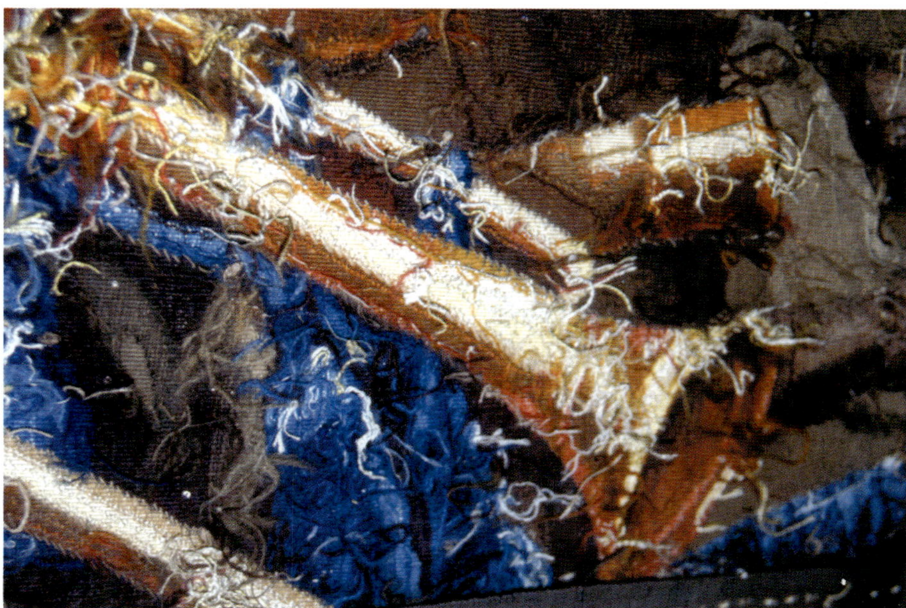

Reverse side of the *Lines of Brabant* tapestry, showing a detail from the border.

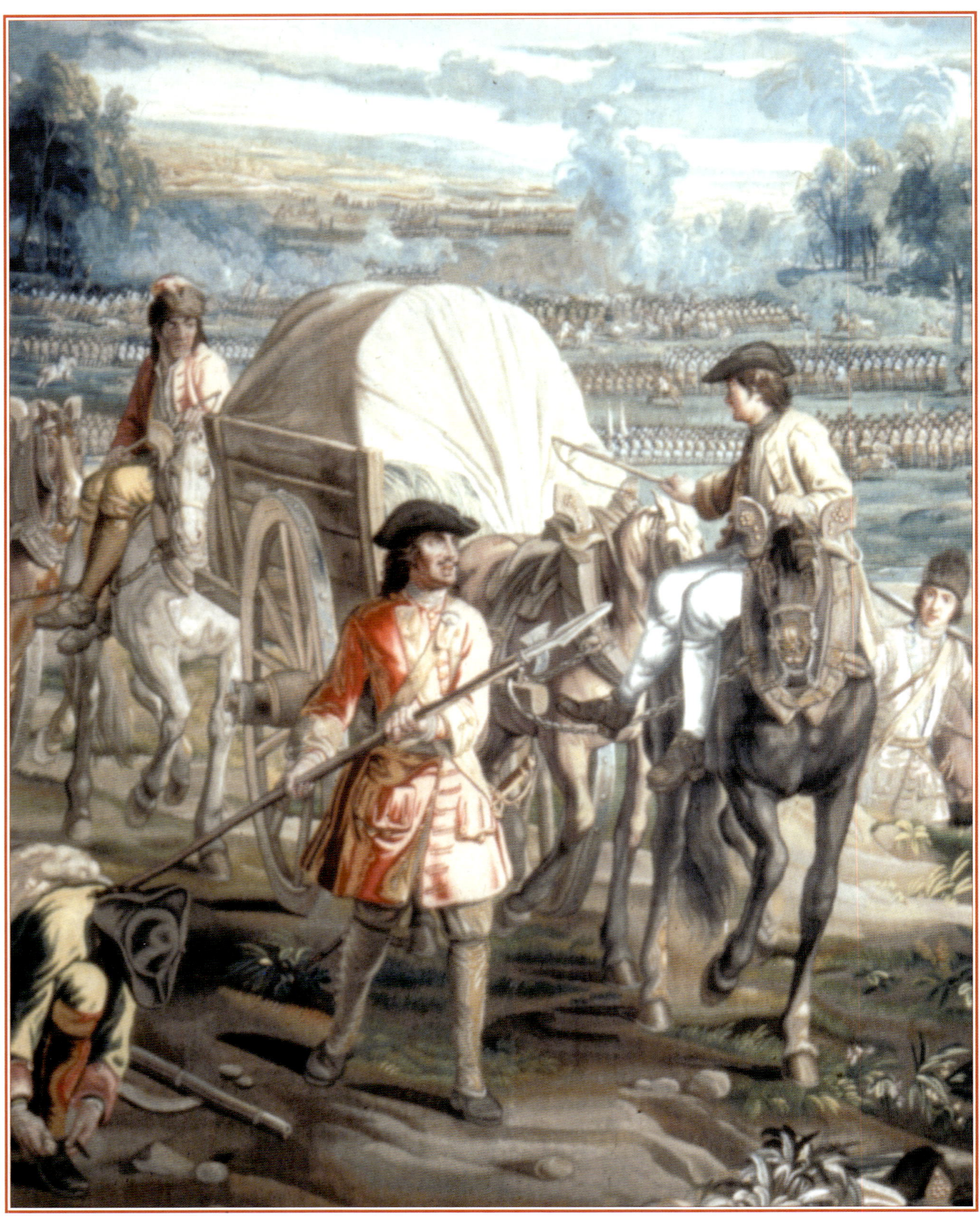

ACKNOWLEDGEMENTS

I make my most sincere acknowledgements to His Grace, the Duke of Marlborough for access to the tapestries at Blenheim Palace, for permission to quote from the Blenheim archives and to reproduce images from the collection.

I am indebted to John Forster for facilitating the retrieval of archival material and for his unfailing encouragement. I am also grateful to Helen Walch for her help and kindness in the early stages of my research. Amongst other friends and colleagues at Blenheim, I would like to thank Connie Ellis and Elspeth Nairn for reading and commenting on draft versions of the text; Linda Heikema and Christine Gadsby who translated Dutch and German extracts for me; Timothy Mayhew and David Samuel for their assistance with the photography.

Many individuals have been generous in sharing their knowledge in their respective areas of expertise. I am grateful to Professor Emeritus Guy Delmarcel for responding to my enquiries. I have enormously profited from my correspondence and conversations with Dr. Koen Brosens of the Katholieke Universiteit Leuven, I owe him many thanks. Dr. Thomas P. Campbell of the Metropolitan Museum of Art, New York generously took the time to read an early draft and offered many helpful comments. Dr. David G. Chandler guided me in appreciating the difficulties of eighteenth century warfare and in recognising the great Duke of Marlborough's military genius. I deeply regret that he did not survive to see the publication of this book but am fortunate to have had the benefit of his knowledge and advice up to a late stage.

Mrs. Minnie S. Churchill is sincerely thanked for providing material from the resources of Churchill Heritage. I am grateful to Mr. and Mrs. R.J.G. Berkeley for permission to examine the tapestries at Berkeley Castle and Mrs. Elizabeth Halls for facilitating my visit there. I must also thank Clare Brown, Curator of Textiles at the Victoria & Albert Museum, and Heather Fordham of the Royal School of Needlework. James Falkner provided some interesting insights on a tour of three battlefields. I am indebted to Sandra Lizioli for her kind hospitality during visits to Brussels and Antwerp. Bernard Guillaume and Jessie Lane are also owed many thanks for their patience, generosity and unreserved support.

The staff at the British Library, the National Archives and the National Art Library have been unfailingly helpful. Particular thanks are due to Emma Lloyd at the Paul Mellon Centre for British Art and to Marijke Booth at Christie's. I express my gratitude to Robert Jones of the Government Art Collection. I must also thank John Saddington at the Commonwealth Institute for the repeated access I have been allowed to Marlborough House in the course of my work and Harold Yexley whose knowledge was invaluable. Sadly he too did not live to see this work completed.

PHOTOGRAPHIC CREDITS

All photographs are copyright of the author with the kind permission of His Grace the Duke of Marlborough, except those listed below. On page 49, with the kind permission of Mr. R. J. G. Berkeley. On page 133, copyright Churchill Heritage, with the kind permission of the Lady Soames. On page 24, copyright Queen's Printer and Controller of HMSO, 2004, UK Government Art Collection. On page 53, copyright Kunsthistorisches Museum, Vienna. On page 59 and 109, copyright Schloss Schleissheim, Bavaria. On pages 82, 98, cover and frontispiece, copyright Jeremy Whitaker. On pages 88 and 89 copyright Blenheim Palace. On pages 29, 52, 125 and 114 copyright Harold Yexley. On page 30, with the kind permission of the Manufacture Royale De Wit.

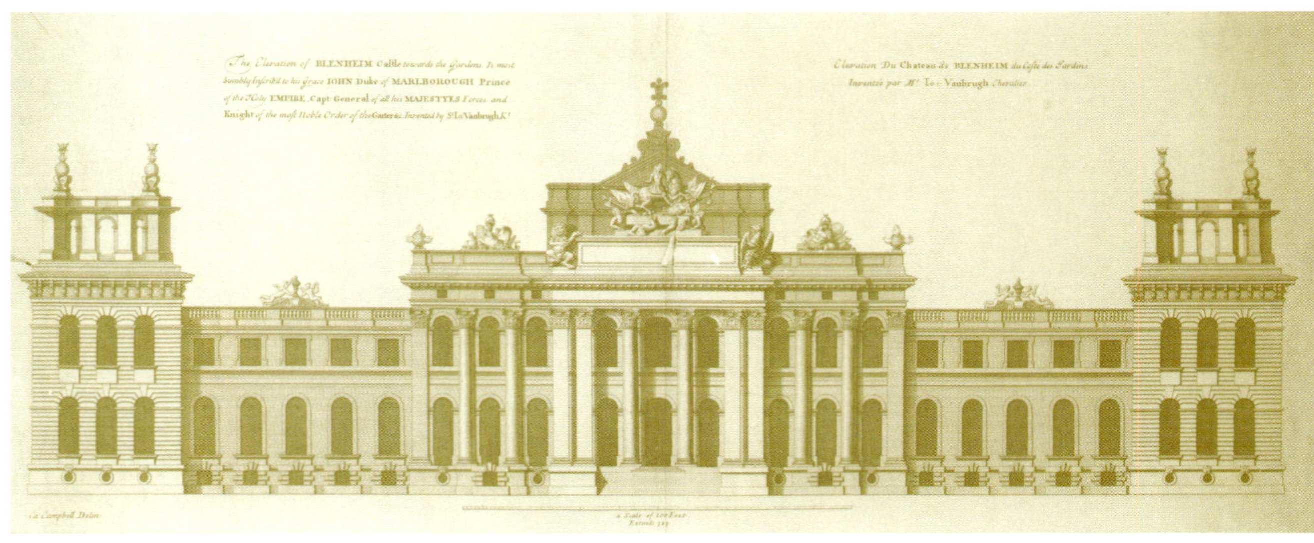